Gloucester and Newbury 1643

Gloucester and Newbury 1643

The Turning Point of the Civil War

Jon Day

Pen & Sword
MILITARY

Pen & Sword Military
an imprint of
Pen & Sword Books Ltd
47 Church Street
Barnsley
South Yorkshire
S70 2AS

ISBN: 978-1-84415-591-0

A CIP catalogue record for this book is
available from the British Library

Typeset in 10/12pt Ehrhardt by Concept, Huddersfield
Printed and bound in England by Biddles Ltd

Pen & Sword Books Ltd incorporates the Imprints of Pen & Sword Aviation, Pen &
Sword Maritime, Pen & Sword Military, Wharncliffe Local History, Pen & Sword
Select, Pen and Sword Military Classics and Leo Cooper.

For a complete list of Pen & Sword titles please contact
Pen & Sword Books Limited
47 Church Street, Barnsley, South Yorkshire, S70 2AS, England
E-mail: enquiries@pen-and-sword.co.uk
Website: www.pen-and-sword.co.uk

Contents

Preface

Late summer 1643 was the military high tide for King Charles I and his armies. Battlefield victories in the North and West were followed by the storming of England's second city, Bristol, and deep political crisis among his enemies in London. A year after England had descended from politics into conflict, this was the king's only realistic chance of winning his civil war. Yet within two months, the opportunity had been squandered. The Royalist armies failed to take the Parliamentarian stronghold of Gloucester, failed to prevent the Earl of Essex from relieving the city, failed to entrap the earl's army in the Severn Valley and finally failed to defeat the Parliamentarians in battle at Newbury. Essex returned in triumph to a politically reunited London, the king's court descended into acrimonious recriminations and Parliament's eventual victory took on an increasing air of inevitability. If the Civil War had a turning point, this was surely it.

Despite its military and political importance, the campaign has been neglected by historians. At the strategic level, the apparent certainty of Parliament's victory has clouded judgements about its vulnerability during the campaign. With some honourable exceptions, 1643 is consequently seen as a dull period of stalemate between the more important battles of Edgehill and Marston Moor. The siege of Gloucester acquired the status of a romantic and symbolic myth, and in doing so became disconnected from the wider context and especially the consequent fight at Newbury. Because that battle did not follow the popular image of Civil War combat, and the complexities and contradictions of contemporary accounts were thought to defy detailed synthesis, it became seen as a tedious draw rather than a decisive combat, and was either ignored or misinterpreted.

For those seeking to fill this gap, there is a wealth of material on which to draw. Seventeenth-century accounts include a surprising number of eyewitness narratives, although all of them have a political or personal agenda of some kind. Much day-to-day correspondence has survived from both sides, offering fascinating though incomplete glimpses of individual perspectives and decision-making processes. Although Royalist intelligence material has to be deduced from the assessments contained in these letters, Sir Samuel Luke's letter book for the period contains the source material, raw intelligence reports from his network of Parliamentarian scouts and spies recorded as they arrived back at Essex's headquarters. It therefore shows what Essex knew of his enemies' strength, intentions and movements throughout most of the campaign and can be tested against other information to assess the accuracy and impact of Luke's previously derided organisation. On logistics I have, I hope, made judicious use of Ian Roy's selection from the Royalist Ordnance Papers; sadly, their Parliamentarian equivalents in the National Archives have not yet been similarly analysed. By contrast, Parliament's journals are complete though often tantalisingly sketchy, useful mainly for establishing chronology. The Oxford and London news books offer vivid pictures of how both sides reacted to events and sought to mould public opinion. They are often reflected in Venetian diplomatic reporting, which was generally shrewd though sometimes gullible and over-reliant on trusted but untrustworthy sources.

As with diplomatic despatches, landscape evidence should not be taken at face value. On close examination, virtually all of the campaign's key sites have changed beyond easy recognition, even where superficial similarities remain. It is, however, disappointing to discover how few modern writers seem to have visited the scenes of their imaginative reconstructions. The same omission applies to many early maps which I have found invaluable for interpreting events in pre-enclosure, pre-industrial England.

I have for the most part attempted to place my narrative in a contemporary context, concentrating on what was known then rather than relying on hindsight. My aim has been to weave the political, strategic, intelligence, logistic and tactical aspects of the campaign together more comprehensively than past histories, and explain what happened and why more clearly, especially in relation to the day-long encounter battle at Newbury. In doing so, I am suggesting a change to the traditional site of much of the fighting, away from Newbury's modern suburbs to the neighbouring fields of Enborne. My account is not, however, definitive. Although Gloucester's defences and siege works have been partially excavated, my analysis of Newbury is (like all of its predecessors) unsupported by any archaeological evidence of the kind that is transforming our understanding of Naseby, Marston Moor and Edgehill. As I have emphasised in the final chapter, I hope very much that this gap can be filled in the coming years and that this book will help provide the stimulus for doing so.

I began work on Gloucester and Newbury in 1999 in the margins of a Ministry of Defence International Relations Fellowship at Harvard University, where a treasure trove of seventeenth-century material on the British civil wars kindled my interest, first in making sense out of the dense and apparently contradictory narratives of Newbury and then of the wider campaign. I am not a member of the academic or re-enactment communities, and have not therefore had the benefits (or disadvantages) that accrue from such networks. I am, however, extremely grateful to Glenn Foard of the Battlefields Trust for responding so positively to my cold call, and for the expert help and advice he has provided. I am also grateful to Stephen Ede-Borrett for reading and commenting on a draft of the text. The British Library, the various libraries at Harvard University, Winchester Library and the Berkshire, Gloucestershire, Hampshire and Wiltshire county record offices have all provided invaluable assistance. Steve Bloomfield at the Weatherhead Centre at Harvard gave me the latitude to go off-piste. Otherwise, I have relied on friends and family for everything apart from any errors, which are mine alone. Geoff Hocking designed the maps. Peter Ryan gave invaluable feedback on the text. Gill Comley was my equine expert. Assorted Hawkheads, Ryans and Comleys provided R&R. My brother Andrew also commented on a draft. My mother gave great moral support. Most importantly, my daughter Catherine was an occasional paid and unpaid research assistant, my wife Sandra tolerant and encouraging in equal measure, and they and my brother helped proof read and produce the index. I could not have completed the book without their inspiration and it is therefore dedicated to them both with my love.

One aspect of this book is art for art's sake, an aspiration to tell the story according to my reading of the evidence and put Gloucester and Newbury, and the people who argued, fought and died during the campaign, in their proper place. Another is to set down my re-interpretation of the Newbury battlefield at a time when the site is coming under the threat of urban expansion. But the campaign is also an example of that modern phenomenon, war amongst the people. You do not have to believe that history repeats itself, or draw fanciful parallels between very different epochs, to see in the debates, decisions and actions of King Charles, John Pym and politicians, advisers and generals on both sides, many of the hallmarks of civil war in the post-Cold War era, whether in the Balkans, Africa, Iraq or Afghanistan. For Britons today, Gloucester and Newbury are little-known episodes in a heritage war. Yet for Britons in 1643, they were the turning point in an unprecedented civil and religious conflict, a matter of weeks during which for the first and only time royal absolutism had the means and opportunity to re-impose itself on the battlefield. Other societies today face similar challenges in the face of absolutism of different kinds. For them, the choices between military action and negotiation, restraint and escalation, compassion and atrocity are real and unavoidable. We have been there too. For all these reasons, the history of the siege of Gloucester and the battle of Newbury deserves retelling.

List of Plates

Maps

List of Maps

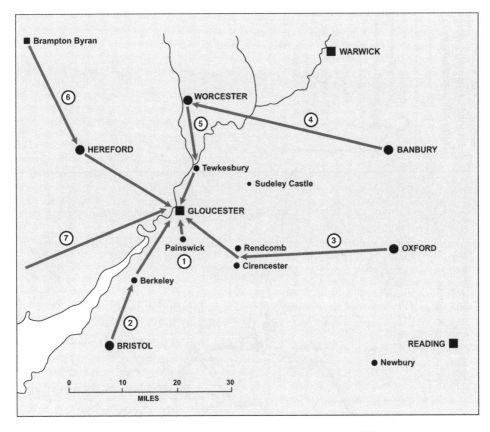

MAP 1 - Royalist concentration against Gloucester, early August 1643

① Aston and Charles Gerard forward based around Painswick

② Rupert's infantry and artillery from Bristol via Berkeley

③ Forth's infantry, cavalry and artillery from Oxford via Rendcomb

④ Infantry from Banbury via Worcester

⑤ Infantry, cavalry and artillery from Worcester via Tewkesbury

⑥ Vavasour's infantry and cavalry from Brampton Bryan

⑦ Basset's infantry from South Wales

● Main royalist garrisons

■ Parliamentarian garrisons

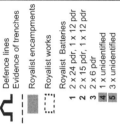

MAP 2 - Gloucester defences and siege works (after Atkin and Laughlin)

Defence lines
Evidence of trenches
Royalist encampments
Royalist works

Royalist Batteries
1 2 x 24 pdr, 1 x 12 pdr
2 2 x 15 pdr, 1 x 12 pdr
3 2 x 6 pdr
4 1 x unidentified
5 3 x unidentified

YARDS
0   240   480

Vavasour's Camp
Kingsholm

5

4

Alvin Gate

Outer
Northgate

Whitefriars Barn

East
Gate

Cathedral

Friar's
Orchard

3

2

1

Gaudy Green

Southgate St.

South
Gate

Castle

Astley's Camp

Barton Hill

The Pen

West
Gate

Quay
Head

Alney sconce

River Severn

*Forth's
Camp*

Lianthony Priory

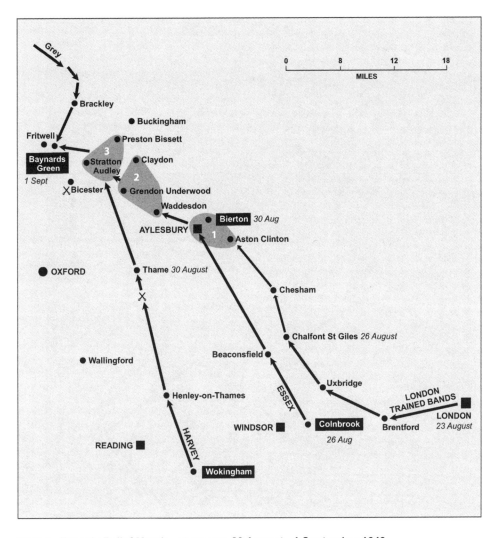

MAP 3 - Essex's Relief March - stage one 23 August - 1 September 1643

Grey

Brackley

Buckingham

Fritwell
Preston Bissett

Baynards Green
1 Sept

3
Stratton Audley

Claydon

2

Bicester

Grendon Underwood

Waddesdon

Bierton *30 Aug*

AYLESBURY

1

Aston Clinton

OXFORD

Thame *30 August*

Chesham

Chalfont St Giles *26 August*

Wallingford

Beaconsfield

Uxbridge

Henley-on-Thames

ESSEX

LONDON TRAINED BANDS

LONDON

HARVEY

WINDSOR

Colnbrook
26 Aug

Brentford

LONDON
23 August

READING

Wokingham

0   8   12   18
MILES

Bierton	Assembly areas
	Overnight dispositions
1	28-29 August
2	30 August
3	31 August
X	Skirmishes

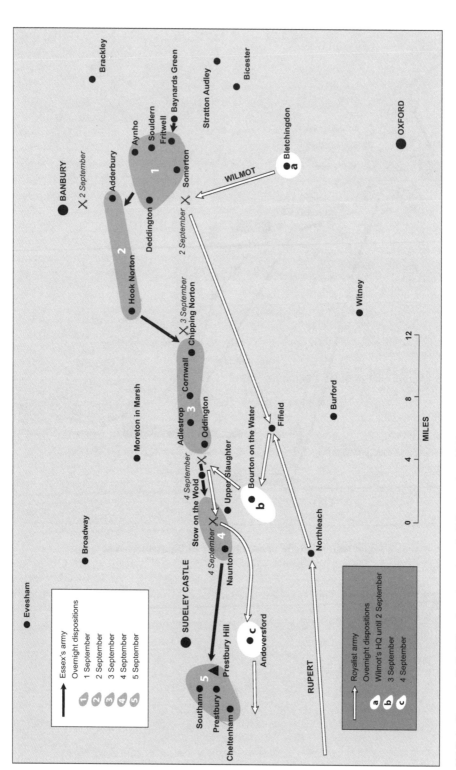

MAP 4 - Essex's Relief March - stage two 1- 5 September 1643

Essex's army

Overnight dispositions
1 September
2 September
3 September
4 September
5 September

Royalist army

Overnight dispositions
Wilmot's HQ until 2 September
3 September
4 September

Evesham

Broadway

Brackley

Baynards Green

Bicester

Stratton Audley

Souldern

Fritwell

Aynho

Somerton

BANBURY
X 2 September

Adderbury

OXFORD

Bletchingdon
a

WILMOT

Deddington

X 2 September

Hook Norton

2

Witney

Moreton in Marsh

X 3 September
Chipping Norton

Cornwall

Adlestrop

3

Oddington

Burford

Fifield

MILES
0   4   8   12

Stow on the Wold

4 September
X

Upper Slaughter

Bourton on the Water

b

SUDELEY CASTLE

4 September
X

4

Naunton

Northleach

RUPERT

Prestbury Hill

Southam

Prestbury

5

Andoversford
c

Cheltenham

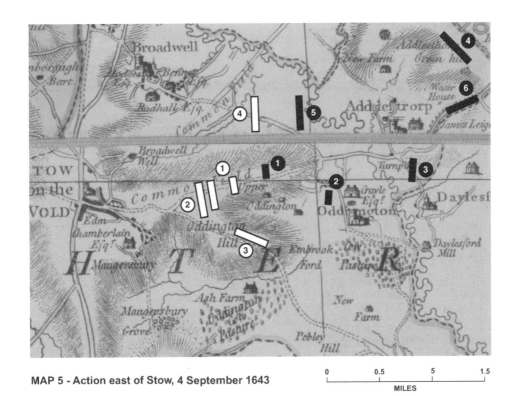

MAP 5 - Action east of Stow, 4 September 1643

| 0 | 0.5 | 5 | 1.5 |

MILES

Based on Taylor's "Map of the County of Gloucester" published 1786.

Royalists

1. Forlorn Hope
2. Rupert's main force on Martin's Hill
3. Brigade detached on southern spur
4. Urry's detachment

Parliamentarians

1. Red Regiment
2. Blue Regiment
3. Auxilliary Regiments
4. Harvey's brigade on Adelstrop Hill
5. Ramsey's brigade
6. Essex arriving from Chipping Norton

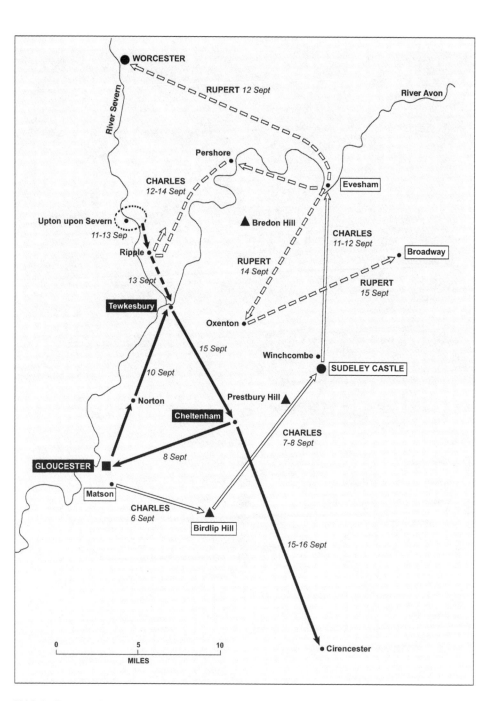

MAP 6 - Essex's feint, 6- 16 September 1643

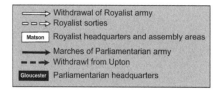

→ Withdrawal of Royalist army
⇢ Royalist sorties
Matson Royalist headquarters and assembly areas
→ Marches of Parliamentarian army
‑ ‑ ➤ Withdrawl from Upton
Gloucester Parliamentarian headquarters

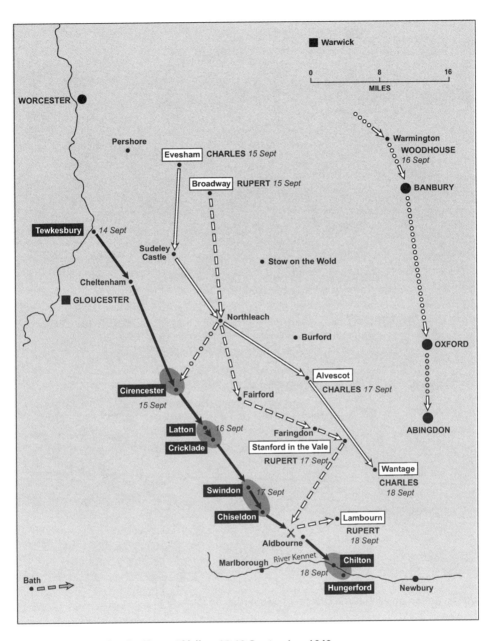

MAP 7 - The race for the Kennet Valley, 15-18 September 1643

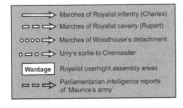

→	Marches of Royalist infantry (Charles)
☐☐⇨	Marches of Royalist cavalry (Rupert)
○○○○⇨	Marches of Woodhouse's detachment
○☐○⇨	Urry's sortie to Cirencester
Wantage	Royalist overnight assembly areas
☐☐⇨	Parliamentarian intelligence reports of 'Maurice's army'

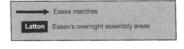

➡	Essex marches
Latton	Essex's overnight assembly areas

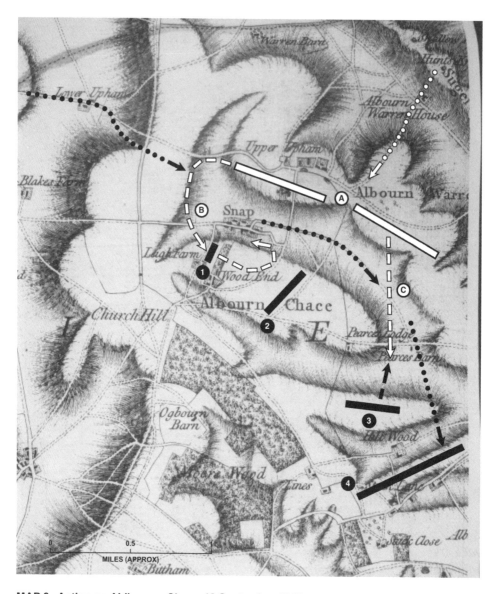

MAP 8 - Action on Aldbourne Chase, 18 September 1643

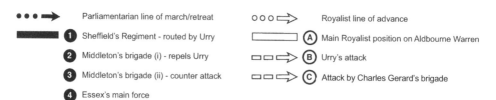

●●● ➡ Parliamentarian line of march/retreat	○○○ ⇨ Royalist line of advance
▬▬ ① Sheffield's Regiment - routed by Urry	☐☐☐ Ⓐ Main Royalist position on Aldbourne Warren
② Middleton's brigade (i) - repels Urry	☐☐⇨ Ⓑ Urry's attack
③ Middleton's brigade (ii) - counter attack	☐☐⇨ Ⓒ Attack by Charles Gerard's brigade
④ Essex's main force	

Based on Andrews and Dury map of Wiltshire, 1773

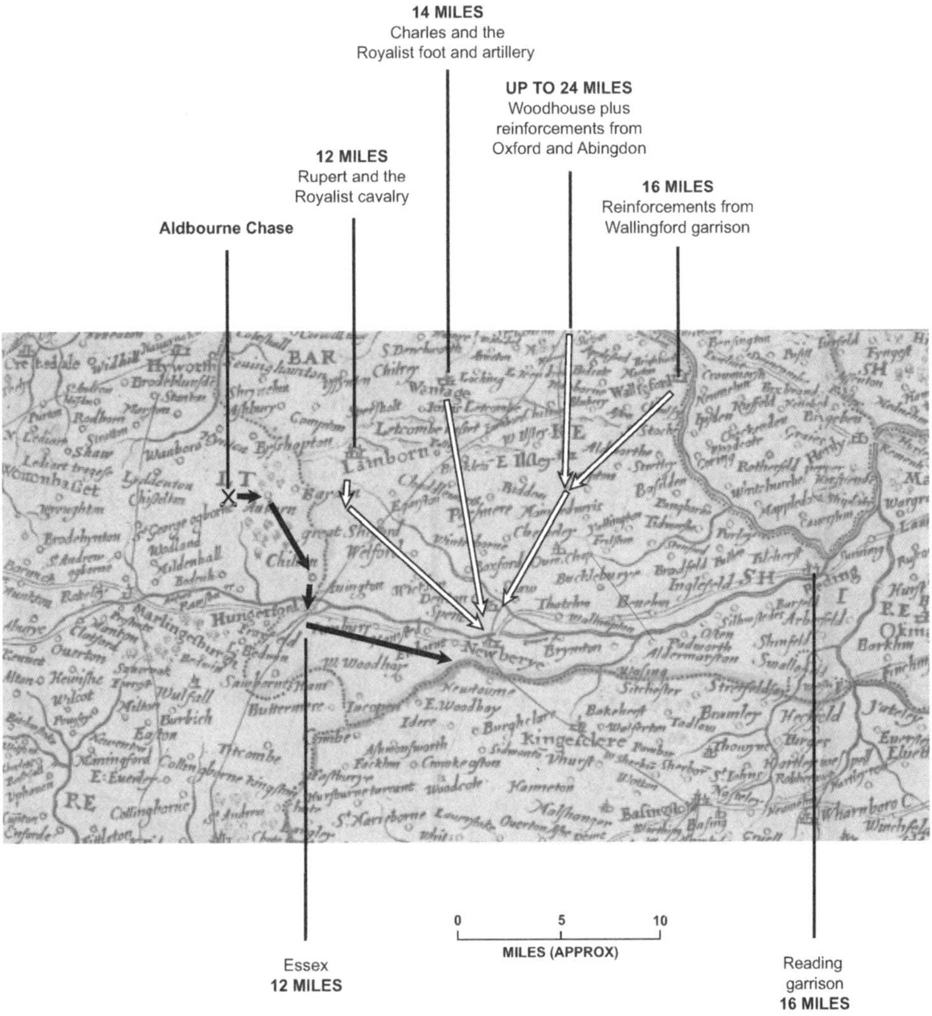

14 MILES
Charles and the
Royalist foot and artillery

UP TO 24 MILES
Woodhouse plus
reinforcements from
Oxford and Abingdon

12 MILES
Rupert and the
Royalist cavalry

16 MILES
Reinforcements from
Wallingford garrison

Aldbourne Chase

Essex
12 MILES

0   5   10
MILES (APPROX)

Reading
garrison
16 MILES

**MAP 9 - The race for Newbury, dispositions and distances
early morning, 19 September 1643**

Based on "A Mappe of Kent, Southsex, Surrey, Middlesex, Berke and Southampton Shire..." by John Garrett, 1688

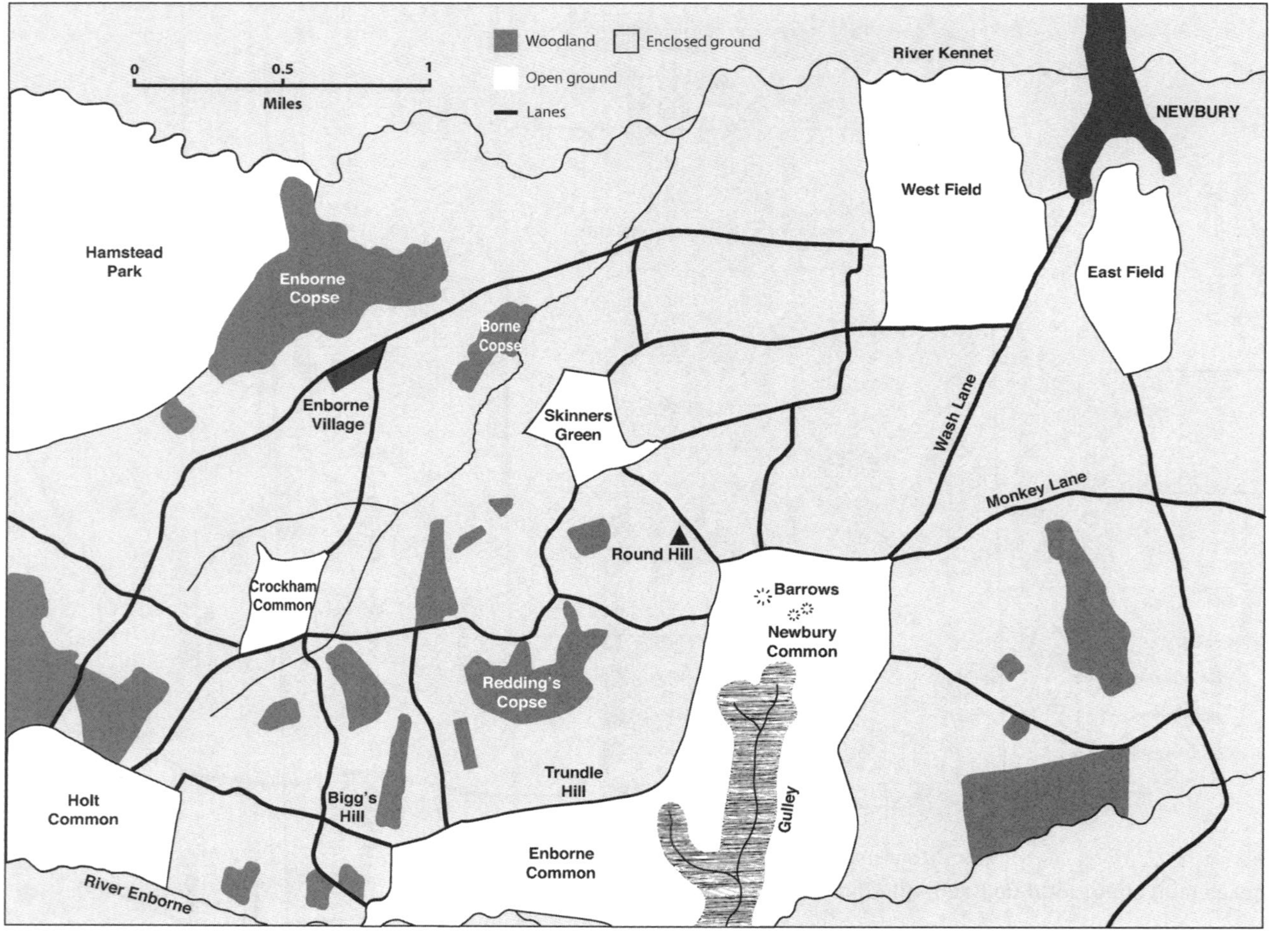

MAP 10
The Newbury
landscape

Woodland
Enclosed ground
Open ground
Lanes

Miles
0   0.5   1

NEWBURY

River Kennet

East Field

West Field

Wash Lane

Monkey Lane

Barrows

Newbury
Common

Gulley

Round Hill

Skinners
Green

Borne
Copse

Redding's
Copse

Trundle
Hill

Enborne
Common

Enborne
Copse

Enborne
Village

Hamstead
Park

Crockham
Common

Bigg's
Hill

Holt
Common

River Enborne

MAP 11 - Battle of Newbury (i) - position prior to the final cavalry action on Newbury Common, mid-morning

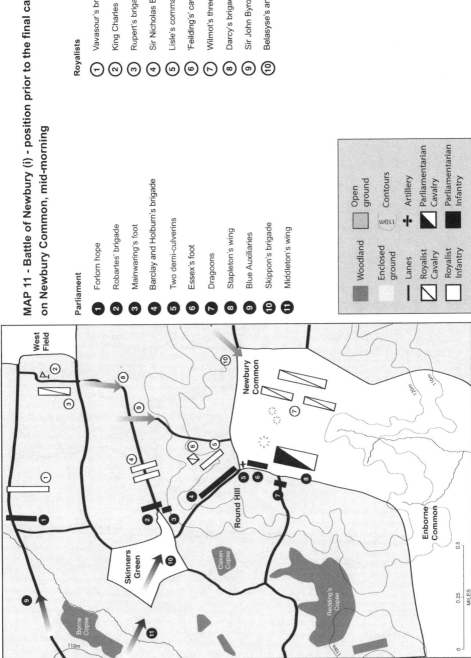

Parliament

1. Forlorn hope
2. Robartes' brigade
3. Mainwaring's foot
4. Barclay and Holburn's brigade
5. Two demi-culverins
6. Essex's foot
7. Dragoons
8. Stapleton's wing
9. Blue Auxiliaries
10. Skippon's brigade
11. Middleton's wing

Royalists

1. Vavasour's brigade
2. King Charles
3. Rupert's brigade
4. Sir Nicholas Byron's brigade
5. Lisle's commanded musketeers
6. 'Feilding's' cavalry detachment
7. Wilmot's three brigades
8. Darcy's brigade
9. Sir John Byron's brigade
10. Belasyse's and Sir Gilbert Gerard's brigades

Woodland

Enclosed ground

Lanes

Royalist Cavalry

Royalist Infantry

Open ground

Contours · 110m

Artillery

Parliamentarian Cavalry

Parliamentarian Infantry

West Field

Skinners Green

Round Hill

Newbury Common

Enborne Common

Oaken Copse

Borne Copse

Reidding's Copse

110m

120m

MILES

0   0.25   0.5

MAP 12 - Battle of Newbury (ii) - position prior to Sir John Byron's attack on Mainwaring's foot, late morning

Parliament

1. Forlorn hope reinforced by Blue Auxiliaries
2. Middleton's wing
3. Robarte's brigade
4. Skippon's brigade plus Springate and Mainwaring's foot
5. Barclay and Holburn's brigades
6. Essex's foot
7. Two demi-culverins
8. Red Auxiliaries
9. Dragoons
10. Stapleton's wing
11. Blue and Red Trained Bands
12. Artillery train

Royalists

1. Vavasour, reinforced by King's Life Guard
2. Rupert's brigade
3. Sir Nicholas Byron's and Darcy's brigades
4. Lisle's musketeers
5. Sir John Byron's brigade
6. Sir Gilbert Gerard's brigade
7. Belasyse's brigade
8. Lucas's horse
9. Artillery battery
10. Wilmot's three brigades
11. King Charles

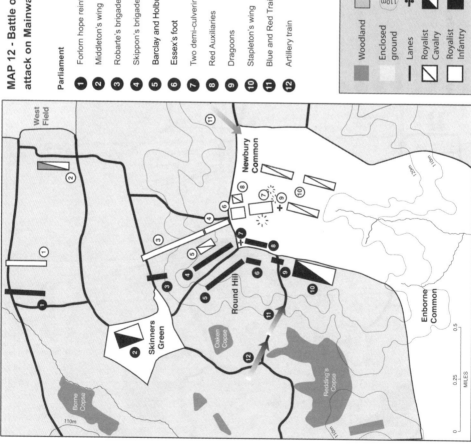

Legend:
- Woodland
- Enclosed ground
- Lanes
- Royalist Cavalry
- Royalist Infantry
- Open ground
- Contours (110m)
- Artillery
- Parliamentarian Cavalry
- Parliamentarian Infantry

West Field

Newbury Common

Skinners Green

Round Hill

Oaken Copse

Borne Copse

Redding's Copse

Enborne Common

0   0.25   0.5
MILES

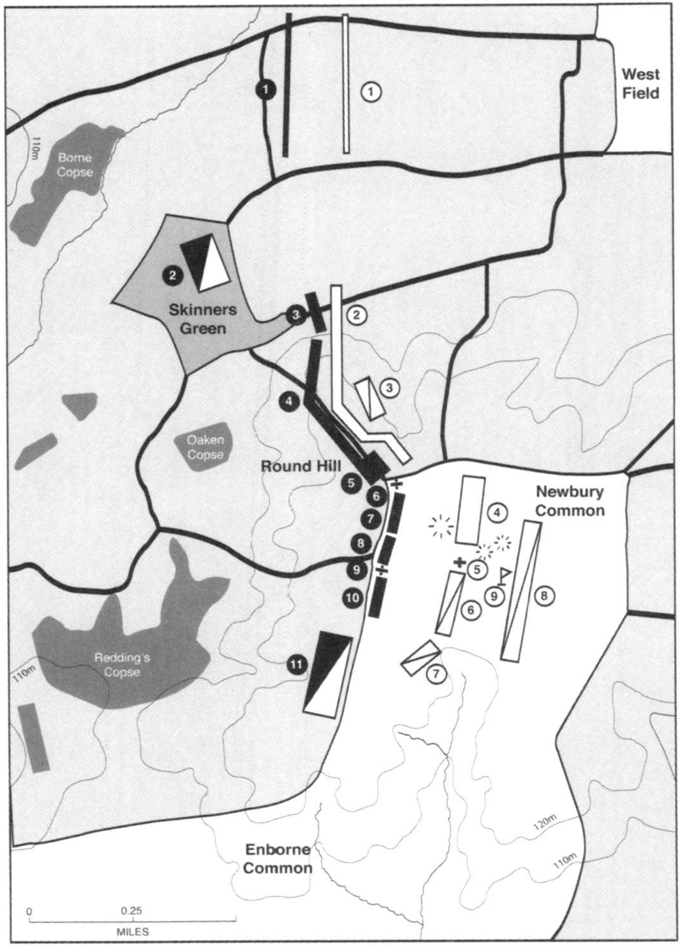

MAP 13 - Battle of Newbury (iii) - position prior to Rupert's attack on the London Trained Bands, late afternoon

Parliament

1. Forlorn hope and Blue Auxiliaries
2. Middleton's wing
3. Robarte's brigade
4. Skirmish line formed by Skippon and Holburn's brigades, plus Essex's, Springate's and Mainwaring's Regiments
5. Barclay's brigade
6. 2 demi-culverins
7. Red Auxiliaries
8. Red Trained Bands
9. Artillery battery
10. Blue Trained Bands
11. Stapleton's wing

Royalists

1. Vavasour and King's Life Guard
2. Skirmish line formed by Sir Nicholas Byron's and Darcy's brigades plus Lisle's musketeers
3. Sir John Byron's brigade
4. Belasyse's and Sir Gilbert Gerard's brigades
5. Artillery battery
6. Rupert's brigade
7. Wilmot's Regiment and Rupert's lifeguard
8. Wilmot's three brigades
9. King Charles

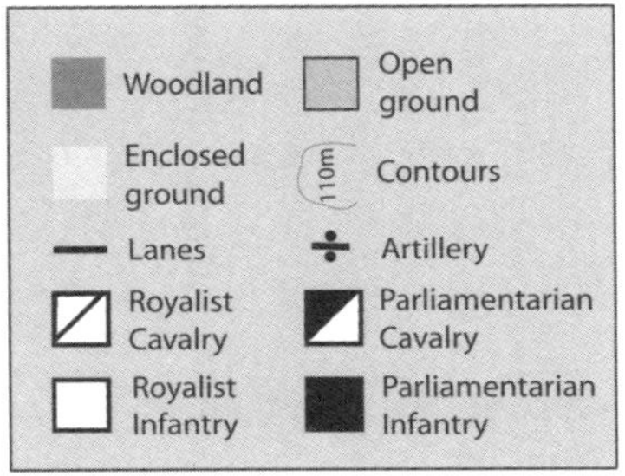

Woodland

Enclosed ground

Lanes

Royalist Cavalry

Royalist Infantry

Open ground

Contours 110m

Artillery

Parliamentarian Cavalry

Parliamentarian Infantry

West Field

Newbury Common

Skinners Green

Round Hill

Oaken Copse

Borne Copse

Redding's Copse

Enborne Common

110m

120m

110m

110m

0   0.25

MILES

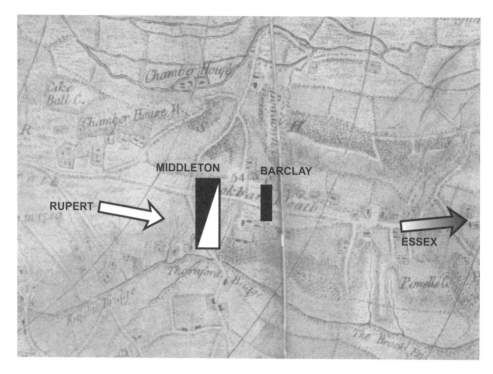

MAP 14 - Action on Greenham Common, 21 September 1643

Based on Rocque 'Topographical survey of the County of Berkshire' 1761

Chapter One

'Gallant men lay on the ground like rotting sheep'

I

Royalist Oxford was congenitally incapable of keeping secrets. Parliamentarian spies working for the Earl of Essex's scoutmaster, Sir Samuel Luke, had been reporting for days that King Charles I would shortly send his nephew and most energetic general, Prince Rupert, with an army into the west of England. When the prince eventually left his uncle's wartime capital on Tuesday, 18 July 1643 with three brigades of infantry, two wings of cavalry and a train of artillery, Luke received details within twenty-four hours. Rupert's immediate objective was reportedly the rich and strategically important Severn valley cities of Gloucester and Bristol, which, only a week before, had formed an apparently secure western bulwark for the king's Parliamentarian enemies from which they could threaten Oxford and restrict access to his loyal Welsh recruiting grounds. Now, however, Parliament's most successful general, Sir William Waller, had lost the army on which their security depended in an unexpected defeat on Roundway Down in Wiltshire and both cities appeared suddenly vulnerable to Rupert's brutal trademark assaults.

On Thursday 20 July, Rupert's army quartered on the edge of the Cotswolds at Minchinhampton, within easy reach of either Gloucester or Bristol. Luke's spies could not decide which was the better target, and in truth the prince had yet to make up his mind between them; Bristol was larger and economically more attractive, Gloucester the southernmost bridging point across the River Severn, closer to the militarily vital route to Wales and less strongly defended. His Colonel General of Foot, Lord Grandison, had argued recently that Gloucester would fall easily to a concerted attack from the land and the River Severn. But at Minchinhampton, intelligence reached the Royalists that Waller had the previous night ridden with some 600 cavalry from Bristol to Gloucester. Rupert thought that Sir William would not abandon the bigger city and on 21 July took part of his army down into the Severn valley to cut the Gloucester-Bristol road. He had, however, misjudged Waller's state of mind. Instead of committing himself to a last-ditch defence of Parliament's position in the West, the general nicknamed 'William the Conqueror' for his previous successes had chosen to quit the field. He spent only one night in Gloucester before cantering off towards Evesham and London.

Further intelligence about the poor state of Bristol's garrison, brought to Minchinhampton the next morning by a defector, tipped the balance for Rupert. His

Flemish engineer, Bernard de Gomme, recorded that 'Sir William Waller having thus parted with the West, the siege of Bristol was now thought the better design'. On 22 July, Rupert advanced to Chipping Sodbury where he held a council with his younger brother, Prince Maurice, who was in effective command of a western Royalist army encamped at Bath. The earlier decision was confirmed: Bristol would be the Royalists' immediate objective; Gloucester, the easier target, would be tackled thereafter; and the Severn valley would become a base for the next stage in the king's war.[1]

Four days later, Rupert's choice seemed vindicated. In the early afternoon of 26 July, the guns in and around Bristol fell silent. Colonel Nathaniel Fiennes, the city's Parliamentarian governor, had sent out a drummer to seek a truce and the prince had agreed, subject to receipt of suitable hostages and a two hour time limit. At around two o'clock, trumpeters passed the order to cease fire and two Royalist officers made their way into Bristol to negotiate terms of surrender. Fiennes' small garrison had fought with unexpected determination but the outer defences had eventually been breached and one of the key inner works abandoned in panic. The Frome Gate into the old city had held out for another two hours while local women worked under fire to build a rampart of earth and woolsacks behind it. Though few casualties had been sustained, the defenders' morale was beginning to crumble, the Royalists were pouring in reinforcements and a successful attack into the centre of Bristol was now inevitable. The rules of war were harsh for defenders who fought on in such circumstances and Rupert's reputation suggested that he would not be lenient.

In fact, however, the Royalists were equally keen to avoid further losses. To the south, the Western Army had filled the dry ditch with carts and faggots, and scaled the old city wall on ladders, but the defenders' fire had been too fierce and about 120 infantrymen, most of them Cornish veterans, had been killed or wounded. Worse still, only one out of three attacks launched by the Oxford Army infantry on the city's northern earthworks had broken through, and the ditches here were also soon filled with Royalist dead and wounded. According to De Gomme, the sole successful attack had relied on a barrage of hand grenades and a spectacular one man charge by Lieutenant Colonel Edward Littleton, who rode 'along the inside of the line with a fire-pike, [and] quite cleared the place of the defendants: some of them crying out "wild fire"'. Casualties had also been heavy in subsequent fighting in front of the Frome Gate and Rupert had asked his brother to send 1,000 Cornish infantry around to the north when the Oxford men had flagged.[2]

For propaganda purposes, Fiennes claimed later that his men had killed almost 1,000 attackers and wounded a further 700. A Royalist report suggested that about 500 infantrymen were killed (if so, it is likely that around the same number would have been injured) and Sir Edward Hyde's history later used the same figure.[3] The number of fatalities was clearly greater than expected, and large enough to justify comment and explanation. For contemporary commentators, however, the most shocking aspect was the high proportion of senior officers on the casualty list. The Western Army had fought a hard campaign from Cornwall through Devon, Somerset and Wiltshire. At Bristol, its core of Cornish infantry lost two of their five original colonels:

> Sir Nicholas Slanning had his thigh broken with a case shot: whereof he died three weeks after. Colonel Trevannion's thigh being shot, it swelled, grew black and stank: whereof he died about midnight.

A third infantry colonel, Brutus Buck, was smashed by a halberd from the top of the city wall into the ditch, where he too died. Trevannion's major had also been killed together with at least three more junior officers. A cavalry officer recalled that 'as gallant men as ever drew sword (pardon the comparison) lay upon the ground like rotten sheep'. Oxford Army losses were no less severe. Lord Grandison was shot in the leg while rallying his brigade and died of his wound in Oxford on 29 September. Colonel Henry Lunsford was shot dead through the heart on the steps at the Frome Gate. Lieutenant Colonel Nathaniel Moyle was shot through the bladder and passed away a few days later. Colonel Edward Fitton died around the same time, either of wounds or disease. In half a day's fighting, nine infantry regiments had their commanding officers killed or incapacitated, and the toll could have been even higher. Lieutenant Colonel Anthony Thelwell was hit on the face bar of his helmet by a bullet that glanced off and wounded a nearby captain in the arm. Another bullet bent Colonel John Belasyse's sword blade back into his head. Colonel John Owen was shot in the face but survived. Lieutenant Colonel Bernard Astley received a gunshot through the thigh, and Lieutenant Colonel Walter Slingsby was knocked unconscious and lived only because a party of his men stayed behind under fire to rescue him. Another eight more junior officers are recorded as killed or injured, and Rupert himself had a horse shot from beneath him.[4]

The Royalists were nonetheless in a position to dictate terms. Fiennes' only option was to withdraw into the castle and burn the city behind him. But the castle would hold less than half of the garrison and not even the staunchest Bristol Parliamentarian was prepared to put his city to the torch. Rupert did not enforce his two-hour deadline, and late in the evening a ten-point agreement was reached. Its terms were lenient. The garrison would surrender their firearms but could march away the next morning with their swords, an escort to Warminster and a guarantee against molestation for three days. Carts would be provided for the wounded and personal baggage, and Parliament's civilian supporters were free to leave at the same time. Nor would Bristol be sacked. In a prudent act of reconciliation, blame for the city's revolt against the king was laid squarely at the door of the soldiers. All inhabitants were to be protected from plundering, violence or other wrongs and the civil authorities in the city were confirmed in their position, although Rupert's public leniency had been purchased at a price, variously described at the time as £140,000, £50,000 or £9,000 and clothing for 15,000 soldiers.

Terms of surrender were one thing, the actuality of capitulation very much another. Controlling a victorious army which had suffered heavy losses and which, under the rules of war, could now expect to take its revenge and reward, would be difficult in any circumstances. In this case, the officers on whom Rupert relied to keep his word were as likely as their men to be set on revenge for lost comrades. The Oxford soldiers in particular had a score to settle because many of them had been pillaged in similar circumstances when the king's Reading garrison had surrendered to the Earl of Essex in April. Indeed, discipline broke down even among troops no longer at the scene. Sir John Byron, who had been sent by Rupert from Bristol with two brigades of cavalry to counter Parliamentarian activity north of Oxford, wrote in frustration to the prince that

> I have sent my lieutenant colonel back to Bristol to fetch back those men of these brigades who are stayed behind, and went this morning in so great

numbers, that there are very few left with the colours, the reason whereof is their discontent, in that they think they are sent away at this time to lose their shares in the pillage of Bristol.[5]

As a result, the capitulation on 27 July was chaotic. During the night many of the garrison had escaped from the city, some to enlist in the Royalist army. A number of Royalists had gone in the other direction in search of loot, often aided by their erstwhile enemies. Perhaps as a result of the deteriorating security situation, Fiennes seems to have opened the gates up to two hours before the agreed time of nine o'clock, and to have drawn up his men at the wrong (or at least a different) gate. When the garrison marched out, the escort and convoy was not there but a mob of Royalist soldiers was waiting to plunder them. Royalist writers tried to play down the treatment of the Parliamentary garrison, blaming 'stragglers and sharks, that follow armies merely for spoil and booty', newly liberated prisoners of war and disgruntled Bristolians. Rupert, however, was incensed at this clear breach of his instructions, and was credited by both sides with confronting the mob and laying about him with his sword to restore order. Inside the city, friend and foe suffered alike. Sir Edward Hyde described later how

> one whole street upon the bridge, the inhabitants whereof lay under some brand of malignity, though, no doubt, there were many honest men among them, were almost totally plundered; which, because there was but little justice done upon the transgressors, was believed to be done by connivance from the officers.[6]

As the two Royalist armies took possession of the battered city, the remnants of Parliament's garrison limped back to London where Colonel Nathaniel Fiennes, scapegoat for the latest in a series of military disasters, was found guilty of surrendering Bristol prematurely and sentenced to death. In the light of Waller's flight to London and the weakness of Fiennes' garrison, this was an absurd decision and Parliament's Captain General, the Earl of Essex, intervened to ensure that the sentence was commuted.

II

Sir Arthur Aston, Rupert's Major General of Horse, carried the news of Bristol's capture to Oxford on 27 July. Thanks were given to God for the victory but King Charles sent his nephew only a short and belated letter of congratulations and the overall response was surprisingly muted. Despite Bristol's political, strategic and economic importance, the capture of much-needed munitions, and the acquisition of eight merchant ships and a warship in the harbour, the main Royalist newspaper, *Mercurius Aulicus*, made much less of the victory than other smaller successes and, uncharacteristically, did not seek to refute Parliamentarian claims about the despoiling of the garrison.

Sir Edward Hyde's post-war account was similarly downbeat, reflecting the fear of political moderates that heavy casualties would harden negotiating positions and prevent a compromise settlement with Parliament. King Charles was less committed to compromise but he was increasingly squeamish about casualties. He had written recently to Rupert rebuking him for his capture of Birmingham, which Parliamentarian propaganda was portraying as a brutal bloodbath: the prince should 'mingle severity with mercy, that your ... carriage and behaviour towards our subjects may gain upon their opinions, and take their affections rather than their towns'; and in besieging the nearby city of Lichfield, he should 'have a care of spilling innocent blood, which is amongst them, but spare where you may destroy, save where time and opportunity gives advantage'. This letter might appear to be an exercise in reassurance, to mollify Royalist moderates in the face of the Parliamentarian propaganda offensive, were it not for Sir Edward Nicholas' stern footnote: Rupert should 'understand by this letter his Majesty's real intention how your princely thoughts ought to be steered ... in all your warlike affairs and enterprises'. So when Hyde mused that after the taking of Bristol, 'the king might very well have said, what King Pyrrhus heretofor did ... [when] he won his victory; "if we win another at this price, we are utterly undone" ', he may well have been reporting Charles' views or even his words. Moreover, he makes it clear that when the king called his privy council together to consider the implications of Bristol, their remit was to ensure that 'this might be the last town he should purchase at the price of blood'. Concern about casualties was widespread; on 30 July, Lord Percy wrote from Oxford to Rupert warning him that it 'is said here you are not careful of your foot'.[7]

The victory was further tarnished by a bitter, public quarrel between the king's generals. Although Rupert had led the storming of Bristol, the operation had been a joint one between two Royalist armies, and the titular commander of the Western Army, Edward Seymour, Marquis of Hertford, now felt himself to have been marginalised. Hertford was a middle-aged grandee with no military experience who had been appointed commander in the west because of his political influence. Effective control of the army had been wielded by Sir Ralph Hopton, until he was injured after the battle of Lansdown when a powder wagon was ignited by a pipe match. Thereafter Prince Maurice had assumed control. Hertford does not appear to have opposed these arrangements but he certainly resented Rupert's actions after the two armies were united for the attack on Bristol, alleging that he was not consulted about the terms of surrender. That is unlikely since one of his officers helped to negotiate them and he was certainly prepared to put his name to them. A more substantive disagreement was caused by both generals' surreptitious efforts to gain control of the military administration of Bristol. This was not simply an honorary position. Bristol was the country's second city, a major provider of wealth, military supplies and other resources, and a source of considerable political influence within the Royalist establishment.

Rupert and Hertford each had persuasive arguments in their favour. The Marquis was regional commander, Lord Lieutenant of the city and represented the political establishment; moreover, as a brother-in-law of the Earl of Essex he also had potentially useful links with the king's enemies. By contrast, the prince was a young, foreign professional soldier whose abruptness and influence had already alienated many of the king's supporters, and whose elder brother was a potential alternative candidate for the English throne. But his leadership had won the prize, and King Charles' cause relied increasingly on his military skill and energy. The argument was further complicated because Hertford had cleverly nominated Hopton as his candidate, a man whose merits Rupert recognised and whose contribution to the western campaign clearly justified such a reward. Finally, Rupert was keen that his brother Maurice should supplant the lethargic Hertford as commander of the Western Army. For political moderates, that would be yet another unpalatable indication that waging war was taking priority over the search for peace.

The immediate question was the governorship of Bristol. Hertford wrote privately to the king asking him to appoint Hopton. Rupert had, however, written in parallel trumping Hertford's request by asking for the post for himself and Rupert's letter arrived first. As a result, the king agreed to the prince's apparently reasonable proposition (probably by word of mouth to Sir Arthur Aston) before he was aware that there was a simmering dispute among his generals. Hyde's detailed account, which is partial to Hertford's position but gives both sides of the argument, suggests that the problem was debated at length among the king's advisers. The decision to confirm Rupert's position was eventually taken only as part of a package to keep both soldiers and courtiers happy. Although Rupert would be governor, Hopton was to be his deputy and would control the garrison. Maurice would take command of the Western Army with an English nobleman, the Earl of Carnarvon, as his deputy. Hertford's wounded pride would be assuaged with a court appointment as a gentleman of the king's bedchamber so that 'he would always have his company and advice about him', a standard line to mollify influential grandees turned unsuccessful generals.

Details of the compromise were passed to Rupert in the king's congratulatory letter of 28 July. In compensation for his demotion from governor to deputy, Hopton received a fulsome letter of praise from the king, signed on 29 July, and a peerage confirmed six days later. Despite some short-lived public gossip about the quarrel, the issue appeared to have been resolved.[8] Rupert was certainly developing plans for the second phase of his campaign, against Gloucester. The Royalist commander in the Welsh marches, Sir William Vavasour, wrote to him on 26 July asking for advance warning of his next operation and Parliamentarian spies reported from Oxford that Rupert would go quickly to Gloucester.[9] Suddenly, however, in a letter to Rupert dated 31 July, the king announced out of the blue that he had decided to travel to Bristol. Hyde explains that, having heard both sides of the argument,

> the king discerned that all depended upon his own royal wisdom; and therefore resolved to take a journey in his own person to Bristol, and there give such a rule as he should find most necessary; to which, he presumed, both persons would conform themselves, as well cordially, as obediently.

This makes little sense unless the compromise was facing resistance, probably from a disappointed Hertford. *Mercurius Aulicus* hinted as much when it reported that Hertford 'came to court on Sunday [30 July], which was conceived to draw on His Majesty's journey'. Either Hertford combined with those at court who had argued against Rupert to reopen the issue of governorship or, more likely, he helped them convince the king that his nephew should be reined in to prevent a repeat of the Bristol bloodbath at Gloucester, and that only the king in person could achieve this.

Although there is also a suggestion in surviving correspondence that Bristol's civil government was reneging on the cash deal agreed with Rupert and that only the king could sort out the problem, it seems improbable that the king would have made such a journey simply to apply pressure to a recalcitrant local authority. Whatever the cause, the king would be in Bristol by 2 August and it can be deduced from what happened when he arrived that the presumption now was that there would then be a re-examination of Royalist strategy for the remainder of 1643. The limited aim of securing the Severn valley would be tested against other options that reflected the changed strategic situation elsewhere. Charles had already written to his general in the North, the Earl of Newcastle, asking him to march south to co-operate in a joint operation against London. After a year of civil war, Prince Rupert's success at Bristol, for all its flaws, represented 'a full tide of prosperity' for the king's cause and perhaps the opportunity for that most elusive of unholy grails, an outright military victory.[10]

Chapter Two
'The next design'

I

King Charles' initial response to the fall of Bristol was political. In the final days of July, the Privy Council agreed that to exploit the favourable military situation, Charles should issue a new appeal to moderates and neutrals throughout the country. The king's 'declaration to all his loving subjects' emphasised his attachment to Protestantism and the liberty of his people, and offered a pardon to those who had been misled by his opponents. Though the declaration had little wider impact, it was an important indication of revived Royalist self-confidence as the king set out for the West. Accompanied by key political advisers, he rode to Malmesbury on 1 August, and made a triumphal entry into Bristol the next day. Once the ceremony was over, Charles moved quickly to resolve any lingering doubts about the city's governance and command of the Western Army, speaking privately to Hertford to tell him to stand aside.[1] The stage was now set for one of the most important occasions of the Civil War: a council of war to decide on the future course of operations in 1643. This meeting was to last, on and off, for five days and its conclusions would influence fundamentally the remainder of that year's campaign and the eventual outcome of the conflict itself.[2]

The council's starting point was the strategic situation as it appeared to the king and his advisers in early August. For them, war had been born of unacceptable political and religious differences between a divinely anointed monarch and a rebellious faction within his overreaching parliament. Following the indecisive Edgehill campaign in autumn 1642, the rebels had gained the upper hand so that by the following spring, the king's writ in the South ran only in Cornwall, Wales and part of the Marches, and a pocket in the Thames valley around Oxford. He had lost the strategic town of Reading through suspected treachery and though disease delayed the Parliamentarian advance, the threat to Oxford was still real and immediate. Rupert did his best to reduce the pressure by raiding the Earl of Essex's lines of communication and the Royalist infantry were encamped at Culham to block the Thames valley but ammunition was in such short supply that consideration was given to abandoning Oxford and retreating into the west or north.[3] Yet much of Yorkshire was at best disputed and the Royalist position in Lancashire disintegrated in April when the Earl of Derby was defeated so decisively that he fled to the Isle of Man.

The tide first began to turn in the Southwest. At Stratton on 16 May, Hopton's Western Army gained an unexpected victory over the Earl of Stamford, whose much larger force was destroyed when the Cornish infantry stormed his hilltop encampment, and then advanced into Somerset. Hertford returned to his command with reinforcements and Prince Maurice to lead the cavalry. In response Sir William Waller, Parliament's best-respected general, moved down from the Severn valley and, after a drawn battle at Lansdown near Bath, hustled the Royalists back into the Wiltshire town of Devizes. But Hertford, Maurice and the horse broke out and rode overnight to Oxford to seek help. Two days later, Lord Wilmot and three Oxford Army cavalry brigades appeared on Roundway Down above the town. Though Waller outnumbered Wilmot by at least five-to-two, his army was defeated in detail and destroyed as a fighting force. Parliament's military self-confidence had received a shattering blow while the already inflated self-image of the king's cavalry had been given a major boost. Both factors would have an important impact on the deliberations at Bristol and the subsequent campaign.

Rupert was able to take most of the Oxford Army to Bristol because of another equally dramatic change in the king's fortunes. The catalyst was Queen Henrietta Maria, who had been in the Netherlands procuring arms and returned to Yorkshire in early February with munitions, professional officers and foreign volunteers. Her arrival made little impact on the tit for tat conflict in the north-east, but a convoy of ammunition and other supplies sent south helped deter the Parliamentarian offensive against Oxford following the fall of Reading. A second convoy left York on 4 June with 3–4,000 reinforcements, artillery, and another 100 wagon-loads of munitions and supplies. Parliament's efforts to intercept the convoy were hampered by quarrels among its commanders and an aggressive covering operation by Rupert. King and queen were reunited on the Edgehill battlefield on 13 July, and escorted into Oxford the next day. The arrival of the convoy was both powerful propaganda and a vital boost to the king's material assets, giving him enough men to release the majority of the Culham infantry regiments to Rupert, and sufficient supplies for a summer campaign.

Meanwhile, at Adwalton Moor on 30 June the Earl of Newcastle inflicted a comprehensive defeat on the Yorkshire Parliamentarians and penned their commanders, Lord Fairfax and his son Sir Thomas, into the port of Hull. When Newcastle captured Gainsborough at the end of July, there was widespread speculation that his next move would be into the Parliamentarian heartland of East Anglia where local Royalists seized King's Lynn. In early August 1643, the military balance was therefore more favourable to the king's cause than at any time since the beginning of the war. The stalemate had been broken in the north and west, and in the Thames valley Essex's army appeared even more debilitated by disease than the Oxford Army. There had even been a Royalist rising in Kent, which sent shock waves throughout London before it was suppressed in late July.

Politically, the king's opponents also seemed to be in disorder and decline. London was in perpetual crisis, with simmering discontent fanned by real and imaginary Royalist plots. The machinery created to run the war was failing in its task and a peace party of moderate peers looked increasingly to be in the ascendant at Westminster. Early in July they had received the public support of an increasingly discontented Earl of Essex, who appeared rudderless after the death of his principle lieutenant, John Hampden, at Chalgrove Field. Meanwhile, Parliament's hawks had lost faith in Essex as a general and a figurehead, and were known to be plotting to replace him with Waller. Even the debacle of Roundway Down seemed only to have delayed Sir William's ascendancy, and the internecine struggle for power was debilitating the overall war effort.

In a God-fearing and superstitious age, the divine support which all sought and Parliament's adherents believed they enjoyed, had apparently been withdrawn. In desperation, its leaders turned for aid to temporal powers, and in particular to Scotland, whose armies had twice humbled King Charles in the Bishops' Wars of 1639 and 1640. An official delegation had been sent north in mid-July to negotiate military intervention. Despite widespread scepticism about the likelihood of an agreement, this was, from the king's perspective, potentially disastrous. Not only would a substantial Scots army change fundamentally the military balance (cancelling out secret negotiations in Ireland to release reinforcements to serve the king in England), his advisers feared that, politically, Scots intervention would be worse than English rebellion. Further-more, in the longer term Parliament held the strongest economic cards, controlled the main sources of wealth and manpower, occupied the capital and enjoyed interior lines of communication. Adwalton Moor, Roundway Down and Bristol had tilted the balance in the king's favour but unless they could be exploited quickly the likelihood was that Parliament would recover and the king would eventually be forced into an unsatisfactory compromise, or even brought to defeat.

II

The second critical factor in the Royalist decision-making process was the size, quality and condition of the king's armies. Size mattered because seventeenth century battles were generally won by the largest army. But the larger the army, the more demanding was the logistic challenge; 10,000 men needed almost 100 tons of food every week, plus wagons to carry it. Strategic and tactical choices were often dictated by logistic calculations of this kind. And God was not always on the side of the big battalions. Leadership, training, morale and equipment could sometimes offset numbers, as demonstrated at Stratton and Roundway Down. The equation was complex and unpredictable but an understanding of the forces available to King Charles at the beginning of the campaign is essential to explain why the council of war reached its decisions and how the campaign then developed.

The Oxford Army: Infantry

On paper, the Oxford Army was formidable. In late July 1643, almost thirty infantry regiments can be identified in its order of battle, each with a theoretical strength of 1,200 officers and men. The reality was very different. A month after Edgehill, pay warrants show that eighteen of the king's twenty-four regiments together comprised only 10,950 soldiers, no more than fifty per cent of full establishment. During the winter and spring, three regiments were sent back to the regions and total numbers fell further still from desertion and disease. By April 1643, the remaining twenty-one regiments (now known collectively as the 'old foot') were divided between garrisons in and around Oxford, and a marching army of fifteen regiments camped at Culham. A note in the Royalist Ordnance Papers dated 2 May states that these regiments were together only 6,000 strong. In the following weeks, Parliamentarian spies assessed that the Culham units totalled as few as 3,000 soldiers, reflecting the growing impact of sickness; another Ordnance document from mid-June shows that at least 1,032 soldiers had been stricken by a 'new disease', probably typhus, and removed from the camp. Many others were in physically poor condition: on 10 June, a spy estimated that half of the king's foot were 'sick and weak ... scarce able to march away'.[4]

Yet march away they did. The three brigades taken to Bristol by Prince Rupert comprised fourteen regiments of 'old foot' from Culham and the Wallingford garrison. Parliamentarian spies and officers from the Bristol garrison put the whole force, including cavalry, at no more than 7–8,000 strong. Given the strength of the Culham units and the number of sick men, the best estimate for the fourteen infantry regiments at Bristol is at most 4,500 all ranks. Seven remaining 'old foot' regiments garrisoned Oxford, Abingdon, Banbury Castle and Wallingford. The only hard evidence for their strength is correspondence from February showing that the King's Lifeguard numbered about 600 and Parliamentarian intelligence that the garrison at Wallingford, including a small dragoon regiment, was 400 strong. If, as seems probable, sickness rates were lower away from the insanitary conditions at Culham, and recruits easier to attract to stable garrison life, the active strength of the 'old foot' in the Thames valley could have been as high as 2,500 all ranks. Eight further regiments had arrived from the north and midlands. A detachment of around 1,000 escorted the queen's first ammunition convoy in May, and were then formed into two regiments as part of the Oxford garrison. A second batch of 2–3,000 infantrymen arrived with the queen in mid-July. Allowing for sickness, the eight new regiments would still have been well over 3,000 strong by early August, some in garrison while others formed a marching brigade.[5]

When Prince Rupert marched to Bristol, the Oxford Army's twenty-nine active infantry regiments could therefore field only 10,000 active soldiers, less than the previous year and with a reduced deployable component because of garrison duties. Another 1,500 or so were sick or recuperating. For Rupert's fourteen regiments, the storming of Bristol provided much-needed combat experience but the human cost had been heavy by the standards of the war thus far. About 500 infantrymen were dead and a similar number injured, all but 120 from the Oxford Army. Worse still, according to Hyde, the period of indiscipline following the Parliamentarian surrender cost the king's army as many men as the assault itself, suggesting that another 500 men disappeared from the ranks, again primarily from the Oxford Army infantry. An eye-witness report of a muster on 28 July suggests that the largest brigade was only 1,400 strong. Two of the smaller regiments were so reduced that they were added to the Bristol garrison to rebuild. Even with the addition of the lightly wounded, plus another 469 men who had recovered from sickness and left Oxford to march to Bristol on 1 August, Rupert is unlikely to have had more than 3,500 infantrymen at his immediate disposal, too small an army with which to mount a major campaign. A further 5,500 men were in Oxford and the surrounding garrisons but the majority would be needed to guard against another Parliamentarian thrust along the Thames valley. Hyde gave a total figure of 6,000 Oxford Army foot available for operations and the evidence is that this was a fair estimate.

Although military theory recommended that two-thirds of the soldiers should be musketeers and one-third pike-men, continuing materiel shortages meant that the Oxford Army ratio was less than one-to-one. When infantry weapons belonging to sick soldiers removed from the Culham camp in mid-June were returned to the Oxford magazine, the proportion of muskets to pikes was only 466–566; and the 469 returnees after sickness were provided with 173 muskets and 227 pikes (the other 69 were probably officers). As there is no evidence that weapons captured or produced at Bristol made a difference so soon after its capture, the 3,500 infantrymen at Bristol probably comprised in the region of 400 officers, 1,400 musketeers and 1,700 pike-men.[6]

Table 1: *Oxford Army Infantry Regiments, late July 1643 (all numbers approximate)*[7]

Oxford Garrison	Marching Army
Colonel Charles Gerard	*First Tertia*
Sir William Pennyman	Sir Ralph Dutton
Lord Percy	Sir Gilbert Gerard
Colonel Thomas Pinchbeck	Lord General
Queen's Lifeguards	Lord Molyneux
Marching Units (including Northern Tertia)	Colonel John Owen
Sir Thomas Blackwell	Earl Rivers
Colonel Conyers Darcy	*Second Tertia*
Colonel William Eure	Sir Jacob Astley
King's Lifeguards	Colonel Richard Bolle
Colonel Samuel Sandys	Sir Edward Fitton (probably became Grandison's)
Sir Thomas Tyldesley	Colonel Richard Herbert
Sir Henry Vaughan	*Third Tertia*
Abingdon Garrison	Colonel John Belasyse*
Sir Lewis Dyve	Colonel Charles Lloyd
Banbury Castle Garrison	Colonel Henry Lunsford (became Rupert's)*
Earl of Northampton	Sir Edward Stradling
Wallingford Garrison	*Total strength pre-Bristol 4,500*
Colonel Thomas Blagge	
Active Thames Valley units 5,500	*Total strength post-Bristol 3,500*
Sick and recovering soldiers 1,000	(* transferred to Bristol garrison)

Could quality compensate for quantity? The evidence of the war's opening campaigns is that the combat performance of most infantrymen was at best variable and often poor. Exceptions such as Hopton's Cornishmen generally reflected some form of homogeneity at unit level, subsequent campaign experience and a taste of operational success. Most of the original Oxford Army regiments had been recruited from the north, north or west midlands, and Wales but not necessarily from within communities or by local officers. At Edgehill, half of the king's infantry regiments broke and ran during the battle, and the remainder were worsted in hand to hand fighting with the Parliamentarian foot. Thereafter, volunteers attracted by pay rates well above labourers' wages were rapidly demotivated when money dried up and desertion became endemic. Impressed prisoners of war kept numbers up but undermined unit cohesion further still.

In practice, understrength infantry regiments became administrative rather than fighting formations. On campaign, they were grouped together in tertias or brigades commanded by a general or senior colonel. Some brigades such as that brought south by the queen stayed together on a semi–permanent basis; most changed composition for different missions, which cannot have encouraged a cohesive spirit. An added complication was the significant number of Welsh units in the Oxford Army; seven regiments had been raised wholly or partly in the principality and reinforcements had been trickling into Oxford since early 1643. Although reputedly good fighters, Welsh soldiers faced widespread English prejudice ('poor Welsh vermin') and almost all of the rank and file spoke only their native tongue. Somewhat surprisingly, little effort seems to have been made to group the Welsh units together. Religion was also a divisive factor in an army that was avowedly Protestant but inevitably attracted Catholics from both home and abroad.

Good leadership might have ameliorated many of these problems and the officer corps had certainly become more professional since Edgehill. Regimental commanders still included inexperienced county gentlemen such as Thomas Blagge and Sir Ralph Dutton, or courtiers like Sir Lewis Dyve, but eight of the fourteen regiments at Bristol were led by men with some military expertise. Richard Herbert had commanded a cavalry troop against the Scots; Charles Lloyd had learned his trade in the Dutch army, been appointed engineer-in-chief and quartermaster general in 1639, and seen further service in Ireland thereafter; and Earl Rivers had recruited John Boys, a veteran of Irish campaigns, as his lieutenant colonel. The northern reinforcements also included English professionals such as Colonel Thomas Pinchbeck and a party of French mercenaries.

Despite this injection of expertise, the overall standard of infantry training and discipline had improved very little. Prior to Bristol, the only major operation since Edgehill had ended in the humiliating loss of Reading. Disease and equipment shortages had only added to their malaise. The officers felt themselves so neglected, especially by comparison with the cavalry, that in late May a set of 'Humble Desires' was submitted to the council of war by thirteen of the Culham regiments. They asked for wagons, money for provisions, ammunition bandoliers, 'a physician and an apothecary', designation of a village outside Oxford in which sick men could recuperate, shoes and stockings for their soldiers, an end to the poaching of trained officers by regional commanders and of foot soldiers by cavalry regiments, the payment of arrears (especially to quartermasters, carriage masters and long-serving officers), and that priority be given to bringing the 'old regiments' up to strength instead of recruiting new units because 'the mixing of new and old soldiers together will sooner be made serviceable than any new raised regiment can possibly be'. Although the council of war met some of these requests at its meetings on 29 May and 20 June, others required an injection of resources that simply did not exist.

Contemporary references to the quality of the Oxford Army foot are generally disparaging. Earlier in the year, Sir Arthur Aston had complained to Rupert:

> I do wish with all my heart that either I had some German soldiers to command, or that I could infuse some German courage into them, for your English common soldiers are so poor and base that I could never have a greater affliction light upon me than to be put to command any of them.

Parliamentarian intelligence reports consistently supported this view and Rupert himself was under no illusions about the quality of his troops. According to Hyde, one of the main arguments the prince had used in favour of an assault on Bristol rather than a formal siege was that soldiers' morale was suitable only for a short operation. In the event, even an assault proved almost beyond their capacity; the attacks on the city's northern defences largely failed because of the reluctance of soldiers to advance under fire and, unlike their Cornish counterparts, most of the dead or wounded senior Oxford Army officers were hit not in close combat but while gathering their men together or urging them forward.

Morale suffered further from Rupert's refusal to grant his soldiers licence to plunder the captured city, and then by their collective decision to ignore the prince and loot both the city and their defeated enemies anyway. A Parliamentarian intelligence report called this a mutiny; Hyde wrote that 'those soldiers, who had warmed themselves with the burden of pillage, never quietly again submitted to the carriage of their arms'; and Hopton described these events as 'much to the prejudice of the future service'. In May, the Culham officers complained that the Oxford foot were 'much weakened by continual service'. Nothing had happened since to improve that pessimistic analysis.[8]

The Oxford Army: Cavalry

By contrast, the Oxford Army cavalry had prospered. Rupert and Wilmot had spent the winter and spring building up a much larger, more professional and better equipped force than the nine regiments of 2,800 men fielded at Edgehill. Based on a core of aristocratic and gentlemen officers and volunteers, leavened with experienced soldiers from the European battlefields of the Thirty Years War, the cavalry suffered not from poor morale but from a surfeit of self-confidence that made them difficult to restrain in and out of combat. Indeed, their spectacular success at Roundway Down may have increased the arrogance of the Oxford cavalry to dangerous heights since it obscured the harsh fact of mid-seventeenth century military life that infantry were increasingly the masters of the battlefield, even in open country.

Away from the battlefield, this arrogance spilt over into routine plundering, of friend and foe alike, and equally routine indiscipline. On 16 May 1643, Lord Wentworth reported to Rupert from a cavalry raid into Buckinghamshire: 'Our men are not very governable, nor do I think they will be, unless some of them are hanged, for they fall extremely to the old kind of plundering'. At times the cavalry appeared a greater danger to themselves than to the enemy. Four days earlier, Sir Edward Nicholas had written disconsolately from Oxford that:

> Sir James Mills was lately shot by an officer upon a private quarrel: and the last night Lieutenant Cranfield was wounded by one Captain Hastings upon the like occasion. There is no punishment, and therefore nothing but disorder can be expected.[9]

Six of the Edgehill regiments still formed the core of the Oxford horse. Some came close to the theoretical 500-strong establishment of a cavalry regiment; in December 1642, Prince Rupert's comprised seven troops, 465 men and 630 horses, and Lord Wilmot's 355 men and 450 horses. Many of the rank and file came from the gentry or their servants, tenants or yeoman farmers, giving them a much greater degree of cohesion (although Sir Thomas Dallison's troop seems to have been officered by resting actors). With the spring, a wave of fresh cavalry regiments was formed. Some came from within existing units: Sir William Pennyman based his regiment around one of Rupert's troops, and the Earls of Northampton and Crawford around troops from the Prince of Wales' Regiment. Others were created from scratch. Politically influential new arrivals at Oxford, such as the wealthy merchant Sir Nicholas Crispe and the courtier Sir John Digby, seem to have been positively encouraged to raise regiments. Although a few were able to recruit, train and keep enough soldiers to fight effectively as front line units, many soon withered away or were used primarily to escort convoys, forage and collect taxes. Yet more regiments appeared as unsuccessful regional commanders such as Sir Thomas Aston were recalled to Oxford. Lastly, the queen brought a brigade of six regiments with her from the north and midlands. Most had battle experience, and the newly formed Queen's Regiment contained a high proportion of French officers and other volunteers. The foreign (or 'outlandish') influence in the brigade was so strong that, inflamed by London propaganda and the sacking of Burton-upon-Trent, Parliamentarian intelligence reports suggested that 'most of them [were] either Walloons or Frenchmen'.

Contemporary sources suggest that around twenty regiments joined and remained with the Oxford Army between Edgehill and the Bristol council of war. Others such as Prince Maurice's Regiment and a brigade commanded by the Earl of Crawford transferred to the Western Army. Detailed records of unit strength have not survived, but some snapshot statistics do exist: at Chalgrove Field, Rupert's brigade of three regiments was at least 1,100 strong; the six regiments brought south by the queen were 1,000–1,500 strong (her own regiment alone numbered 500); at Roundway Down, Wilmot's three brigades comprised about 1,800 men; and Rupert seems to have had around 2,500 cavalrymen with him at Bristol in two wings totalling three brigades. Given that there were now around twenty-five regiments in the Oxford Army, Hyde's recollection that 6,000 cavalrymen were available in early August is a reasonable estimate. Received wisdom seems to have been that this was the maximum that could be maintained as a single coherent force because of their fodder requirements.

King Charles had therefore doubled the size of his cavalry arm since Edgehill. Although a considerable achievement, this created problems as well as opportunities. Feeding 6,000 horses required 840 acres of grazing every week; equipment was expensive and often had to be imported; and intensive training was needed to ensure that the Royalist horse were able to compensate for lack of firepower by controlled shock action. As with the infantry, the small size of many individual regiments meant that a brigade structure was needed to employ them effectively. Five brigades were operational at this time. Brigading seems to have posed fewer difficulties in terms of cohesion than with the infantry, perhaps because the social makeup of the cavalry arm was less diverse. More significant was the severe imbalance between the Oxford Army's horse and foot. According to most contemporary theorists, the ideal ratio between infantry and cavalry was not the Royalists' 1:1 but from 2:1 to 4:1 or even 5:1, depending on the campaign circumstances. Although a higher proportion of cavalry-men conferred advantages in mobility and in controlling territory or imposing a blockade, for siege warfare or battle in enclosed countryside, they added little military value while increasing substantially the army's logistic demands. Whether the Royalist investment in cavalry was deliberate or an unintended consequence of the social composition of the king's support, it imposed major constraints on strategy for the coming campaign.

There were in addition a number of dragoon regiments, classified as part of the cavalry but in reality musketeers who travelled on horseback and dismounted to fight on foot. Rupert had used dragoons extensively during his winter, spring and summer raids in the south and midlands; their mobility suited his strategy and at one stage at least there were five regiments in the Oxford Army. However, only two went to Bristol and they are unlikely to have numbered more than 400 men. Another small regiment was in garrison at Abingdon. In the coming weeks, perhaps because the expansion of the cavalry arm proper made it more difficult to obtain mounts, dragoon regiments seem to have been used as infantry and to have become almost indistinguishable from the foot.

As the council of war met, most of the Oxford Army cavalry was positioned in the Thames valley to guard against a renewed offensive by the Earl of Essex. Rupert had returned two of the brigades that had been with him to Bristol to reinforce Wilmot, and probably retained only the northern brigade under Colonel Charles Gerard and some regiments with West Country connections. It is therefore likely that there were around 1,500 cavalrymen at Bristol and another 4,500 in and around Oxford.[10]

Table 2:   *Oxford Army Cavalry Regiments, July 1643 (those marked * seem to have remained at Bristol)*[11]

Edgehill veterans	Formed Winter/Spring	Queen's Northern Brigade
King Charles' Lifeguard	Lord Andover*	Queen's*
Prince of Wales	Sir Arthur Aston*	Thomas Dalton*
Prince Rupert	Lord Chandos*	William Eure*
Sir Thomas Aston	Charles Gerard*	Lord Molyneux*
Sir John Byron	Lord General	Samuel Sandys*
Lord Digby	Sir Charles Lucas	Sir Thomas Tyldesley*
Lord Wilmot	Earl of Northampton	*Recently formed*
Dragoons	Sir William Pennyman	Sir Nicholas Crispe
Thomas Hooper	Lord Percy	Sir John Digby
Sir Robert Howard*	Sir George Vaughan*	Thomas Morgan
Henry Washington*		Lord Spencer

The Oxford Army: Artillery and Munitions
The final element of the Oxford army was artillery. Seventeenth century nomenclature was confusing and imprecise but there were broadly four kinds of weapon: heavy battering cannon firing iron balls weighing between twenty-four and sixty pounds for use in siege warfare; field guns for battlefield employment, usually in batteries, firing balls of five to eighteen pounds; light battalion guns often deployed at regimental or brigade level and firing balls of as little as three-quarters of a pound or tin containers of musket balls known as case-shot; and stubby mortars to lob incendiary bombs onto towns or fortresses. Battering and field guns were long, heavy (those in use in 1643 weighed up to 4,500 pounds each), difficult to move and demanding to supply. Most pieces were cast in brass; although iron guns were cheaper, they were heavier still and more dangerous to use. Some guns, known as drakes, had short, tapered barrels and reduced powder charges, and were therefore lighter than the norm for their calibre (while the barrel of a 9-pounder demi-culverin might weigh around 2,500 pounds, a demi-culverin drake was only 1,500 pounds). Rates of fire rarely reached ten rounds an hour and though theoretical ranges exceeded 1,500 yards, battering guns had to be emplaced within 200 yards or so of their targets to be effective and case shot seems to have had a maximum range of little more than 150 yards.[12]

Numbers were not the problem. In late May, nineteen brass guns plus a mortar were 'to be ready upon all occasions for to march', and the queen brought another six guns and two mortars from the north. Rupert took a train of nine pieces to Bristol including six of the largest in the Oxford magazine: two 24-pounder demi-cannon, two 15-pounder culverins, two 12-pounder quarter-cannon, two 6-pounders and a mortar. Each demi-cannon had forty-two rounds of iron ammunition; the other guns had fifty iron rounds each. When the column left Oxford on 20 July, the artillery and ammunition train alone required fifty-two carts and 364 horses. The Royalist Ordnance Papers suggest that about twenty field guns, a similar number of small battalion guns and three mortars were left at Oxford, either for future deployment or to defend the city, but they included eight pieces in such poor condition that they were melted down in early August and used to cast three new 6-pounders. And though Bristol yielded the extraordinary total of ninety-eight artillery pieces, the vast majority were battalion guns or suitable solely for use on wall-mounts. What the Oxford Army lacked was the large battering train of heavy cannon needed to destroy fixed defences quickly. The artillery used at Bristol had been inadequate in this respect; only the two 24-pounder demi-cannon were genuine battering guns and could therefore be relied upon to breach masonry walls. As a result, Rupert had been obliged to compensate for a shortfall in firepower with the blood of his infantrymen.[13]

Table 3: *Oxford Army Artillery, types, specifications and numbers early August 1643*[14]

Type	Calibre (inches)	Weight (lbs)	Range Level/max (yards)	Crew	Horses	Numbers ( ) actually deployed
24-pounder Demi-cannon	6	4,500	340/1,600	9	17–19	Bristol 2
15-pounder Culverin	5	4,000	400/2,000	6	13–15	Bristol 2 Oxford 1
12-pounder Quarter-cannon	4.75	3,200		6	9–11	Bristol 2 Oxford 2
9-pounder Demi-culverin	4.5	2,500	320/1,600		5	Oxford 2
6-pounder	3.75			2	5	Bristol 2 Oxford 8 (5)
5-pounder Saker	3.5	1,600	300/1,500	2	5	Oxford 9 (1)
3 or 4-pounder Sakeret/Minion	3	1,100	280/1,400	2	3	Oxford 7 (4)
2-pounder Falcon or smaller	2.75	700	260/1,200		3	Oxford c12
Mortar	Various			3–5	10–14	Bristol 1 Oxford 2 (2)

In the longer term, Bristol's resources meant that the Royalist's perennial problem of shortages of powder and ammunition would be reduced. The queen had brought seventy-eight barrels of powder from the north, but Rupert had taken seventy with him to Bristol, together with three tons each of match and musket balls, 384 iron cannon balls and eighty rounds of case shot, and used a proportion in storming the city. So the most important windfall surrendered by Colonel Fiennes was the contents of Bristol's magazine. When Fiennes was put on trial in the autumn, he said the total was fifty barrels of powder, but his enemies argued sixty plus more in the outlying forts. The true figure could have been ninety or more since deliveries appeared to have included 126 double-sized barrels from France. De Gomme reported that Bristol, Berkeley Castle, Dorchester and Weymouth together produced 120 barrels of powder and 1,500 muskets. Equally important, Bristol had the industrial capacity to manufacture up to eight barrels a week; according to Hopton, its gunsmiths could within a month produce 200 muskets a week as well; and on 15 August a Dunkirk frigate was claimed to have delivered 6,000 muskets, 2,000–3,000 hand grenades and thousands of carbines, pistols and other arms. The key question now was how quickly these munitions could be supplied to the Oxford Army's front line regiments. As for the Oxford magazine, stocks had been replenished to the extent that, within a week of the fall of Bristol, orders could be given to prepare a convoy carrying 260 heavy cannon balls and 50 hundredweight each of powder, match and musket shot. Compared to the powder famine of the spring, this was a feast indeed.[15]

The Oxford Army: Leadership[16]

Command and control of Civil War armies was an amalgam of feudal hierarchy, political necessity and practical experience, informed by a growing literature of military theory. At the pinnacle was the monarch, the Royalists' Captain General. In 1643, King Charles had beneath him two Lord Generals, the Earl of Newcastle in the north and the Earl of Forth with the Oxford Army in the south. From Forth, the command chain should then have travelled down separate lines for cavalry, infantry and artillery, with Prince Rupert as General of Horse, Sir Jacob Astley as Major General of Foot and Lord Percy as General of the Ordnance. In practice, Rupert had obtained from his uncle a clause in his commission exempting him from receiving orders from anybody but from the king himself. Hyde thought the prince's autonomy was divisive though there is no evidence at this stage of significant difficulties between these key personalities. Both at Oxford and in the field, the king and his senior generals were advised by the council of war which brought them together approximately twice a month with experienced middle-ranking officers, civilian officials and trusted courtiers to debate and decide military policy, strategy and supply. Not surprisingly for a monarch fighting to preserve his divine right to rule, difficult decisions were often taken privately by the king and his immediate entourage. Nonetheless, this structure was perfectly adequate to manage the war, provided that the people placed in positions of power and influence were competent and able to work cooperatively together.

The tone was set from the top. Though physically unsuited for combat, King Charles played a major role at the grand strategic level, marched with the Oxford Army and interfered regularly in the day-to-day responsibilities of deployed generals. In May, Secretary of State Sir Edward Nicholas had written, part in apology and part in despair, to Prince Rupert that he

> could wish that ... the king would leave every officer respectively to look to his own proper charge, and that his Majesty would content himself to overlook all men to see that each did their duties in their proper places.

Micromanagement intruded into tactical decision-making. Two months later, as Rupert tried to cover the queen's advance towards Oxford, Nicholas was passing on the king's 'inclination ... that your Highness should not advance before the Earl of Essex's army, or towards ye Queen until you know certainly where her Majesty was'.

This interference was not simply irritating for the king's generals. Charles displayed little strategic or tactical vision, and veered between stubbornness and indecision, pessimism and optimism. Having sent Rupert north in early April to bring the queen and her reinforcements to Oxford, and confirmed the plan as late as 15 April despite reports that the Earl of Essex was marching against Reading, the king sent the prince a personal recall letter on 16 April ('I have resolved to desire you to come to me with what diligence you may'), a second more urgent letter later the same day ('desiring you to use all possible diligence to come away'), a further personal letter on 20 April followed by one from Sir Edward Nicholas the next day ('to desire you to use no delay') and yet another one from 'your loving uncle' at seven that night ('to desire you to make what haste ye may to me'). Although some of this correspondence can be explained by fear that letters had been intercepted, the growing stridency suggests complacency overtaken by panic.

The king's other striking characteristic as Captain General, his reluctance to sustain – or inflict – casualties, might be considered a strength if he were moving towards a negotiated settlement but he was not prepared to offer the concessions necessary to make compromise a realistic outcome and therefore hamstrung both his peace negotiators and his generals. Whether in peace or war, the king was a poor judge of people. Loyalty counted more than ability and perceived betrayals were neither forgotten nor forgiven: after Colonel Richard Feilding surrendered Reading to save its precious garrison, the king condemned him to death for abandoning Parliamentarian deserters to the Earl of Essex. Even the usually sycophantic Hyde accused him of placing undue weight on personal prejudices instead of professional competence and quality of advice. This was not being wise after the event. Queen Henrietta Maria had recently complained that 'if a person speaks to you boldly, you refuse nothing'. He will have taken her criticism seriously. Charles' devotion to his French Catholic wife was admirable but in Civil War England his willingness to defer to her partisan judgement and promote the interests of her favourites was a dangerous weakness. All of this encouraged an unhealthy atmosphere of factionalism in the Oxford court in which amateur politicians and strategists thrived: Nicholas grumbled that 'I could wish that some busy-bodies would not meddle as they do with other men's offices'.[17]

Suspicion of Charles' French queen reflected one of the main criticisms of his peacetime rule, his reliance on foreigners at court and in government. This trend continued into the conflict. The king's most senior general was seventy year-old Patrick Ruthven, Earl of Forth, a Scot who had served for almost half of his life abroad with the Swedish army. Returning to Britain, he had held Berwick for the king in the Bishops' Wars and taken over as Lord General after Edgehill. Yet despite his formal role, Forth was not at Bristol for this vital council of war but at Oxford, presumably to deal with any Parliamentarian counter moves. Although that may reflect the king's nervousness about threats to his capital, it was also indicative of Forth's declining powers. Undoubtedly an excellent fighting soldier in his day, Hyde recalled that his understanding 'had never been quick and vigorous; he having been illiterate to the greatest degree that can be imagined', and that he 'usually delivered that as his opinion, which he foresaw would be grateful to the king'. Deaf, gouty, a hard drinker 'spoiled with the scurvy' at Berwick, where many of his teeth had fallen out, the king's premier general was past his prime, and lacked energy and drive at key moments.[18]

Prince Rupert, Count Palatine of the Rhine, Duke of Bavaria, Knight of the Garter and General of all His Majesty's Forces of Horse was the antithesis both of Forth and of the devil-may-care cavalier of Victorian legend. Brought up in exile in the Netherlands while his father, the deposed King of Bohemia, schemed to regain his throne, Rupert was tall, physically powerful and intelligent. After spending three years brooding and studying the military sciences as a prisoner in Austria, he had been released at Charles' initiative but obliged to promise never again to take up arms against the Holy Roman Emperor. That left him indebted to his favourite uncle and at a loose end when England slid into civil war. Still only twenty-three, arrogant yet reserved, a professional who made up for what he did not yet know with energy, personal bravery and good luck, Rupert rapidly became the dominant personality in the Royalist camp. He could be inspiring on the battlefield; he had turned the Royalist cavalry into the most feared fighting arm on either side; he was already showing promise as an administrator; and he was gathering around himself a coterie of like-minded youngish officers, selected by merit not rank. Parliamentarian propagandists tried to turn Rupert into a German butcher surrounded by hordes of bloodthirsty outlanders but, for his own side, the prince had become a talisman. Sir Philip Warwick recalled that he 'put that spirit into the king's army that all men seemed resolved'.

Despite this totemic quality, Rupert's influence on policy and strategy was neither paramount nor unchallenged. The queen mistrusted Rupert's influence over her husband, and the prince did little to placate her. Lord Percy felt so torn between them that he wrote to Rupert in Bristol on 29 July pleading with him not to 'forget your civility to Ladies' and reply to her letters. Meanwhile, political moderates such as Hyde sought to rein in any military action which could pre-empt a negotiated peace. Hyde also blamed Rupert for creating 'faction and designs in the army'. The prince was certainly unwilling to practise diplomacy on Royalist grandees, but his neglect of key relationships within the army and council of war caused greater damage. He alienated professional soldiers like Lord Wilmot, and was careless of allies with political influence such as Percy and Digby. If he did not create factions, neither did he discourage them. When most of his cavalry officers wanted to execute Richard Feilding for the surrender of Reading, Rupert ignored them by arguing for the colonel's life, placing himself firmly on the side of the army's socially inferior infantry officers. Because Rupert had few close friends on the council of war, there was a growing risk that he would find himself in a minority in discussions of strategy among an unholy coalition of political moderates and the queen's hard-liners. He displayed no gift for the political aspects of command and remained an outsider, unwilling to do what was necessary to gain the assistance of those less talented but just as proud as he was.[19]

By contrast Lord Henry Wilmot, Rupert's Lieutenant General of Horse, actively pursued popularity in the army and influence in Oxford. Hyde liked him no more than the prince, leaving a picture of 'a man proud and ambitious, and incapable of being contented ... He drank hard, and had a great power over all who did so, which was a great people'. This unfavourable portrait reflected Wilmot's hostility to the king's civilian advisors. He had

> from the beginning of the war, been very averse to any advice of the privy
> council, and thought fit that the king's affairs ... should entirely be governed
> and conducted by the soldiers and men of war.

Wilmot was certainly experienced. He had learned his trade as a cavalry captain in the Dutch army and been wounded at the siege of Breda in 1637. In the Bishops' Wars he had been Commissary General of Horse and the sole English hero at the disastrous battle of Newburn, charging unsupported into the advancing enemy. Now he was basking in the glory of Waller's defeat, the queen's arrival had boosted his influence and the king had recently created him a baron.

There is, nonetheless, a sense of insecurity about Wilmot throughout this period. During the First Bishops' War, he was imprisoned for drawing his sword on a fellow officer in a violent dispute over who was responsible for the army's commissariat. He resented Rupert's appointment over his head and in December 1642 had replied to the prince's orders to march to Wantage with an almost mutinous letter of complaint: 'give me leave to tell your Highness, that I think myself very unhappy to be employed upon this occasion'. If, however, Wilmot tended towards paranoia, he had genuine grounds for feeling hard done by. Hyde recalled that the king 'had no kindness for him upon an old account, as remembering the part he had acted against the Earl of Strafford'.

Prior to Edgehill, Wilmot was accused unfairly of ill conduct in not attacking a party of retreating Parliamentarian troops and blamed for the Royalists' subsequent failure to capture Coventry. For a man who had displayed almost suicidal bravery at Newburn, it would have rankled when civilians such as Hyde suggested that he had 'a colder courage than many who were under him'. Meanwhile, Rupert displayed an 'irreconcilable prejudice' against Wilmot and in council his 'personal animosity against him, made any thing that Wilmot said or proposed, enough slighted and contradicted'. A letter from Percy recording the king's wish to reconcile his two senior generals of horse shows that their antipathy was a cause for real concern.[20]

Third in the cavalry's command chain was Sir Arthur Aston, Commissary (or Major) General of Horse since the previous December. Aston had fought as a mercenary for the Orthodox Russians against the Catholic Poles, the Poles against the Moslem Turks and the Protestant Swedes, and then the Swedes against his Imperialist Catholic co-religionists. Though he evidently wore his Catholicism lightly, he seems only to have been commissioned by the Royalists when word spread that he had opened negotiations with Parliament. According to Hyde, 'there was not in [the Royalist] army an officer of greater reputation, and of whom the enemy had a greater dread', but Anthony Wood described him as 'a testy, forward, imperious and tyrannical person, hated in Oxford and elsewhere by God and man'. Politically, Aston's Catholicism put him in the queen's camp but his surviving correspondence with Rupert suggests that they were on good terms. In addition to their responsibilities as generals, Rupert, Wilmot and Aston all commanded cavalry brigades together with Sir John Byron, an energetic if brutal regimental colonel with little command of higher tactics; and Colonel Charles Gerard, one of Rupert's protégés who had been promoted to command the northern brigade ahead of older and better connected officers. The final senior officer in the command chain beneath the prince was the Major General of Dragoons, Thomas Lord Wentworth, a competent soldier whose influence was limited by the declining importance of his dragoons.

Sir Jacob Astley, the Major General of Foot, was a thorough-going professional in his mid-sixties. A small man, called affectionately 'little monkey' by Prince Rupert's mother, he had served first in the 1597 Azores expedition and thereafter in the Netherlands, with Dutch, Danish and Swedish armies in Germany, and as King Charles' Major General of Foot in his two wars against the Scots. Between times he had been Rupert's military tutor. Reappointed Major General in 1642, Astley's voice was listened to with respect by soldiers and politicians alike. Even Hyde thought well of this 'honest, brave, plain man' though his appreciation probably reflected Astley's reticence in council where he 'was not at all pleased with the long speeches usually made there'; so while his views carried weight, his strategic influence was limited. It is also unclear what his precise role was at this period. Wounded at Edgehill and removed from front line command in November 1642 to be Oxford's governor, he returned to lead the infantry in the following spring and was present at Reading but did not march with Rupert to Bristol and does not seem to have been involved in the debate on strategy that followed. As with Forth, age and injury may have been taking their toll; in 1640 he had suffered from stress and exhaustion ('a shrewd sickness') defending Newcastle against the Scots.

Indeed, the Royalist high command may already have been grooming a younger man to replace Astley. William, Viscount Grandison, who had commanded Rupert's marching regiments as Colonel General of Foot, was a nephew of the Duke of

Buckingham, a friend of Hyde, a protégé of Rupert and a capable soldier with prior service in the Low Countries and Ireland. Wounded in the right leg at Bristol, he was expected to recover (and seems to have taken over one of the infantry regiments that had lost its colonel) and was therefore carried back to Oxford to recuperate. Of Grandison's two fellow infantry brigade commanders at Bristol, Colonel Henry Wentworth, brother of the Earl of Cleveland, was an experienced soldier who had led a brigade since Edgehill but disappeared from the records during the siege of Gloucester, probably as a result of illness; while Colonel John Belasyse, a younger son of Lord Fauconburg, had led the protest by the Culham camp officers, brimmed with self confidence but was not recovering from wounds he too had received at Bristol and would not return to service for some weeks.[21] Potential replacements were not of the same quality; senior colonels Sir Ralph Dutton and Sir Gilbert Gerard were middle-aged provincial gentlemen without significant prior experience. As the campaign progressed, professional officers from outside the Oxford Army were brought in temporarily to command infantry brigades, Sir William Vavasour from the Welsh marches and Sir Nicholas Byron from the west midlands. The implication is that the pool of leadership talent among the Oxford Army's infantry colonels was not very deep.

A similar problem existed with respect to the army's logistic support. King Charles had appointed the quintessential amateur to the post of General of the Ordnance. Henry Percy, a younger son of the Earl of Northumberland and, since June 1643, Baron Percy of Alnwick, was one of the queen's close circle of courtiers. Despite experience in the Bishops' Wars, he was known primarily for his role in the abortive military coup known as the Army Plot. Hyde thought Percy 'generally unloved as a proud and supercilious person' and even the queen had recently warned her husband that although 'it is I who always speak for [Percy] ... I see now that he acts of his own head, and that he fancies he has a power over you which ... he has not yet deserved'. Far from pushing Percy's case as General of the Artillery, she hoped the appointment 'is not for ever, but only for this time'. Percy evidently ingratiated himself with the king and then asked for the post. That plausibility appears to have convinced most of the people some of the time; an anonymous letter written in Oxford in July lamented that Rupert was 'not the gallant man we took him for; you may judge it by Percy's being his chief favourite'. Untested in meeting the myriad demands of a large army on operations, Percy would have to neglect his political intrigues and concentrate on the mundane mechanics of military logistics if the king's cause was to prosper.[22]

By contrast, Percy's deputy was the epitome of expertise. Sir John Heydon, a fifty-five year old artilleryman with continental experience and more than a decade's service as Lieutenant of the Ordnance, ran the main Royalist magazine at Oxford with dedication and efficiency. The third officer with a key logistic role was Hopton, now Lieutenant Governor of Bristol under Prince Rupert. According to Hyde, Hopton's appointment reflected concern about his recovery from the injuries he had suffered after Lansdown, but there may also have been a recognition that his administrative talents were needed to exploit Bristol's potential as an arsenal and recruiting centre.

The king's staff officers were similarly competent in managing day-to-day operations. Charles signed much correspondence himself, supported by Edward Walker, a herald who became Secretary at War in 1642 and accompanied his master on campaign. However, the driving force of the Oxford Army's central nervous system was Sir Edward Nicholas, one of two Secretaries of State and the main coordinator of the war effort in 1643. A professional military administrator, reputed to be unusually capable, honest and devoted to the king, Nicholas ran a complex network for gathering and disseminating information, and for giving orders and guidance. His letters mixed assessed intelligence, direct instructions to Royalist commanders, glosses on the king's wishes and chatty advice to Prince Rupert, to whom he was evidently close. But he remained in Oxford when King Charles was with his army, perhaps because of poor health, and he therefore had little direct influence on the Bristol council of war. The intelligence reports on which Nicholas drew were presumably provided by Sir William Neale, a shadowy figure identified as Royalist Scoutmaster-general in a list of officers at Cirencester in February 1643 and by John Aubrey at his death forty-eight years later.

Other influential figures were the king's cousin, James, Duke of Richmond, Rupert's friend at court who represented the prince's interests when uncle and nephew were apart; George, Lord Digby, seen by many as the author of the king's confrontational strategy which had provoked civil war, and now rebuilding his position on return from exile with the queen while spreading his energy and intelligence widely as a cavalry colonel, staff officer and occasional editor of *Mercurius Aulicus*; and Lucius Cary, Viscount Falkland, the Lord Privy Seal and second Secretary of State alongside Nicholas. Falkland was the intellectual leader of moderate Royalism and had worked tirelessly for a negotiated settlement but was deeply depressed by the increasing polarisation of the king and his opponents. A number of other civilians played important roles in strategic decision making. Sir Edward Hyde was Falkland's close political ally and, as Chancellor of the Exchequer, charged with generating the revenue needed to pay for the king's war effort. He therefore had a strong interest in where, when and how the army mounted its operations. Sir John Colepeper shared similar politics but whereas Hyde was a cultivated lawyer, Colepeper was a country squire whose sharp intellect was masked by an aggressive, confrontational manner. According to Sir Philip Warwick, Colepeper 'had an eagerness or ferocity, that made him less sociable than his other colleagues'. Unlike Hyde, Colepeper had military experience and little compunction about engaging in debates on strategy beyond the scope of his formal position as Master of the Rolls. The king evidently thought highly of his advice and took him to Bristol, where he was to exert a major influence on the council of war.

Although not at Bristol, Queen Henrietta Maria also had a powerful voice in the formulation of policy and strategy. Daughter of the great French war-leader, Henry IV, she was a shrewd politician, devoted to the king (despite rumours of serial infidelity with young cavaliers) but pursuing her own agenda, including Catholic interests. Loathed by many Protestants, her return from the continent had been a mixed blessing. While the reinforcements she brought south facilitated the summer campaign, the widespread perception that her forces were overwhelmingly foreign and Catholic, no matter how exaggerated, damaged the king's cause among moderates on both sides. Equally unsettling was the sense that the queen ruled the king, opposed compromise and invariably advocated the use of force. Even Hyde eventually admitted that Charles often deferred to her judgement, and following her triumphant relief of Oxford, the 'she-majesty generalissima' was determined to push for a rapid military solution to the revolt of 'this perpetual parliament'.[23]

Notwithstanding the Oxford Army's leadership flaws, especially in the infantry and logistics, the age of some continental veterans, and the debilitating effect of political factionalism, the key questions hanging over the king's generals was not whether they were capable of leading their troops to victory on the battlefield, but whether Charles and the council of war could give them direction and achievable campaign aims, and whether their complex mix of egos and agendas could then work effectively in harness together. As for the forces at their disposal, success at Bristol could not disguise potentially serious weaknesses in training, equipment and morale, especially among the infantry; the numerical imbalance between cavalry and infantry which limited tactical options while increasing logistic burdens; and the lack of a siege train.

Regional forces

The king's advisors recognised that the Oxford Army was incapable of exploiting the capture of Bristol without reinforcement. Over 14,000 men had failed to obtain victory in 1642; 12,000 men were unlikely to be more successful in 1643. The Royalists had, however, built a number of regional armies which might now be called upon in support. Nearest to hand was Prince Maurice's Western Army, recovering from an arduous three-month campaign. Though Hyde disliked him even more than his elder brother and was dismissive of his leadership ability, Maurice was a capable soldier, even if closer to the caricature of the wild young cavalier. But casualties and desertion had reduced the Western Army to fewer than 3,000 infantry and 1,000 cavalry; some units would be needed to garrison Bristol; others needed time to rebuild after heavy losses; and morale, especially among the Cornish foot, was worse even than that of the Oxford soldiers. While the Cornishmen had not taken part in the looting of Bristol (Hyde explicitly exonerates them), they were now so opposed to marching still further from home that there was a danger that their regiments would disintegrate if added to the Oxford Army.[24]

In south Wales and the Marches, Lord Herbert of Raglan was Lieutenant General but Sir William Vavasour, an experienced soldier with no local ties, was in effective command. By late July he had raised 300 cavalry and almost 2,000 infantry, and was laying siege to Brampton Bryan Castle in Herefordshire. Further reinforcements were promised from the seemingly inexhaustible pool of manpower in south Wales (a figure of 2,000 would later be used in a Royalist letter), although they would have to be equipped from the arms captured at Bristol. Vavasour was clearly expecting to be summoned. Having written to Rupert on 26 July asking for advance notice, he wrote again on 30 July and 4 August with details of his preparations. Arthur, Lord Capel, Herbert's opposite number in north Wales, Cheshire, Shropshire and Worcestershire, had fought a series of unsuccessful local campaigns but had preserved his army in being and could, if required, provide significant reinforcements including a new infantry regiment being recruited by Colonel Michael Woodhouse, already 700 strong, and 800 infantry and a regiment of cavalry from the Worcester garrison.[25]

Potentially most significant of all was the Earl of Newcastle's victorious northern army, estimated at up to 15,000 strong (although probably rather smaller – in May the queen put it at 7,000 infantry and 69 troops of cavalry). His main opponents, the Fairfaxes in Hull and the Eastern Association south of the River Humber, were too weak to face him in the field, though the Fairfaxes were conducting an active campaign of harassment against his rear. The king had already asked him to bring his army south towards Oxford and was awaiting a reply. If he came, the military balance in the south would be transformed. That would, however, require Newcastle to act from a national rather than a local perspective, leaving Yorkshire at risk from the Fairfaxes in the same way that Hopton had left the Devonshire Parliamentarians in control of Plymouth and Exeter. The difference in this case was that Hopton was not a Cornishman while Newcastle had a strong sense of semi-feudal responsibility to Yorkshire and, according to Sir Philip Warwick, the king's envoy, a reluctance to subordinate his army to the king's southern generals.[26]

Even if Newcastle failed to appear, the Royalists could choose to reinforce the 12,000-strong Oxford Army with up to 6,000 infantry and 1,500 cavalry from the west, south Wales and midlands, plus another 2,000 unarmed Welsh levies and, in an emergency, contingents from the Thames valley garrisons. By contrast, their intelligence told them that the Earl of Essex deployed no more than 5,500 fit soldiers, the rump of Waller's army comprising only 600 cavalry and the part-time London Trained Bands, which had a pre-war establishment of 8,000 infantry, were unreliable and unwilling to fight except in defence of the capital. From Bristol, this looked to present the king with a substantial short term advantage, especially if Newcastle's army could be brought into play and a decisive action fought before the longer term prospect of hostile Scottish intervention became a reality.

III

Three factions, all loose coalitions, competed for the king's ear in the council of war.[27] What might be called the limited war party aimed to restore Charles to his lawful position through a compromise that engaged the moderates on Parliament's side, healed rifts and rebuilt the status quo. Military action was a means to that political end, embraced without enthusiasm and with distaste for the professionals whose service had now become essential. Recent victories were welcome as a stimulus to negotiation on favourable terms and future operations were seen primarily in the context of their impact on Parliament's political response. Some in this camp such as Falkland and Hyde were political moderates and reformers, others were among the most reactionary of the king's supporters, upholders of the status quo and therefore reluctant to escalate the war in ways that could be permanently damaging to the societies in which they lived. Despite a public rebuke from the king, Lord Herbert refused to make use of free quarter for his lifeguards at Gloucester but provided their food himself so that his men 'would not leave a grudge in the people'.[28]

The second faction, perhaps best described as ultra-Royalists, were determined to crush the king's enemies and were generally relaxed about the means needed to do so. Their motives also varied, from personal commitment to the sovereign or the Anglican Church to selfish concern for wealth or position. Some were Catholics who could not expect to prosper if Parliament dictated peace terms. Paradoxically, these advocates of total war often shared with Hyde and the moderates a belief in the primacy of political factors in prosecuting the conflict, and a mistrust of most professional soldiers, who were usually more willing to compromise on political issues. At this stage, the queen was their leading light, and Percy and Wilmot their chief sympathisers in the army. Their war aims had been stated succinctly in a letter from the queen to her husband during peace talks earlier in the year: 'Remember that you are lost if you consent to a peace before this parliament be dissolved'.[29]

The third faction comprised military professionals whose political views took second place to a common (usually implicit) belief that the war needed to be fought more effectively and that political goals should be subordinated to this aim. Most were outsiders to the Royalist political establishment as it had evolved at Oxford. Hyde's dismissal of Charles Gerard as a man 'who used to hate heartily upon a sudden accident, without knowing why' is indicative of the gulf between the Royalist political class and the professionals on whom they now had to rely.[30] The quintessential professional and outsider was Prince Rupert, and it was around him that this group was centred and on his relationship with the king that it relied.

Outside the circle of decision makers were single issue lobbies pressing for their particular interests. Most significant were the groups of local gentry arguing for military resources to be employed to restore their positions against local rivals. Parochial concerns of this kind could not easily be dismissed without the risk of undermining the Royalist cause in these areas. Of particular relevance at Bristol were the lobbies from Gloucestershire, Dorset and Devonshire. As for the king himself, all three factions could convince themselves that at heart he was on their side but none of them could be certain that was the case or that royal sympathy today guaranteed royal support tomorrow. Factionalism was inherent in court politics but there was a fundamental incoherence about the aims and perceptions of the members of the council of war that met on 3 August.

Sir Edward Hyde described the council's main agenda item: 'whether both armies [at Bristol] should be united, and march in one upon the next design? And then, what that design should be?'.[31] The first decision was taken relatively easily: the Western Army should remain an independent command and be given a separate mission. Though Devon's Parliamentarians had regained control of most of the county, such was the psychological impact of Roundway Down and Bristol that local lobbyists argued that the Royalists would only have to appear before the Parliamentarian strongholds for them to surrender. A similar case was made by Dorset gentry. The council therefore concluded that the Cornish infantry would be better employed in re-establishing Royalist control in their own back yards than being forced to march with the king and then melting away. As for the cavalry, the council felt that the 6,000 or more horse in the Oxford Army were all that could be sustained logistically for a single operation. A final factor, unacknowledged according to Hyde, was that an expedition into the West was the only way to give Prince Maurice an independent command. This smacks of sour grapes at a further stage in the professionalisation of the Royalist command structure.

Maurice's deputy, Lord Carnarvon, was already in Dorset and took Dorchester bloodlessly on 2 August. Maurice would now join him, leaving Hopton with six weak infantry regiments (the non-Cornish units plus two from the Oxford forces, together only 1,200 strong) and Maurice's cavalry regiment (fewer than 200 men) to garrison Bristol and build up reinforcements. Although Maurice might be expected to bring his army to cooperate with the king once the south-west was cleared, that would take weeks even if the optimistic assessments of Parliamentarian morale proved correct. For the time being, the Western Army had ceased to be part of the equation for the forthcoming campaign.[32]

The second decision, to identify 'the next design', was far more difficult. The starting point was Rupert's pre-existing Severn valley strategy, the second stage of which was to be the capture of the remaining Parliamentarian stronghold of Gloucester. It is fair to assume that the Prince intended to take the city by storm. That had been his style of operation throughout the first part of the year and even Bristol had not been unduly costly by continental standards. Meanwhile, Rupert was continuing his preparations. On 3 August the Governor of Sudeley Castle, north-east of Gloucester, reported confidently that the city would surrender on demand, and Vavasour was ordered to bring his forces from Brampton Bryan to within a day's march of Gloucester by the evening of 7 August. Next day, Sir Arthur Aston provided an order of march to a rendezvous at Painswick, only six miles from Gloucester; and Vavasour replied on 4 and 6 August confirming that he would have 1,500 men a day's march from Gloucester by the seventh, by which time Royalist cavalry were already harassing the Gloucester garrison. It is inconceivable that these preparations had not been agreed with the king. Only Charles could have ordered Forth at Oxford to begin preparations to deploy more infantry, extra ammunition and a mortar, all of which would be required to take Gloucester and all of which were summoned in a letter from Bristol dated 3 August; and the letter of the same date to Vavasour set out a detailed plan to concentrate forces from Bristol, Oxford and Worcester under Forth's command 'to reduce our City of Gloucester to its loyalty and due obedience'.

It was at this stage that the different agendas of the three Royalist factions came fully into play. Rupert's plan was well within the compass of the forces available at Bristol and Oxford. In London, Colonel Nathaniel Fiennes warned that taking Gloucester would make the king 'master of all that tract between Shrewsbury and the Lizard's Point in Cornwall ... [and] master of all the traffic of that inland sea the Severn', while opening up the route into South Wales 'will from time to time supply him with a body of foot'. The so-called Prince Rupert's Diary states that the Welsh infantry would not march beyond the Severn until Gloucester was taken and suggests that the next step would be an advance into the east midlands or East Anglia ('ye Associated Counties'), which would cut London off from one of its main areas of political support and logistic supply, winter Royalist troops in enemy territory and facilitate cooperation with Newcastle's army. The Gloucester option was therefore a strategy of consolidation. It would give the king a stronger hand to play politically, rectify his shortage of infantry and provide a secure hinterland in which to prepare for next year's campaign.[33]

By contrast, to the ultra-Royalists Gloucester was a diversion from their goal of bringing Parliament to its knees as quickly as possible. It would neither win the war nor compensate for the impact of possible Scottish intervention. What the queen and her supporters wanted was a second march on London to achieve in 1643 what the king had failed to achieve the previous year after Edgehill: the military defeat of Essex's army, the re-occupation of the capital and the consequent political demise of their enemies. They believed that the time was ripe for such an offensive because of what they perceived to be fundamental splits in the Parliamentarian ranks and growing Royalist support in London itself. On 5 August, a Parliamentarian intelligence report warned that the Royalists would move quickly against London 'where they hope to be let in without much cost or trouble, because they conceive they have more in the city for them than against them'.

An advance on London had been under consideration from the beginning of the year. What was now at issue was whether the strategic environment yet suited its implementation. The plan has often been interpreted as a complex three-pronged attack with the king advancing down the Thames valley, Maurice through Hampshire and Newcastle through East Anglia, which would have been difficult to co-ordinate and therefore risked the separate armies being defeated in detail. Moreover, given that Maurice was now marching west, his role in it seems at best questionable. This does not mean, however, that an advance into the south-east was impossible or had already been ruled out by the king and his advisers.

The key issue is where the Royalist armies were to converge and what their aim would then be, and the critical evidence is a Venetian report from earlier in the year that recorded a conversation with a Royalist emissary called Herne. In late January, Herne (perhaps the dancing-master Jeremy Herne) told Venetian diplomats that by March the king expected to have gathered 40,000 troops and planned

> to divide into two armies, and closing the river above and below, to scour the country with his cavalry, reducing London to extremity for food and thus force the people to revolt against the present Government.

The weakness of the Oxford Army had put the concept onto the back burner but there is no contrary evidence to justify dismissing it. Herne was believed by the Venetians, otherwise they would have at least caveated the report with a query about his credibility (as they regularly did on other occasions). Provided that the king could field a large enough army, the strategy was militarily coherent, including its emphasis on cavalry; and it was consistent with the recurring Royalist illusion that a popular rising was simmering below the surface in London and the claims of Royalist cavalrymen later taken prisoner at Cirencester that their regiments had been raised for a descent into Kent.[34]

From the queen's perspective, here at last was the chance to put this plan into effect, using Newcastle's army to compensate for the lack of numbers in the south. The king appears to have been thinking along similar lines when he wrote to Newcastle the previous week. According to Hyde, the Earl had been commanded to abandon the siege of Hull and march through the associated counties of East Anglia towards London while the king advanced from the west. Who argued this case at Bristol is not recorded. As a good bureaucrat, Hyde emphasised consensus, minimised disagreements and omitted to identify dissenting voices. Nor is it certain who argued against the proposition although the Earl of Sunderland later wrote to his wife that 'all of the people of quality' favoured the London option, which implies that some moderates had made common cause with the queen's supporters. They may have felt that Rupert's strategy was an inadequate way of exerting the military pressure needed to obtain a satisfactory political settlement.

Whatever the course of the debate, by 6 August Prince Rupert's Severn valley strategy was widely known to have been abandoned in favour of the return of the forces at Bristol to Oxford as the first stage in a campaign against London. Sunderland's letter, written three days later, is explicit on this point: 'when I went from Bristol on Monday morning [7 August, the king] ... was resolved to come hither [Oxford] this day and to that purpose sent his troop before'. Gloucester was to be blockaded by garrisons, probably under the command of the injured Lord Grandison; on 6 August, he was ordered to take his infantry regiment to Tewkesbury in place of Sir James Hamilton's Worcester horse and dragoons, who would join the army around Bristol to take part in the advance eastwards. It is, however, also clear that other options had not yet been foreclosed. That may in part be because Newcastle had not yet replied to the king's letter but, as Hyde explained, there 'was not a man, who did not think the reducing of Gloucester ... of mighty importance to the king, if it might be done without great expense of time, and loss of men'. Rupert appears to have still been fighting a rearguard action to preserve his campaign.

Rupert evidently had allies at court because Hyde's version of the argument for moving first against Gloucester was couched as much in political and financial as in military terms. Control of Gloucester and the River Severn would enable the important garrisons of Worcester and Shrewsbury to be supplied from Bristol, Bristol's economy would benefit and Gloucestershire, which was populous, wealthy and had supported Parliament, could be taxed till the pips squeaked in retribution. Moreover, with Gloucester in Royalist hands, Welsh soldiers and money could be redirected to Oxford so that 'the king would have had a glorious and entire part of his kingdom, to have contended with the rest'. Strong support for an early move against Gloucester was given by local Royalists, who were plainly a vocal lobby in the margins of the council, promising 'great levies of men'; cavalry captain Richard Atkyns resigned his commission so that he could repossess his estates once the city fell.[35]

The critical issue seemed to be time: 'all of these motives were not thought worth the engaging ... in a doubtful siege' that would give Parliament the chance to reunite and rebuild its army. Even without Newcastle's support, the queen's supporters argued that in these circumstances it would be better to advance on London in the hope of stimulating a rising. Debate therefore focused on whether Gloucester could be taken quickly. Rupert would have argued that a swift operation was possible. Gloucester was less well defended than Bristol, which he had taken in three days, and its garrison was hardly bigger than Cirencester, which in February had fallen in a matter of hours. It was now that the king's opinions were certainly engaged, and against his nephew's well known preference for assault operations. Hyde was unambiguous: 'all thoughts of storming were laid aside upon the loss at Bristol'. Sir Richard Bulstrode, Wilmot's adjutant, agreed: the king 'had intentions of storming [Gloucester], but fearing to lose the best part of his infantry in that action, and being assured it could not be relieved ... [lost] the opportunity of taking it'. Charles' comments after hearing of the casualties sustained at Bristol had hardened over the intervening days from sentiment into policy. He had joined the advocates of limited war in putting a higher premium on lives and the possibility of political progress than on rapid military success. This was a crucial turning point in the conduct of the war in 1643.

Consideration was given instead to an alternative means of taking cities quickly: subversion. Betrayal was in the air. The Royalists had failed by a whisker to capture Hull through the treachery of its governor, and the first year of civil war had been marked by the flexible loyalty of some combatants. Professional soldiers appeared especially vulnerable and Gloucester's governor seemed to be of that mould. Lieutenant Colonel Edward Massey was young, ambitious and reputed to be so unpartisan in his political affections that he took service with Parliament only after failing to secure a sufficiently senior Royalist post. There was also judged to be a strong if so far silent party of Royalist sympathisers in the city to whom he could look for help; Edward Walker had drawn up a list of 104 names. Meanwhile Sudeley's governor was reporting that the locally recruited members of the garrison had already decided not to resist. Massey's actual loyalties and the degree of Royalist support will be considered later. At this stage what is important is that some at Bristol thought that he might be willing and able to sell Gloucester to the king.[36]

Massey was not the sole target. Gloucester's town clerk, John Dorney, reported a paper bombardment by 'diverse of the king's army of no mean quality'. On 4 August, Thomas Pury, Gloucester's puritan Member of Parliament and an implausible Judas, was approached by letter 'full of persuasive oratory for the yielding up of this city, with great promises . . . of preferment' and, by his own account, sent no reply. But it was on Massey that real hopes were pinned. The approach was made through Rupert's major, William Legge, who had served with Massey in the Bishops' Wars. Legge sent a message to his former comrade, couched in friendly language, inviting him to surrender Gloucester to his lawful sovereign. There is persuasive evidence, discussed later, that the approach was made on 6 August under cover of a parlay to recover some stolen horses. Massey received the messenger before witnesses and his formal response was a brusque rebuff. But the messenger reported that Massey subsequently met with him a second time in secret, and asked him to

> tell Will Legge, that he was the same man he had ever been, his servant; and that he wished the king well; that he heard Prince Rupert meant to bring the army before that town; if he did, he would defend it as well as he could; and his highness would find another work than he had at Bristol; but if the king himself came with his army, and summoned it, he would not hold it against him: for it would not stand with his conscience to fight against the person of the king; besides that in such a case, he should be able to persuade those of the town; which otherwise he could not do.

Notwithstanding the impression given to Sunderland, final decisions had been delayed until Legge's messenger returned and the council reconvened when he arrived in Bristol. Since the meeting with Massey almost certainly occurred on 6 August, and the revised decision had not been taken when Sunderland left on the next morning, this critical session must have taken place later on 7 August. Hyde is emphatic that Massey's answer:

> turned the scale; for though it might be without purpose of being honest, yet there was no great objection against the king's marching that way with his army; since it would still be in his power to pursue any other counsel, without engaging before it.

Massey's failure to hang or imprison the messenger was taken as a sign of goodwill. There was supporting evidence for Massey's inclinations, although it appears not to have arrived in time to influence the decision. On 8 August, Sir Edward Nicholls wrote to the king from Oxford that a Captain Presland Molyneux, an old friend of Massey's, was convinced that his 'affections are to serve your Majesty'; furthermore, Massey's father, a Royalist prisoner in Cheshire, was offering to persuade him to surrender.[37]

The issue was not, however, resolved without argument. That is apparent from the efforts to attribute and escape blame later on. Indeed, the debate seems to have been intense because the outcome was a compromise that met the aims of none of the main parties. The Oxford Army would march to Gloucester but neither to storm the city nor to besiege it. Instead the aim would be for the king to appear in sufficient strength before the walls to give Massey the excuse he said he needed to capitulate. If that did not work, there is no record of what the next step would be. Presumably the queen's supporters, whom Sunderland described as most unhappy with the result, would insist on moving quickly on to Oxford and then London. Bulstrode later summed up the mood: 'if the king had then marched to London, he had, in all probability, made an end to the war. But he was ill (if not maliciously) persuaded to besiege Gloucester'. Rupert was equally dissatisfied. A letter to him from Sir Arthur Aston, dated 7 August, suggests that the prince did not believe that the Royalists could deploy in sufficient strength to make Massey live up to his commitment; and that he felt so strongly about the compromise decision that he had withdrawn from any involvement in the operation: 'I understand your Highness does not intend to come hither . . . and yet I cannot choose but approve of your Highness's absence in this business'.[38]

Who was the architect of this unpopular compromise? Sunderland and his friends did not know but Sir Philip Warwick later recalled that 'the king pitched upon that fatal resolution, recommended to him by Lord Colepeper, of besieging Gloucester'. Hyde agreed. Intelligent and influential with the king, Colepeper was a former Chancellor of the Exchequer and therefore knew how important Gloucester and its affluent hinterland could be in refilling the treasury's bare coffers. He was also a pragmatic politician, skilled at building consensus on difficult issues yet abrasive when agreement proved illusive. Since Rupert thereafter bore him an enduring grudge, it is likely that he found himself on the receiving end of Colepeper's blunt debating skills. Hyde sought to defend him from the allegations that arose even before the siege of Gloucester had ended, conceding that the Master of the Rolls favoured the Gloucester option and spoke most in the debate, but emphasising that his views were honestly held. That seems, with the benefit of hindsight, most like a plea in mitigation.

A decision had at last been taken. Rupert's mission to complete the subjugation of the Severn valley had been set to one side. The original strategy for 1643, of starving London into revolt against Parliament, was preferred but it depended on the cooperation of the Earl of Newcastle who had not yet agreed to move south. In the meantime, taking Gloucester had military, political and financial attractions yet only if it could be done rapidly and without losses. If Lieutenant Colonel Massey delivered the city, those criteria would have been met; if he would not or could not, the king would then have to decide what to do next. In either case Newcastle's letter would be the vital factor. It was not an elegant strategy. Cobbled together between factions whose aims were fundamentally different, even at the time it appeared capable neither of producing a decisive military victory quickly nor of giving the king a stronger platform from which to wage a prolonged war. The presence of the council in the west also seemed to have given their deliberations an unduly provincial dimension. Had the king remained in Oxford and summoned Rupert to him, it is unlikely that Gloucester would have loomed so large in their calculations.

Colepepper's compromise drove even deeper rifts between the factions. From Oxford, Sunderland wrote acidly about the 'king's sudden resolution' and a livid queen complained to Newcastle that the decision 'gives no little dissatisfaction to everyone here; and with reason, to see [the king] take such hasty councils'. The military professionals felt they had been ignored and blamed a key member of the moderates for a decision they disliked. Worst of all, the king's nephew and best general, whose energy and enthusiasm had been crucial in what little success the Oxford army had thus far enjoyed, was sulking in his metaphorical tent.[39]

Chapter Three
'A civil, courteous and religious people'

I

Five weeks before Prince Rupert stormed Bristol, another young soldier had been in the national spotlight, though in very different circumstances. Lieutenant Colonel Edward Massey had only recently been appointed governor of Gloucester. Although a professional officer and de facto military leader in the city since the previous December, he owed his promotion to the influence of Sir William Waller, Parliament's regional commander, who had overruled the local authorities when they 'thought well of a man near home . . . a known patriot'. Perhaps in an effort to convince the doubters of his worth, on 21 June Massey had led a detachment of his garrison on an ambitious raid deep into Royalist-controlled territory in the Cotswold Hills. It went terribly wrong.

Massey's objective was the quarters of Colonel Charles Gerard's Royalist cavalry regiment in the villages around Stow on the Wold. He had with him 120 cavalry and dragoons, virtually the entire mounted component of Gloucester's garrison. At dawn on 22 June, they descended upon the villages of Upper and Lower Slaughter, and took a surprised lieutenant and twelve of his men prisoner. Skirting around Stow, Massey moved on to Oddington where a troop of forty men was beaten up and their quarters looted. But the alarm had been sounded and Massey's men now faced a twenty-five mile withdrawal in the face of increasing Royalist opposition. The remainder of the regiment, five troops under Gerard's second-in-command, Lieutenant Colonel David Walter, caught up with Massey near the Slaughters and attacked the rear of his party, but the Parliamentarians turned about and beat them off.

Here overconfidence got the better of Gloucester's governor. His chaplain, John Corbett, usually a strong partisan, later wrote critically that Massey 'being confident he was able to fight with them on any ground, made no haste to march off'. By the time that the Parliamentarian force reached Andoversford, still a dozen miles from Gloucester, Walter had been reinforced by a detachment of Lord Chandos' cavalry regiment from Sudeley Castle. Massey drove back another Royalist charge, but instead of continuing his retreat he then dismounted the dragoons in three bodies, with the cavalry on their flanks, to counter-attack his pursuers. At this stage, however, the courage of his cavalrymen failed. As Massey advanced at the head of the dragoons, he looked back and 'saw the greater part in a strange hurry, occasioned by the facing about of some cowardly spirits'. Walter seized his chance and charged once more. The dragoons were overwhelmed; Massey fought until he was in danger of capture and then followed the rest of his men towards Gloucester. Others were not so fortunate.

The Parliamentarians admitted losing four dead, many wounded and twenty-seven prisoners, including Colonel Henry Stephens, the newly commissioned commander of Gloucester's second infantry regiment and perhaps the 'known patriot' that Massey had beaten for the governorship. Stephens died of 'poisonous air' (probably typhus) in Oxford.

The Royalists were jubilant. At the cost of three dead and four or five wounded they had routed the enemy, rescued their prisoners and liberated their belongings. The Oxford newspaper *Mercurius Aulicus* gave the skirmish more space over two days than it gave to the fall of Bristol. Andoversford was by no means a major action, even by the standards of local skirmishing, but it highlighted two potentially fatal weaknesses in the Gloucester garrison. Many of its soldiers were unreliable and Edward Massey's judgement was sometimes suspect. Neither can have given the City's leadership great confidence when the king's army began its short march north from Bristol less than two months later.[1]

The view of the war from Gloucester was a mirror image of that seen from Oxford and Bristol. Parliamentarians everywhere had watched the deteriorating strategic situation with mounting gloom, but in Gloucester the rising tide of Royalism was now lapping at their very doors. No-one could be sure how the city would respond. In London, Bristol's former governor, Nathaniel Fiennes, was predicting that Parliament's remaining Severn valley stronghold would last for no more than two days should Prince Rupert choose to storm it. Against that background, four questions arise. Why had Gloucester become a Parliamentarian stronghold and therefore a potentially important target? What was the city's military capacity to resist the king? How strong was its political resolve to do so? And was its governor, Edward Massey, as vulnerable to subversion as the Royalist council of war believed?

II

At the outbreak of civil war, there were few doubts about where the loyalties of Gloucester and its 5,000 inhabitants would lie. Although influential local Royalists might contest control of the surrounding countryside, close trade links with the king's opponents in London, political radicalism and strong Puritan religious beliefs combined to make Gloucester itself one of Parliament's main political bastions in the west.[2] Puritanism was seen by most contemporaries to be the driving force behind Gloucester's political allegiance. During the previous half century, the Puritan community had gained control of most of the city's levers of power and created, nationally and in their own minds, the impression that Gloucester was a city apart, a Godly place in an otherwise wicked world. This was partly wishful thinking. As a focus for inland trade, a distribution centre for consumer goods and the administrative capital of the county, Gloucester had its share of alehouses and other forms of vice, and a large, potentially unstable underclass of urban poor. Nonetheless, a high proportion of its citizens, especially among the ruling elite, thought of themselves as God's elect and looked upon the king's efforts to roll back Puritan reform of the established church as a very real threat to their way of life.

Religious belief was reinforced by equally real economic and political differences between this Puritan elite and the government. A major economic downturn in the 1620s and 30s created widespread and endemic poverty, exacerbated in 1638 by an outbreak of plague. The clothing industry felt especially hard-pressed and civic bankruptcy loomed. King Charles' governments appeared to be making things worse and striking at the heart of local freedoms; taxation such as the Forced Loan and Ship Money was seen as unreasonable and excessive, while the billeting of soldiers for unpopular wars built up resentment. The queen's Catholic favourites were convenient scapegoats when pleas for redress were unsuccessful and Gloucester's elite increasingly felt themselves to be targets of a hostile and aggressive monarch. This trend combined with the city's traditionally poor relations with its immediate rural neighbourhood (known as the inshire), and resentment at interference by the county authorities and the regional council in the Marches of Wales, to feed a growing sense of isolation and militancy. As a result, from the mid-1630s Gloucester's sullen hostility hardened into covert and overt resistance to the king and his ministers.

Nonetheless, Gloucester played little part in the political crisis that escalated eventually into civil war. It submitted petitions, including one urging the abolition of episcopacy that was at the centre of a key Parliamentary debate in 1641; it worried about Catholics in south Wales and the Forest of Dean; and the city authorities made half-hearted efforts to stock up with gunpowder and repair the dilapidated old walls. A few individuals also played a part in the wider political ferment, especially Thomas Pury, the city's MP, but at home there were so few instances of disorder that the Puritan preacher Richard Baxter could delight in Gloucester's 'civil, courteous and religious people' when Royalist mobs hounded him out of Worcestershire. War, too, came slowly. Not until mid August 1642, when Lord Chandos tried unsuccessfully to rally the county's Royalists in Cirencester, did the Parliamentarian majority among the gentry and merchant classes take effective political control. A county committee was established and the militia was mustered, but there were no immediate threats and the arrival of regular soldiers to provide Gloucester with its first garrison in November was greeted less with relief than by complaints about the cost of food and accommodation.[3]

Lieutenant Colonel Massey arrived in early December with the Earl of Stamford's infantry regiment from Hereford, and was appointed Deputy-Governor to the absentee earl. It was only then that the war began to impinge directly on Gloucestershire. Royalist cavalry regiments in winter quarters at Burford plundered Parliament's supporters across the Cotswolds, and exacted taxes from friend and foe alike. In response, the Gloucestershire Committee garrisoned nearby Cirencester with militia plus two of Massey's regular companies. This was a constraint the Royalists could not tolerate. On 2 February, Prince Rupert appeared before Cirencester to give the amateur militia soldiers a lesson in professionalism. With a small artillery train and fewer than 2,000 infantry and dragoons, he stormed the town in ninety minutes, capturing 1,200 prisoners in the process. Royalist soldiers turned loose to plunder 'that night, all the next day, and on Saturday ... showed all the barbarous insolence of a prevailing enemy'. In panic, Massey and the committee abandoned their other forward posts at Berkeley, Sudeley and Tewkesbury.

Rupert followed up by leading his cavalry and dragoons on to Gloucester, where on 3 February he summoned the garrison to surrender. It was bluff yet, according to John Corbett, only Massey, his officers (who could see that Rupert again had no artillery with him) and Mayor Dennis Wise were resolutely against giving in. Massey would not surrender to a 'foreign prince' and Wise would not break his oath to hold the city for king and Parliament. It seems to have been a close run thing. There were rumours of betrayal and had Rupert launched even a token attack, the resolution of the minority might have crumbled as well.[4] Worse was to follow. Faced now by a hostile garrison at Cirencester to the east, Gloucester's leaders soon confronted an even more direct threat from the west. In mid-February, a 2,000-strong Welsh army paid for by Lord Herbert of Raglan marched through the Forest of Dean and entrenched themselves on the west bank of the Severn, within sight of the city. Herbert's army was not big enough to force its way across a wide defended river but its presence suggested that Rupert or his brother might soon appear with reinforcements from Oxford.

According to Corbett, who had been a local Puritan clergyman before becoming Massey's chaplain, morale in the city collapsed: the civilian population were 'extremely dashed at this strange turning of things . . . the hearts of many sunk very low and began to lie flat'. This was not surprising in view of the state of the garrison. Defences were

> not half finished, the soldiers within mutinous and desperate; no monies came from the state, and but small supplies out of the country, that the vilest mutineers were to be dealt with by entreaty, their insolence to be suffered with patience.

Corbett was generally sympathetic to Massey and the garrison's professional officers, which suggests that Gloucester's first experience of unpaid regular soldiers under pressure was an unpleasant lesson.

On this occasion, the crisis proved containable. The city authorities took emergency measures to raise money and introduced free quarter. With his men paid and discipline restored, Massey began to harass the enemy fieldworks. No Royalist army appeared from the east and morale among Herbert's Welshmen began to fall; Herbert himself found Oxford more congenial and became another absentee commander. On 23 March, Parliament's new general in Gloucestershire and the surrounding counties, Sir William Waller, crossed the Severn below Gloucester and the next day attacked the Royalist field works from the rear. Herbert's 'mushroom army, which grew up and perished so soon' capitulated with hardly a shot fired.[5] Waller rapidly established Parliamentarian control over the lower Severn valley. Although Prince Maurice was sent from Oxford to contest the region, and defeated Waller at Ripple Field in April, he was withdrawn soon afterwards to take part in the abortive relief of Reading. Meanwhile, Waller used Gloucester as a base to build up his army, recruiting new regiments locally and from Welsh prisoners, including one to reinforce the city's garrison. Money was extorted from neighbouring nominally pro-Royalist areas, military administration was put on a better footing, and an effort was even made to redress local grievances against the military and to tackle corruption.

Waller's preparations were interrupted by Sir Ralph Hopton's victory at Stratton and the rapid march north-east of his Cornish army. Sir William was ordered to protect Bristol. Before leaving, he did his best to ensure the security of his Severn valley base by capturing the Royalist stronghold of Worcester, which posed a perennial threat both to Gloucester and its satellite garrison of Tewkesbury, but his attack was repulsed. Back in Gloucester, money was again a problem. On 3 June, the Gloucestershire Committee informed the House of Commons that the 'want of money hath bred such mutinous dispositions in the soldiers that no arguments will make them stir'. Waller's efforts to raise extra resources met with robust resistance. From Cirencester, Lord Crawford reported to Prince Rupert that 'Waller had sent out his orders for bringing in of contribution; but I gave the constables strict order to the contrary, threatening fire and sword if they paid him a penny'. The greater burden therefore fell on Gloucester and the surrounding area within Parliament's direct control. When the army finally left on 6 June, the city's population would have been relieved to see them go.[6]

Six weeks later Waller returned, briefly, his army crushed at Roundway Down, his destination London. His defeat and the loss of Bristol had been so unexpected that Corbett wrote of a 'sudden surrender ... which was almost beyond our fears'. For Gloucester, the strategic situation was transformed and the future was bleak. Since the outbreak of war, the city had been in the front line in theory but at risk only briefly after the loss of Cirencester and during Herbert's stay on the far bank of the Severn. In neither case had the Royalists possessed the military capacity to capture Gloucester. Nor had the city stood alone. Royalist control of the surrounding area was by no means absolute; to the south was the Bristol garrison and the Parliamentarian-dominated counties of Somerset, Wiltshire, Dorset and Devon; and Waller had shown that it was possible to deploy an army from London in time of crisis.

In those circumstances, Gloucester had been strategically valuable. It protected Bristol from the north, enabled Parliament to exploit the relatively affluent Severn valley up to Tewkesbury and beyond, provided a base for extorting money from the Royalists in Worcestershire, Herefordshire and the Welsh borders, and blocked the most direct route between Oxford and the king's fertile recruiting grounds in south Wales. With hindsight, much of that value had disappeared with Waller's army. Instead of forming the northern point of a large swathe of Parliamentarian territory, Gloucester was now a vulnerable enclave within the king's new heartland, absorbing rather than generating resources. In the longer term, it might as Corbett described (also with the benefit of hindsight) act as a focus for harassing the Royalists in that heartland but for the time being, and certainly in the context of the coming campaign, Gloucester's objective military importance to Parliament was marginal. Only the reluctance of Welsh Royalists to release infantry reinforcements until the city fell was a critical factor in the military balance and that was not apparent either in Gloucester or London. Neither side would admit it after the event, but the campaign of August and September 1643 did not begin as a contest for a militarily significant objective.[7]

III

Gloucester's limited strategic value was reflected in the size and state of its garrison. The county's part time militia, dismissed by Corbett as 'effeminate in courage and incapable of discipline', had been destroyed at Cirencester and was not rebuilt. That left a core of professional soldiers detached from Parliament's main field army, reinforced by local volunteers who were increasingly professional but owed their loyalty first and foremost to the city authorities. In the former category was the Earl of Stamford's Regiment of Foot, commanded by Massey (Stamford himself had been stranded at Exeter by Hopton's rapid advance from the west) and one of Parliament's original twenty infantry regiments, recruited from London and Stamford's home county of Leicestershire. The regiment was not at Edgehill, having been detached to Hereford to help contain the king's march south. At that time it mustered nine or ten companies with 778 private soldiers and perhaps 100 or more officers, NCOs and drummers against an establishment of 1,200. By August 1643, Stamford's blue-coated musketeers (there was little call for pikemen in defending a city) had amassed considerable experience in the sieges, storms and skirmishes that characterised garrison warfare. Discipline was an enduring problem, especially when money was short, and few among the officers or other ranks were likely to put their lives at risk unnecessarily. Numbers had also declined, including a company lost at Cirencester, but the soldiers that remained were probably as good as any on either side, Massey was not the only experienced officer. His deputy, Major Constantine Ferrer, had served in the Scots Wars and rejected an attractive offer to defect while at Hereford. Of the others, three of the seven company captains had been with the regiment since the beginning of the war, two of the replacements had been promoted from within the regiment and one of the outsiders was Massey's brother George.

The second regiment, nominally commanded by Colonel Henry Stephens who was now dead or dying in Oxford, was led in practice by the lieutenant colonel, Humphrey Matthews. Raised locally under Waller and often known as the Town Regiment, it consisted of eight or nine companies, again almost certainly of musketeers. The officers were drawn primarily from Gloucester's Puritan elite, and included both the MP Thomas Pury and his son of the same name. Most of the soldiers had little experience but, in theory at least, they had the additional motivation of defending their homes and families, although reports from Royalist Sudeley suggested that some had decided not to resist the king.[8] Neither of the two infantry regiments was at much more than half strength, around 600 men apiece. Serving alongside them was a company of trained band foot and the 100-strong remains of a dragoon regiment formed by Waller under a Scots officer, Colonel Forbes, and withdrawn from Berkeley Castle after the fall of Bristol. Its second-in-command, Lieutenant Colonel Nicholas Devereux, was a cousin of the Earl of Essex who had arrived in Gloucester with the garrison's most singular military asset, Essex's bridging train, left behind after the Edgehill campaign. There was also a troop of cavalry commanded by a local lawyer, Captain Robert Backhouse, and a gaggle of unemployed officers known as 'reformados'. This was by any standards a small garrison, totalling no more than 1,500 soldiers. By contrast, Cirencester had been defended by 1,700 men and Bristol by 1,800, and neither had been able to mount more than a single day's resistance.[9]

At Bristol, Fiennes had been able to compensate for his shortage of manpower with over 100 cannon of different sizes. Massey had only a fraction of this total. 'Some pieces of ordinance' had been obtained from London and Bristol as the political crisis deepened, apparently including two 9-pounder demi-culverins and four 6-pounders. One of the latter was lost at Cirencester but Waller probably captured some light pieces in compensation during his operations in the Severn valley. Evidence by Thomas Pury given at Fiennes' trial suggests that there were only seven or eight guns at Gloucester during the siege. However, an assessment of the garrison's strength made six months later identified a dozen guns in addition to those delivered after the siege, and referred to an unspecified number of others. A total of around twelve, including small pieces that Pury may have ignored, is probably about right. Whatever the exact number, this was too small a battery to defeat a determined attack.[10]

Military stores were also in short supply. Fiennes had justified his surrender on the grounds that in heavy fighting he had used sixty barrels of gunpowder and had only twenty left. In early August, Gloucester's stock was 32–50 barrels (the sources differ), plus the capacity to produce a further three barrels a week from two mills inside the city. Powder was therefore a potentially fatal constraint on the garrison's ability to resist either an assault or a prolonged siege.[11] There were, however, ample supplies of other kinds, much of which was stripped from the surrounding countryside including a herd of over 200 cattle and hay to feed them, corn and alcohol. Water pipes from springs on Robinswood Hill to the south could easily be cut and the River Twyver, which drove the corn mills, could be diverted but there were wells within the city, the Severn was too wide to block or divert, and horses could be used to grind flour.

Compared to Cirencester and Bristol, Gloucester's greatest advantage was its location.[12] Although it had spread beyond the original medieval walls, it was still a compact city while, to the west, the River Severn was a barrier against all but amphibious attack. To the north and northeast, the ground was marshy and therefore unsuitable for heavy artillery, mining or other engineering operations; and the River Twyver and a tributary stream formed a potential obstacle against attack. Only to the east and south, where the ground was higher and drier, were conditions entirely favourable for siege or storm. This meant that the garrison could focus its resources on this section and be fairly confident that major threats were unlikely to emerge elsewhere.

The city's natural advantages were not significantly enhanced by its man-made defences. The medieval works, reinforced by a Norman castle, had survived into the first half of the sixteenth century when John Leland described Gloucester as strongly defended. But John Speed's map of 1610 shows that the subsequent century of peace saw the rapid degeneration of both walls and castle. By 1643, the castle was a ruin and only the stretch of wall from the South Gate to the Inner North Gate remained, and parts of that were falling down. Massey seems to have had some engineering experience and this had been put fully to the test in frantic efforts to reinforce these defences, originally in the face of Herbert's investment and now as the strategic picture had deteriorated again. The garrison believed that the most likely points for attack were the drier south and south-eastern approaches to the city. To meet this threat, a strong earthwork defence line, including a narrow water-filled ditch, was built from the Severn to the South Gate in front of the dilapidated castle, with an artillery battery at the old castle barbican.

From the South Gate to the East Gate, the old walls were two stories high but only six feet or so thick, and therefore extremely vulnerable to modern artillery and mining. Although wooden blinds provided protection for musketeers firing from the top of the walls and the defensive ditch continued along in front, neither the South Gate nor the old walls had yet been reinforced with earth to strengthen them against artillery fire. The walls and ditch continued northeast from the East Gate as far as Whitefriars Barn, but then turned west towards the Inner North Gate, well inside the city's boundaries. Another earthwork had consequently been built in the period immediately before the siege to enclose part of the northern suburbs. This ran north from Whitefriars to the Outer North Gate and Alvin Gates and then west towards the Severn. The ground in front was very marshy and the line probably followed the course of the River Twyver and its tributary, which would have formed a wet moat. These defences were not as strong as those to the south but they were reinforced by an earthwork bastion at the Outer North Gate and one or two more at the Alvin Gate. A second line of defence was provided by the final section of the old wall and a ditch or earthwork running from the Inner North Gate under the cathedral walls to St Oswald's Priory. The effort put into defending the city's northern edges suggests that Massey was concerned more with assault than with artillery bombardment, and that the dampness of the ground did not appear an insuperable handicap.

To the west were small earthwork forts or sconces at the Vineyard, the old Bishop's palace on the far bank of the Severn, and on Alney Island, a strip of land between the river's two arms. They were reinforced by north-facing earthworks running from the Twyver to the Severn at the West Gate, and incorporating an artillery battery. Finally, a half-moon bastion was built on the riverside as a second line of defence in the unlikely event of the West Gate being captured and the enemy attempting to storm across the Severn.

Beyond these defences, Speed's map and a later one of 1624 show that Gloucester's suburbs had expanded to the north, south and especially east. Efforts had been made to clear fields of fire but to be fully effective, these buildings would have to be levelled. That would be a difficult decision for any civic authority and one that at Gloucester was delayed until the last possible moment. Preparations were, however, made in advance to fire the houses when the time finally came and a committee was set up to re-house the affected families. There may also have been some artificial flooding of the north and north-west approaches. By the standards of the day, and compared even to Bristol, Gloucester's defences were far from formidable. Though Massey would continue to strengthen the earthworks and walls, and prepare to deal with incendiary bombardment of the predominantly wooden buildings inside the city, neither at the time nor with hindsight did it appear that the defences were adequate against an attack or a more deliberate investment.

The final element in Gloucester's defences was the command arrangements. As governor, Massey was the undisputed military leader inside the city. His leadership style tended to be autocratic and there are few references from this period to a council of war. However, the governor's powers were not absolute and had to be shared with the civilian authorities. Gloucester had created a committee of defence in the previous summer. A county committee to run, and in particular to fund, the war on Parliament's behalf had been established in December, dominated by a small group of activists. As 1643 progressed, the rate of attrition among them increased. Of the nine most prominent committee men, one had been captured at Cirencester and two at Bristol, and Sir Robert Cooke, the most influential man in the inshire, had been mortally wounded at Worcester. Of the others, only Thomas Pury, Gloucester's own MP, is mentioned in contemporary accounts as being in the city at the time of the siege and it is difficult to avoid the impression that most of Parliament's civilian leaders in the county were either conveniently in London or keeping their heads down elsewhere.

That left the city's representatives. The forty-strong common council was in theory the main civic body but power was exercised in practice by an inner circle of mayor and aldermen. When efforts were being made to stiffen the city's resolve, the common council met in formal session but when the king's ultimatum was considered, no more than fifteen civilians were involved in drawing up the reply. In both cases, however, officers from the garrison took part in large numbers. That may have been a reflection of the dual roles of some local leaders, who were both aldermen or council members and officers in one or other of the garrison units. Nonetheless, it seems that during the siege, Gloucester's political and military command structures were for all practical purposes integrated. This is in stark contrast to the situation later in the war when relations between the military and civilian authorities degenerated into bitter disagreements.[13]

Taken overall, Gloucester's military condition was not hopeless. The garrison had strengths as well as weaknesses, and the much shorter perimeter under threat compared to Bristol was a significant advantage. Yet the probability was that however well the soldiers fought, they would be submerged by one of Rupert's trademark assaults. If that option remained closed, it was uncertain how the city would resist a prolonged investment. Here the key factor was the will of the people to resist their king. Should civilian morale collapse, it would be difficult for a relatively small garrison, drawn in large part from the local population, to carry on regardless.

IV

Political resolve is difficult to judge in any circumstances but especially when the events concerned rapidly enter the realm of popular mythology. In fact, Gloucester was not as unusual as the myths would suggest. It was not exceptional for towns loyal to either side in the civil war to resist a field army, which is why Prince Rupert had already acquired a reputation for brutality in capturing them. Nor were sieges extraordinary events; Portsmouth, Hull and Reading had refused to submit quickly to opponents, with varying degrees of success. Gloucester's ubiquity was a product of the disparity between what contemporaries expected to happen and what eventually took place; and what appeared thereafter to be unique was the perceived imbalance between the king's main army and the small Parliamentarian garrison, and the very fact of successful resistance in the wake of a series of defeats. In addition, Parliament encouraged a perception of highly motivated heroism for propaganda purposes.

At the time, negotiated surrender was widely anticipated, yet with hindsight it is surprising not that Gloucester resisted but that it came so close to capitulation. Given the combination of factors that had delivered it into Parliament's camp, robust resistance to a Royalist army was to be expected. Contemporaries pointed to the city's Puritanism, its record of opposition to the Crown and fear of its savage Welsh Royalist neighbours. Today, we can add the strong feelings of community among the city's ruling elite, their well-developed sense of victimisation and isolation, and their fear of social disorder. We can also identify the machinery that enabled the often unpopular elite to maintain social order in peacetime and could now be used to impose their will on the rest of the city's population.[14]

Nonetheless, following the storming of Bristol it is clear that there was, yet again, a spectacular collapse of civic morale in Gloucester. Corbett, whose account put the lie at a very early stage to the myth that Gloucester was a homogeneous community, united in opposition to tyranny, wrote that the 'minds of people were filled with amazement, and the failing of such a promising government made most men infidels'. He also identified the many and various culprits: 'malignant spirits ... [who] questioned the passages of state', the 'weak and faint hearted', and 'the viler people ... [whose mouths] were filled with curses against the authors of our engagement'; while beyond the walls, the 'whole country forsook us'. This was not solely the post hoc prejudice of a member of the civic elite, nor was it entirely Corbett's attempt to present his patron, Massey, in the best possible light. The Royalists believed they had identified 104 potential supporters and this cannot all have been wishful thinking. Moreover, on 29 July, two days after Bristol's surrender, Massey himself wrote to the Speaker of the Commons in what seems a state of despair about the condition of civilian morale in the city: 'Alderman Pury and some few of the citizens, I dare say, are still cordial to us, but I fear ten to one incline the other way'. Massey was making a last minute attempt to obtain reinforcements and, perhaps, to put on record advance justification for the loss – or surrender – of Gloucester so that he would not face the same opprobrium as Fiennes. But it was a public report and Massey would have found himself in domestic difficulty with the city's civil authorities had he misrepresented the situation.

Despair infected the garrison as well. In his 29 July letter, Massey warned that he could not enforce loyalty because of 'the general discontent of both [regiments], of the city soldiers and our own'. As noted previously, the Royalist commander at Sudeley was reporting a similar message to Bristol, suggesting that the locally recruited soldiers had decided not to fight; in a separate letter, he mentioned that Stamford's 'blue-coats' were deserting in numbers. Massey told Parliament that unless they sent help, he had lost all hope of saving Gloucester. He was not the only one. Mayor Dennis Wise, who had played a prominent role in past crises, is almost invisible during this period and, perhaps not coincidentally, received little credit thereafter for his city's achievement. Indeed, the only individual that we know of whose nerve certainly held was alderman and MP, Thomas Pury.[15]

Pury was a long standing opponent of the king, best known nationally for a blistering attack on episcopacy in 1641. His background was described succinctly by a political enemy during the 1640 elections: 'once a weaver, now an attorney, whom I think, nothing has so much endeared as his irreverence in God's house, sitting covered [in a hat] when the rest go bare'. Another Royalist later complained that he 'bears no goodwill to gentlemen'. As a clothier and a Puritan, Pury had strong grounds for fighting the king. As someone who could expect little mercy if captured, he also had ample justification for keeping his head down in London; he was sufficiently notorious to be excluded from the king's pardon in 1642. But he seems to have combined conviction with personal courage and by 29 July he had returned from London. The nineteenth-century historian John Washburn believed Pury's influence to have been crucial in stiffening the city's resolve:

> some were wavering; and there is good ground for suspicion that [Pury] and his party counteracted any thing like a return towards loyalty in the other authorities; for both the mayor and governor seem to have hesitated, the former upon his oath, and the latter upon his ancient service and allegiance.

The evidence for Pury's role is circumstantial but strong. It was only following his return to Gloucester that the city's military and civilian authorities began to prepare in earnest for the coming onslaught; he was identified as one of the leaders standing out against surrender on 3 August; and it was during the first ten days of August that a fundamental change took place in the attitudes of the leadership and in public mood. The broad and enthusiastic support for resistance emphasised by Parliamentarian sources, but also remarked upon by Royalists and neutrals, was in such marked contrast to the situation in late July that it required sustained leadership of the kind that no-one else seems capable of providing.[16] The first steps were also primarily political rather than military in nature.

Pury cannot have acted alone. Without Massey, he could not have persuaded the garrison to fight and he must therefore have won his public support at an early stage. At Sudeley, they thought that only Pury, Massey, Singleton and Nelmes stood in the way of Gloucester being 'delivered up without a stroke'. Singleton was probably William, an alderman, Pury's predecessor as MP in the Short Parliament and a captain in Stephen's Regiment; Nelmes was one of his fellow officers. If this was Pury's party, they took the initiative quickly and effectively. A common council meeting was called to which the garrison officers were invited, and both officers and civilians were asked to confirm the oaths of allegiance to Parliament that they had taken only weeks earlier. To do otherwise would have been political suicide for the civil leaders and tantamount to resignation for the officers since taking the oath was a condition of soldiers receiving their pay. With one possible exception, no one appears to have declined and the officers 'vowed never to see within the gates the face of a conquering enemy'.

Next, measures were agreed to underpin the oath with financial incentives. The lesson of February had been well learnt and soldiers were therefore to be paid, including the officers whose loyalty and example would be essential in winning around the civilian population. It was also decided to give doubters the opportunity to leave, thereby reducing the likelihood of action by covert Royalists. The two measures were linked in that anyone departing had to place their money and valuables in a newly established treasury that could be used to pay the troops. How many left is uncertain. The single senior officer who seems to have decided to go was the Scottish professional, Colonel Forbes. Although there is a record of his being paid during the period before the siege, the Royalists at Sudeley reported that he had gone towards Warwick, his dragoon regiment was described thereafter as 'broken' (or leaderless) and there are no subsequent references to him serving in Gloucester.[17]

To restore morale among the remaining people in the city, Pury and Massey used a mixture of example and mobilisation. Officers loudly 'vented themselves in sharp and cutted speeches, which ... were received for good prognostics', and Massey took to riding through the streets 'with a cheerful aspect ... [giving] assurance of safety, concealing the danger, or lessening its esteem'. A second request for help, as urgent but less apocalyptic than the first, was sent to Parliament on 5 August. In parallel, civilians of both genders, all classes and all ages were conscripted to work round the clock on the defences. This was militarily essential but it also kept potential malcontents busy and encouraged the community spirit that had previously been lacking. All the evidence is that the initiative was a great success. Dorney could write without contradiction of the 'cheerful readiness' of even the 'inferior sort of people' to labour on preparations and Hyde would comment with grudging admiration that 'they in the town behaved themselves with great courage and resolution'. Although fear of looting and reprisals would have probably stiffened resolve once the Royalist threat materialised, that would have been too late to complete the city's defences. The contrast between the positions in late July and on the king's arrival was therefore both a tribute to the determination and political skills of Pury and his supporters, and an essential precursor if Gloucester was to have any hope of surviving the coming storm.[18]

V

Yet for all Gloucester's renewed commitment to Parliament's cause, the fact remains that the Royalists were about to march north because they believed that it would not resist the king and, in particular, that Colonel Edward Massey was prepared to surrender the city. Rumours were insistent. In London, Venetian diplomats heard that the 'people of Gloucester are ... parlaying, but they want to make a bargain with the king in person'. In Oxford, *Mercurius Aulicus* eagerly anticipated victory 'on the first assault' because of 'the backwardness of the people to make good [the defences] ... or contribute to the work'. More specifically, an unidentified Royalist recorded only days later that Massey had written to 'Major Legge, that if the king came before the town, he would bring him in with a thousand men'. At Sudeley, they thought instead that Major Ferrar might desert.

According to Hyde, though the rumours were right, Massey's offer was not genuine but 'craftily and maliciously written to amuse the king'. They were, in other words, a deception. Two centuries later, Gardiner disagreed. Massey was guilty of a 'contemplated act of treachery' and changed his mind only after Parliament's true supporters regained effective control of the city. Subsequent accounts have tended to follow Gardiner or to sit on the fence.[19] After such a lapse of time, one cannot say with certainty what were Massey's motives. It is, however, possible to construct a chain of events consistent with the evidence and what happened subsequently, and to adduce from it a plausible explanation for his actions.

There is undoubtedly a case to answer. Writing some years later, Hyde had no reason to invent Massey's message to Legge, which was to the discredit of a man then working for the Royalists, and Massey had been and would in future be prepared to serve the king against Parliament. His reply was sufficient encouragement to those that knew him to justify putting him to the test and, in the circumstances of the time, there was clearly merit in a prudent and ambitious man leaving open all possible options until the last moment. By the same token, it seems most unlikely that a commander in Massey's position would have done anything to incite the king to move against his weak garrison. Yet that is precisely what Hyde suggests happened.

Massey was young (in his early twenties) and, according to his critics, arrogant and impetuous. Even his admirers did not pretend that he was anything but self-confident and a risk taker. That is what made him so attractive to Parliamentarian propagandists, who were scraping around for successful generals with what would later be called star quality. Playing a double game requires confidence and appears to have come naturally to him, whether as a Royalist agent during the Interregnum or as Gloucester's garrison commander during the following winter when he conducted a prolonged deception of Sir William Vavasour, the so-called Backhouse plot, which led to another series of rumours about the loyalty of the garrison, a risk that he clearly thought worth the potential gains. Nor were secret negotiations foreign to the climate of civil war. The Earl of Essex's apparently hardline cavalry commander, Sir Philip Stapleton, had only recently been in correspondence with the apotheosis of his beliefs, the queen; while Sir John Hotham, Hull's turncoat governor, argued at his trial that correspondence with the enemy was a trick commonly used by professional soldiers in Germany to gain time when their garrison was in difficulty. It is therefore entirely conceivable that Massey was indeed acting out of loyalty to Parliament in responding to Legge's initiative. That he received the messenger openly for the first of their meetings suggests that he was confident that this would not be misinterpreted in Gloucester. After his bout of panic in late July, there is none of the equivocation in his actions that might be expected from a potential traitor, especially one that would have to carry some of his fellow officers with him. Nor is there any of the suspicion in Parliamentarian quarters that rightly surrounded Hotham before his arrest.

The weakest link in the case against Massey is, however, in the timing of his message to Legge. Gardiner's argument that Massey intended to betray the city when he sent the message and changed his mind only when Pury's party took control is inconsistent with what we know of the timetable of events. Legge did not receive Massey's reply until 7 August. It is likely that the messenger was a trumpeter sent by Colonel Charles Gerard, who is recorded by Dorney as entering Gloucester the day before on the pretext of negotiating with Massey for the return of four cavalry horses.[20] By that time, the shakiness of late July was past, Pury was well in control and Massey was playing a key part in preparing the city for battle. On the other hand, when the message arrived it would have appeared inevitable to Gloucester's leaders that the king would march against them. In these circumstances delaying tactics such as covert negotiations would have been an attractive and legitimate stratagem. Only Essex could save them and a relief march would take time. Massey's reply is consistent with that approach. Far better to have the king in command of the army than his nephew, who was more likely to storm the city than to negotiate or besiege it, and less likely to restrain his troops after any eventual surrender. And from Massey's point of view, if negotiations provided him with an insurance policy in case the city had second thoughts or his men refused to fight, then so much the better.

The evidence therefore suggests that Massey may have been prepared to sell Gloucester but only during his period of despair in late July. At that time, the Royalists were still squabbling about the governance of Bristol and Rupert's plans involved the storming of Gloucester, not its capture by betrayal. When the Royalist council of war eventually began considering other options, Massey's resolve had been stiffened, the militants were back in control and the time for treachery had passed. By then, however, Gloucester's leaders had strong motives for pretending that their governor was open to negotiations. When Legge made his approach, they had nothing to lose and perhaps something to gain from this routine but often effective ruse. Massey received no criticism thereafter because he had been acting with the agreement of his colleagues.

Whatever the true motives of Massey and Gloucester's other leaders, there can be little doubt that the king and his army would advance northwards on a wild goose chase. The basis for the council of war's decision was that Gloucester could be taken quickly, by subversion from within or as the result of a collapse of the defenders' will to resist their sovereign. Either response might conceivably have greeted a Royalist army in the immediate wake of Bristol's capture. By the time the army finally marched on 8 August, it was too late. Any traitors had left or were lying low. The city's political will to resist had been restored. Militarily, the garrison was incapable of defeating a full-scale assault but they were better placed to wage a battle of attrition. At worst, they could delay the king for days, perhaps weeks, until relief came, Rupert's solution was adopted or they ran out of food and ammunition. Gloucester was not in control of its own destiny yet its leaders were, unconsciously, already pulling some of the king's strings.

Chapter Four
'No good news'

I

As the summer of 1643 progressed, the self-confidence of King Charles' enemies melted away. All the theoretical advantages of economic strength, population, local organisation, military resources and interior lines of communication were failing to achieve significant or sustained success. The righteousness of their cause had counted for little in the face of Wilmot's cavalry, Hopton's Cornish infantry, Newcastle's resources and Prince Rupert's brutal assaults. In diaries, letters, speeches and newspapers, there is a growing sense of despair about the military situation: 'I fear we shall see sorrowful times'; 'Many expect the storm ere long to come upon us'; 'This week hath produced no good news, the City of Bristol is lost to our great grief'.[1] To contemporary chroniclers of the war, these dark days were the nadir of Parliament's cause. Subsequent descriptions of the achievements of Parliament's leaders, John Pym and Robert Devereux, Earl of Essex, have reinforced that impression of prior weakness and danger. Such an approach brings structure and coherence to the events of the summer of 1643. If this was indeed the turning point of the war, it makes sense for the period immediately before it to have been the time when Parliament was most at risk. Because of the importance of that assumption, it needs to be re-examined to provide the baseline for what Pym, Essex and their colleagues did actually achieve, starting with the eruption of a major crisis in London in early July.

Although the crisis was primarily political, its origins lay in military failure and disappointed expectations. In April, Essex had been applauded for his almost bloodless capture of Reading but the public mood changed quickly when that success proved to be the high water mark of his campaign. MP Sir Simon Dewes believed that had Parliament's Captain General and his forces moved immediately against Oxford, 'the king's army would have disbanded before they had come up to them'. London newspapers agreed: 'the glory of the action ... seems to be eclipsed by our staying there so long without advancing'. A Venetian diplomatic report talked of Essex 'wasting money and men in sloth'. What was the earl doing with his army of, reportedly, 30,000 men?

In truth, the army was never more than 19,000 strong, even according to Royalist estimates, and had reached that number only temporarily by calling on regional commanders for assistance. Nor was the army, which had been rebuilt over the winter from the wreckage of the Edgehill campaign, in good shape psychologically or physically. Fragile morale was weakened further by the earl's honourable refusal to sanction the pillaging of Reading or its garrison. As at Bristol, discipline collapsed, and many soldiers broke ranks and their general's word to attack the departing Cavaliers. Parliament then turned Essex into a liar by failing to provide him with money to pay the twelve shillings per man compensation he had promised them in lieu of plunder. At the same time, the typhus epidemic hit the army, and sapped its morale and capabilities still further. Normal pay dried up and desertion became rife.[2]

Under pressure from Westminster, Essex finally resumed his advance. In early June his crippled army crawled to Thame, only a dozen miles east of Oxford but an infinite distance from capturing it. Royalist intelligence sounded almost sympathetic:

> The chief cause of their moving is supposed to be for fresh quarters, and for the relief of their sick, which die in great abundance; four hundred of them were sent this day in barges for London, and great numbers remain behind unable to stir, and many who have the use of their legs employ them in running away from the misery that follows their army. They are certainly in great confusion, and are possessed by marvellous fears.

The earl made one half-hearted attempt to outflank the Royalist capital to the north before Prince Rupert began to harry his quarters to encourage him to retreat. In a skirmish at Chalgrove, John Hampden, John Pym's representative at the army's headquarters, and Essex's friend, advisor and reputed successor, was mortally wounded and died on 24 June. Without hope of defeating the Royalists in front of Oxford, and plagued alike by disease and Rupert's cavalry, there was little Essex could do in the Thames valley. The Royalists therefore switched their attention to ensuring the safety of the queen's northern convoy. On 30 June, Rupert's cavalry moved to Buckingham and four days later Essex shadowed him north-east to Great Brickhill.[3] From here, in the strategic wastelands of north Buckinghamshire, the earl wrote a letter to Parliament dated 9 July that ignited the simmering political crisis.

His correspondence with Parliament was already bad tempered and confrontational. In late June, he had complained that the House of Commons was criticising him unfairly, undermining his plans by insisting on prior consultation and failing to provide adequate funding. In early July, twelve of his colonels refused to take the new loyalty oath. On 5 July he demanded 500 horses immediately and 200 a month to keep his cavalry operational. By 9 July, the tone of this further letter suggests that he was close to despair. Without Hampden's astute political advice, it was certainly maladroit. First, Essex admitted that his sick and shrinking army could not counter Rupert's marauding cavalry; indeed, he implied that he had moved to Great Brickhill to escape from them. Second, the letter threw his clumsy political weight behind peace proposals being developed in the House of Lords that looked to most observers to verge on capitulation. Finally, it suggested, quixotically, that if peace talks failed the civil war should be decided by a single set-piece battle while the king sat to one side awaiting the outcome. To the peace party in the House of Lords, the letter was welcome support for a negotiated settlement. To John Pym and the advocates of continuity in the war effort, it was at best ill-judged and at worst called into question the earl's commitment. To Essex's many critics, this was a heaven-sent opportunity to attack the man who most symbolised what they saw as Parliament's half-hearted war. Puritan preachers and pamphlets accused the earl of 'carnal self love', graffiti pictured him as a latter day Nero, newspapers suggested that London's money would go much further 'were there fewer officers and more common men' in the army, and MPs ridiculed and vilified the proposals in equal measure.[4]

Military events underlined Essex's impotence. For critics, it was bad enough that the withdrawal to Buckinghamshire appeared from the map to leave London open to the king. Most of them were unaware of the strategic niceties but they could fairly link the earl's withdrawal from the Thames valley with Wilmot's canter south to Roundway Down and Rupert's march west to Bristol. Those who knew that Essex's main target had been the queen's convoy could ask equally legitimately why it had danced between the various components of Parliament's blockade with such apparent ease. Then on 16 July, London was terrified by a Royalist rising in Kent.

Treason was in the air. A Royalist plot to take London had been exposed at the end of May. The governor of Hull had been arrested in late June. Royalist plans to use Catholic troops from Ireland to extend the war to Scotland were uncovered. Nathaniel Fiennes would soon be accused of betraying Bristol. The Venetians reported the rumours surrounding Essex:

[Parliament's] suspicions of his behaviour have reached a climax ... he has got [his leading officers] secretly to promise loyalty to himself ... he is preparing a manifesto ... it is clear that His Majesty apprehends nothing from his forces.

Instead of closing ranks, Parliament's generals were at each other's throats. Essex complained that although Lord Grey and Colonel Cromwell had 'many strict commands to have fought with the queen's forces and stopped her passage ... for which design they had a competent force ... it was not done'. Sir William Waller was thought to blame Roundway Down on Essex's failure to assist him, and support was growing for Waller to replace him or be put in command of an autonomous new army. In Oxford, *Mercurius Aulicus* commented smugly that Essex

knows not either what to do with his forces, or where to dispose of himself; not daring to go towards London ... for fear of being excoriated and put out of office by the headstrong multitude.

Discontent went well beyond the political classes. A new excise ordinance to raise money to pay Essex's soldiers would affect the standard of living of everyone under Parliament's control. London was suffering from food and fuel shortages and all were at risk from uprisings such as that in Kent, where Royalist mobs were looting and threatening to 'make every man a Roundhead that hath anything to lose'.[5]

Whether prompted by Pym or recognising belatedly that he had blundered, Essex wrote a follow-up letter to Parliament on 12 July, again setting out his problems but with no mention of peace negotiations. In an attempt to rebuild bridges, he asked for a Parliamentary committee to investigate the army's condition and invited the younger Sir Henry Vane, one of his bitterest critics, to help review the military situation. The political initiative was, however, passing beyond Westminster. Fuelled by concern about wasted money and abandoned Puritan principles, pressure was growing to revitalise Parliament's war effort separately from the earl's army. On 8 July, a pamphlet appeared advocating the creation of a 'godly' army of volunteers commanded by 'some godly nobleman'. Ten days later, London's City Council petitioned Parliament to transfer sole control of the London Trained Bands and other City units to the Militia Committee. This placed severe practical constraints on Essex, who already had London regiments in his army and would rely on the Trained Bands if the king marched on the capital. Yet Parliament acceded. On 20 July, a second petition from the City appeared seeking even more radical measures, a new 10,000 strong volunteer army controlled by a House of Commons committee packed with radical MPs. This was a blatant affront both to Parliament (which was being told who to appoint to its committees) and to Essex (whose post and army were in danger of being marginalised). But the Earl's political enemies, a coalition of militant war makers including radical republican Henry Martin and London's puritan Lord Mayor Isaac Pennington, had taken control of the Commons, and the sense of despair and the need for a fresh start were so great that Parliament again acceded.[6]

Having created the machinery for raising and controlling a new army, the militants needed a general to command it. With impeccable timing, their preferred candidate, Sir William Waller, entered London with the rump of his western army cavalry on 25 July. Although Waller was a tarnished hero, the London crowds (presumably orchestrated by Martin, Pennington and their friends) gave him a victor's welcome; two days later he was appointed by the Commons as general of the new 'Flying Army' with the express task of recapturing the west for Parliament. The City of London followed suit and made him commander of their forces as well. Meanwhile, on 28 July, news of Bristol's loss was received and on 1 August, when Lieutenant Colonel Massey's letter arrived from Gloucester pleading for help, Parliament's immediate response was to make Waller responsible for sending 'some force of men' to his assistance.[7] This was a considerable coup for Henry Martin, Isaac Pennington and their allies. They had exploited the circumstances adeptly to pursue the goal of a politically more congenial commander, and one who they believed would prosecute the war more vigorously and to better effect.

II

Waller's rival, Robert Devereux, third Earl of Essex, was a man moulded by betrayal and radical rebellion who took refuge in loyalty and conservatism.[8] His father had been executed for treason, his two wives both cuckolded him, and his king had cashiered him during the First Bishops' War and forced his resignation as Lord Chamberlain during the crisis of April 1642. Politically, he believed in monarchy, aristocracy and episcopacy yet he was the military figurehead of an alliance, many of whose members he despised, against a king he was sworn to uphold. The common strand in Essex's political life was loyalty to Parliament, where he had been one of King Charles' most consistent opponents, and to the soldiers he commanded during his sporadic military career. He was at home in both environments, though an inspired performer in neither. Despite decades at the centre of English political life, Essex displayed extraordinary naivety at the worst possible times in his relations with the Parliament he served. The 9 July letter was only the most recent example. His military experience had been gained in the 1620s in unsuccessful campaigns of attrition in the Netherlands and Rhineland, and in the Cadiz debacle. He planned carefully, looked after his men and displayed personal courage but had so far shown little strategic insight, a reluctance to take the initiative and a tendency to procrastinate. In his early fifties, Essex was cautious and bruised, jealous of potential rivals and (notwithstanding occasional threats to resign) desperate to preserve his status and position.

Waller, known popularly at that time as 'William the Conqueror', had made his reputation in secondary operations in the south and Severn valley. Less experienced than Essex, Sir William appeared to have a better grasp of what it took to fight battles and win campaigns. Although his armies were notoriously undisciplined, they moved quickly and he showed an unusual tactical ability to exploit terrain. Until Roundway Down, he had held the upper hand against the Royalist Western Army. Thereafter, he had escaped with surprisingly little criticism for his defeat by Wilmot or his flight back to London. For some, Waller's main asset was that he was not the earl nor of the earl's party. But that does not mean that he was a cipher. Although politically moderate and personally pious, he was astute, not without ambition and, according to gossip, driven forward by his domineering second wife.[9]

Neither Essex nor Waller was blessed with exceptional talent as a commander. Essex had been unimaginative and ponderous but he was trusted by and popular with his officers and soldiers. He had yet to lose – or win – a major battle and he had accumulated more experience of managing and controlling a large army than any of Parliament's other generals. Yet if Waller were to replace him and the necessary resources were made available, there was no reason why a new broom should not revitalise the jaded army. On balance, what mattered was not so much who commanded Parliament's main army but how quickly the rivalry could be resolved, and whether that commander would be given the men and money to be able to deal effectively with whatever political instructions he was then given. The key influence in this respect was John Pym, King Charles' most enduring enemy, a Somerset Puritan who was the first Englishman to become a national figure through Parliament, though he was neither a fluent debater nor a gifted interpreter of MPs' moods. Pym's strengths were his inner certainty, religious passion, intellect and organisational skills. A long-time ally of Essex, he had created and managed Parliament's war machinery (based around a joint Committee of the Lords and Commons for the Safety of the Kingdom and an ad hoc network of tax gathering and disbursement run by Sir Gilbert Gerard, cousin and namesake of one of the king's colonels) but now faced as deep a crisis as any in his political career. Military failure and political dissension were exacerbated by the near collapse of Parliament's finances[10], reflected in the critical under-funding of its armies. Pym faced these challenges with the added burden of fatal disease, 'a large abscess' that was probably bowel cancer. The earl's future depended on Pym's ability to stave off his illness and cast his spell over the factions competing for control of Parliament's strategy.

III

Although the war between Parliament's generals was good political theatre, the more important decision taken in those bleak weeks of July was Parliament's hasty, almost offhand, adoption of a policy of offensive operations by giving Waller a specific remit not only to reinforce Gloucester but to recapture the west.[11] As a longer-term aim, this was unobjectionable, if ambitious given the state of Parliament's armies. Mature reflection might also have suggested other, higher priorities for military action. Bristol's fall and Massey's letter focused political attention on the west but should in parallel have highlighted the potential risks of an early offensive campaign. While the Kent revolt had been suppressed before the Royalists could exploit it, the general expectation was that Bristol's loss would be followed by invasion of the south-east. Now the Earl of Newcastle looked to be moving south and Gloucester to be little more than an appetiser for Prince Rupert's cavaliers on their way towards London. Unless Parliament was extraordinarily well informed about the true state of the king's armies, and there is no hint of that in surviving intelligence reports, or there were other reasons to take the fight into the west, an offensive strategy seems an unduly risky enterprise.

The main reason for that conclusion is the state of Parliament's own forces. Their condition had, after all, caused the political crisis to which the western strategy owed its origin and it is inconceivable that even the most un-military MPs could have harboured illusions about Essex's troops. On 22 July, they received an emotive letter from the earl's council of war reporting that the army was 'much decayed very suddenly' and risked 'destruction and overthrow'. That was followed by yet another letter from Essex himself, dated 28 July and read in Parliament three days later. From Beaconsfield, Essex described the condition of his army in stark terms:

> 1. The number of foot three thousand marching men, at least three thousand sick, occasioned by the want of pay, ill clothing, and all other miseries which attend an unpaid, sickly army. 2. The number of horse two thousand five hundred (three thousand last muster) occasioned by loss of horses upon hard duty and service, recruit of horse though often desired not performed; beside, by reason of a new army, the present regiments much lessened, ... and great discouragements and scandals put upon his Excellency, the officers, and the army.

There was little exaggeration in Essex's surprisingly frank assessment. Surviving pay warrants confirm that the army's eleven infantry regiments between them comprised only 4,681 private soldiers in July/August and therefore had a total theoretical strength (including those too sick to march) of around 5,900. Typhus, under-funding and desertion had reduced Major General Skippon's regiment from 1,133 private soldiers in early April to 516; Lord Robartes' Regiment from 723 to 365; and Colonel Langham's from 908 to 431. The cavalry seem not to have lost as many men from disease but they started from a much smaller base; records suggest that the eight cavalry regiments were paying a maximum of only about 3,200 men during this period. Without substantial reinforcements, new clothing and equipment, and pay, the truth was that Essex's army was incapable of offensive operations. No other existing force could compensate. Waller's old army was broken, plans to build up the Eastern Association's forces under the Earl of Manchester were as yet on paper only, and Parliament's forces in the east midlands and Lincolnshire were hard pressed to prevent Newcastle's army from marching south. Although London's part-time Trained Bands had been expanded to over 20,000 strong, they were not expected to deploy away from the capital.[12]

Despite the seriousness of the military situation, defeat was not an immediate danger. In an emergency, the remaining field armies together with the London Trained Bands and the Tower's powerful artillery train should have been able to fight a successful defensive battle, either in front of or behind London's defences. Blockade and starvation was a threat if Newcastle joined the king, though difficult to enforce while the Navy remained loyal to Parliament. Rupert's raids and the rising in Kent caused panic in the capital and there was deep depression about the overall military situation, but the abiding impression is one of frustration or weariness, not fear of imminent attack. This view is supported by the public response to Waller's return and promotion; the political primacy of the militants who wanted to win the war rather than the advocates of a negotiated compromise; and Venetian assessments that the king had lost an important opportunity by not supporting the Kent rising.

If, however, survival was not enough and Parliament wanted to take the initiative either by recapturing lost ground in the west or forestalling an offensive against London, then additional forces would be needed, in large numbers and quickly. And it is clear from the decisions taken by Parliament in late July and early August that retaking the military initiative was a very high priority. From today's perspective, it is difficult to put a convincing motive to this imperative. On 19 July, Vane was commissioned by Parliament to take a team to Edinburgh to negotiate Scottish military intervention, Pym's scheme for breaking the military stalemate which promised much better prospects of victory in the new year, provided of course that Parliament was not defeated in the interim.[13] Against that background, a low risk defensive strategy appears far preferable, at least until the outcome of the Scots negotiations became clear. There may of course have been factors driving Pym and his colleagues of which we are not aware. They may have been so concerned about London's loyalty and susceptibility to Royalist subversion that they considered it safest to meet the Royalist threat as far as possible from Parliament's heartland, or judged that positive action was necessary to bolster morale and frustrate the Lords' peace initiative. Given the timing, however, it seems more likely that if the offensive strategy was the product of deep thought of any kind, it was imposed on Pym by those who were looking for an early home-grown victory to pre-empt Scottish intervention and influence. Religion was an important factor in this respect. Henry Martin and his allies were opposed to replacing episcopacy with Scottish-inspired Presbyterianism; the City of London had declined to take part in Vane's negotiating team. Religion aside, City purses would be stretched still further by the inevitable high costs of a Scottish army. Martin would self-destruct in mid-August when Pym was able to exploit his ill-judged advocacy of regicide to have him imprisoned in the Tower. But by then the strategy was not only in place, it was being implemented.

IV

A citizen army of volunteers (known as the Army of the General Rising) was at the heart of Martin's plans. In theory, London and the south-east provided Parliament with overwhelming superiority in manpower. However, Essex had already discovered that the well had run dry after the enthusiastic response of the previous summer and although money now came in freely from the City, people did not. They were happy to turn out to applaud Sir William Waller and to listen to rousing speeches at the Merchant Tailors' Hall, yet not to become soldiers in Parliament's cause – or at least not in this army. Within a week, Martin had to report to the Commons that the flood of recruits had failed to materialise. According to the Venetians, recruiting proceeded slowly

> not from lack of money, as the citizens vie with each other in their zeal to do their utmost, but of men, of whom there are few left who are ready to take service.

Sir Simon Dewes put the number of volunteers as low as 300. The coalition between the City and the radical MPs proved fragile when put to this test; Martin's army found itself in competition for recruits with the City's new forces, and the City could offer much better terms. When Martin's committee suggested some form of coercion, the Commons gave a stony response. As a result, Waller, as commander of both forces, found himself in the midst of an increasingly bitter row between his two sets of employers.[14]

Pym exploited the divide between Martin and the City to counterattack with skill. His renewed energy may reflect a period of remission from the cancer that was gripping his body. The catalysts were Essex's more measured letter of 28 July and second thoughts on all sides about how to respond to Massey's plea for assistance. After describing the appalling state of his army, Essex asked for six specific remedies – money to pay arrears and attract recruits, and 1,000 uniforms per regiment; 500 horses plus 200 per month for recruits; no recruiting for a new army until his requirements had been met; both Houses of Parliament to pass a declaration of support vindicating his actions and those of his officers; no commissions for raising or commanding forces to be granted except by Essex himself; and an investigation into the causes of Parliament's defeat in the west. These requests were not new; some money and horses had already been voted in response to the plea from Essex's council of war. But by 2 August, a step behind Martin's initiative, Pym had obtained agreement to most of the other requests and at the same time undermined almost everything that Martin had achieved.

On 31 July, only three days after Waller's nomination as commander of the Army of the General Rising, both Lords and Commons confirmed Essex's contention that all commissions should come from him. Waller therefore had to go through the additional hoop of the Captain General's approval before he could take up his new posts. Parliament further agreed that Essex should get his horses and be able to recruit 4,000 new soldiers, thereby adding to the already fierce competition for manpower, although they also introduced forcible impressment to compensate for the decline in volunteers. The next day, they agreed to cover Essex's pay arrears and to provide the clothing he had asked for. For potential recruits, the earl's army suddenly looked more attractive than Waller's under-funded regiments. Then, on 2 August, the Commons approved all of Essex's remaining requests, with the unsurprising exception of the potentially divisive inquiry into Waller's western debacle. To ensure that this was more than symbolic support, a supporting money bill was also passed. Pym was clearly back in the driving seat. On the same day he made sure that control of the conflict could not in future be snatched from his hands by pushing through the Commons the creation of a council of war to advise the House on military issues and coordinate military planning for all of the main Parliamentarian armies. As Martin's committee had been packed with militants, so this was composed of Pym's reliable friends.

Pym's final coup was more important still. Further differences had emerged between Martin and the City of London, this time over command of their western venture. News from Bristol and Gloucester concentrated the minds of Isaac Pennington and his fellow civic leaders. Whereas on 1 August they agreed with Martin that Waller must lead the expedition, leaving Essex to atrophy around London, a day later Pym's nephew predicted to a supporter that the City would side with Essex on the morrow. It is not certain whether the City leaders wanted a politically reliable general close at hand if the king marched east or had decided belatedly that Essex was a sounder bet for such a large scale operation. Whatever their motive, Pym was able to exploit this change of heart. On 3 August, only two days after Waller had been ordered to reinforce

Gloucester, Parliament decided that he should instead be given command of the army for the defence of London while Essex led his troops, reinforced by almost 5,000 new volunteers, into the west. A committee for the relief of Exeter and western parts (not explicitly Gloucester) was established to debate strategy and Pym was invited to lead a delegation to tell Essex that his demands had at last been met – and ask the earl to approve Waller's subordinate appointment. That day, when Martin reported the failure of his recruiting drive, Parliament was no longer sympathetic. The shift in power is evident from his complaints that one of the reasons for failure was that Essex had yet to grant Waller a formal commission. In similar vein, the City took the humbling decision to send two aldermen to apologise to Essex 'for the lack of respect shown by the people'. This was not, however, a return to the status quo ante. As a consequence of Martin and Pennington's short-lived alliance, and its conjunction with the loss of Bristol and cries for help from Gloucester, Pym and Parliament had been saddled with a commitment to relieve Gloucester and recapture the west.[15]

It is impossible to say for certain whether Pym personally favoured early offensive action in the west. He may have judged that Essex could delay his march until negotiations with the Scots were resolved or considered that another indecisive campaign in the Thames valley was a price worth paying for his victory over Martin and the militants. The fact was, however, that although Pym was back in control in Westminster, he was no longer in control of the timing of this key element of Parliamentarian strategy. A public commitment meant that the value of Gloucester could not simply be judged in military terms. Massey's garrison was already a political symbol, and its loss would have a disproportionate impact on morale and perhaps even the talks on Scottish intervention. Unfortunately, however, the problems of recruiting Waller's regiments had shown that who commanded the army was less of a challenge to Parliament in those early days of August than finding their generals sufficient soldiers to lead into battle.

V

Another internecine political battle in Westminster came to the fore during these critical few days before the king and his council of war took their decision on the future focus of the conflict. In early August, the peace party in the House of Lords launched their final attempt to achieve a negotiated settlement of the conflict. Because the Earl of Holland later opened his heart to Sir Edward Hyde, their initiative has often been accorded disproportionate importance.[16] With hindsight, the timing suggests that when firm proposals eventually emerged after the fall of Bristol, they were out of kilter with the temper in Westminster and less of a threat to Pym's management of the war than Martin's assault from the opposite end of the political spectrum; Pym and his allies did not lose control of the Commons – or of the Earl of Essex – during this crisis. That does not mean the threat did not exist but the danger point had been after Essex's endorsement of a negotiated settlement in early July. Had he continued to give even covert support, Holland and the peace party might well have garnered sufficient support in the Commons to push proposals through. Thereafter, the opportunity disappeared. Although despair among Parliament's supporters in the country was at its height following the loss of Bristol, by then the main question in Westminster was not whether to treat with the king but how best to defeat him.

Holland knew that Essex's endorsement of the peace plan was a key factor and on 3 August he visited the earl, his cousin, at his new headquarters at Kingston to seek his support. The deteriorating military situation had, paradoxically, forced Parliament to act in ways that lightened the gloomy picture that had affected Essex's judgement at Great Brickhill. Parliament was restoring his position within the military hierarchy, all but one of his long-standing requests was in the process of being satisfied and, thanks to Pym, he, not Waller, would lead the forthcoming campaign in the west. Moreover, once the Commons learned of Holland's visit, they added Pym to a delegation due to discuss Waller's commission with the earl, to stiffen his resolve. As a result, Holland failed to win Essex's support (indeed, according to Hyde, he 'expressed such a dislike of the Earl of Holland for proposing it that he [Holland] thought it high time to get himself out of his reach') and the initiative was to all intents doomed.

Holland and his colleagues went ahead anyway. Their proposal, endorsed by the Lords on 4 August and considered by the Commons the following day, was tantamount to capitulation, exchanging an act of oblivion for the king's opponents for control of the militia and the placing of issues of religion in the hands of a synod. Though a first vote to continue the debate on the following Monday went in favour of the peace party, supported by Waller, Essex's silence was deafening and he subsequently contributed, albeit indirectly, to pressure outside the House to reject the proposals by at last granting Sir William his commission. It was too limited for Martin's taste and would be subject to further negotiation but the message it sent was clear – Essex favoured carrying on the fight. When the Commons resumed consideration of the plan the next day, there was a militant London mob at the door and though the ballot was still a close run thing, the plan was defeated by eighty-eight to eighty-one, with Waller among the swing voters.[17]

So with coincidental symmetry Parliament had by 7 August, the day that the king's council of war decided at last to march north to Gloucester, cleared its political decks for the consequent campaign. It had done so not in response to Royalist action against Gloucester but as part of an ambitious, even rash, offensive strategy for the west as a whole. The roots of that strategy remain obscure but since it had been adopted while attention was focused on political infighting, it is most likely that when Pym and Essex regained control of the levers of power they found themselves committed to a military adventure which they had not thought through and for which Parliament's armies were ill-prepared. The need to consider the implications of the new commitment also helps to explain why it took over a week before Pym and Essex met to work out how the strategy should be implemented. By then, the military landscape had changed yet again.

Chapter Five
'Insolent and seditious answers'

I

From the outset, the late summer campaign of 1643 was characterised by incoherent thinking and ad hoc planning. Parliament now had a strategy that was inconsistent with its political priorities and no army to implement it, while the king had an army but no strategy worth speaking of; and the Royalists' military capacity was more impressive from a distance than it appeared in the council of war at Bristol. In moving north against Gloucester, Charles and his council had adopted a course for which rapid action and decisions were paramount. If Lieutenant Colonel Massey was to be put to the test before he could reconsider his offer to surrender, they had to get the army on the road from Bristol, summon reinforcements from Oxford and regain the services of their best general, Prince Rupert, as quickly as possible. Should Massey prove unreliable, they would then need to decide whether to take Gloucester or to move east against London as the queen wanted. The prevailing assumption was that the latter option would be adopted. Here, too, speed would be important to avoid losing the momentum of the past month and exploit Parliament's perceived fragility.

Thanks to Rupert's preparations, the army was already deploying northwards. Sir Arthur Aston, Colonel Charles Gerard and a strong body of cavalry were quartered around the village of Painswick, only six miles from Gloucester. Although Sir Arthur was complaining about his lack of infantry, records show that at least one regiment was based nearby at Nympsfield. The rest of the Bristol forces faced a thirty-mile march up the Severn valley or a longer journey along the Cotswold scarp. Local tradition is that the route chosen was through the Cotswold villages of Tetbury, Minchinhampton and Painswick to approach Gloucester from the south-east but to march infantrymen, guns and carts for an extra eight or so miles across hills and deep, steep valleys rather than along the flat Severn valley floor makes little sense. The cavalry screen was well able to prevent any interference by Gloucester's tiny mounted contingent, which is what the Royalists reputedly feared. According to intelligence received in Gloucester, the infantry, artillery and supply train quartered overnight on 8 August at Berkeley, eighteen miles north of Bristol, a very respectable day's march implying either that the column left Bristol on 7 August, immediately after the decision was taken or, more likely, that they spent the night of 8 August strung out between Bristol and Berkeley.[1]

The king did not accompany the main force but rode across the Cotswolds to meet the reinforcements from Oxford. A rendezvous had been designated at North Cerney and Rendcombe, north of Cirencester. Since the Oxford forces (including infantry and a supply train) arrived there on the evening of 9 August after a march of over thirty miles, they too must have left Oxford on 7 August, which means that news of the decision to move against Gloucester was received in Oxford on the same day that it was taken and that the column departed almost immediately. Lord Forth had been under notice to move since at least 3 August although his preparations seem to have been conducted in ignorance of the variations to Royalist plans that had occurred in the intervening days. An order issued in Oxford on 6 August to send a shipment of muskets after the reinforcements that had marched to Bristol on 1 August clearly presumes that they would be operating in the west, not moving eastwards.

The Oxford infantry still had another fourteen-mile march to Gloucester and are unlikely to have been given much rest before setting off again. By contrast, the king rode to Painswick to spend a more comfortable night. He had by that time achieved the third major precondition for success. Prince Rupert was, however reluctantly, prepared to stay with the army. The prince had accompanied his uncle from Bristol on 8 August and in the subsequent two days the king was able to convince him to take part in the coming operations in his formal post as commander of the cavalry. But until the later stages of the campaign, Rupert played a subordinate, at times almost peripheral, role in the Royalist decision-making process. Orders had also been sent to other commanders to join the king at Gloucester. Sir William Vavasour was marching from his siege at Brampton Bryan, almost forty-five miles away in north Herefordshire, leaving up to 700 men to maintain a blockade. Part of the Worcester garrison, including artillery, was preparing to move south, for the most part by boat down the Severn to Tewkesbury and, according to Parliamentarian intelligence, accompanied by a detachment from Banbury Castle. Meanwhile, Lord Wilmot remained in the Oxford area with most of the cavalry to guard against any demonstrations by the Earl of Essex's depleted army.

On the night of 9 August, the Royalists were therefore spread out over a substantial part of four counties. The more senior officers followed the king's example and sought bed and board with the local gentry. Rupert was at Prinknash, only four miles short of Gloucester, Lord Chandos dined nearby with Lady Guise at Brockworth. They had succeeded in concentrating a significant part of the army within striking distance of Gloucester after only two days but it was essential to the plan agreed at Bristol that Massey, his garrison and the civilian leaders should be overawed and intimidated when the king appeared before Gloucester on the following day, and there were as yet no indications that the approach of the Royalist forces was achieving that aim.[2]

II

From Gloucester's parochial perspective, there had been little doubt that the king would turn upon them once Bristol had fallen. The letter sent to Thomas Pury threatened Rupert's forces, 1,500 Welsh foot and 2,000 'clubmen' to be armed from Bristol, 800 foot and a cavalry regiment from Worcester, and 5,000 foot and a cavalry brigade from Oxford. It was, however, the appearance of the Royalist cavalry at Painswick on 5 August that convinced them (prematurely given the then state of debate in the council of war) that their nightmare was now close at hand. A final appeal was sent to London and preparations for a siege were redoubled. Soldiers and civilians worked side by side to strengthen the city's defences and to store supplies. When the surrounding countryside was scoured for food, the reaction of Gloucester's rural neighbours was predictably unfavourable. 'The whole country forsook us' complained John Corbett 'and employed some to ... persuade us to make our peace with the enemy', arguing that if Gloucester resisted, the king's army would devastate the area, whereas if it surrendered, they would be 'far from spoil and plunder' in the heart of Royalist territory.

It was hardly surprising that the neutral majority wanted the least possible disturbance to their lives. Local gentlemen wrote to the king asking him to spare the property of Royalist sympathisers when the city came to be sacked. Even Parliamentarian activists were prepared to temporise. Sir Arthur Aston reported that clothier Samuel Webb, a known supporter of the garrison, had obtained a letter from Prince Maurice testifying to his loyalty to protect him against plundering. From Sudeley Castle, the Royalist commander wrote to Rupert that 'Nat Hill, who was under-sheriff, and a great collector for the Parliament, and a cornet in their army ... promises to do the king good service in information against the rebels'. But the position was rarely straightforward. Aston also complained that Webb was still sending cloth to Gloucester and Hill's father, Tewkesbury's town clerk and one of those who went to the city to try to persuade them to surrender, was 'there laid up in prison, but ... by his own consent'. Some indeed were going even further and resisting the Royalist cavalry. Aston warned that 'I am forced to keep our horse upon perpetual duty ... the country being so generally evil affected unto his Majesty ... the country people do themselves assault some of our quarters'.

Corbett's account demonstrates the sense of isolation felt in Gloucester during the final days before the Royalist army appeared. On the morning of 6 August, Colonel Charles Gerard appeared with his northern brigade directly in front of the city's southern defences in Tredworth Field. As argued earlier, it is probable that his lame request to trade captured horses was a cover story to enable his trumpeter to meet Massey and pass on Major Legge's message. In the afternoon, when Gerard had departed, a Parliamentarian patrol captured ten Royalists at Wootton, presumably left behind to keep the city under observation or indulging in some private venture plundering. Next day, Royalist cavalry were reported to be looting the village of Tuffley, two miles south of the city. Acting on their own initiative, Captain Evans and the younger Captain Pury, local men of Stephen's Regiment, took forty infantrymen and some cavalry to intercept them but the Royalists had withdrawn to Brookthorpe, where there was a brief skirmish. When Royalist reinforcements appeared, the party withdrew, losing one man prisoner and meeting Massey at the head of a detachment of musketeers marching to their rescue. Although he is unlikely to have approved of their independent action, it was a welcome indication that the town regiment was ready and willing to fight.

Final preliminaries took place on 9 August. Learning that Chandos was dining at Brockworth, no more than four miles away, Massey sent a raiding party to snatch him, a characteristically flamboyant gesture that does not suggest either treachery or defeatism. In the event, there were already Royalist soldiers en route at Barnwood, and after an exchange of fire the Parliamentarians withdrew. But the mythology of the siege received an early contribution from 'a little boy of Captain Nelme's company, [who] having shot away all his bullets, charged his musket with a pebble stone, and killed a commander therewith'. Many equally far-fetched stories would appear in the coming weeks.[3]

There was now little that the garrison could do but wait. Gloucester's defences had been substantially improved, with water and storm poles in the moat and ditches, and turnpike barriers on the approach roads. The suburbs were prepared for destruction to open up fields of fire for artillery and muskets. Earthworks at the gates and along the northern half of the perimeter were primitive by continental standards but sufficient to require a formal assault and assisted by the damp ground around much of the northern sector. Massey's failure to reinforce the old curtain wall to the south and east suggests that he did not expect a prolonged artillery bombardment and siege. One of Rupert's trademark assaults appeared the more likely threat, in which case the garrison's weakness in artillery meant that Massey would need to be able to transfer men quickly between threatened points. The garrison's few cavalrymen would have been vital in this role; Bristol's loss was being blamed in part on the failure of Fiennes' cavalry to mount a counterattack and Massey would not want to repeat that mistake. Finally, although the stores contained less powder than Fiennes had expended, Gloucester had only a tiny proportion of Bristol's ninety-eight cannon, and even the lowest estimate of thirty-two barrels was adequate to meet an assault, which would succeed or not in a relatively short time.

Massey's plans were of course based on a false supposition. An assault had been ruled out and Royalist strategy was based on intimidation and bluff; and that strategy now faced a formidable obstacle. Contrary to the information on which the king's decision had been based, neither Gloucester's leaders, the garrison nor the civilian population were displaying the symptoms of fragile morale that would be expected to accompany an impending capitulation. Since late July, Pury and like-minded militants had restored the cohesion of the Puritan elite and galvanised in them a renewed, almost bloody-minded determination to resist this latest royal assault on their righteous city on a hill. Pury had also stiffened Massey's resolve at a critical time and they had between them ensured the loyalty of both elements of the garrison, Stamford's regulars and the local forces. Thereafter, the city's well-established mechanisms for social control, together with the example set by Massey and his officers, had suppressed dissent and bolstered morale among the less politically committed majority. All of this did not mean that Gloucester's collective will would hold when confronted by their sovereign and his army. It did, however, make resistance much more probable than it had looked less than two weeks before and therefore called into question the assumptions that had carried the king north rather than east, with an army intended to frighten rather than to fight.

III

Parliamentarian propaganda rapidly mythologised the events of 10 August and Hyde's account is demonstrably inaccurate in key respects. All sources agree, however, that Charles and his army appeared in front of Gloucester on that Thursday morning, and deployed on open ground in Tredworth Field to the south and Walham to the north-west. According to town clerk John Dorney writing immediately after the siege and chaplain John Corbett writing two years later, 6,000 infantry and cavalry were drawn up within a quarter mile of the city in Tredworth Field, and a further 2,000 cavalry within cannon shot of the defences in Walham. Yet an anonymous account written in Gloucester before the siege was raised stated that the king had only 3,000 horse and foot with him at Tredworth, together with another 300 men on the city's north side.[4]

Both figures were probably correct. Because of the distances involved, it is improbable that the infantry components of either the Bristol or Oxford columns reached Gloucester before noon. The king therefore seems to have taken the vanguard of cavalry and infantry regiments already deployed in the area with him in the morning, and then waited for the remainder of the army to march in later in the day. Twelve of the fourteen infantry regiments that had accompanied Rupert to Bristol marched north to Gloucester with a combined strength of around 3,500 all ranks. Forth brought with him from Oxford another 2,500 men in seven regiments (the figure of 5,000 used earlier in the letter to Pury was propaganda). The Royalist Ordnance Papers show that this force was combined into four brigades for the Gloucester operation, commanded at the outset by Lord Forth and Colonels Wentworth, Dutton and Darcy, though only three brigades were present and issued with ammunition at Gloucester on 10 August. The fourth, Dutton's, arrived the next day and was probably escorting the slow moving supply train from Bristol. Rupert's cavalry and dragoons from Bristol comprised some 1,500 men, while Forth's column had been escorted by a further brigade from Oxford, giving a cavalry force of about 2,500 and an army very close in size to the assessments made inside Gloucester.[5]

While the regiments assembled, the king rode with his senior commanders and engineers to view the city's defences. On their return, at about 2 pm, the Somerset and York Heralds, escorted by a detachment of 1,000 musketeers, were sent forward to begin the formal business of negotiation. Inside the gate, the two emissaries were taken to the exchange or Tolsey where the Somerset Herald, John Philpot, read out the king's summons to a 26-strong meeting of the Common Council and senior garrison officers. In addition to Massey, Pury, Mayor Dennis Wise and town clerk Dorney, the group included five professional officers from Stamford's Regiment, five local officers (some of whom were also peacetime politicians) and civilian Council members. The king's summons was a predictable mixture of threats and promises. If Gloucester's inhabitants and soldiers submitted to their monarch, he would pardon them all, without exception, prevent the army from causing any damage to people or property, and leave only a moderate garrison. If they refused, he would be compelled to take the city by force and the inhabitants would have only themselves to blame 'for all the calamities and miseries that must befall them'. A reply was demanded within two hours. Having delivered the king's ultimatum, Philpot asked to be able to make a second, public announcement of the terms outside in the street. Massey refused. Morale had improved but there was little merit in testing the city's resolve unnecessarily.

The heralds withdrew to a side room. There can have been nothing of great surprise in their summons. Nonetheless, Mayor Wise appears to have resurrected his worries about the implications of his oath of office, especially whether he could with clear conscience resist his sovereign's demand to surrender the city. If there were other waverers or potential traitors, this was the opportunity to try to swing the meeting away from resistance and towards capitulation. No-one seems to have done so. Dorney recorded simply that 'after some debate in satisfying Mr Mayor's scruples touching his oath of mayoralty, an answer was drawn, and unanimously agreed unto by citizens and soldiers'. Gloucester would fight.[6]

The decision was reached and the reply agreed and signed by all twenty-six leaders within or shortly after the two hour deadline. Two representatives, one civilian and one military, were selected to deliver the city's robust reply. Tobias Jordan was a bookseller and alderman who had taken part in the discussion. Major Marmaduke Pudsey appears neither on the list of participants in the meeting nor on Dorney's list of senior garrison officers during the siege. His selection is a mystery. Perhaps lots were drawn among all the garrison officers or perhaps Pudsey, who was probably a reformado officer, volunteered to help press his case for a permanent post in the garrison. In mid afternoon the two men accompanied the heralds out of the gate and across the open ground to the Royalist army. During the negotiations, there had been fraternisation between Royalist musketeers and Parliamentarian soldiers on picket duty at the turnpike barriers. Yet again the Royalists were left with the impression that the garrison was not prepared to resist the king. These Parliamentarians 'swore if they knew the king were in the field, though their officers made them shoot, they would drop their bullets, and [they] vowed to drink the king's health on their knees'. The truth was rather different.

With characteristic pomposity, Hyde described Jordan and Pudsey as having

> lean, pale, sharp and bald visages, indeed faces so strange and unusual, and in such a garb and posture, that ... it was impossible such ambassadors could bring less than a defiance. The men, without any circumstances of duty, or good manners, in a pert, shrill, undismayed accent, said 'they had brought an answer from the godly city of Gloucester to the king'; and were so ready to give insolent and seditious answers to any questions, as if their business were chiefly to provoke the king to violate his own safe conduct.

An anonymous Royalist recalled that Pudsey

> came at the king, slightly kneeling, tendered him their brief answer in writing. Their backs turned scarce thirty yards, on clap they their hats in the king's presence, with orange ribbons [Essex's colours] in them.

Whether these affronts to Charles' dignity were the product of nerves, ignorance or self-confidence is impossible to say. There was, however, no doubt about the tenor of Gloucester's reply, which was short and unambiguous:

> [The inhabitants, magistrates, officers and soldiers] do keep this city according to our oath and allegiance, to and for the use of his majesty and his royal posterity, and do accordingly conceive ourselves wholly bound to obey the commands of his majesty signified by both houses of parliament; and are resolved by God's help to keep this city accordingly.

In the language of the day, this was an absolute repudiation of everything for which the king was fighting.

Corbett recorded that Gloucester's reply was received by the king 'with all mildness ... only to wonder at our confidence, and whence we expected succour, adding these words, Waller is extinct, and Essex cannot come'. But as Jordan and Pudsey walked back to the city, the Royalist strategy lay in tatters. The king had appeared yet Massey had failed to deliver his promise. Gloucester had not been overawed. Contrary to expectations, its gates were shut against the king and its leaders had delivered a rebuff that smacked both of confidence and insolence. And as its representatives disappeared behind their defences, smoke and flames began to rise from around the city's periphery.[7]

III

While Massey completed Gloucester's defensive preparations by torching the suburbs, Charles and his advisers tried to extemporise a new strategy for their campaign. The participants in this resumed council of war were not recorded but the balance of argument and the queen's subsequent reaction suggest that the advocates of a march on London were not effectively represented. That in turn implies that the council was predominantly a military gathering and the influence of the professional soldiers, lacking confidence in their own army and nervous of an ambitious offensive against London, will have been reinforced by the arrival of the king's senior general, Lord Forth. Much of the debate was familiar from Bristol. The queen's views were well known and intelligence from London stressed the continuing political turmoil. Local gentlemen were warning that Gloucester could pose a threat to the king's lines of communication if he marched east without subduing it, and making extravagant promises of reinforcements to help conduct a siege and then join the march on London. Reinforced by Forth, military concerns about the numerical strength of the Oxford Army seem at last to have struck a chord with the king: 'Upon the drawing up of his army, he found it much weaker than he thought it to have been'.

Events had, however, moved on and four new factors also affected the debate. The first was royal pride and dignity. Having come so far, could the king ignore the affront that Gloucester had given to his personal reputation? Hyde explicitly used the words revenge and honour, and the king was notoriously sensitive about prestige and loss of face. The robust attitudes of Jordan and Pudsey were an additional provocation. Despite his mild response, the king had been 'exceedingly incensed' by their 'sauciness'. Secondly, based on the morning's reconnaissance of the defences and intelligence about the garrison's food and ammunition stocks, and morale inside the city, the professional military advice was that Gloucester could be taken quickly without an assault. 'Soldiers of the best experience', which suggests Forth and Astley, were confident that they could capture the city within ten days. Particular emphasis was laid on the alleged existence of 'many well affected people in the town, who, with those who were incensed by the burning of the suburbs, and the great loss they must sustain thereby, would make such a party, that as soon as they were distressed, the seditious party would be forced to yield'. These closet Royalists were probably the 104 on the list drawn up by Sir Edward Walker, many of whom had in fact left Gloucester or were under detention.

Linked to this argument was an optimistic though not unjustified assessment of Parliament's ability to save their garrison. Parliament 'had no army; nor, by all intelligence, was like to form any soon enough to be able to relieve' Gloucester. According to Hyde, it was also agreed that if Parliament raised an army

> it was much better for His Majesty to force them to that distance from London, and to fight there, where he could be supplied with whatsoever he wanted, could choose his own ground, and where his brave body of horse would be able to defeat any army [Parliament] could raise, than to seek them in their own quarters.

Here at last was the germ of a coherent military strategy. If Essex or Waller did not come, the Oxford Army would be able to reduce Gloucester at its leisure. If they did come, their army would be weak and the balance of advantage would favour the

Royalists more strongly than in the south-east. Because this is presented by Hyde as a fresh argument, it is tempting to attribute it to Forth.

These factors were not, however, decisive. What tipped the scales in favour of staying at Gloucester was the long awaited reply from the Earl of Newcastle to the king's request to advance south against London. With Newcastle's army in support, there was a chance of defeating Essex or at least of imposing a blockade on London and applying political pressure on the capital and Parliament. Without it, the professional soldiers were undoubtedly right that the Oxford Army alone was too weak to mount a credible campaign of that kind. Newcastle's reply appeared at 'the very time that His Majesty came before Gloucester, and before he took the resolution to sit down before it'. It will have been a grave disappointment to the king. The earl was sorry but the Yorkshire gentry, who provided his best regiments and officers, refused to march south until Hull had been taken. Sir Philip Warwick, who was used by the king to deliver messages to Newcastle and was with the earl at the time, alleged later that Newcastle did not want to be subordinated to the main Royalist army and to serve under Rupert. His decision to besiege Hull was on the advice of his lieutenant general, James King, a Scot whose motives were suspect. In Warwick's opinion, Newcastle could have persuaded the Yorkshire gentry to agree to a move south provided that some of their local forces were left behind to blockade Hull, and then recruited reinforcements in Lincolnshire. Warwick believed that the king should have commanded Newcastle to join him. But the fact was that he had not done so and any further orders could not be implemented soon enough to influence the current campaign. Although the Oxford Army could draw on regional forces from the south and midlands, that would still not produce sufficient men to make the queen's brainchild a viable strategy.

As usual, Hyde stressed consensus. 'All thoughts of storming put aside', the king decided on a siege that his generals said would take less than ten days, and there was 'not one man in the council of war dissuading it'. Forth would command the operation and one of two main approaches, with Astley controlling the other. Rupert was given prior refusal but declined so that 'he might not be thought accountable for any accidents which should attend the service'. More likely he was still smarting from Bristol and continued to hanker after a more direct attack.[8] The discussion, rushed though it must have been, produced a wiser strategy than five days' heated debate at Bristol. Political differences among the king's advisers were not as apparent. Besieging Gloucester should be within the capacity of the Oxford Army, though with their limited artillery train the ten-day timetable might prove to be ambitious, especially if the king continued to insist on an absolute ban on assault operations. But without the prospect of help from Newcastle, time was no longer important. Unless Parliament proved able to mount a credible relief operation, the only real deadline was the onset of winter weather. Indeed, if the Royalists were confident of their ability to defeat the Earl of Essex in Gloucestershire, the bait provided by a prolonged siege could turn to their advantage.

IV

Outside the council of war, the focus was on Gloucester's burning suburbs. For Massey, destruction of the buildings outside the city's defences was militarily essential to provide his artillery and musketeers with fields of fire, and to deprive the Royalists of cover for assault troops or siege operations. Preparations had been made and the decision to begin torching the houses was an inevitable consequence of refusing the king's summons. According to the Royalists, flames were rising while their heralds were still inside Gloucester's walls. Once Jordan and Pudsey had returned, the process of destruction could start in earnest. All three suburbs, to north, east and south, were razed, requiring a substantial effort by the garrison. 241 houses of all sizes, with values ranging from £10 to £500, and a church were set alight. Although some buildings survived, including one large house within musket shot of the eastern walls, the Royalists conceded that the suburbs were 'burnt quite off'. Destruction was not limited to the east bank of the Severn. Although Vavasour's army had not yet appeared from Herefordshire, the garrison was abandoning its fortified defences on the west bank so that the river would form an impenetrable barrier and the soldiers could be redeployed to reinforce the other more vulnerable sectors. Highnam House and the old Bishop's Palace at the Vineyard, opposite the city, were destroyed and two earthwork sconces on Alney Island were slighted.

Some Royalists thought that Massey had made a mistake in burning down the suburbs and that it would mobilise public opinion in Gloucester against resistance. There is no evidence of that. Promises of compensation and fear of what Royalist soldiers would do to houses that were not burnt were probably enough to mollify those who lost property and possessions.[9] For everyone else, the blaze must have been a spectacular sight. At some stage in the late afternoon or evening, however, the Royalists ceased to be spectators and began to advance towards the city's defences. Most of the action took place outside the East Gate around a building known as Issold's House that had escaped the flames (Dorney explained that the surrounding garden had acted as a firebreak). The eastern side of the city had been made Astley's responsibility and Darcy's northern brigade was to be encamped there. Astley was evidently keen to secure a lodgement close to the defences from where his men could start engineering operations, and in particular to build artillery emplacements and trenches.

Darcy's regiments, with Astley in close attendance, made two attempts to establish themselves in and around Issold's House. The first occurred while the fires were still burning strongly and this together with musket fire from the East Gate defences drove the Royalists back, killing a Lieutenant Colonel Edwards. Once the flames had died down, the Royalists returned and were able to occupy Issold's House, from where musketeers opened a heavy fire on the East Gate. In response, the defenders mounted a cannon on the wall and sent five or six rounds into the house, at which the Royalists again withdrew. The anonymous Royalist eyewitness wrote that towards evening 'the enemy shot . . . with small and great shot fiercely. Sir Jacob Astley was shot at first, in the arm'. Exchanges of musket fire probably continued until nightfall because Darcy's men were again replenished with ammunition the next day. On the other side of the city there was another, briefer, skirmish when a Parliamentarian cannon near the West Gate fired at Royalist cavalry threatening a working party of women collecting turf to line the defences. These incidents were quickly magnified by rumour into pitched battles and Royalist disasters. Parliamentarian intelligence reported stories that almost a complete cavalry regiment had been destroyed on the first day of the siege and the king forced to summon all of the surgeons in Oxford to treat hundreds of casualties.[10]

Hasty logistic and administrative arrangements were certainly being made to provide for the Royalist army's needs. Even a short siege would place immense pressure on the local economy and the army's supply arrangements, and this was the first time since

Edgehill that the Oxford Army as a whole had operated away from its home base in the Thames valley. On the first day alone, 36 hundredweight barrels of gunpowder, similar quantities of match and shot, and 310 cannon balls had been issued to the infantry and artillery. Maintaining a constant supply of ammunition would be a great challenge for Lord Percy and his team at Oxford. Food would be an equal problem. As a first step, the king issued a proclamation announcing the establishment of daily markets in the camp where soldiers could buy food at reasonable prices, and threatening death to those who tried to interfere with farmers and merchants bringing produce to sell. And although the weather was for the present seasonably good, accommodation would be needed for officers and men alike if the siege lasted more than a few days.[11]

As night fell on 10 August, siege operations began in earnest. Around Issold's House to the east and on Gaudy Green to the south, engineers and soldiers started the laborious task of digging the fieldworks from which the investment would be conducted, aiming to get as close as possible to the city's defences before dawn broke. On Robinswood Hill, two miles to the south-east, a party was at work destroying the pipes that brought spring water into Gloucester's conduits. Elsewhere, the River Twyver (more of a stream than a river) that drove the city corn mills was being diverted. For his part, the king had retired with his two sons to their new lodgings at Matson House. Despite Newcastle's disappointing letter and Massey's unexpected obduracy, the Royalist mood was confident: the soldiers had got their way and expected that Gloucester's 'old stone wall ... would fall upon an easy battery'. Inside the city, the mood can only have been sombre. Their only hope of relief, an army from London, appeared a remote prospect at best. The Puritan elite may have been convinced that what they were doing was right but most of the civilian population did not have their commitment or optimism; and the soldiers, especially the more experienced officers, will have known that they could defeat neither an assault nor a prolonged siege.[12]

Chapter Six

'This business may draw into a greater length than was imagined'

I

Soldiers are as prone to fads and fashions as any other group, and no more so than in arcane fields of military theory and novel means of delivering high explosive. In the 1640s the model for modern military thinkers was the late Swedish king, Gustavus Adolphus, who had re-ignited the Protestant cause in Germany during the previous decade and revolutionised the art of war in the process. Although remembered today primarily for his battles, Gustavus' success was built at least as much on siege warfare and Prince Rupert had copied his approach at Brentford, Cirencester and Bristol. The traditional Dutch style employed a methodical mix of bombardment, mining and blockade to wear down the defenders over weeks, months or even years. By contrast, the Swedish king had concentrated on intimidation, rapid investment, heavy bombardment and early assault with overwhelming force to carve his way through central Europe in the early 1630s.

Compared to the modern fortresses reduced by Gustavus and the Dutch, Gloucester's patchwork defences seemed to pose little challenge. King Charles' officers clearly believed that a siege in the Swedish style would bring success within a matter of days. The method was well established. First trenches would be dug within musket shot of the defences. Then artillery batteries would be constructed as close as possible to the walls. While cannon battered the wall to make a breach, the moat would be mined and drained, and wood faggots prepared to fill it in so that troops could cross. Throughout this process, the defenders would be harassed with musket fire from the trenches and mortar bombs, which were filled with explosives or 'wildfire' and lobbed over the walls to destroy morale, especially that of the civilian population. When the wall was breached, assault troops supported by cavalry would be drawn up ready to storm through the gap. If the defenders refused to surrender, the gap in the wall would be raked with case shot from the attackers' cannon and the assault troops would be unleashed. This method would not be cost-free but the losses should not be anything like as great as in an unprepared assault such as Bristol. Once inside the walls, in the absence of a citadel into which the garrison could withdraw and with cavalry to ride down any opposition in the streets, it was only a matter of time before the defenders capitulated or disintegrated. Then the looting, in compensation for the effort and casualties, could begin.

At Gloucester, Swedish theory would require some modification to take account of British reality. In his 1630 campaign, Gustavus had carried with him two 48-pounder cannon, six 36-pounders and twenty-five 24-pounders. But Rupert's reputation for launching unprepared assaults was due in large part to the weakness of the Royalist artillery train and Forth, who had served for years under the Swedish king, had just eight guns at his disposal, of which only the two 24-pounder demi-cannon were proper siege guns. The Royalists also set great store on the physical and moral impact of mortars, the latest fashion in artillery, which the Dutch had famously used in 1636 to recapture the Schenckenschans fortress. The Dutch had, however, hurled up to sixty mortar bombs a day at the Spanish garrison for six months while Forth had brought a single mortar and twenty bombs from Oxford to join a second used at Bristol and however many bombs remained after that operation. Now that the Earl of Newcastle had declined to cooperate, time was no longer pressing and the weakness of the Royalist artillery train might have made the sedate Dutch model of siege warfare a more attractive option. That would, however, take longer than the ten days promised by the king's generals and it was therefore the Swedish approach that the Royalists again adopted.[1]

II

At first, things appeared to go according to plan. At dawn on 11 August, the garrison discovered that trenches had already been dug on both the southern and eastern sides of the intersection of the old wall, from Gaudy Green around to Issold's house, within musket shot of the walls (archaeological evidence suggests they were about 130 yards distant). Work was continuing between the burnt out houses and behind protective earth-filled gabions. In response, Massey lined the wall with musketeers who started an intensive fusillade to try to disrupt the pioneers. They failed. Forth and Astley deployed musketeers of their own to provide covering fire (from Darcy's Regiment on the east side, and Owen's and Vaughan's Regiments to the south) and the trenches grew longer, deeper and nearer. The ground on the southern side of the city, from the Severn to the East Gate, was higher and dryer than elsewhere, and therefore better suited to constructing entrenchments and artillery batteries. Here too the thin medieval walls were more vulnerable to artillery fire than the hastily built earthworks around the rest of the perimeter, and the right-angled intersection of the south and east walls provided the perfect target for gunners, enabling them to bring crossfire to bear on both the walls and the defenders.

Behind the fieldworks the garrison could see the Oxford Army beginning to settle in for the siege. Although they did not build an outer line of circumvallation to prevent a relief army from interfering in their operations, Forth did follow best Swedish practice by constructing a fortified leaguer south of the city, behind a low rise in the ground to the rear of the ruined Llanthony Priory. Astley set up his camp around an undamaged house to the east. There were other encampments further away, including one for the cavalry at Barton Hill; the main magazine seems to have been installed in Matson church. Some regiments were already being dispersed to quarters in surrounding towns and villages to spread the logistic burden; Parliamentarian intelligence reported a detachment at Malmesbury and 1,000 cavalrymen at Cirencester.

While work continued in the trenches, the first Royalist reinforcements began to arrive. Sir William Vavasour's army of 1,200 infantry (mainly pikemen) and 300 cavalry appeared on the west bank of the Severn, and eventually occupied the abandoned

Vineyard palace. The defenders fired a demi-culverin at them from the West Gate and Dorney later mocked their nervousness, reflecting the traditional antipathy between Gloucester and its Welsh neighbours. There was little for Vavasour's men to do on the west bank and arrangements were soon made to bring the infantry at least across to take a more active part in the operation. On 11 or 12 August, they were joined by a regiment of cavalry and 800 infantry from the Worcester garrison accompanied by another 400 infantrymen from Banbury Castle (the foot seem to have travelled down the Severn by boat). The Worcester soldiers established themselves to the north in the suburb of Kingsholm where they occupied a number of houses that had survived the fire.[2]

From Massey's point of view, nothing had yet happened to suggest that the Royalists did not intend an early assault. His options were in any event extremely limited. The only sensible choice was a Micawberish strategy, waiting for something to turn up, preferably a relief army and preferably quickly. He therefore needed to delay the Royalist operations for as long as possible. During the first day's operations, valuable ammunition had been expended but work on the trenches had continued. Once darkness fell, the garrison changed tack. During Lord Herbert's half-hearted investment in the spring, the Gloucester garrison had used offensive defence tactics against the Royalist camp at Highnam, with considerable success. Massey now decided to employ similar means against this much more formidable opposition, to disrupt and delay their work, undermine their morale, and force them to expend time and effort protecting themselves against his attacks rather than prosecuting the siege. If successful, this strategy would also bolster spirits and confidence within the garrison and the city. Characteristically, however, it was high-risk because failure and casualties could have a potentially fatal affect on the garrison's morale and military capacity.

The first raids were pinpricks. At midnight a small party commanded by Massey's captain lieutenant, James Harcus, attacked the Royalist trenches on Gaudy Green. No casualties were claimed on either side but shovels and pick axes were stolen and the work disrupted. The Royalists retaliated with sallies against the East Gate, where six men were claimed to have been killed by Parliamentarian cannon fire, and to the south around the castle barbican. Next day's raids were more serious affairs. During the morning, Harcus led another party through a salley port constructed surreptitiously in a house adjoining the south wall at the Rignall stile, crossed the moat on ladders, stormed the trenches on Gaudy Green and came away with prisoners, tools and weapons. A thirty-minute firefight followed as the raiders withdrew. In the afternoon, Captain Edward Gray, another of Stamford's company commanders, led 150 musketeers over the earthwork defences at the Little Mead to the north-west and attacked the newly arrived Worcester forces at Kingsholm. This was a more ambitious attack. After a fierce skirmish, Gray's men claimed to have killed a captain and eight or nine soldiers, taken five prisoners and a supply of weapons, set fire to the buildings being used as guardhouse and quarters, and withdrawn without loss.

Although a welcome boost to Gloucester's morale, these attacks had not significantly disrupted Royalist preparations. As 12 August wore on, Forth's men completed a square earthwork battery on Gaudy Green about 130 yards from the walls, and began to line it with gabions. They also started work on a second battery further west towards the riverbank together with a supporting breastwork. Even faster progress was made in front of the east wall. By nightfall a battery had been completed just out of musket range, two 15-pounder culverins deployed and a preliminary bombardment opened. The impact was limited as culverins fired too light a ball to knock down masonry and some rounds reportedly overshot, but the implications were clear: the Royalists were already in a position to mount a major effort of some kind the next day. There can be little doubt that had Rupert been in charge, he would have stormed Gloucester on 13 August (the Diary suggests that he had already fallen out with Forth and Percy over tactics) and Massey certainly reacted as if he expected an imminent attack. Corbett suggests that the garrison thought at first that the attack would come from the north, across the recently constructed earthwork defences, but seeing where the engineering effort was concentrated, they now feared a breach in the old walls followed by an assault that would give the Royalists control of the higher part of the city and make further resistance impossible. A last minute attempt to reinforce the old walls with earth therefore began. This buttress was 'some four or five feet deep' and reached up to the top of the wall. According to Dorney the work was completed quickly, which implies that Massey threw every possible resource into it to pre-empt a more effective bombardment on the following day.[3]

Although the Royalist plan for 13 August in fact envisaged bombardment rather than an infantry attack, extra powder was issued to Forth's three infantry brigades in case the walls were breached so completely that an assault could be launched without undue risk of heavy casualties. The operation did not get off to an auspicious start. Forth had emplaced the two mortars and intended to use them during the night to begin the process of intimidating Gloucester's garrison and citizens. The barrage had little material effect and the larger mortar, reputedly the biggest weapon of its kind in the country, itself exploded when its first round was fired. Nothing daunted, the main bombardment began at 11 am on Sunday 13 August. Two 24-pounder demi-cannon at the Gaudy Green battery, the heaviest guns in the Oxford Army's inventory, together with a smaller 12-pounder maintained a methodical battering of Gloucester's antiquated defences throughout the day. But the earth-reinforced wall held firm, only a single defender was killed and the garrison became sufficiently confident that there would be no immediate attack that they began work further along the same wall to improve the fortifications at the South Gate.[4]

This lack of early success appears to have persuaded the Royalist generals that the task of reducing Gloucester might be more difficult than they had envisaged. Lord Percy sent to Oxford for a further 50 barrels of powder, a replacement mortar, additional bombs and spare wheels for the guns, especially the vital demi-cannon. A convoy of twenty-four wagons was despatched to carry the munitions back to the siege. In parallel, Gloucestershire's sheriff, Sir Baynham Throckmorton, was ordered to send to his native Forest of Dean for forty skilled miners in case the artillery train proved inadequate for the job, and the High Constable of Barton Hundred to find thirty woodmen to make faggots to fill in the defenders' moat. Meanwhile, a bridge of boats had been constructed across the Severn and most of Vavasour's regiments marched across to join the Worcester contingent at Kingsholm, where an infantry leaguer was built with perhaps another for cavalry at Walham. Vavasour, an experienced soldier, assumed command of operations to the north of the city, although some of his men remained on the west bank to maintain a blockade, including at the Vineyard and one of the Alney Island sconces. Vavasour would soon receive a valuable reinforcement of artillery by boat from Worcester. Rumours of their arrival had already reached the garrison and during the following morning, 14 August, Massey sent 150 musketeers under Captain Mallery of Stamford's Regiment to find and spike them. After a fruitless search, they set fire to yet more houses being used as quarters, skirmished with Vavasour's men, took two prisoners and then retreated.[5]

However, the day's main focus was again on the south wall. Prince Rupert himself had spent the night working in the trenches, which suggests that the Royalists were determined that this should be a day of maximum effort. In one respect they succeeded. The trenches at Gaudy Green had now reached the moat near the Rignall stile. During the day, engineers were able to make 'a kind of mine to drain the moat, which much sunk the water of the moat between the south and east ports'. This was one of the key preconditions for reducing the effectiveness of defences prior to a breach and Massey must now have been expecting an attack at any moment. The artillery bombardment was also beginning to show signs of success. Parliamentarian guns mounted on the wall had failed to suppress the Gaudy Green battery and iron shot from the Royalist demi-cannon had finally penetrated the wall. The defenders worked frantically to seal the breach using woolsacks and gabions, and Massey probably sited some of his own cannon behind it to fire case shot into the attackers. Yet the assault did not come. No Royalist accounts refer to these events so it is difficult to be sure why the breach was not exploited. Corbett says that there was an attempt to build a bridge across the half drained moat by filling it with faggots but that the attackers were driven off by musket fire. Perhaps the breach was not wide enough, or the moat still too much of an obstacle. What is most surprising is that no attempt was made by the artillery to widen the breach. It seems in fact that the bombardment came to a halt that day and did not resume for five days, until 19 August. The evidence is that Forth had run out of ammunition; not powder but 24-pounder cannon balls.

According to the Royalist Ordnance Papers, 204 round shot for demi-cannon had been issued for the Bristol and Gloucester operations. Rupert had taken eighty-four to Bristol, where the two guns had taken part in a six hour preliminary bombardment. Forth had brought a further 120 rounds from Oxford and these had been issued on 10 August. Even at a leisurely rate of fire of five rounds an hour, 120 cannon balls would have lasted only ten hours. If the Bristol bombardment had consumed no more than half of the original supply, a further four hours would have been possible. At any event, the demi-cannon would have exhausted their ammunition by around the middle of 14 August at the latest. To Gloucester's Puritans, this must have appeared an almost divine delivery. Corbett, presumably reflecting the views of the garrison's professional officers, thought that the Royalists were being unduly cautious and husbanding the lives of the infantry. To the king and his generals, it was yet another disappointment.

The immediate question was what to do next. Percy does not seem to have written to Oxford for an immediate re-supply of demi-cannon round shot, which suggests that he knew that the magazine did not have any to send. Indeed, they would not even be able to satisfy his request for a further fifty barrels of powder; the next convoy would bring only five. Meanwhile, though there were plenty of cannon balls for the smaller guns, they were too light to cause significant damage, even to Gloucester's old walls. Though orders for new supplies of shot for the siege guns appear to have been placed with Soudley iron furnaces in the Forest of Dean, for the time being the artillery would have to take a back seat. The primary alternative short of an unprepared assault was mining. Rupert's mine at Lichfield had been the first seen in England but miners with the right skills were plentiful and many were looking for alternative employment now that war had disrupted the economy. Throckmorton already had his agents recruiting in the Forest of Dean mining areas.[6]

In the meantime, there was little the Royalist army could do except refine their fieldworks and make their lives in the siege lines more comfortable. The following day, 15 August, was therefore taken up primarily with housekeeping, including moving tents and carts into the Llanthony leaguer. Further reinforcements also appeared. Vavasour's command was strengthened by 500 Glamorgan militia men under Colonel Richard Bassett, who was knighted for his efforts, and 450 experienced musketeers arrived from Bristol. They were placed under the command of Lieutenant Colonel Theophilus Gilby from Bellasyse's Regiment, issued with ammunition and some were sent immediately into the trenches. Hopton wrote to Rupert that a frigate load of munitions bought by the queen had arrived in Bristol and the first Parliamentarian spy to penetrate the Royalist camp noted that the king received a shipload of wines and sweetmeats. In the trenches, work and skirmishing continued. The garrison used hand grenades to attack the pioneers. Rupert was narrowly missed on one occasion but the tactic rebounded when Captain Lieutenant Harcus was killed while peering down from the wall at the results of his grenade. Massey used the unexpected respite to further improve the city's defences. At the South Gate the drawbridge and adjacent buildings had been lined with earth, and a cannon-proof breastwork built between the draw-bridge and the gate. During 16 August the houses next to the North Gate received similar treatment and the bastion on the east side at Friar's barn was strengthened when the Royalists began to extend their trenches northwards from the East Gate.

Shortly before sunset on 16 August, the garrison mounted its most ambitious raid yet. Captain Peter Crisp of Stamford's Regiment took 150 musketeers out of the North Gate and attacked the eastern trenches. Although accounts differ, this was evidently a bitter battle with cannon from both sides involved. Dorney and Corbett claimed that the raiders escaped with only two injured men and killed more than 100 of Darcy's soldiers, but the anonymous Royalist described 'a desperate sally ... They left twenty-four bluecoats in one ditch, besides wounded men. They brought out a drake [cannon], [which] killed four of ours that ran over the field'. On this occasion, the Royalist version sounds more plausible.[7]

Neither the king nor Rupert was there to witness the fighting but in Oxford, having ridden in at midday. High politics had intruded on the campaign and the lull in operations enabled them to respond to two urgent matters at court. Queen Henrietta Maria was by all accounts livid that her views had been ignored at two successive councils of war. On 13 August, she wrote to Newcastle complaining bitterly that the king had 'gone to Gloucester in person, which gives no little dissatisfaction to every one here; and with reason, to see him take up such hasty councils: and all those very persons who have advised him disown it'. She appears to have written to the king, presumably in similar terms. According to Hyde, Sir John Colepeper was the immediate target of the queen's wrath, inflamed by rumours from London that Parliamentarian leaders feared an early march on the capital and saw a diversion against Gloucester as their best hope of avoiding defeat; some talked of treachery. But she was also

> inflamed with a jealousy that there was a design to lessen her influence with the king, and that Prince Rupert was chief in that conspiracy, and meant to bring it to pass by keeping the king still in the army and by hindering his coming to Oxford.

Percy's correspondence shows that Rupert had contributed to the queen's suspicions by ignoring repeated requests to write to her. Now her husband had brought the prince to Oxford to put her fears to rest. This reconciliation was achieved (Rupert was, after all, not the architect of the king's current strategy) but not all rifts were healed since the queen remained unhappy about the siege and 'reproaches were publicly cast upon those who gave the advice'. Rupert left Oxford that evening to return to the more congenial surroundings of the army. The king remained throughout the next day, 17 August, to deal with the second major political problem.

In the wake of their failed attempt to launch a peace initiative in early August, Lord Holland and six similarly inclined peers had felt their position in London so insecure that they had decided to flee the capital. Some retired to their homes but Holland and the Earl of Bedford appeared at the Royalist garrison at Wallingford asking to be allowed to go on to Oxford to seek the king's mercy. This was not an unalloyed political victory for the king because in his absence the queen refused their request. Now, in another bitter debate in the Privy Council, Colepeper again stood out against the queen's partisans, this time arguing for pragmatic civility towards the penitents. Surprisingly, Colepeper once again won the day. The king concluded that it would not be sensible at that time 'to make any persons desperate' and that the peers should be permitted to stay in Oxford without constraints. Hyde made much of this episode, in large part because he seems to have befriended Holland after his arrival, but the peace peers had already been marginalised and were no longer important players in the political game.[8]

Back at Gloucester, the Royalist generals were showing increasing signs of nervousness at their lack of success. In an extraordinary letter to the king dated 17 August, Lord Percy set out at Forth's request 'the condition of your affairs' at the siege. After accusing one of the engineers of deceiving Forth, and then blaming the engineer and Forth for any further errors in his assessment, Percy conceded that 'this business hath and may draw into a greater length than was imagined' and that he was running short of powder. More than 120 hundredweight barrels had been used and only 70 remained, sufficient had the demi-cannon been able to exploit their initial breach, but the requirement would now increase as the siege progressed. This part of the letter may have been inspired by the arrival that day of only five of the fifty powder barrels ordered on 12 August. Shortage of powder was already biting. Rather than full twelve-shot bandoleers, Gilby's musketeers from Bristol had been issued with no more than six rounds per man on 15 August. Turning to the mining operations, it seems that the plan was to build a bridge across the moat from which engineers would be able to mine the bottom of the old wall. Percy set out two choices. The moat was 'twelve foot deep and near thirty broad'. At present the miners were working in the trench under a gallery and behind protective blinds, and filling up the moat with earth. Although relatively safe for the miners, it was a slow process and would take them a week to reach the wall. The alternative was to cast caution to the winds and fill the moat with wood faggots. This would take two nights and require constant covering fire from musketeers, but casualties would nonetheless be heavy. Forth intended to continue with the slower, safer course that night, although they would start throwing faggots into the moat as well, and they would seek further direction when the king returned. Percy's letter contains all sorts of implications, including that the king was playing a direct role in the conduct of the siege, a complex art in which he had no experience; that his continuing aversion to casualties was inhibiting Forth's operations; and that

Forth and his colleagues had been genuinely surprised by the difficulties they were encountering.

By the time the king returned, the position had deteriorated yet further. During the night the Royalists did indeed make a concerted attempt to fill the moat with faggots but they were beaten off by musketeers firing from the walls. Much worse, Sheriff Throckmorton wrote a distraught letter to Percy that evening with the news that most of the Forest of Dean miners had deserted. Perhaps they found the prospect of the more direct approach to bridging the moat too risky or the pay unsatisfactory. Throckmorton had sent men after the deserters with orders to burn the houses of those who would not return immediately and begged Percy to 'judge charitably of this unhappy accident, for never man had such rogues to deal with'. Even the deployment of the new mortar was a damp squib. Four bombs filled with incendiary material fell onto houses but did little damage, another fell in the street near the South Gate where, according to Dorney, 'a woman coming by with a pail of water, threw the water thereon, and extinguished the fuse thereof, so that it did not break, but was taken up whole'. Mortars were intended to attack morale as much as materiel and half-hearted efforts such as this inevitably undermined their value. Letters sent to Thomas Pury, again trying to persuade Gloucester's leaders to surrender, also smacked of growing Royalist frustration and weakness.[9]

Massey seems to have sensed that for the moment he held the initiative. Early the following morning, 18 August, he mounted the garrison's largest attack by far against the Royalist lines. The target was once again the artillery brought downstream from Worcester to reinforce Vavasour's forces to the north of the city. By this time four cannon had been deployed (another was reported to have slipped its chains on the boat and fallen into the Severn), three in front of Vavasour's main quarters at Kingsholm and the fourth close to the Alvin Gate defences. While fifty musketeers under Lieutenant Pincock launched a diversionary attack from the Little Mead, Major Pudsey and 400 musketeers took the Alvin Gate cannon from both front and rear, disposing of the Royalists with the butt-end of their muskets before driving a nail into the cannon's touchhole to disable it. The raiders then marched on to the main Kingsholm battery where, according to the anonymous Royalist, the Welsh defenders were driven from their positions but counterattacked and drove the Parliamentarians back to the city. Dorney claimed that Pudsey's attackers killed more than 100 Welshmen and took five prisoners, while losing only two dead and four captured. The Royalist account admitted that the cannon had been nailed and conceded eleven dead, sixteen wounded and one taken prisoner but claimed to have killed twenty-seven of the garrison. This was undoubtedly a nasty little battle. Vavasour's men needed a major re-supply of ammunition as a result and it gained a short reference in *Mercurius Aulicus* (which was otherwise giving few details of the siege). Later that day, a second raid was launched by 150 musketeers and forty cavalry against Astley's positions in front of the eastern defences, the only reported use of Parliamentarian cavalry during the siege and to little apparent effect.

Rupert had already returned and the king was on his way with infantry reinforcements from Oxford. Parliamentarian intelligence reported that all sick soldiers who could march, plus ten men from every company in the garrison, were on their way. Up to 1,000 men may have been involved, probably commanded by Colonel Thomas Pinchbeck, though not all left at once; Captain Challoner of Lloyd's

Regiment was ordered to take twenty to thirty recovered typhus victims to Gloucester on 18 August, yet they were still in Oxford a week later.[10]

Meanwhile, the ten days within which the king's generals had undertaken to capture Gloucester would soon be up and the evidence is that the Royalists were determined to make a last effort to meet the original deadline. Charles was presumably under intense spousal pressure to produce early results; the queen was said to have given a four shillings bonus to all of the men at Gloucester to encourage them to complete the operation quickly. For their part, Forth and the other generals had their reputations on the line, especially now that accusations of treachery were flying at court. Notwithstanding the growing powder shortage highlighted in Percy's letter and Throckmorton's problems with miners, the decision seems to have been taken to concentrate both on bombardment and crossing the moat. That could mean that the demi-cannon had received a further supply of iron round shot, but there is no record in the Ordnance Papers and it is more likely that the generals decided instead to compensate for lack of quality of artillery with quantity of guns. Even if they failed to breach the walls, a massive barrage might finally intimidate Massey into surrender or provide sufficient covering fire for the moat to be filled with faggots. *Mercurius Aulicus* reassured its readers that 'His Majesty's having approached so near, that they have battered the works in many places with their ordnance, so that it cannot possibly be long before the town be generally assaulted'.

Preparations began on 18 August. Rupert spent the night in the trenches, where he was hit on the helmet by a stone. By the next morning, the Royalists had completed a third battery opposite the East Gate and now had eight cannon deployed in three batteries against Gloucester's old walls. To the east, the original battery had been increased from two to three guns, probably with the addition of the second 12-pounder. This was where the gallery was sited to bridge the moat and it was here that the day's main effort would be made. Despite their earlier disappointing performance, the two 15-pounder culverins were now the Royalists' best bet for bringing down the walls. Forty iron shot and four barrels of powder were issued to them during the day. Because the eighty culverin shot brought from Oxford had been issued at the beginning of the siege, they were probably the last of the 100 rounds taken to Bristol. Even at the slow rate of five shots an hour, the culverins would run out of ammunition after no more than five or six hours. The new battery at the East Gate was presumably occupied by the pair of 6-pounders, which would have little impact on the walls but could engage Parliamentarian guns and musketeers if they tried to disrupt the operation. To the south were the two demi-cannon, probably with little or no ammunition, and the 12-pounder.

At 10am on Saturday 19 August, the tenth day of the siege, the Royalist artillery began what the defenders described as a 'furious' bombardment but which must, by the standards of the day, have been either intensive but short or prolonged and desultory, as Dorney recorded that only 150 rounds were fired, fewer than twenty per gun. If the bombardment continued until the evening, as seems to have been the case, no more than around fifteen rounds an hour can have been delivered. And if the culverins are assumed to have used all of their available ammunition, say 110 iron shot at most, the contribution of the other cannon was extremely limited, although the two mortars joined in and continued their bombardment into the next night. The material effects were derisory. Some damage was caused to the corner of the walls but, reinforced with earth, they stood firm. Inside the city only slight harm was caused, mainly by mortar bombs, and the sole fatalities were a man, a woman and a pig. Indeed, the Parliamentarians seem to have had the better of the day's exchanges. The Royalists claimed to have dismounted two of the garrison's small cannon but admitted losing two of their gunners (Dorney put the figure at three and Corbett at four) and the defenders' morale improved as the impotence of the Royalist artillery became apparent. Corbett wrote that

> neither were the people daunted at the noise of cannon, which by the slender execution, became so contemptible, that at that very time women and children wrought hard in lining the walls and repairing the breaches.

Nonetheless, Massey was still concerned that the walls might not hold. He therefore began the urgent construction of an earth breastwork across Friar's Orchard, the open ground behind the intersection of the south and east walls across which the Royalist attackers would come if a breach were made. Pending completion of this second line of defence, he concentrated his reserves at the city's south-east corner and kept them at high readiness throughout the day. Towards evening, drummers beat the alarm in expectation of an assault under cover of darkness and an attack was indeed launched. According to Dorney, the Royalists 'attempted to make a passage over the moat at the place they had battered, but being descried by our sentinals, they were beaten off with some loss by our musketeers'.[11] This failure meant that after ten days, the Swedish model of siege warfare had failed to deliver anything approaching the desired results. The city's resolve and Massey's disruptive tactics had contributed towards this failure but Forth had ultimately been thwarted in his attempt to deliver Gloucester quickly by the inadequacy of his artillery train and the unwillingness of his sovereign to countenance substantial casualties.

III

In the wider world, speculation and rumour about events at Gloucester were already rife. The mayor had been hanged, Massey had expelled all the women, children and old men, and the king was determined to burn the city down. Parliamentarian newspapers told their readers that the Royalists had lost up to 2,000 soldiers killed and another 800 wounded. *Mercurius Aulicus* took pains to refute the casualty figures, admitting fewer than sixty dead by 19 August, but could not disguise the delay. More reliable Parliamentarian intelligence reports tended to support the *Mercurius Aulicus* line on Royalist casualties ('about 100, and very few killed in the town' on 19 August, and 'not above 300 men' three days later). But from Banbury, they also told of many Royalist deserters from the siege who had left 'by reason of the hot service there . . . and say they will be soldiers no more'. Morale was undoubtedly a continuing problem for the besieging army. One of Rupert's reasons for storming Bristol had been his concern that the Oxford Army would not respond well to a prolonged investment and Gloucester was now proving him right.

Royalist garrisons were ordered to arrest deserters and return them to Gloucester for Forth to hang. A soldier under Lieutenant Colonel Lunsford was to be executed for mutiny having refused to march without pay. There were recurrent stories of reluctant Royalist infantry being driven into the attack by their own cavalry. Inside the city, the Royalists' declining enthusiasm was attributed to the slow progress of their operations, the priority attached to preserving the infantry and harassment by the defenders. It was not unusual for Civil War soldiers to be compelled to fight. More striking are the accounts of mass Royalist indiscipline, not simply in Parliamentarian propaganda. Hyde recalled that a 'very great licence broke into the army, both among officers and soldiers; the malignity of those parts being thought excuse for the exercise of any rapine, or severity among the inhabitants'. As early as 12 August, orders had been issued to senior cavalry officers to apprehend and hang soldiers who 'wander about the country robbing and spoiling our subjects'. Kidnapping became widespread: 'many countrymen [were] imprisoned by officers without warrant, or the least knowledge of the king, till they had paid good sums of money, for their delinquency'. But Hyde was being disingenuous in suggesting that these were all freelance activities. Although the king had forbidden the seizure of goods without payment or the plundering of houses, on 17 August he issued harsh articles of inquisition that enabled his men to punish those who withheld rents or fled to garrison towns such as Gloucester. At Frampton, a Parliamentarian supporter had his house plundered for doing just that, a 'butcher's man' was hung for refusing to say God bless the king, allegedly on Rupert's orders, and on 25 August a Parliamentarian spy at Gloucester was told that the king had promised his soldiers free licence if they could take the city.

Conditions in the Royalist camp were not the explanation for the indiscipline. The high summer weather had been fine, sickness was not a major problem and there are no suggestions of food shortages. To supplement the markets set up at the beginning of the siege, food convoys had been organised, commissaries were seizing further supplies as necessary and cavalry sweeps through the Cotswolds rounded up thousands of sheep for slaughter (although Hyde portrayed this as wanton destruction). Vavasour's regiments were being provisioned from south Wales using a fleet of boats and barges on the Severn. Around the city, encampments of tents and huts had been thrown up to provide accommodation for the soldiers. Officers were even better off, quartering in cottages in the surrounding villages and entertaining each other to supper in the evenings. At Matson House the king presided over an itinerant court at which the Marquis of Montrose argued the case for widening the war to Scotland, the Earl of Carnarvon complained about Prince Maurice's behaviour in the south-west, the playwright William Davenant was knighted, and the bored young Princes of Wales and York famously carved chunks out of the window sill. There was hard work and casualties in the trenches, and not everyone shared the Earl of Sunderland's pleasure at 'so much good company, together with the noise and tinta-marre of guns and drums', but by the standards of the time the Royalist army was not badly off. So while it is tempting to link the decline in Royalist morale to the failure to meet the ten-day deadline, it is more likely that the Oxford Army infantry regiments brought their discontent with them from Bristol and that the cavalry simply carried on the behaviour for which they were notorious.[12]

Nor were conditions intolerable inside the city. Massey's worst fear, a full-scale assault, had not been realised and his garrison had proved equal to the demands of siege warfare. With only 1,500 soldiers, he could not mount a strong defence at all points but once it became clear that the Royalists were digging in and that the focus of their operations was the south and east walls, he could concentrate the garrison on disrupting the progress of engineering work, defending against the occasional artillery bombardments and raiding the Royalist trench lines; and the garrison could safely be dispersed to some eighteen posts (probably a company per post), plus a main guard of 120 men in the centre of the city near the Cross. Morale seems generally to have held up among both the soldiers and the civilian population. Corbett's picture is in marked contrast to the position before the siege started:

> No great complainings were heard in our streets, no discontent seized on the soldiers, at other times prone to mutiny; men of suspected fidelity did not fail in action; every valuable person was active in his own place: the usual outcries of women were not then heard.

There were few desertions, and work on the defences was sustained throughout the siege and undertaken quickly in emergencies, often under fire. Even Hyde conceded that 'they in the town behaved themselves with great courage and resolution ... the discipline within was very good'. Although Massey and his officers were credited with playing a key role in keeping spirits high, only Pury and the Puritan elite could have delivered this level of active support by Gloucester's civilians.

In the long term, however, the logic of siege warfare was that where a city could not be resupplied or relieved, it would eventually fall. Food was not yet a major problem and no epidemics had broken out, but the siege was only ten days old, and hunger and disease could both be expected in the coming weeks. Massey's most immediate concern will have been powder. His raids, the harassment of the Royalist trenches and the exchanges with the Royalist artillery all consumed more than the garrison could afford, and local production of three barrels a week (the equivalent of about five rounds per musketeer) did not compensate.[13] Difficult choices would soon present themselves. If powder stocks were used at the same intensive rate, the garrison would quickly run out and the Royalists would launch an assault. Yet if powder was hoarded, the garrison could no longer harass the Royalists' siege operations and a prepared assault would come that much sooner. Massey could only trust that the Royalists had an exaggerated view of his available stocks.

IV

Unfortunately for Massey, on 20 August the king received an authoritative, up to the minute intelligence assessment of conditions inside Gloucester. While the Royalists returned to work on their mine across the moat at the east wall, Hatton, one of the garrison's gunners, launched himself into the River Severn and swam to the Royalist lines. This was no case of war weariness but a straightforward defection. According to camp gossip, Hatton revealed that Gloucester was short of bread and had ammunition for only three days' fighting. He also seems to have identified a number of potential targets and weaknesses in the defences. Reporting this rare piece of good news from the siege, *Mercurius Aulicus* emphasised the garrison's exhaustion after the previous day's bombardment.

Nonetheless, Massey's strategy of disruption remained for the moment unchanged. At dawn on 21 August, a two-pronged raid was launched to spike the Royalist guns in front of the south and east walls. The plan was extremely ambitious, involving an amphibious landing and a coordinated attack from opposite ends of the Royalist lines, and for the first time, a local officer from Stephens' Regiment was given command of one of the parties. The more daring element of the operation in fact went according to plan. Under cover of darkness, Captains Blunt and White from Stamford's Regiment took a strong detachment by boat down the Severn and landed between Forth's main leaguer and the Severn Street artillery redoubt. While the garrison's artillery opened a diversionary barrage from the barbican battery, Blunt and White marched their musketeers up to the redoubt and stormed it. Taken by surprise, Major Wells and a number of soldiers were killed, and one prisoner captured. The next step was to roll up the Royalist trench line from the west while the second party did the same from the north, covered throughout by artillery and musket fire from the walls.

To the north, however, darkness had worked against the raiders. Two hundred musketeers left the city from the North Gate. They were drawn primarily from Stephens' Regiment under Captain-Lieutenant Robert Stevenson, but Captain Moore and a detachment of Devereux's more experienced dragoons accompanied them. Their initial target was the battery at the East Gate. Unfortunately their guide lost his way and led them instead into the midst of Darcy's brigade in their quarters around Barton Street. The raiding party promptly disintegrated. Most seem prudently to have hesitated but forty musketeers pressed on and attacked a Royalist force claimed by Corbett and Dorney to have been five companies strong. Here too, surprise worked in their favour for they drove the Royalists back, taking two officers prisoner. The Royalist unit was probably Sandys' Regiment, which seems to have lost over twenty men in a raid on its quarters at about this date. Flushed by this success, the Parliamentarians advanced still further before running into eight more Royalist companies at Barton Court, where a firefight developed. These were probably Eure's and Tyldesley's Regiments, both of which reported themselves to be 'destitute' of ammunition that day. Heavily outnumbered, the Parliamentarians at last began to withdraw.

From the walls, Massey could see that the plan had miscarried and trumpets sounded the retreat. To the south, Stamford's men had advanced to the Severn Street turnpike before the recall came but supported by the cannon from the Barbican they suffered only two men wounded in pulling back to the South Gate. To the east, Stevenson's party were outnumbered by the Royalist infantry and threatened by two troops of cavalry when, according to Dorney, 'Ensign Matthews facing about, charged them, and forcing them to retire, made good our retreat'. The Parliamentarians admitted a further two dead, three wounded and a sergeant taken prisoner. If true, they were fortunate to have escaped so lightly for the Royalists clearly thought they had inflicted a serious reverse on the garrison. *Mercurius Aulicus* claimed many Parliamentarians killed and reported that prisoners 'were most purely drunk . . . as the only means to make them stand'. Hyde later quoted captured soldiers as saying 'the governor always gave the party that made the sally, as much wine and strong water as they desired to drink'.

Massey was evidently disappointed with the outcome and the degree of justification offered by Corbett implies that he was also criticised inside Gloucester. Tactics certainly changed; this was the last large-scale raid mounted by the garrison. Offensive defence had run its course, and was now too wasteful in ammunition and risked unacceptable losses. The Royalists soon noted the reduction in tempo. On 25 August, the Earl of Sunderland wrote to his wife that the Parliamentarians did not dare 'to sally any more, being so well beaten the last time'. Disruption could, however, take many forms and musketeers continued to snipe at the Royalist trenches, killing a dragoon captain later on 21 August. That same day, Massey adopted another traditional delaying tactic by making two attempts to call a truce, first to recover three dead Parliamentarian soldiers and then to exchange prisoners. The first was granted, the second refused. Finally, small parties of Parliamentarian musketeers began to make short sallies against the various Royalist positions to keep them on alert and encourage them to waste ammunition. Though these irritations were good for the city's morale, they are unlikely to have caused more damage than a few sleepless nights in the trenches.

Both sides had now been obliged to change their strategy. For their part, Forth and the king had little option but to maintain the siege. To march away now would be a major propaganda victory for Parliament and the past ten days had demonstrated that the army was not as powerful as some of the king's advisers had argued, which weakened further still the case for an advance on London. The siege had, therefore, become a long-term commitment. A rapid conclusion was of course desirable but what mattered most was to take Gloucester, however long that took. As a result, a lull descended upon Gloucester and the Royalist lines. The rhythm of a regular siege was less frenetic than the pace of Forth's original Swedish-style efforts, and greater stress was required on the accumulation and husbanding of munitions and other supplies.[14]

Strenuous efforts were being made to replenish artillery ammunition stocks. Following Massey's final flurry of raids, Percy urgently asked the Oxford magazine for case shot for all of the cannon. Case shot consisted of musket balls inside tin boxes and was ideal for dealing with infantry at close range. The tin boxes were despatched on 22 August. On 23 August, a consignment of cannon balls (120 for the culverins, 234 for the demi-culverins and 300 for the smaller sakers) arrived by boat from Bristol, the first re-supply since the beginning of the siege. Two days later, a further seventy-one iron shot for the culverins arrived from Bristol and another fifty culverin shot were delivered as part of a convoy of thirty wagons of arms, ammunition and clothing from Oxford. Unfortunately, the guns concerned were those proven by harsh experience to be too light to bring down the walls. On 24 August, Throckmorton delivered twenty-one 'bars of English iron', makeshift ammunition (they were heated to red-hot temperatures and fired over the walls) which enabled the demi-cannon to re-enter the battle, but more significant was the arrival on 26 August of thirty-two iron shot for the demi-cannon from the Soudley furnaces in the Forest of Dean, the harbinger of a restored battering capability. Replenishing powder stocks was more difficult. Thirty barrels arrived from Bristol on 27 August but Royalist magazines in southern England were still incapable of satisfying the demands of a large field army. The king had consequently turned to the Earl of Newcastle, who seems to have been as tardy in responding to this request as he had been to the call for a march on London, for on 22 August the king sent him a rather plaintiff reminder: 'I desire you not to forget my 200 barrels of powder'.[15]

The main focus was therefore on mining the city's old vertical and vulnerable walls. One mine was already well advanced. Under cover of a wooden gallery, the moat was being bridged and, as Lord Percy had reported on 17 August, it was expected that the wall would be reached by around 24 August. At some stage the decision was taken to expand this effort by starting work on two additional mines. One appears to have been another surface mine, directed against the south wall. The second was a more ambitious underground mine near the East Gate. This was carried out in secrecy and the garrison did not suspect its existence until 28 August. An underground mine was technically more demanding and complicated in this instance by springs that rose even on the higher ground to the east of the city. Ten midlands miners who had served with Rupert at Lichfield refused to take on the work and 100 or so miners recruited in Wales did not arrive until 29 August. In the interim, Throckmorton may have succeeded in press-ganging some of the Forest of Dean miners to return but progress underground was at best very slow and the main focus remained on the original operation against the east wall.

The problem of bridging Gloucester's outer moat and ditch so as to avoid casualties on the scale suffered at Bristol was passed to the ingenious academic mind of Dr William Chillingworth to solve. His solution was dismissed by Corbett as

> unperfect and troublesome engines ... [that] ran upon wheels, with planks musket proof placed on the axle-tree, with holes for the musket shot and a bridge before it, the end whereof (the wheels falling into the ditch) was to rest upon our breast works.

In fact, provided that they were long enough to cross the ditch, 'sows' of this kind were a sensible means of reducing losses during a prepared assault. For the time being, however, the Royalists' emphasis was on attrition. During the evening of 23 August, the mortar battery resumed its desultory bombardment and was joined the next day by the cannon, some of which seem to have been redeployed back to Llanthony so that they could lob their rounds over the wall without overshooting, but little damage was done.[16]

Persuasion and subterfuge were also employed. On 24 August, two local men (Mr Bell of Sandhurst and Mr Hill of Tewkesbury) asked by letter for a meeting. They were admitted to the North Gate where they tried unsuccessfully to persuade the garrison to surrender in the face of overwhelming odds, the impossibility of relief and the growing burden being placed on the surrounding countryside. That night, in a more devious stratagem, Colonel Charles Gerard took his cavalry brigade to Wainlode Hill where they 'feigned to skirmish with one another and made fires'. The aim, according to the anonymous Royalist, was

> to draw out the besieged, upon intelligence that it was believed in Gloucester that Waller would come that night and give signs of it by fires: but they stirred not out of the town; for Massey knew he had but gulled his soldiers with the hopes of it, to hold out.

Worse still, the incident was quickly distorted by rumour into a Royalist defeat in which Gerard was said to have been killed.

Even the weather seemed to have turned against the Royalists. For the first time since the beginning of the siege, the skies opened and torrential rain lashed the trenches, which cannot have helped Gerard's men to keep their fires alight. A Parliamentarian spy reported that it also soaked the king, who had ridden to Robinswood Hill to watch the opening of a new stage in the artillery bombardment. His trip was wasted as it was too wet to fire the guns. Next day, 25 August, the weather cleared and the Royalists began their first intensive artillery attack for almost a week. Massey attempted to forestall it with a raid from the North Gate but Royalist cavalry were on hand to drive the Parliamentarians back into the city. Although a Royalist powder barrel was ignited during the skirmish, the bombardment began in the afternoon and continued through the evening into the night.

Intimidation was the objective. During daylight, the main weapon seems to have been mortar bombs filled with high explosive or incendiary material (the so-called 'wildfire'). A woman was killed when two fell in Southgate Street. Others 'shrewdly battered' several houses. Here too, shortage of ammunition was a constraint. Only fifty bombs had been delivered from Oxford and Captain Fawcett was therefore obliged to intersperse bombs with 'great stones ... which did little hurt, and killed none'. After dark, the demi-cannon joined in, sending about twenty red-hot iron bars 'flying in the air like a star shooting'. They 'passed through stables, and ricks of hay, where the fire by the swiftness of the motion did not catch, and falling on the tops of houses, presently melted the lead, and sunk through; but all the skill and industry of the enemy could not set one house on fire'. In one case, it was a close run thing. A bar

> came through three houses, and fell into a chamber of Mr Comelin, the apothecary, and being perceived, many pails of water were cast upon it to quench the same, but that little availing, it was cast into a cowl [or tub] of water, where after a good space it cooled.

Conventional iron shot were also used to try to extinguish lights that had been set on the College Tower as a sign that Gloucester continued to resist, though again without success.[17]

V

Disappointment at yet another unrewarding day was compounded by disturbing news from London. The evidence suggests that despite setbacks and delays, the Royalists had until now remained confident that they would eventually succeed in taking Gloucester unhindered by Essex or Waller. In his final journal entry on 24 August, the anonymous Royalist described Gerard's abortive attempt to lure Massey into a sortie in terms that leave little doubt that relief was not in prospect. On the following day, the Earl of Sunderland wrote optimistically to his wife that the gallery in front of the east wall 'will be finished within this day or two, and then we shall soon despatch our mine, and them with it. Many of the soldiers are confident that we shall have the town within this four days'. Around the same time, however, Parliamentarian intelligence began to detect traces of pessimism on the Royalist side. At Malmesbury soldiers complained that the king's army was 'still as far from the taking of Gloucester as they were at the first'. At Oxford, it was said that despite losing only 100 casualties, undermining the walls and threatening to blow up the city, the Royalists expected it to 'hold out longer yet'. Indeed, the siege might even be raised because 'they are devils in Gloucester'. And from the camp at Gloucester itself came a report that 'they were digging and shooting against the town, but there was no possibility of taking it'.

More importantly, there was intelligence from Gloucester that the Royalists believed that:

> they must despatch presently for if they cannot take it presently they must be compelled to leave the siege and meet with his Excellency [Essex] who they heard was advancing either to Oxford or to the relief of Gloucester.

This was a potentially critical new factor. According to Hyde, the possibility that Essex was about to mount a relief operation 'would not at first be credited at the leaguer ... and therefore they were too negligent upon the intelligence, and suspected rather that he would give some alarm to Oxford'. There was certainly scepticism about the earl's capabilities and intentions. *Mercurius Aulicus* mocked claims that he had mustered

10,000 soldiers on 22 August, and the gossip in Oxford was that he had only five or six thousand men and would do no more than repeat his feeble advance to Thame.

Nonetheless, Charles and his generals were sufficiently concerned about Essex's movements for the king and Prince Rupert to ride to Oxford on 26 August for a two-day council of war. As a result, a planned further reinforcement of the army at Gloucester was reduced in scale (Colonel Feilding went 'with very few forces'); the frontline garrison at Abingdon was replenished with powder and match; the defences at Wallingford and Oxford itself were strengthened; Hopton was ordered to send 'as many horse and foot as could well be spared' from the Bristol garrison to join the siege; and plans were drawn up to blockade Gloucester in case the siege had to be lifted. This was prudent contingency thinking but Hyde recalled that the council also concluded that Essex was in practice unlikely to attempt a march on Gloucester

> over a campaign near thirty miles in length, where half the king's body of horse would distress, if not destroy his whole army, and through a country eaten bare ... and if he should, without interruption, be suffered to go into Gloucester, he could neither stay there, nor possibly retire to London, without being destroyed in the rear by the king's army.

Charles and his generals therefore decided to continue with the siege while Lord Wilmot and 2,000 cavalry mustered around Banbury, prepared to mount a delaying action in the Cotswold Hills in the unlikely event that Essex moved against Gloucester, in which case Rupert and the rest of the cavalry would join them.

Though prudent and coherent, Royalist planning was predicated on a judgement that Essex could not raise a force capable of challenging the Oxford Army, which in turn reflected intelligence about the size of the Parliamentarian army and its fighting quality, and a prejudice that Essex was inherently a timid commander. If, however, the earl did march westwards, Hyde states explicitly that the king's army 'should nevertheless not engage itself in the hazard of a battle'. This stricture makes little military sense as the Cotswolds were open cavalry country and can only be explained as yet another manifestation of the king's sentimental aversion to casualties. It certainly helps to explain some of the more impenetrable decisions that Royalist commanders would make in the coming days.[18]

Chapter Seven
'I am tomorrow, God willing, beginning my march'

I

Contrary to common prejudice, conducting war by committee has many benefits, especially in a democracy, but the rapid implementation of decisions is rarely one of them. Having adopted a twin-track strategy based on reconquering the west of England while negotiating for Scottish intervention, and despite the prospect of losing their key strongholds of Gloucester and Exeter, Parliament's leaders turned their attention to other issues. While the Royalist armies gathered around Gloucester, Parliament did little more than pass a resolution that the city should be encouraged to hold out, and that only on 10 August, by which time it was too late to get the letter through. In part, MPs may have been in a state of shock at events on their own doorstep. The Commons' vote on peace proposals had been taken on 7 August against the background of a mob of 5,000 in the Palace Yard clamouring for a continuation of the war. When next day another mob appeared, mainly of women 'with their children in their arms, to soften the hardest hearts and implore peace' or 'dirty and tattered sluts' according to political taste, soldiers opened fire, first with noisy volleys of powder, then a volley of shot, which killed two men who had been inciting the mob. Eventually a troop of Sir William Waller's cavalry cleared the yard at sword and pistol point, killing a bystander in the process. *Mercurius Aulicus* gloated that the enthusiasm for war of the militant mob had again not been reflected in their willingness to volunteer for Waller's fledgling army.

Despondent and fearful for their safety, the Lords' peace party disintegrated; some fled to their homes, others like the Earls of Holland and Bedford defected to the king. In London, public order was the immediate priority. According to the Venetians:

> Every effort, not omitting violence, is used to purge this city of the pacific royalists and neutrals. Many of the women who went to implore peace have been imprisoned, as well as their husbands, the mere suspicion of desiring it being considered the last degree of criminality. For this reason they have made a fresh general search in the houses, and taken away arms of every sort, even swords, from those not actually serving the parliament. Many have been arrested without any evidence about their sympathies save the indiscretion of soldiers.

This is a vivid picture of the lengths to which the Parliamentarian leadership was prepared to go to prevent the kind of rising envisaged by the queen and her supporters. By mid-August, any internal threat had been crushed.

Jockeying among Parliament's generals continued unabated. Essex was quite happy to issue the Earl of Manchester with a commission to command the Eastern Association's new army but continued to cavil over Waller's role and commission. Essex had moved his headquarters to Uxbridge and Parliament sent a four-man delegation to flatter him into agreeing that Waller should be appointed commander of the 'New Army' of twenty regiments. They failed. The earl would release some of his heavy artillery but 'would not show any sign of regard' for his fellow general. None of this was a secret. London newspapers reported 'discontents' between Essex, Waller and the City authorities, and predicted that Gloucester had no more chance of holding out than had Bristol. To the Venetians, it seemed that the earl was still hankering after a negotiated settlement. They certainly did not expect him to move towards Gloucester, reporting on 11 August that though 'the people there [were] showing the utmost determination to hold out until the last gasp ... it will have to capitulate soon, as it cannot be relieved'. A week later they noted further Parliamentary pressure for Essex to act but concluded that 'he has no more than 3,000 men, and is not yet disposed to move as they would wish'.

Nonetheless, a change in mood and tempo had occurred during that week. The catalysts were confirmation that Gloucester had not fallen and the arrival at Essex's headquarters of yet another delegation from Parliament. On 15 August, Pym and the older Sir Henry Vane visited the earl to discuss whether his army should be directed against Gloucester, Oxford or Exeter. It has been argued that their real aim was to persuade Essex finally to issue Waller's commission. In fact, however, the two issues were inextricably linked. Essex was determined that he would lead any major operation that summer and he was therefore stalling with regard to agreement of his rival's commission until it was impossible for Parliament to change its collective mind once more and appoint Waller to command that operation in his stead. The 15 August meeting established beyond doubt that the objective would be Gloucester and that Essex would lead the relief army. Waller would remain behind to defend London, a task that would only become relevant should Essex be defeated. Wrestling Sir William's commission from the earl would still take time but the parties were now simply haggling over the details. A second issue was the composition of the relief army. If as the Venetian report suggests Essex had been asked to march with only his own stricken forces, he was undoubtedly right to have resisted. Now, however, the political pressure to save Gloucester meant that he could name his terms. Given the contrast between Parliament's inactivity before the meeting and the rapid steps taken afterwards, it is hard to resist the conclusion that, until 15 August, the judgement in Westminster was that Gloucester would fall quickly and that the campaign in the west would therefore be fought for different objectives and in longer time. Only when news arrived that Massey had not surrendered and Rupert had not then stormed the city was serious consideration given to going beyond rhetorical support to practical assistance.

Essex had in his own terms gained an important political victory. Two days later, Parliament published the formal vindication of his past actions (Pym having presumably shown him the text at their meeting): the earl was a true patriot who had been falsely maligned and suffered the insubordination of some of his officers. His recent disappointments had been the result of circumstances beyond his control.

Mercurius Aulicus commented wryly that Essex was 'willing to continue still a rebel', but the truth was that thanks to Pym's political manoeuvring he was now once again in control of his own destiny and Parliament's military fortunes. The mood of London's newspapers lightened in parallel; if Gloucester could keep the Royalists at bay for another two weeks, Essex and Waller 'will put a fire in their breeches'.[1]

II

If Gloucester was to be saved, a sense of greater urgency was only the starting point. Parliament was therefore fortunate that if Essex had thus far demonstrated a military forte it was in building armies quickly from unpromising beginnings; first in the previous summer to fight the Edgehill campaign and then in spring 1643, before that army was destroyed by disease and indiscipline after the capture of Reading. Now, however, the challenge was even greater. Gloucester could not be expected to hold out for many weeks and a relief march meant accepting the probability of a battle on substantially less favourable terms than if the king advanced towards London. Even more daunting was the apparent lack of raw material from which to build the new army. The Edgehill army had been based on the officers and organisation assembled for an abortive expedition to Ireland. Despite the losses during and after Edgehill, there were still firm foundations in the following spring upon which to work. By early August, the spirit of Essex's regiments may have been willing but their military capacity was extremely weak.

According to surviving pay records, Essex had eleven of his own infantry regiments available for an operation of this kind. Compared to their combined theoretical establishment of 12,200 men, their maximum actual strength in the period prior to Christmas 1642 had been 8,558 private soldiers plus some 1,000 officers, NCOs and drummers, but as the result of the privations of the spring and early summer, only 4,681 privates were being paid in July and August. Even if the regiments retained a disproportionate number of officers, NCOs and drummers, total manpower would have been less than 6,000 and the reality was that because of continuing sickness, the figure capable of marching and fighting was little more than 3,000. Three other regular regiments were employed as garrisons at key strategic points (Aylesbury, Windsor and Chichester) and could not be released; four more had been raised locally in London and Kent but they were currently engaged in suppressing the Kent uprising. Without substantial reinforcement, Essex simply did not have enough infantrymen to mount a credible challenge to the Oxford Army. The same applied to the earl's cavalry. Following a reorganisation earlier in the summer, they had been grouped into nine regiments, one of which seems to have been retained in or around London. Pay records for the cavalry are less comprehensive than for the infantry but it appears that the eight available regiments consisted of a total of about forty-eight troops and some 3,500 cavalrymen, including a small number of dragoons. Although disease does not seem to have ravaged the cavalry as badly as the infantry, their military effectiveness had been undermined by a critical shortage of suitable horses; at the end of July, Essex claimed that he could mount only 2,500 men. Only in artillery did Essex enjoy an undoubted superiority over the Royalists as the Tower of London magazine could provide all of his requirements for guns and ammunition.[2]

Essex had already set out his requirements: £10,000, horses for his cavalry and 5,000 extra infantry. Money was relatively easy to provide if the City of London was agreeable, which it now was; commissioners were appointed on 19 August. Horses were also being rounded up across south-eastern England. Producing large numbers of additional soldiers at short notice was a much more difficult problem. In the time available, there were two potential solutions. The first was to reinforce his existing regiments. Waller's dismal experience suggested that volunteers were most unlikely to appear in anything like adequate numbers, so conscription was the only credible alternative. Parliament had approved impressment legislation, and the pool of potential recruits in London and the south-east had not yet been properly tapped. On 18 August Essex's soldiers were ordered to return to their units on pain of death and on the following day Parliament authorised conscription of 4,000 men from London and the surrounding counties to reinforce the infantry regiments. What seemed a good idea in theory proved a failure in practice. Four days later, *Mercurius Aulicus* reported that

> the pressed men (being in all 1,000) which were sent to Kingston, being so intractable, and watching all advantages to escape away ... it was work enough for the rest of the army to keep them from dispersing in the open field, and hinder them from running home.

Gossip in the Royalist lines at Gloucester was that if Essex forced the conscripts to serve 'they all intend to run to the king's side'. This was not simply propaganda. The Venetians wrote on 25 August that for the past week 'they have been pressing men with so much inhumanity that many of the objectors have been injured and five killed'; and subsequently confirmed that Essex had sent the conscripts home before setting out on the march.[3]

Sick men will have recovered, and some volunteers and perhaps even some conscripts will have filled out the eleven infantry regiments. By 25 August the record of a shoe distribution suggests that their actual strength was around 4,300 all ranks. If the four Kent and London regiments were made available, Essex could therefore deploy in excess of 6,000 regular infantry, but intelligence suggested that there were 10,000 Royalist infantry at Gloucester, a fatal imbalance in a pitched battle, so he did indeed need to find an extra 5,000 men. Waller's army still existed primarily on paper and it was rumoured that what soldiers he had refused to serve under Essex. Manchester's new 20,000-strong Eastern Association army did not yet exist as a coherent force and from 23 August was diverted by a Royalist uprising in Norfolk. That left only one other source: the London Trained Bands.

Here was the major test of Pym's control of Parliament's factions. If he had re-imposed his influence but alienated the City of London, his victory in early August would have been at best pyrrhic. In fact, Pym's confidence in the renewed strength of his position was demonstrated in his destruction of Henry Martin, the City's erstwhile ally against Essex. With poor judgement and timing, Martin implicitly advocated the king's execution in a Commons speech on 16 August and, following a powerful speech by Pym, was expelled from the House and imprisoned in the Tower. Only two weeks before, this would have set Pym at odds with the City of London authorities. Now, however, they were part of the new consensus working frantically to provide Essex with whatever he desired. On 21 August, the City of London Militia Committee announced that it was contributing forces to the army that was being sent to relieve Gloucester because London 'cannot be long in safety if that city be lost'. Lots would be drawn to choose which London Trained Band regiments would be sent. The names of soldiers who would not go, and of volunteers from other units, should be passed to the

Committee. All shops within the 'lines of communication' would be shut so that London's inhabitants could help prepare defences in case the expedition failed. Two days later, the commitment was formalised in a Parliamentary ordnance committing London to contribute six infantry regiments of up to 8,000 men and 1,500 cavalry.

Although the Venetians commented unfavourably on the Trained Bands' in-experience, *Mercurius Aulicus* cast doubt on whether they would actually march and numbers eventually fell well short of the commitment, the six regiments were an invaluable reinforcement without which Essex could not have envisaged challenging the Oxford Army. None of the regiments had seen combat but all were well equipped and by contemporary standards the two original Trained Band units had undergone intensive peacetime training. Some London soldiers were evidently reluctant, and the Militia Committee seems to have resorted to courts martial and the threat of the death penalty to encourage doubters. Yet many others were enthusiastic and, in contrast to most men fighting on either side, committed politically to their goal.

Strengthening the cavalry was if anything a harder task. There was no untapped pool of Trained Band regiments, Waller's forces were weak and unwilling, and diverting units from local armies risked defeat in the north and midlands. Nonetheless, four additional regiments were found, two each from the south-east and east midlands, plus a handful of independent troops, and every effort was made to provide the regiments with their full complement of mounts; Hertfordshire was reported almost emptied of horses at the orders of the Militia Committee. Horses were also needed to tow the guns and supply wagons. It was rumoured that the Parliamentary commissioners tried unsuccessfully to persuade Essex not to take heavy artillery with him, probably to reduce the requirement for horses. That they failed is not surprising; the earl's military education had been in the Netherlands where artillery was a vital component of any army. Despite the undoubted shortfalls, the achievement of Parliament, and especially of John Pym, was considerable. In a matter of days, he had scraped together an army comparable in size to that which had fought at Edgehill, an army that Parliament had not possessed when the king laid siege to Gloucester.[4]

III

What did Essex plan to do with his army? Observers such as the Venetians and *Mercurius Aulicus'* London agents were unsure of his intentions, but it was in Essex's interests to keep the king and his sympathisers guessing. With the benefit of hindsight, there is sufficient circumstantial evidence to recreate an outline of the earl's strategy. His aim was less ambitious than in previous campaigns or compared to the objective adopted by Parliament at the end of July, re-conquest of the west. The task now was simply to relieve Gloucester. Nor was Essex searching for a decisive battle; the idea of deciding the war by trial by combat belonged to the days of his depression at Great Brickhill in July. If he could relieve Gloucester and return to London without meeting the king's army, so much the better.

Indeed, it might be possible to save Gloucester without going anywhere near it. Earlier in the year, the king had shown himself determined to defend Oxford. Now that the queen was based there, his resolve would be all the greater. A large-scale attack up the Thames valley should therefore bring the king's army scuttling from Gloucester to Oxford's defence, at which Essex could pull back towards London and declare his job done. That would certainly have been the prudent option, which is probably why the Royalists expected Essex to adopt it. But it was also the easiest threat for the

Royalists to counter. Even with only a reduced garrison, Oxford's defences could not have been breached quickly. The king could have ignored the threat until he had taken Gloucester, or marched against Essex once he was committed to a siege, out-manoeuvred or defeated him, and then taken Gloucester at his leisure or advanced on a demoralised London.

Since no other potential targets were likely to divert the king, Essex was left with little choice but to advance on Gloucester itself. Ideally he would have hoped to trap the king's army in its siege lines between his troops and Gloucester's guns but that would require a level of incompetence that the earl could not expect from professional soldiers like Forth and Rupert. At the other extreme, he had to avoid allowing the Royalists to exploit their advantage in cavalry so the longer he could spend in enclosed country, where infantry had the upper hand, the better his chance of success. The Venetians thought that Essex might attempt to interpose his army between the king at Gloucester and the queen at Oxford, but that would oblige him to stay in the Cotswold Hills where Rupert's cavalry should have reigned supreme.

The best clue to the earl's intentions is his intemperate letter of 9 July from Great Brickhill in which he complained about the superiority of the Royalist cavalry:

> it is impossible to keep the counties from being plundered, nor to fight with [the enemy cavalry] ... but when and where they list; we being forced, when we move, to march with the whole army, which can be but slowly.

In July his main concern had been the army's failure to protect the local population. Now the circumstances were very different. If Essex could keep his army together while it was at its most vulnerable, moving through open country, he should be able to fend off Rupert's cavaliers. The king would then have to raise the siege to mass his infantry against the advancing Parliamentarians. Although Essex might be forced to give battle, it would be on better terms and, if he could escape from the open hills into the enclosed Severn valley, on more suitable ground.

This judgement appears to have dictated his chosen route. Of the two options for bypassing Oxford, that from the south by way of Reading, Newbury and Cirencester involved the longest march through unenclosed country. From Newbury until the Cotswold scarp, a distance of some forty-five miles, Essex's army would have had Rupert's cavalry regiments snapping at their flanks. By contrast, the northerly route past Aylesbury and Bicester, and then across the Cotswolds, was vulnerable only during the stretch between Banbury and Prestbury, a shorter march of some thirty miles. There were still risks in this strategy. Essex did not take large quantities of food with him, either because it would take too long to procure or, more likely, there were insufficient draught animals to pull the wagons, and all accounts agree that the Parliamentarian army lived off the land during its advance. Or at least it tried to do so. The Royalists had, through indiscipline or policy, conducted a scorched earth operation throughout north Gloucestershire. If Essex's army moved too slowly, his men would begin to starve, and if they moved in a single concentrated body for fear of the Royalist cavalry, they would be unable to forage. The worst possibility of all was that the king would be able to block the Earl's progress as he attempted to cross the Cotswolds and that his isolated army would then fall apart as the result of hunger.

For Parliament, the defeat or disintegration of Essex's army represented potential disaster. In the longer term, its ability to wage war was inherently greater and negotiations with the Scots, which were progressing satisfactorily, promised a major injection of military might in the coming months. Until then, Essex's soldiers were the only guarantee against Royalist victory. At the Royalist council of war outside Gloucester on 10 August, one of the key arguments for mounting a siege was the possibility that any relief army could be met on favourable terms, but nobody seems at that stage to have thought a relief operation was likely. As a high-risk option it was out of character for Essex and his political masters. The earl must have been aware of the stakes. In truth, the safety of Gloucester was a secondary consideration; its loss would not be a fatal blow to Parliament's cause. If on the other hand Parliament's main field army, reinforced by a significant proportion of London's Trained bands, until now Parliament's untouchable strategic reserves, was lost, the impact would be incalculable. Waller might be able to scrape together enough soldiers to man London's walls (there were still thirteen Trained Band regiments in the capital), but it was questionable whether the will to resist the king's triumphant army would have remained among the soldiers, the politicians or the London mob. A de facto capitulation along the lines of that proposed by the Earl of Holland would have appeared an increasingly attractive solution to the nation's ills. Whatever his strategy, Essex could not win the war at Gloucester but he could certainly lose it.[5]

IV

On 22 August, while Massey's garrison licked its wounds after the over-ambitious attempt to spike the Royalist guns, Essex held a muster on Hounslow Heath. It was not an impressive sight. The Venetians estimated that the Parliamentarian army was 10,000 strong but *Mercurius Aulicus'* sources counted only 2,000 cavalry and under 3,000 infantry ('with all their diseases'), to which could be added the 1,000 disaffected conscripts at Kingston. In fact, of course, a significant number of other units were also absent, including the Trained Bands, the units in Kent and reinforcements from the south and midlands, and the muster may therefore have played an unheralded part in shaping the campaign by reinforcing the Royalists' preconception of the relative weakness of Parliament's army. Essex seems to have revised his own overall assessment to 5,000 foot (plus 2,000 sick) and under 3,000 horse, to be reinforced by another 4,000 foot and 2,000 horse.

According to Robert Codrington, who may have served with the army, the earl 'thanked them for their love, and applauded them for their courage, and ... forthwith marched to the relief of Gloucester'. In practice, however, it was far from that simple. A complex concentration of forces had to be orchestrated, and the demanding logistic task of preparing the army for active service had to be completed. It is clear from surviving records that Essex was particularly unhappy about the physical condition of his own eleven infantry regiments. Loyalty to his men was an enduring characteristic throughout his military career, and remedying the state of their equipment and clothing was a necessary precondition for the march. More pragmatically, the army as a whole had to be paid before it could be depended upon to fight. The first leg of the journey was therefore an overnight stroll to Colnbrook, where camp was made for the next three days. Money arrived and the troops received two weeks' pay. Some clothing arrived but Essex refused to issue it because, as he wrote to Parliament, the 'shirts, shoes, coats and snapsacks ... are so unevenly provided that I know not how to dispose of them without a damage to the army by a mutiny, there being no stockings and so few shirts'. Here too the unwilling conscripts were released.[6]

Parliament also had unfinished business to complete before the earl disappeared. Waller was now Parliament's senior commander in the south-east yet was still without a formal commission. If Essex failed, Sir William would be their last line of defence and he therefore required confirmation of his status. After the months of bitter infighting, Essex was disinclined to be gracious. On 25 August he sent a message taking exception to some of Waller's proposed new colonels. In response Pym was sent to Colnbrook to obtain a signed commission. Essex signed it the next day but still refused to write Waller's name and left the space blank. The Commons finally brought the charade to an end by ordering their clerk to insert Waller's name and the Speaker passed him the commission as general of the 'New Army'. More positive was the stirring declaration of intent with which Essex concluded his letter covering Waller's commission: 'I am tomorrow, God willing, beginning my march, and if the army be as willing to march as I shall be to lead them (and the town hold out until we can release them), I shall endeavour it, or perish in the act'. True to his word, on 26 August the earl led the core of his force from Colnbrook towards Beaconsfield. Not everyone was convinced of his determination. The cynical Venetians thought that he had moved only under pressure from Pym.[7]

The advance was conducted not in a single formation but across a broad front in a series of smaller columns, to spread the burden of feeding and housing the troops overnight. Dispersing the army in this way may incidentally have helped to further mislead the Royalists about its total size. Essex and the main force marched through Beaconsfield and then on to Aylesbury, where most of the army would assemble. Further east, the London Trained Bands were making their way along a parallel route. Sergeant Henry Foster of the Red Regiment described how his regiment was mustered at the City Artillery Ground on 23 August and then marched through the night to Brentford. Some part-time soldiers were extremely reluctant to serve: 'the next day many of our citizens, who seemed very forward and willing at first to march with us, yet upon some pretences and fair excuses returned home again, hiring others to go in their room'. This last minute injection of new faces cannot have helped unit cohesion. From Brentford, the Red Regiment advanced to Uxbridge on 25 August and to Chalfont the following day, where a soldier was killed by an accidental musket discharge. On 27 August, five of the six London regiments mustered for the first time near Chesham. More memorably for Foster, that night 'we were well accommodated for beer, having great plenty'. The London brigade reached the Aylesbury assembly area on 28 August and was quartered in and around Aston Clinton.

Trained Band soldiers were well equipped and clothed and not therefore involved in the mass issue of weapons and clothing that took up much of the next two days. Coats, shoes and snapsacks were distributed to the eleven ragged infantry regiments from Essex's own army at St James church at Bierton, just north of Aylesbury. There were insufficient shirts to go round and they were all kept on the wagons, presumably to avoid charges of discrimination. In view of the coming march and the uncertainty of future supplies, it is reasonable to assume that the 4,260 pairs of shoes issued was a close approximation to the total active strength of these eleven regiments.[8]

At Aylesbury, Essex received the first hard information from inside the besieged city of Gloucester. Massey had been trying to get messengers out and Major John Bridges, Parliament's governor of Warwick Castle, had been attempting to pass messengers in. Neither succeeded until at midday on 28 August two 'substantial men from the town' appeared at Warwick having somehow evaded the Royalist cordon.

Bridges wrote immediately to Sir Samuel Luke at the earl's headquarters and the letter arrived at Aylesbury on the following day. The news was far better than might have been feared: 'the town was in a very good condition and full of courage, having every day put the enemy to much loss ... the town hath not lost above ten persons, of men, women, and children slain'. Sir Jacob Astley was yet again reported to have been killed but more substantively Bridges reported that 'the king's foot there are few, and those in very ill condition, so that whensoever the town makes a sally, the quarter they fall upon, runs without striking a blow'. This was encouraging and potentially valuable information.

On 30 August, the earl mustered his forces outside Aylesbury and, as the garrison artillery fired in salute, conducted a formal inspection. Not all of the disparate forces had yet arrived but numbers were edging towards respectability and the newly clothed regiments must have looked considerably more impressive than before. That evening, the army split up again to seek quarters. The main force advanced along the Bicester road to Waddeston while the Trained Bands marched on to Claydon, where the Red Regiment spent the night in the house of Sir Ralph Verney, the Roundhead father of King Charles' standard-bearer who had been killed at Edgehill.[9]

V

Aylesbury marked the boundary of territory controlled by Parliament. Westward lay Oxford and Henry Wilmot's covering force of Royalist cavalry. At the council of war at Oxford on 26 August, Wilmot had been ordered to 'wait about Banbury, and to retire before the enemy, if he should advance towards Gloucester, and to give such impediments to their march, as in such a country might be easy to do'. Since then, he had not been idle. The Venetians reported that he had led 2,000 of his cavalry to scatter fifteen companies of trained bands marching from Surrey to join the Parliamentarian army. This action probably occurred on 30 August south of Thame. The evidence is that a third Parliamentarian column, comprising the four London and Kent infantry regiments returning from the Kent uprising, plus two cavalry regiments, all commanded by Colonel Edmund Harvey, had marched north from Wokingham through Henley-on-Thames towards Thame and Bicester. The Venetian report exaggerated Wilmot's success because he claimed only to have killed some of the advance guard and taken five prisoners, from whom he established that the column was 2,500 strong, including the escort. Undeterred by the skirmish, Harvey continued his march from Thame on 31 August and joined Essex's main force near Bicester.[10]

On 31 August Wilmot wrote to Prince Rupert from his headquarters at Bletchington, north of Oxford:

> this day, I am informed, [Essex's] rendezvous is near Bicester. I shall not fail to attend him with as much diligence as I am capable of, and daily to give your Highness an account of his and my motions.

Cavalry from both sides did indeed spend the day skirmishing around the small town of Bicester. The official report, authorised by Essex and published in October, recorded that 100 Parliamentarian cavalrymen under Captain Robert Hammond, commander of the earl's lifeguard, chased a party of Royalists through Bicester and for two miles beyond. When a larger Royalist force appeared, they were in turn driven off by the rest of Essex's Regiment and that of Colonel Dalbier. Wilmot's cavalry do not seem to have delayed the advance or obliged Essex to concentrate his forces. Sir Philip Stapleton's cavalry were at Bicester, the London brigade were quartered at Stratton Audley with Harvey's column nearby at Preston Bisset, while the remaining infantry seem to have been further north again towards Brackley.

For the Royalists, intelligence was arguably more important at this stage than delay. On 28 August, *Mercurius Aulicus* was still scornfully mocking Parliamentarian claims that Essex had marched with more than 10,000 men. At Gloucester it was being said that the earl had at most 2,000 cavalry and 6,000 infantry. During 31 August, Wilmot attempted to get up-to-date eyewitness evidence by sending a trumpeter to Essex's headquarters under a flag of truce. The excuse was 'procurement of a pass for some lady, though many presumed his intent might be to view the army'. Essex played along and blindfolded the trumpeter until he came near to the London brigade, which was paraded for the purpose. The earl then removed the blindfold, assured 'him that these were only the Londoners, added to, and no part formerly of his army, and then sent him out of us'. By the time that news of this incident reached London, it had been magnified into a covert peace offer from the king to Essex, rejected to shouts of 'no propositions' from the soldiers. Meanwhile, Wilmot should have been realising that the earl's army was substantially larger than had hitherto been assumed.[11]

VI

On the following day, 1 September, the Parliamentarian army received its final reinforcements when Lord Grey of Groby rode in from Leicester at the head of a detachment of midlands cavalry. The army was now almost due north of Oxford. So far, Essex had succeeded in keeping opponents and observers in the dark about his strategy; even a week later the generally well-informed Venetians were still speculating that his real objective was Oxford. But at Gloucester the siege was entering its fourth week and, despite the heartening news from Warwick, the earl will have known that ammunition would be running low. He would, therefore, shortly have to show his hand. Before he did so, a third and final muster was held, this time at Baynard's Green, north of Bicester. Sergeant Foster described 'great shouting and triumph as [the earl] passed by to take a view of our regiments'. Good news from Gloucester and Exeter was announced to help stiffen the soldiers' determination, and after about an hour the army began the second, most difficult stage of its march.[12]

Some reorganisation took place at about this time to integrate the newly arrived units. The army thus took on the broad shape it was to retain throughout the campaign. At its heart were twenty infantry regiments of very different sizes and backgrounds but all equipped with muskets and pikes according to the optimum two-to-one proportion. Biggest and best equipped were the two London Trained Band and three Auxiliary regiments. Drawn traditionally from householders with a vested interest in public order, war had widened their recruiting pool (the Auxiliaries targeted London's apprentices) and the refusal of some to march had further diluted cohesion, yet the London part-timers were still close-knit, well motivated and better trained than most other militia units. Another London regiment was added to the brigade, Mainwaring's regulars who had arrived with Harvey and had so far been used solely for internal security in the capital and Kent. These six regiments between them totalled 5,000 men. The remaining fourteen regiments were wartime regular soldiers. Four had performed creditably at Edgehill; one had missed the battle; and six had been raised in late autumn 1642 by the Earl of Warwick. This was the rump of the army which had taken

Reading. Muster rolls and the shoe distribution at Bierton suggest that only two regiments were more than 500 strong and their combined strength was about 4,300 men. Although infected by disappointment, indiscipline and disease, they were now experienced soldiers in well-established units with newly issued equipment. Their English officers seem to have had no greater expertise than their Royalist counterparts, but two regiments (Barclay's and Holburn's) were commanded by highly competent Scottish professionals, and there seem to have been significant numbers of veteran Scots serving in more junior posts and as reformadoes following an active recruiting campaign during the previous winter. The final three infantry regiments had been raised more recently, two from Kent and one probably from London; they were neither well trained nor seasoned and unlikely to have totalled more than 1,200 men. It is therefore a fair estimate that Essex began the campaign with around 10,500 infantry, 1,500 fewer than he had fielded at Edgehill.

Like the Oxford Army, the main tactical formation was the brigade. At Edgehill, Essex had followed the Dutch three-brigade model. For this campaign, he appears to have adopted the Swedish approach of five brigades, though the larger regiments were big enough to operate on their own. Professionals commanded three of the brigades, Major General of Foot Philip Skippon and the Scottish colonels, Harry Barclay and James Holburn. In contrast, John, Lord Robartes, the Earl of Warwick's son-in-law, had no military experience before Edgehill, and Randall Mainwaring, Major General of the London Trained Bands, was a middle-aged merchant and political activist known primarily for using excessive force to suppress dissent in the capital.

Skippon was a considerable asset. A professional soldier in the Palatinate and the Netherlands, he had risen no higher than captain before returning to England in 1639. Nonetheless, the king had recommended him to lead the Honourable Artillery Company, a decision he must subsequently have regretted when Skippon employed his part-time soldiers against royal interests in the pre-war political crisis. Parliament appointed him commander of the London Trained Bands in January 1642 and at Turnham Green, his 'brave boys' were decisive in halting the king's advance on London. In November 1642, Skippon became Essex's Major General of Foot in place of Sir John Merrick. Though it is commonly assumed that this was at Essex's instigation, Merrick was his friend and protégé, and Hyde alleged that Skippon was appointed 'without the cheerful concurrence of the earl'. Whatever the truth, Essex and Skippon worked well together, and Skippon became extremely popular with the rank and file. But it was his hard-earned experience, his good sense as president of the army's council of war, and his abilities as a battlefield commander with a breadth of vision beyond his immediate responsibilities, that made Skippon especially valuable to Essex. He was also, somewhat surprisingly, the author of devout religious books and seems to have seen himself as a 'Christian Centurion'.

There was no equivalent to Skippon to command the Parliamentarian cavalry. The nominal commander, the Earl of Bedford, was one of the peace party Lords currently defecting to the king. His deputy, an able Scots professional, Sir William Balfour, had gone abroad because of his health and would not return until after the campaign. Another experienced Scot, Sir James Ramsey, was Commissary-General but had been widely suspected of either cowardice or treachery at Edgehill, and was not a credible successor. Politician turned colonel Arthur Goodwin had died, probably of typhus, in August. Command of the cavalry therefore devolved temporarily upon Sir Philip Stapleton, a Yorkshire landowner who had thrived in both Westminster and the army.

He had served his political apprenticeship alongside Hampden, taken command of Essex's cavalry regiment, fought bravely at Edgehill and Chalgrove Field, and thereafter replaced Hampden as Essex's main confidante and adviser. A friend described him as having 'a thin body and a weak constitution, but full of spirit ... quick of apprehension, sound of judgement'. Though undoubtedly courageous, Stapleton had no prior military experience, his actions were often rash and his advice sometimes naïve (he was the originator of Essex's idea for a trial by combat to decide the outcome of the war).

Parliamentarian cavalry regiments seem to have been divided into wings or brigades on an ad hoc basis, with command shared between Stapleton, Ramsey and their senior subordinates. John Dalbeir was a German who had been paymaster to the mercenary Count von Mansfeld in the 1620s before taking service with King Charles. When war broke out Dalbeir was languishing in prison for debt, from where he transferred his loyalty to Essex in return for his liberty and was now Quartermaster General. Hans Behr was another German professional and John Middleton a young Scot who had been fighting on the continent and for the Covenanters for more than a decade, and had acquired a reputation for bravery and generosity on both sides. By contrast, Edmund Harvey was, like Mainwaring, a London mercer without prior experience, and twenty-one year old Lord Grey of Groby owed his position as Parliament's commander in the east midlands to the influence of his father, the Earl of Stamford. The foreign presence in the cavalry was very marked and a matter of political controversy. Officers such as Croatian Captain Carlo Fantom were valued by Essex because they taught his cavalry 'the way of fighting with horse' but Fantom was in England 'to fight for your half-crown and your handsome women', and 'outlanders' of all kinds were mistrusted even within Parliament's higher command.

At the end of July, Essex had claimed that his nine regiments numbered only 2,500 mounted men, down from 3,000 at the previous muster. One of these regiments, Balfour's, remained in the south-east but the others had been reinforced and a combined strength of 3,000 is consistent with surviving muster records. Four regiments had joined them, one each from London and Hampshire plus Grey's two midland units. From the fragmentary evidence, it is unlikely that they totalled many more than 1,000 men. Even taking account of three independent troops and three companies of dragoons, Essex started the campaign with at most 4,500 horse. Quality did not compensate for quantity. Most regiments had a core of professional officers; those of Dalbeir, Behr and Middleton were further stiffened by foreign mercenaries; and all ranks seem to have been well armed (a few troops were still wearing full armour). But though Oliver Cromwell's famous critique of the poor quality of Parliament's cavalrymen ('decayed servingmen and tapsters') may have been unduly harsh, the standard of some troopers and mounts still left much to be desired. As a result, the Parliamentarian cavalry remained, on paper at least, inferior to their Royalist counterparts.[13]

With the artillery, the opposite was the case. Essex had a substantial train of field guns, no apparent shortages of powder or other ammunition, and a competent commander. Although no breakdown of the Parliamentarian ordnance has yet been discovered, between forty and fifty guns were taken on the Edgehill campaign, and almost fifty were lost before and at Lostwithiel in 1644, so a similar number is likely to have gone to Gloucester. From primary accounts, it is possible to identify at least five 'great guns' of culverin size and above, three demi-culverins and ten lighter guns, and each of the five infantry brigades seems to have had up to five small drakes allocated to it. Royalist reports of powder taken at Lostwithiel in 1644 after a three month campaign ranged from 100 to 300 barrels, so it is unlikely that the army started this operation with any less. Extrapolating from the Royalist ordnance records, this train would have required something in the region of 140 wagons and 750 horses.[14] At Edgehill, the artillery had been mishandled by a Frenchman, M Du Bois. He had since disappeared and the nominal General of Artillery, the Earl of Peterborough, had died of consumption. Instead, Essex had appointed the displaced Sir John Merrick, a professional for a dozen years on the continent and a good friend who appears to have done his job quietly and conscientiously, and was probably the earl's closest military confidant. Artillery aside, Essex did not take a large supply train into the Cotswolds. There are repeated descriptions of hungry soldiers, and Sergeant Foster would later complain of marching for days with little or no food. Senior officers had carriages but there are no indications that the army was accompanied by the cloud of camp followers (servants, wives, partners, prostitutes and children) that generally accompanied early modern campaigns, slowing progress and consuming precious supplies. By the standards of the time, this was a lean and mobile fighting force.[15]

Command arrangements were simpler than the Royalist model. Once away from London's political manoeuvrings, Essex was the undisputed Captain General and there seem to have been no challenges to his authority. What little evidence exists suggests that the council of war met regularly and was supportive. In late July, it had consisted of fourteen officers including Skippon, Stapleton, Merrick, Dalbeir, Middleton, Barclay, Holburn and Luke. Ramsey, Robartes, Mainwaring, Harvey and Grey were probably added once the army was assembled. Though Essex's secretary, a Mr Baldwyn, seems not to have exerted significant influence, the journal of Sir Samuel Luke (a working document) implies that the feisty and diminutive Scoutmaster also acted as de facto chief of staff. Captain Charles Pym, commander of a cavalry troop and son of the more famous John, often provided an informal link between the earl and his political masters in Westminster. On this occasion, however, once the army moved beyond Oxford, Essex and his men would be very much on their own. With that in mind, the muster was a considerable success as a morale-raising exercise. Sergeant Foster wrote that 'it was a goodly and glorious sight to see the whole army of horse and foot together'. Essex now had an interest in exaggerating his numbers to persuade the king to abandon the siege and deter the Royalists from seeking battle, and some London newspapers talked of an army of 18,000 soldiers. Foster gave a more conservative figure of at least 15,000 and, as set out above, that is broadly supported by the various records.[16]

The earl was still not sufficiently alarmed by the Royalist cavalry to order the concentration of the army. From the final muster, the regiments marched west to quarter in villages south of Banbury. Essex spent the night at Aynho, the London brigade was at King's Sutton (where they were 'very much scanted of victuals'), other infantry regiments were at Fritwell and Harvey's cavalry were at Somerton. A large party of Wilmot's cavalry kept Harvey's men from their beds for some hours but did not venture too close. Further north, Middleton had to chase some Royalists from his quarters at Deddington and there were skirmishes between scouts. Wilmot was reported to have 2,000 or more men at a pass towards Oxford (probably one of the bridges across the River Cherwell). As yet, however, he remained content to observe rather than attack.[17]

Twenty-three days had elapsed since the king had appeared in front of Gloucester. By the standards of the day, this was not a prolonged siege. But England was not the Netherlands where sieges routinely lasted for months and sometimes years. Massey had to be relieved quickly or not at all. Since inactivity was no longer politically acceptable in London and the king had chosen to ignore any indirect threat to Oxford, Essex was now committed to the final stage of his relief march. Despite the confident tenor of subsequent accounts, this was an extraordinarily dangerous venture. Not only did it give the king the opportunity to recover the strategic initiative he had lost during the past three weeks, it gave him the chance for the first time in the war to meet Parliament's main field army on potentially favourable terms. If the king's generals could then defeat Essex in battle, Parliament's overall strategic advantages would melt away and the king could look forward to dictating a political settlement or even military victory.

Chapter Eight
'We shall do little good upon this town'

I

The siege had settled into a routine of attrition. On 26 August, while the king and Rupert rode to Oxford to consider the threat posed by the Earl of Essex, pioneers working four abreast inside the wooden gallery beneath Gloucester's east wall were filling the moat with earth and wooden faggots. North-west of the city's defences, hayricks were burnt to prevent the garrison from collecting them. For most Royalist soldiers, however, the day was probably more notable for the issue of new coats from Oxford. That night, a desultory artillery bombardment played against the south wall and three mortar bombs were lobbed into the city, all with little effect. Under cover of darkness, the two Parliamentarian messengers destined to reach Warwick on 28 August slipped away, the first men to penetrate the Royalist lines since the siege began.

The underground mine against the East Gate was evidently now a priority and on 27 August the battery there began a preparatory softening-up bombardment, firing twenty rounds at the 'house' over the gate, perhaps to divert attention from what was happening below. If that was the intention, it failed. On 28 August the garrison concluded that the East Gate was indeed being attacked and Massey ordered counter-mining to begin to flood or collapse the Royalist tunnel. Two countermines were started, yet they soon hit so many springs that Massey judged that it was too damp for mining by either side and abandoned them. Massey's decision demonstrates the problems faced by the Royalist miners and explains why the work was taking such a long time. King Charles and Rupert returned that day from Oxford but there was no significant increase in tempo as a result, further evidence that the Royalists had still not grasped the threat posed by Essex's army.

Inside the city, the gallery creeping towards the east wall was a visible reminder that time was running out. Massey responded on 29 August by using some of the garrison's precious powder supply to mount a bombardment of the eastern trenches by cannon emplaced at Friar's Barn, and by starting work on a secret gun port from which to attack the gallery itself. Activity of this kind was good for the garrison's morale but an even bigger boost was received that night when the two messengers made their way back from Warwick through the Royalist lines to confirm that Essex's army was on its way. Though Corbett wrote later that the 'report of his Excellency, who then lay under a cloud, did give no great assurance', two scouts were sent out with instructions to light two fires on a hillside if they heard further good news. Powder shortages were now limiting the garrison to little more than passive resistance. On 30 August a public fast day was celebrated, combining prayer with prudent economy. Food stocks had not, however, reached crisis point. Two hundred cattle were being grazed outside the north-western defences in the Little Mead, moving to and fro across the ditch on a bridge of ladders. Vavasour's Welsh and Worcester soldiers seem occasionally to have sniped at them but had made no concerted efforts to kill or rustle them.

This was symptomatic of deteriorating morale among the besiegers. According to the anonymous Parliamentarian account, there was a mutiny by Royalist infantry on the night of 29–30 August provoked by 'a speech among the common soldiers they should have orders to march away, but their next orders was a regiment of horse environed them in, and kept sentry all that night'. Missed deadlines and frustrated expectations did not help morale. Sunderland had forecast on 25 August that Gloucester would fall within days, at Oxford they predicted 29 August while in the Royalist camp Rupert was said to have wagered the huge sum of £5,000 with the king that he would take the city by 30 August. But Sir William Killegrew of the King's Lifeguard was now quoted by Parliamentarian intelligence as saying that the siege would not be over for another week. A further straw in the wind was the departure of most of the Royalist cavalry to reinforce Wilmot in the event that Essex advanced beyond Oxford. Precisely when they moved is unclear but a Parliamentarian spy reported that 100 troops of cavalry were expected in Oxford as early as the night of 29 August, and that there were only ten troops remaining at Gloucester. That timeframe would explain the infantry mutiny the same night.[1]

Meanwhile, Lord Percy had been receiving a steady supply of cannon balls from the Soudley foundries, 454 between 28 August and 1 September, including seventy-four for the invaluable demi-cannon. A small delivery including five demi-cannon shot also arrived from Bristol. Although a sporadic bombardment was kept up against the city to help wear down morale, neither Corbett nor Dorney refer to heavy artillery use during this period and the Royalists must therefore have been husbanding their munitions. When the mines were exploded, the infantry would need covering artillery fire as they crossed the moat.

Mining was clearly the main plank in Royalist strategy. Indeed, since Forth seems to have received a briefing on conditions inside Gloucester from a Royalist spy on 30 August, and cannot therefore have believed that the city was close to surrender, it was now the only plank in that strategy. Work on the mines was undoubtedly intensifying; the Ordnance Papers contain the first reference to the supply of candles to miners at the works. Their task was far from easy. To pass under the moat, the underground mine had to be sunk to a considerable depth. Because of the springs, this in turn necessitated a major effort to pump out water and keep the tunnel tolerably dry. Why then was the apparently less difficult mine across the moat against the east wall, which Percy had estimated on 17 August would be ready in a week, taking so long to complete? John Gwyn, a junior officer in Lloyd's Regiment, later recalled that 'had there been as much care taken in making one mine ready as was in making the other two which stayed for it, probably we had carried the town'. A letter from the king written on 5 September confirms that the primary emphasis had been laid on the underground mine. The implication is that a conscious decision was taken not only to give priority to the mine under the East Gate but to delay completion of the other two as well. Perhaps this was the result of shortages of skilled personnel, miners and engineers; second thoughts about the feasibility of draining and filling up the moat; or even a recurrence of the king's scruples about an attack on the walls in the face of enemy cannon. Whatever the cause, yet another delay had been imposed on the Royalist timetable.[2]

On 31 August Vavasour tried at last to drive off the city's cattle from the Little Mead, but his men were unwilling to close with the Parliamentarian musketeers acting as cattle guards. Alert as ever to changes in his opponents' mood, Massey resumed his harassing tactics. From the southern defences, three snipers crept undetected along the riverbank and opened fire on the leaguer at Llanthony where, according to Dorney, they kept the Royalists pinned down for an hour. When a hundred or so of the besiegers gathered behind a wall ready to advance, the garrison battery at the barbican 'discharged a demi-culverin ... which lighted in the midst of them, made the stones of the wall fly about their ears, and could not but do good execution'. That may have been wishful thinking yet such episodes were bound to lift the defenders' morale. Early the next morning, a sergeant and four regulars from White's company together with John Barnwood, a grenade expert from the Town Regiment, slipped out of a hole made secretly in the East Gate dungeon and made their way silently to the mouth of the East Gate mine. This commando-style operation was intended primarily to discover whether mining was underway. Barnwood was able to creep to the mine entrance, upon which was a wooden board which he removed 'fired and cast a grenade in amongst them, our four musketeers playing at them as they ran out'. Covered by musket fire from the walls, the raiders retreated to the sally port claiming to have killed four and wounded others. Not surprisingly, the Royalists were in 'a great fright, they crying nothing but arm, arm, for a good while after'. More importantly, Massey now knew that his judgement had been wrong. The springs were not preventing the Royalist miners from attacking the East Gate, and countermining had to be resumed.

Massey and his professional officers will have estimated that an assault was inevitable within a matter of days. One or other of the mines would succeed and the garrison would then have to deal with an all-out attack. In those circumstances, Royalist artillery would quickly make the outer defences untenable. A second line of defence was therefore essential to prevent the Royalists, and especially their cavalry, from breaking rapidly into the heart of the city. As a first step, work began during 1 September on building an earth fort or sconce on rising ground in Friar's Orchard from where four artillery pieces could sweep the open ground behind the south and east walls with case shot, or take an attack from the East Gate in the flank. To support the sconce, an earth wall was built across the middle of Friar's Orchard. The impact on civilian morale of work that explicitly recognised that the external defences could not be expected to hold for much longer was potentially serious. Massey must therefore have been in no doubt that the military situation was sufficiently grave to warrant such a measure.[3]

II

The picture from London looked rather different. For the first time, the weekly Venetian report contemplated the possibility that the siege might be lifted, concluding that 'His Majesty now realises how much he has lost through the obstinacy of the governor and inhabitants of that place, of no great consequence, by committing himself to this enterprise' rather than exploiting the rising in Kent and marching against London. From 2 September, the campaign became a race between the Royalist besiegers, determined to capture Gloucester without interference, and Essex's army marching to the city's relief. The equation was straightforward. From Aynho, Essex had thirty-four miles to travel before he reached the Cotswold escarpment, after which he would be into the Severn valley and the Royalists would risk envelopment if they did not lift the siege. Armies rarely sustained more than ten to thirteen miles per day so King Charles had three days in which to take Gloucester and turn on the Parliamentarian army. If Essex could be delayed in the Cotswolds, that would increase the time available still further. However, failure to capture Gloucester before Essex appeared, though disappointing, would not necessarily be a defeat since the king would then have the opportunity to cut the earl off from London and bring the relief army to battle on terms favourable to a decisive Royalist victory. The Venetians were premature in writing off the king's hopes for his summer campaign.

Nonetheless, from the Royalist perspective, the race began with an unpleasant surprise. Overnight on 2–3 September, the garrison's secret gun port close to the gallery against the east wall was finally completed after four days painstaking work. A five-pounder saker was emplaced behind the gun port, sited at an oblique angle so that it could fire directly into the long wooden flank of the gallery. On the wall above, Massey gathered eighty musketeers, some equipped with hand grenades. At eight o'clock, the gun port was quietly unveiled and the saker opened fire. Surprise was again complete. Bolt shot from the saker slammed into the side of the gallery, while grenades and musket fire poured down from the walls, and the cannon at the barn to the north of the East Gate raked the Royalist trench lines. For once, however, the Royalist response was uncharacteristically decisive. Their artillery batteries on the city's eastern side returned a heavy fire against the top of the wall, killing at least one musketeer, while the southern battery bombarded the South Gate defences, presumably to deter further attacks. None of the Royalist cannon were, however, able to train on the offending gun port. For most of the day the Parliamentarian saker pounded away at the gallery. According to Corbett, one of the gallery's main beams was smashed as a result. Eventually, towards evening, the Royalists managed to mount their own cannon opposite the gun port, at which Massey prudently withdrew the saker and closed up the hole. A single smashed beam seems scant reward for such an investment of effort and ammunition. The Royalist engineers had clearly done a good job in building the gallery to withstand prolonged artillery fire and Corbett's claim that the attack set back Royalist plans by three days sounds markedly over-optimistic. The gallery was already long overdue and greater emphasis was being placed on the underground mine.

Despite the previous day's grenade attack, the Welsh miners who had arrived on 29 August were advancing the underground work rapidly. Talk in the camp was that their tunnel had reached under the moat almost to the south side of the gate and was expected to be under the gate itself by the following night. This was not simply gossip. When, soon after, work started again on the countermines, Massey's miners 'could hear them work under them'. The climax of the Royalist investment was at last approaching. After days of lassitude there was a sense of renewed determination among the besiegers elsewhere around the perimeter. To the north there was skirmishing in Walham where a Royalist corporal was killed when he refused quarter. Men and women cutting turf in the Little Mead came under sniper fire from Welsh soldiers hidden in a ditch, and the Parliamentarians expended valuable powder to drive them off with artillery. During the night, the mortars had a rare success when a bomb set light to stables in Eastgate Street.

In the Royalist camp, a Parliamentarian spy was told that the plan was to delay Essex on the Cotswolds for four days while the city was taken. Additional reinforcements were on their way. Those brought from Oxford by Colonel Feilding will already have arrived, Hopton was stripping out the Bristol garrison and Percy had sent urgent orders to Oxford to produce another marching train of artillery, ten field guns plus extra wheels and a team of carpenters, wheelwrights and smiths to make the siege guns at Gloucester mobile should the need arise.[4]

III

North of Oxford, Lord Wilmot and his 2,000 Royalist cavalry were still sitting between the Royalist capital and Essex's army, which had spent the night of 1–2 September spread out in and around Aynho on the banks of the River Cherwell. On the following morning, most of the Parliamentarian army was engaged in crossing the river and was therefore vulnerable to attack by cavalry. To pre-empt this, Essex sent Colonel John Middleton, the young Scottish brigade commander, with his own and Sir James Ramsey's cavalry regiments south to where Wilmot was deployed at one of the lower crossing points (or passes) over the Cherwell. Although considerably outnumbered, Middleton drove the Royalists back from the pass and dismounted some dragoons to hold it. Skirmishing continued until three in the afternoon, by which time the rest of the army was across the river and into the hills beyond, and Essex therefore recalled Middleton, whose men had performed admirably. A Royalist party pursued Middleton's men north through Deddington but were beaten off. Few casualties were suffered on either side yet the king's much-vaunted cavalry had undoubtedly come off second best. It is hard to explain Wilmot's defensive stance in such potentially favourable circumstances unless he was intimidated by the unexpected size of Essex's army or obeying the council of war's orders to the letter by taking no action that could conceivably involve him in battle.

Whatever the reasons, most of Essex's regiments had been able to spend 2 September marching unhindered towards their goal. They seem to have formed a single loose column, extending over five miles, with parties of cavalry scouting their flanks. The London brigade managed nine miles and quartered in the village of Hook Norton. Harvey's cavalry, who had spent part of the day acting as Middleton's reserve, joined them. Wilmot did not trouble the Parliamentarians at all that night, though the rearguard, including Essex's own cavalry regiment, had to beat off a sortie from Banbury Castle. Essex himself can have drawn only satisfaction from this first real day of his campaign. His cavalry had kept the Royalists at arm's length while the infantry and the artillery train had made good progress once across the Cherwell. And among the intelligence reports coming in to Sir Samuel Luke was one that the earl may well have digested and stored away for future reference: the Royalists 'quarter in several places far remote from the siege where they may easily be surprised'.

The next day, 3 September, was a Sunday and Essex began the morning with an open-air church service, after which the main force advanced steadily to Chipping Norton, from where the earl wrote a despatch to Parliament reporting his progress. Wilmot's cavalry continued to shadow them westwards and appeared nearby in the evening until Ramsey took two regiments and drove them off. Chipping Norton was only twenty miles or so short of the Cotswold escarpment but a potentially serious problem was now emerging, created by the differing rates of march of the army's various components. In the absence of significant opposition from Royalist cavalry, the earl had not yet concentrated his column. By Sunday night, those formations unencumbered by slow moving artillery and supply wagons were well ahead of the main force, some in dangerously exposed positions unsupported by friendly units.

Harvey's cavalry quartered in the hamlet of Cornwall, three miles beyond Chipping Norton. Further on, at the head of the column, was the London brigade, desperately seeking shelter as the weather turned unseasonably cold. The brigade had rendez-voused with Essex at Chipping Norton before marching onwards, and when night fell, the leading regiments had reached Oddington, six miles west of Chipping Norton and only two miles short of the next major town, Stow-on-the-Wold. Sergeant Foster gave the strong impression that it was first come first served as far as accommodation was concerned. The Blue Regiment

> marched in the van and took up the first quarter in the [village]; the other three regiments of the auxiliary forces were quartered in the adjacent villages; whereupon our Red Regiment of the Trained Band was constrained to march half a mile further to get quarter.

This was the part of the village known now as Upper Oddington.

Foster had a miserable night:

> we were no sooner in our quarters, and set down our arms, intending a little to refresh ourselves; but presently there was an alarm beat up, and we being the frontier regiment nearest the enemy, were presently all drawn up into a body, and stood upon our guard all that night.

They were only too aware of their exposed position, and especially that no friendly cavalry were nearby. No food had reached them during the day and now they had to stand to arms in an open field without bread, water or fires. The truth of their situation was even less favourable because the London brigade had inadvertently blundered into a major concentration of Royalist cavalry, some of whom were camped less than a mile away. Essex had lost control of his unwieldy column. If Rupert were to discover and exploit the isolation of the London brigade, the earl could lose almost half of his precious infantry when the sun next rose.

Rupert had left the camp at Gloucester earlier in the day. Wilmot must by then have confirmed that Essex was indeed advancing and the plan agreed at the Oxford council of war was therefore being put into effect. A Parliamentarian intelligence report suggests that the two bodies of Royalist cavalry rendezvoused that evening at Fifield and that most of them subsequently quartered only four miles to the south-west of Stow, at Bourton-on-the-Water. Wilmot had presumably ridden from Chipping Norton and the main force had probably come from the Oxford area. Rupert himself spent the night of 3–4 September in nearby Northleach. The prince faced a challenge that should have been ideally suited to his skills and temperament. He now had with him the bulk of the Oxford cavalry, about 5,000 strong, in whose training and organisation he had invested most of the previous year. From Wilmot, he should have gained a fairly accurate picture of the earl's army and its dispositions. On the other hand, this intelligence can only have given Rupert pause for thought. Contrary to previous estimates, the Parliamentarians numbered well over 10,000, and their cavalry was numerous and had been well handled. If Essex kept tight control of his army, the

Royalist cavalry would not be able to defeat or stop him; at best, they could impose delay. If, however, the Parliamentarians lost their cohesion, the relief march could fall apart. Much would depend on Rupert's orders and how he interpreted them.[5]

IV

Back at Gloucester, soldiers and civilians were in the midst of the Sunday morning church service when word came from the East Gate that the Royalists were building a new battery within fifty yards of the defences. Massey took this to mean that the mine beneath the gate was close to completion and the service was abandoned 'without any sermon' so that a second defence line could be thrown up behind the gate. Dorney described how

> we began the lining of the houses over the East Gate, and the making of a
> very strong breast work across the Eastgate Street, with a large trench before
> it, filled by some springs there, intending to raise it up to the eaves of the
> houses, and to plant some cannon there.

The Friar's Orchard artillery sconce was also finished. Both were major engineering tasks and will have required the enthusiastic involvement of large numbers of civilians to complete quickly, further evidence that morale was holding up. Later on 3 September a force of 'straggling horse and foot vapoured ... in the Walham, but darest not come within the reach of our musketeers'. Thomas Pury's battery lobbed a ball at the departing cavalry and claimed to have hit a white horse. Otherwise, the day was marked only by an exchange of propaganda, delivered across the lines by arrows. A Royalist 'well-wisher' threatened

> your God Waller hath forsaken you, and hath retired himself to the Tower
> of London, Essex is beaten like a dog, yield to the king's mercy in time,
> otherwise, if we enter perforce, no quarter for such obstinate traitorly rogues.

By return, 'Nicholas Cudgel You Well' replied that 'Rome's yoke we are resolved never to obey: but for our cabbages which ye have eaten, be sure ere long ye shall be soundly beaten'.

The expected attack did not materialise because the East Gate mine was still not ready; the issue of candles to the miners is evidence of the continuing work. Meanwhile Lord Percy was ordering another twenty barrels of powder plus a double load of match from Oxford, where the marching artillery train had been prepared with ten cannon, thirty cannon balls apiece, fifty barrels of powder, and a ton each of match and shot for the infantry. The convoy comprised nineteen carts and 137 horses escorted by a detachment of the King's Lifeguard of Foot but Essex's army was too close for comfort and its departure was therefore delayed.[6]

V

Next morning, 4 September, Sergeant Foster and his comrades of the Red Regiment at last received food and drink after a cold night shivering in the bleak Cotswold fields outside Oddington. But their breakfast was no sooner completed than a scout galloped up on a wounded horse 'shot in the neck all bloody' with the news that Royalist cavalry were at the edge of the village. Four accounts of the events that followed have survived, three from Parliamentarian eyewitnesses' reports and a detailed Royalist report in *Mercurius Aulicus*, which together paint a consistent picture of the first major encounter of the campaign between the two field armies.

The Red Regiment was commanded by its lieutenant colonel, William Tucker. Concluding that Upper Oddington was indefensible, he advanced the seven companies to an open field at the top of Oddington Hill, where they could be formed up in close order to defend against a cavalry attack. To their obvious disappointment, the Blue Regiment, quartered back down the hill at Lower Oddington, did not join them but drew up outside that part of the village. From their vantage point, the Red Regiment soldiers could see three large bodies of Royalist cavalry to their front and on either flank, the nearest less than a quarter of a mile away. A messenger was sent back to warn Essex, and the London pikemen and musketeers prepared to face an assault. Foster believed that the Royalist plan was to encircle and cut off the Trained Band regiments. He was undoubtedly correct. The London brigade was dispersed on both sides of the River Evenlode, with the Red and Blue Regiments on the west bank and the Auxiliaries on the east in the villages of Adlestrop and Daylesford. Essex and the main force were nowhere in sight; they faced a five mile march from Chipping Norton before they reached the Evenlode valley.

Rupert therefore had the opportunity to destroy the London brigade in detail before the earl could intervene. The Trained Band regiments were equal in numbers to the prince's cavalry but they were spread out and if one regiment could be broken, there was a good chance that the others would disintegrate. Advancing from Bourton-on-the-Water through Stow, Rupert deployed the greater part of his force on Martin's Hill facing the Red Regiment, with a detachment thrown forward as a forlorn hope; he sent another body riding south of the village to a spur of high ground overlooking the valley from where they threatened the Blue Regiment in Lower Oddington; and advanced a third under Sir John Urry, the Scottish turncoat, to the north of Oddington into the Evenlode valley. Yet to Sergeant Foster's surprise, the Royalist cavalry did not attack. The hedges in front of the Red Regiment had been lined with musketeers but there were still no more than 900 Parliamentarian infantrymen facing the bulk of Rupert's cavalry. After half an hour, the Londoners recovered their confidence and six or seven of those with horses rode forward to taunt the immobile Royalist cavalry while a pair of musketeers advanced to snipe at their forlorn hope.

Why did Rupert not take advantage of his clear local superiority? The answer seems to be the early appearance of Parliamentarian reinforcements on the far side of the Evenlode valley. Colonel Harvey's quarters around the village of Cornwall were only two miles east of the River Evenlode, and he arrived on Adlestrop Hill above the Evenlode at about the same time that Urry's men rode down into the valley. Harvey had with him his own cavalry regiment and two infantry regiments (probably the London units he had previously helped to escort up from Kent), plus artillery. This was not a large force but they were in a strong position. A demi-culverin was brought forward and three or four cannon balls were fired into the midst of the Royalist cavalry below.

Urry responded with characteristic aggression, leading his troopers forward towards Harvey's position. Fortuitously, however, a second batch of Parliamentarian reinforcements was now coming up. A brigade of three cavalry regiments under Commissary General Sir James Ramsey was leading the army's advance from Chipping Norton. Although Ramsey had received much of the blame for the poor performance of the

Parliamentarian cavalry at Edgehill, he was an experienced professional and now handled his brigade with canny skill. The west bank of the Evenlode valley was enclosed and therefore unsuitable for dashing cavalry charges. Ramsey advanced steadily down into the valley with his full brigade and some musketeers, pushing Urry's smaller force back towards Rupert's main body on the hills in front of Oddington. When Ramsey's progress was impeded by a hedgerow with only a narrow gap, he sent Captain Gilbert Carr, another Scots professional from Middleton's Regiment, forward with a small forlorn hope and lined the hedge behind him with musketeers. Urry turned on Carr's advance party but his men ran into a volley of fire from the Parliamentarian cavalrymen and musketeers. In a confused skirmish, *Mercurius Aulicus* claimed that the Queen's Regiment killed fifteen, wounded an officer, took a number of prisoners and lost only a single horse. Harvey's report admitted one fatality and half a dozen captured, and the Royalists may indeed have had the better of the hand to hand fighting but the bulk of the three Parliamentarian regiments were pushing their way through the hedge and Urry had no option but to disengage.

Once again, the main Royalist force made no move, either to support Urry or to attack the Red Regiment. Rupert may have been deterred by the enclosed ground or mindful of his orders not to give battle, but the chance of inflicting a quick and easy reverse on the London brigade rapidly disappeared. One or more of the Auxiliary regiments joined the Red Regiment in front of Upper Oddington, 'at whose coming we gave a great shout' according to the mightily relieved Foster, and in the distance Essex and the rest of his army finally appeared. The earl used artillery ('three or four drakes') to drive off the second Royalist advance party from the hills to the south of Oddington and reunited his forces on the slope in front of Rupert's now heavily outnumbered cavalry.

Though an opportunity had been lost, the prince could still inflict delay on the relief army and he did not withdraw his men. Essex would have to lever him out. To do so, the earl adopted the tactics set out in his letter from Great Brickhill, the methodical employment of the whole army to offset the superior mobility of the Royalist cavalry. Behind another forlorn hope, the Parliamentarians advanced slowly up the hill, with the London brigade in the lead supported by Essex's infantry regiment with the earl at their head and two regiments of cavalry. Having escaped a potential mauling thanks to the quick thinking and competence of his subordinates, the Captain General was taking personal control of the second stage of the action. When the Royalist cavalry stood their ground, Essex brought up some of his lighter cannon and opened fire. The tactic worked. Rupert was not prepared to allow his men to stand under artillery bombardment with no means of reply. The Royalists pulled back and reformed further along the narrow plateau leading from Martin's Hill towards Stow. Essex responded in the same way, using two heavier cannon to force Rupert to withdraw again. For a third time the Royalists regrouped, now on the slope in front of Stow itself, and once again the Parliamentarian army tramped forward, deployed its artillery and left Rupert's cavaliers with no choice but to retreat.

For the prince, this must have been an intensely frustrating morning. Parliament's relief army was much larger than intelligence reports had suggested and it was being handled with unusual skill. He therefore led his men westwards to find a more favourable site on which to renew the contest. By contrast, the sight of the feared Royalist cavalry withdrawing not once but three times will have given a tremendous boost to the fragile morale of Essex's army. This burgeoning confidence can be seen in the

Parliamentarian accounts of the afternoon's continuing advance: 'they all fled, and we pursued them and followed them three miles' according to Foster. Essex kept his army tightly concentrated as they moved cautiously forward. Towards evening, they came upon the Royalist cavalry, drawn up three miles from Stow 'beyond a pass on the side of a hill'. The site of this final confrontation was almost certainly the steep western slope of the Eye valley, north of Upper Slaughter.

Essex pushed a forlorn hope of 200 commanded musketeers, forty dragoons, two cavalry regiments and a pair of field guns across the stream, and with himself and Sir Philip Skippon at their head advanced steadily towards the Royalists. Rupert stood firm and there seems to have been something of a standoff, with the Parliamentarians firing ineffectively at the Royalist cavalry, until the rest of the army arrived. Now, in one of the most evocative passages of the entire war, the London brigade formed up and moved forward six deep and eight hundred abreast 'which goodly show did so much the more daunt the enemy, that (as it is reported) Prince Rupert swore, he thought all the roundheads in England were there'. The prince again had little option but to retreat.

Skirmishing continued as the Royalists were pushed westwards in the gathering twilight. At nightfall Rupert disengaged. He had been utterly defeated in his efforts to disrupt the Parliamentarian advance and had failed even to impose a significant delay. By midnight, when his exhausted men sank down to snatch a few hours sleep in the open country around the village of Naunton, Essex had gained an invaluable thirteen miles from Chipping Norton and was within a day's march of the relative safety of the Severn valley. The seven-mile advance from Oddington had been a model of tactical control, with the entire army driving the Royalist cavalry from one position to another, infantry, cavalry and artillery co-operating seamlessly to achieve an almost bloodless victory. For that is what Essex undoubtedly won on 4 September. It was not as dramatic as pitched battles such as Edgehill or Roundway Down, yet in the wider context the Parliamentarian advance through Stow was no less important and displayed a degree of military competence not usually associated with the Earl of Essex or his army.[7]

VI

For besieged and besiegers alike, events at Gloucester during 4 September carried contradictory messages. On the one hand, most of the Royalist cavalry had disappeared and preparations were clearly being made to withdraw other elements of the army. Parliamentarian spies reported that some of the artillery was being dispersed by river to Worcester and Berkeley Castle, and the garrison could see cartloads of incapacitated soldiers being carried from the Llanthony leaguer to boats waiting to take them downstream to Bristol. One spy counted 400 sick and wounded Royalists being evacuated in this way. Yet the traffic was not all in the same direction. On or about 4 September a major reinforcement arrived from Hopton's Bristol garrison. Five regiments of infantry and Prince Maurice's rebuilt cavalry regiment, some 2,000 foot and 500 horse, had been sent northwards in accordance with orders issued at the Oxford council of war on 27 August. To have assembled this force in such a short period is a great tribute to Hopton's organisational abilities. Meanwhile, unfounded rumours abounded that Maurice himself had been recalled from the south-west.

Below the moat, mining and countermining were reaching their climax. During the morning the garrison's countermine reached the outside of the East Gate, only to discover that the Royalist mine was being dug considerably deeper. Massey therefore 'set workmen upon the making of great borers with which we intended to bore through our mine into theirs, and so drown the enemy's mine'. But except for six rounds fired into the city after dark, which as usual caused no casualties and little damage, the artillery was silent on both sides. Inside the East Gate, the garrison had completed their earthwork defences across the street and lined adjacent buildings with soil, turning them into primitive blockhouses. These preparations would, however, avail little if a determined assault were launched. The garrison now had only three or four barrels of powder remaining, less than half a twelve-shot bandoleer per musketeer. If Essex did not come very soon, their resistance would have been a futile gesture and the revenge of the king's frustrated soldiers would be unconstrained and brutal. Yet spirits must have been raised that night when the scouts sent out previously lit the prearranged fires on Wainload Hill to confirm that the relief army was indeed on its way. Unknown to the garrison, in the Royalist camp orders were being given to remove the heavy guns from their batteries in front of the walls so that they could be ready to march at thirty minutes' notice.[8]

VII

At Naunton, Sergeant Foster and his comrades 'lay all in the open field, upon the ploughed land, without straw, having neither bread nor water, yet ... there was not one feeble sick person amongst us, but was able to march with us the day following'. Colonel Harvey's report was grumpier, stressing his 'cold lodging without any refreshment'. Six miles to the south-west, Rupert's cavalrymen were undoubtedly even less happy in the fields around Compton Abdale and Andoversford. But the prince had not given up. According to unusually precise Parliamentarian intelligence, his plan for the next day was to continue his attempts to delay Essex on the Cotswolds and then give battle at the foot of the hills five miles from Gloucester. This has a plausible ring. Descending the steep Cotswold scarp in the teeth of Royalist cavalry attacks would be a formidable challenge and, most importantly, Rupert should have been able to call on a substantial proportion of the king's infantry and artillery.

On the morning of 5 September, Essex gathered his cold and hungry soldiers for a final effort. They set off still in tight formation, although this time the London brigade was at the rear with the Red Regiment guarding the supply train. Contrary to the intelligence report, however, the Royalist cavalry was nowhere to be seen and the army marched unhindered until the evening. From his overnight dispositions around Compton Abdale and Andoversford, and the suggestion that he intended to meet Essex as the Parliamentarian army descended from the Cotswolds within five miles of Gloucester, it seems that the prince expected his enemy to march west-southwest from Naunton directly towards the city. If so, he will have spent at least part of the day in the wrong place. True to his strategy of getting down from the bare Cotswold hills into the enclosed Severn valley as quickly as possible, Essex directed his army almost due west towards the market town of Cheltenham. This was the shortest route to the Cotswold scarp, although it also meant a descent into the valley from Prestbury Hill, one of the highest and steepest parts of the scarp face. According to the anonymous *Journal of Prince Rupert's Marches*, the prince marched with the cavalry straight to Cheltenham. It may therefore be that by the time he learned of Essex's true route, it was too late to interpose his men between the Parliamentarians and the Cotswold scarp without the unacceptable risk of fighting an action with the precipitous slope at his back.

Earlier that day, while Rupert was marshalling his men on the hills, a key meeting had taken place in the king's quarters at Matson. The outcome was recorded in a letter from Charles to his nephew signed at ten o'clock:

> [Lord Forth] is of the opinion that we shall do little good upon this town, for they begin to countermine us, which will make it a work of time; wherefore he is of the opinion, to which I fully concur, that we should endeavour to fight with Essex as soon as may be, after we have gotten our forces together, which I hope will be tomorrow, those from Bristol being already come; the greatest care will be to meet with him before he can reach the hedges: now if this be your opinion, as it is ours, which I desire to know with all speed, I desire you to do all things in order to it, that no time is lost.

This extraordinary document demonstrates just how out of touch Forth and the king were with the events of the past few days, either because Rupert had failed to keep them up to date with Essex's progress or because they had ignored his views. Even more striking is the implication that Forth and the king had reversed Rupert's orders not to engage in combat. If Hyde's recollection was correct and that was indeed the constraint under which the prince had been operating (and this would certainly explain his uncharacteristically indecisive performance in the Cotswolds), to change gear so fundamentally at the last moment was a mark of strategic ineptitude on the part of King Charles and his senior general.

Rupert's reply has not survived but it can only have disparaged Forth's proposal. Now that the Parliamentarians had directed their march further to the north, it would be impossible for the Royalist infantry and artillery to cover the ten miles from Gloucester quickly enough to meet Essex before he descended into the enclosed countryside of the Severn valley. That cannot have been a welcome response. Nonetheless, during 5 September, Forth and the king must have accepted that they could not prevent Essex from raising the siege. Contrary to expectations, the two armies appeared evenly matched so that to remain fixed in front of Gloucester risked a battle at Essex's initiative and therefore on unfavourable terms. Hence the role of the cavalry was now to delay the Parliamentarians while the Royalists broke camp and reached what was for them the relative security of the open Cotswold hills.

The *Journal of Prince Rupert's Marches* records that the prince spent eight hours with the cavalry near Cheltenham. When it became clear that the Parliamentarians would not be able to interfere with the Royalist withdrawal, he returned to Gloucester. By the time he reached the Royalist camp, it must have presented a dismal sight. In early August, failure to take the city had been unthinkable. Now it was harsh reality. First the artillery and baggage trains trundled out of the Llanthony leaguer, then bodies of infantry and cavalry began to follow them. According to a Parliamentarian spy who was there, Rupert covered the withdrawal with three troops of cavalry. Inside the city it was another public fast day and all those who could be spared were at church. Dorney recorded that the news that the Royalists were pulling out arrived 'in the space between the sermons'. Watching from the walls, the garrison and citizens could not believe that this was not a trick 'till we perceived their rearguard to fire their huts and their men to be drawn out of their trenches'. As the Royalists disappeared, Massey sent parties out to torch the mines and artillery batteries, and Chillingworth's siege engines were discovered and taken into the city.[9]

The initial Royalist rendezvous was the king's quarters at Matson House, two miles south-east of Gloucester. Neither Charles nor Rupert was with them, having ridden to Painswick. Most of their soldiers will have had to spend the night in the open. The effect on their already fragile morale when the fine weather that had characterised the siege gave way to a torrential downpour can only be imagined. Corbett described it as a 'tempestuous rainy night'. Royalist John Gwyn agreed, recalling that 'when we drew off, it proved to be a most miserable tempestuous, rainy weather'. Gwyn's view was that the floods would have forced the Oxford Army to leave in any case: 'had not Essex come that very day he did ... the land-flood, which, by a great glut of rain fell that night, had made our labour in vain'. For the sick and injured, the storm must have been a particular ordeal. A Parliamentarian spy reported that 'many of the king's officers are now sick and many of them lately dead'. Some were too ill to move. Hopton wrote sadly of one of his officers who 'falling sick was taken prisoner at the rising from before Gloucester'.[10]

Although he did not yet know it, Essex had achieved the first part of his mission. His concerns that night were, however, also focused on the appalling weather. Notwithstanding the absence of opposition, it took his army the best part of 5 September to travel eight miles from Naunton to the Cotswold scarp at Prestbury Hill. It was not an easy march. Foster explained that the soldiers had received little food for six days and even water was in desperately short supply: the men 'would run half a mile or a mile before, where they heard water was, such straits and hardship our citizens formerly knew not'.

At around six o'clock in the evening, the vanguard of the Parliamentarian army stood on Prestbury Hill from where they could see Gloucester, smoke and flames rising near to the city, and Royalist cavalry drawn up in several bodies at the foot of the slope in front of them. Not surprisingly, Colonel Harvey's report conceded that 'the sight at first a little troubled some'. Essex resumed his tried and tested tactics, bringing forward heavy field artillery to the edge of the hill. A single shot from a demi-culverin prompted the nearest Royalist group to wheel and ride off. Four shots from the culverins, fired primarily to give advance warning to Massey and the garrison that relief was truly at hand, drove off the rest. Rupert was later criticised for allowing the Parliamentarians to descend Prestbury Hill 'without any disturbance' and there was conceivably an opportunity to disrupt their advance at a vulnerable time but having decided to raise the siege there was now more to be gained from drawing Essex into the Severn valley.

The earl decided to descend the hill in the dusk rather than camp for the night at the top of the scarp. His determination to reach the enclosed valley floor as soon as possible coincided with the natural desire of his soldiers to seek shelter from a storm that was now raging around them. However, Prestbury Hill is around 1,000 feet high with a slope of almost one in five, the light was fading, the weather marked by 'the violence of cold and rain', and the soldiers were tired and hungry. Discipline evaporated and the descent became a chaotic race for shelter in the villages below. Essex led the way with a forlorn hope to cover the rest of the army and sprained his leg 'by going down some steep place'. Behind him, troops, horses and wagons slithered through the mud. Gun carriages and supply wagons 'were overthrown and broken, it being a very craggy steep and dangerous hill, so that the rest of the wagons darest not adventure to go down'. Unable to leave the train unprotected, the London brigade had to spend the night at the top of the hill. Foster's unhappiness is palpable: 'it being a most terrible tempestuous night of wind and rain, as ever men lay out in, we having neither hedge nor tree for shelter, nor any sustenance of food, or fire'. At about midnight, the Trained Band regiments stood to in case of attack. Many of the Londoners were terrified, 'fearing his fellow soldier to be his enemy', and one man was shot in error. In the valley, a clutch of officers including Colonels Harvey and Springate rode ahead of their regiments, racing for dry quarters in Southam, but in the village

> Major Bourn and Captain Buller with their troops (mistaking us for cavaliers) dismounted at our quarter, and by a pistol shot (before we could make them understand who we were) wounded sorely, we fear mortally, Cornet Flesher, and we strongly presumed had pistolled more of us had not my colonel seasonably returning, made known himself, and so rescued us.

Soon every building was crammed with wet and exhausted soldiers.

Only in Gloucester could the lifting of the siege be celebrated in any comfort but no-one quite believed that their ordeal was over. No message had yet been received from Essex's army and nobody had heard Essex's cannon. Although prayers were offered for Gloucester's deliverance, Corbett admitted that

> we did not venture upon the rear of the enemy ... but kept as strong and watchful guards as at any time before; presuming that relief at hand had raised the enemy, yet suspecting that in point of honour they would attempt something worthy of a royal army.

For all its military and political significance, the end of the siege was an anti-climax for those directly involved on both sides.[11]

Chapter Nine
'The fools were cozened'

I

By the morning of 6 September, the rain had stopped but a strong autumn gale continued to blow. Neither army was in a state to seek battle. Hyde recalled that the Royalist army had left Gloucester 'in more disorder and distraction than might have been expected'. John Gwyn remembered that 'the unceasing winds ... soon dried up our through-wet clothes we lay pickled in all night (as a convenient washing of us at our coming from the trenches)'. The Royalists had appointed Birdlip Hill, on the Cotswold scarp some six miles south-east of Gloucester, as their rendezvous. Infantry regiments began to move from Matson at around six o'clock and the aim seems to have been to assemble the army by midday. A consignment of powder and match arrived belatedly from Bristol while some of the heavier baggage was sent in the opposite direction.

Essex's exhausted army lay only six miles to the north. Sergeant Foster described how the Trained Band regiments at last descended Prestbury Hill 'being wet to the very skin, but could get little or no refreshing every house being so full of soldiers'. The earl himself advanced gingerly to Cheltenham and the army remained spread through the surrounding villages. Although his intelligence reports suggested that the Royalists were withdrawing towards Bristol, it soon became clear that the king was not retreating. According to Foster, within three hours of their arrival in Prestbury, 'we had an alarm that the cavaliers were near the town with a great body of horse'. Hastily drawn up in formation 'our soldiers began to complain pitifully, being even worn out and quite spent for want of refreshing'. In the event, the Royalist cavalry raided the nearby quarters of Colonel Dalbeir's cavalry regiment instead, and the Blue and Red Regiments marched to the village of Norton between Gloucester and Tewkesbury where Foster conceded 'our soldiers had some reasonable accommodation and refreshment'.

Essex's decision not to march directly to Gloucester reflected the city's inability to feed and house the army. Dispersing the brigades eased supply problems but left them more vulnerable to further Royalist raids. On the following day, 7 September, Lord Wilmot led a successful attack on the quarters of Behre and Goodwin's cavalry regiments at Winchcombe. The Parliamentarians were driven from the village, Major Boza covering the retreat and losing two officers and his standard in the process. *Mercurius Aulicus* broke its silence on events in the Severn valley to claim that three troops of the Queen's Regiment charged seven Parliamentarian troops, killed eighty and took up to forty prisoners, all at no cost; less fancifully, one of Luke's spies reported six dead and nineteen captured. More worrying for Essex, the Blue and Red Regiments refused an order to support their Auxiliary comrades quartered only two miles from Winchcombe, 'it being a very dark night, and our men worn out and spent with their former marching'. Next morning they changed their minds and marched but the implications for morale and discipline were not auspicious.

Wilmot's raid was more than routine harassment. The Oxford Army was moving north-east to take up a blocking position astride the earl's route back to London, and Lord Chandos' home at Sudeley Castle outside Winchcombe had been chosen as the new Royalist base. Wilmot had hounded the two Parliamentarian cavalry regiments from the adjacent village to secure the surrounding area. The march along the western fringes of the Cotswolds was not an easy one. Parliamentarian intelligence reported that 'diverse of their carriages have lately broken and some of them lie upon the ways'. The Royalists' priority now was to prepare for a mobile campaign; the artillery and supply train ordered from Oxford on 2 September was at last on its way, five six pounders, a five pounder saker and four three pounders with thirty iron shot and ten case shot per gun, plus fifty barrels of powder. Hopton sent a further twenty-two barrels via Cirencester to avoid Parliamentarian cavalry patrols. For the time being, ammunition was no longer a major problem.[1]

II

In London, hard news of the earl's relief march had dried up after Essex's despatch from Chipping Norton. On 6 September, rumours spread that Gloucester had fallen. A Venetian despatch written at around that time reported that the siege 'occupies the attention of all' and that Royalist morale was crumbling, noted that the king was gathering reinforcements and speculated that he would avoid a battle with Essex's inexperienced army, which was believed to have reached Stow. The Venetians were already out of date. On the evening of 7 September, two messengers sent from Gloucester the day before brought the first reports of the city's delivery. But the fog of war was still so dense that there was scepticism about their veracity. Surprisingly, Essex and Massey did not write official letters to Parliament until 10 and 11 September respectively, and it was only when these letters arrived on 14 September that Parliament was prepared to declare victory. The London media was less circumspect. Newspapers announced the first messages from Gloucester on 8 September and 'confirmed' that the relief march had been successful as early as 12 September, probably to balance the loss of Exeter, which had surrendered to Prince Maurice on 4 September.

From Oxford, the Royalists tried to put a positive gloss on events. On 12 September, Sir Edward Nicholas wrote to the Venetians explaining that the king 'has driven the rebel Earl of Essex into Gloucester ... [and] has no doubt he will soon destroy the rebel army'. The Venetians were convinced and their next despatch characterised the king's withdrawal as a pre-planned strategy that had left Essex besieged by powerful forces and opened the prospect of a risk-free Royalist victory. That was also the line being peddled in the Royalist camp. A Parliamentarian spy heard talk of reinforcements coming from Exeter, Bristol, Oxford and the north so that Essex would be encompassed: 'they say that no man shall go back alive'. *Mercurius Aulicus* adopted a variation on the same theme, arguing that the king had raised the siege 'on purpose to meet with the Rebels' Army and fight with them' but Essex was 'skulking away (more like a thief than an open Rebel) through woods and enclosed grounds, resolving (if possible) to steal privately away'.[2]

What was the true strategic position? The starting point was that Gloucester had been saved. Massey and Pury had maintained the city's resolve and resistance for just long enough. Town clerk John Dorney attributed Gloucester's delivery to the resolution of the garrison and citizens, the leadership of Massey and his officers, the contribution of all sections of the population, the ineffectiveness of the Royalist artillery, Essex's timely arrival, the hoarding of supplies before the siege, Royalist over-confidence and, of course, divine intervention. Essex gave the credit to Massey, who had 'managed his business with so much judgement and courage', and appears to have promoted him to colonel. From the Royalist side, Hyde later applauded Massey's 'pertinacious defence' and the garrison's discipline, courage and resolution.

But contemporaries recognised that the outcome of the siege had been a close run thing. Massey had been reduced to two or three barrels of powder and if an assault had been launched, the garrison could not have mounted more than token resistance. Essex congratulated Massey for concealing this shortage 'that the enemy, not knowing of such want, had but small hopes of attaining their desires'. Despite this constraint, active defence had been a critical factor throughout. With one or two notable exceptions, Massey had balanced the risks and benefits of offensive actions judiciously, bolstering morale inside the city so there was no recurrence of the collapse in spirits among the officers and city elite that characterised the pre-siege period. Less obviously, the king's letter to Rupert explaining Forth's reasons for raising the siege referred specifically to the garrison's countermining activities.[3]

Parliamentarian accounts identified three other factors. All commented on the inability of the Royalist artillery to cause either damage or casualties. The cannon had made no major breach in the walls and had started no significant fires inside the city. Colonel Harvey reported that 300–400 large calibre cannon balls, more than twenty mortar bombs and 'many' red-hot iron bars together killed only four people, maimed none and lightly injured only 'some few'. The second factor was the disparity in casualties between attackers and defenders. While claims for Royalist fatalities ranged from 1,000 to over 1,500, Harvey put total deaths inside the city at no more than forty, Sergeant Foster was told thirty, and Dorney and Corbett admitted fifty (including prisoners). No-one seriously disputed these figures, which means that the Royalists failed to inflict sufficient losses on Massey's two regiments to affect their effectiveness or morale. Finally, Corbett especially commented on the Royalists' aversion to risking casualties. Time after time, Massey expected assaults that did not happen and had concluded that the king's priority was to prevent losses to his infantry, cautious tactics which had backfired, undermining still further their fragile morale. The conduct of the siege would therefore have an enduring impact on the remainder of the campaign.[4]

Gloucester's place in Parliamentarian iconography was assured, and its soldiers and citizens could take a well-deserved back seat. For Massey, this was an opportunity to rebuild his ammunition supplies. Essex handed over forty barrels of powder, plus match and shot to replenish the dwindling magazine, and left behind three culverins to reinforce Massey's defences, probably because their weight risked slowing down the return march. The city itself reverted to the role it had played under Waller, as a logistic base for local operations. Feeding the Parliamentarian army was an immense burden on top of the city's already swollen population of soldiers and civilians, made

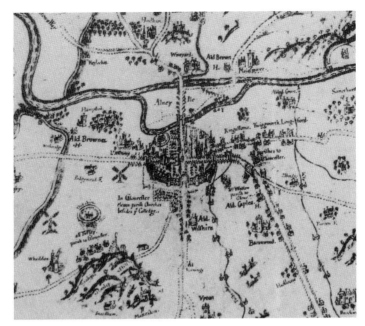

Map of Gloucester, 1624. This near contemporary drawing shows the River
Severn and Alney Island, the city's walls, the castle, the extent of the suburbs,
Inshire villages and the road layout. *(Gloucestershire Archives)*

Cannon in a battery by Stefano della Bella, c1641. Della Bella was an Italian
printmaker who was employed by Cardinal Richelieu in the mid-1640s to record
French military operations. This engraving suggests how the Royalist batteries at
Gloucester would have appeared.
*(Peter Harrington/Anne S K Brown Military Collection, Brown University Library, Rhode
Island, US)*

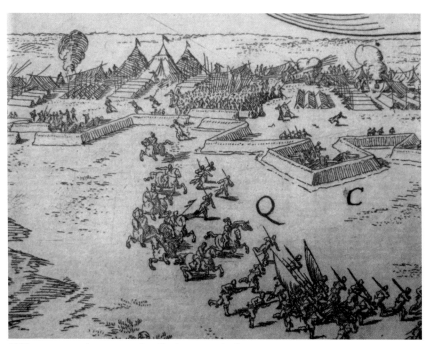

Mid-seventeenth century fortified camp, similar to those built by the Oxford Army at Culham and Gloucester. Detail from 1643 Flemish engraving.

(Author's collection)

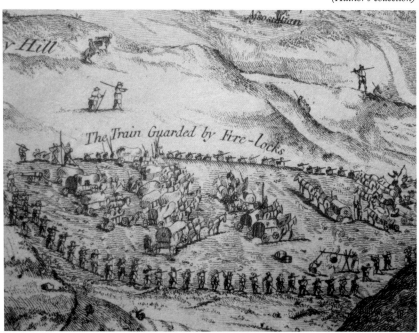

A Civil War baggage train, from Streeter's contemporary engraving of the battle of Naseby.

(Author's collection)

An army on the move; two details from an engraving by Stefano della Bella, mid 1640s. This probably shows the French army but apart from some minor aspects of dress suggests how both Royalists and Parliamentarians would have appeared during the campaign.

(Peter Harrington/ Anne S K Brown Military Collection, Brown University Library, Rhode island, US)

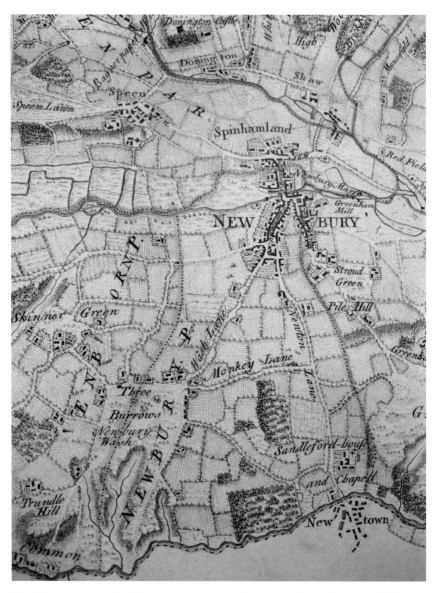

The Newbury battlefield in the mid-eighteenth century, from Rocque's 1761 'Topographical Survey of the County of Berkshire'. *(Berkshire Record Office)*

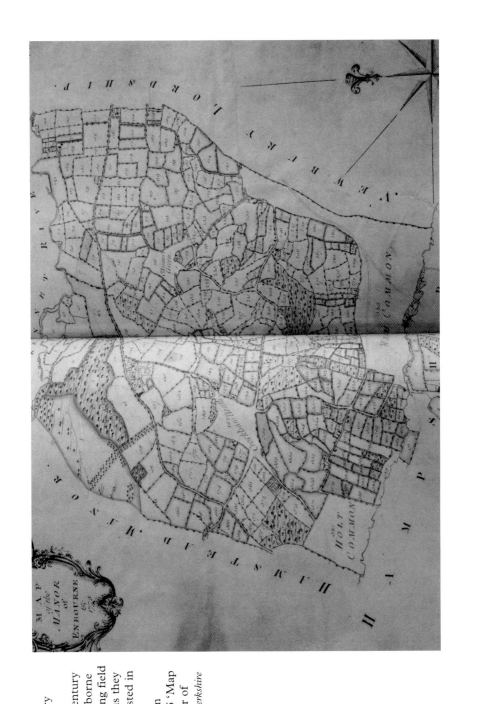

The Newbury battlefield - eighteenth century survey of Enborne parish showing field boundaries as they probably existed in the previous century; from Baker's 1775 'Map of the Manor of Enborne' (*Berkshire Record Office*).

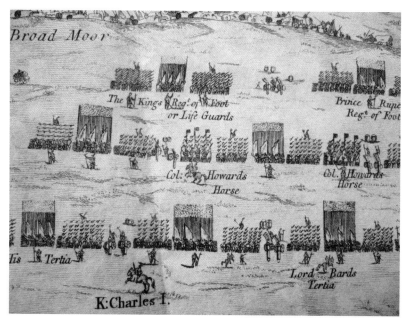

Royalist infantry drawn up in battle formation, from Streeter's contemporary engraving of the battle of Naseby.

(Author's collection)

Newbury Common showing the gulley and stream; detail from Rocque's 1761 'Topographical Survey of the County of Berkshire' *(Berkshire Record Office)*.

Combat in the mid-1640s. Details from a 1643 Flemish engraving suggesting aspects of the fighting on Newbury Common: cavalry in three ranks using firepower as Essex's regiments did early in the day; an infantry regiment under pressure with musketeers beginning to fade away to the rear similarly to the Royalist brigades during the afternoon; and cavalry against infantry combat of the kind experienced by the Trained Bands. Here too only aspects of dress are likely to have differed from contemporary English armies.
(Author's collection)

Greenham Common in
the mid-eighteenth
century, from Rocque's
1761 'Topographical
Survey of the County of
Berkshire'.
(Berkshire Record Office)

more difficult by the continuing depredations of the Royalist cavalry. There is, however, evidence that the Royalists' behaviour had alienated much of rural Gloucestershire so that there was greater enthusiasm in the wake of the siege for helping the king's enemies. During the relief march, one of Luke's spies had reported that 'the country is very much oppressed by [the Royalists], and are exceeding glad to hear of the Parliament's forces advancing that way'. Within three days of the end of the siege, the Royalist governor of Berkeley Castle complained to Rupert that the local people were so hostile that he could not re-supply his garrison. By contrast, it was reported in London that a great market was held in Gloucester on 6 and 7 September, presumably to buy in food for the garrison and Essex's hungry men. Hyde marvelled at the appearance of provisions from areas that the Royalists 'conceived to be entirely spent' and accused the army's commissaries for conniving with the local population to keep supplies hidden. In parallel, Essex's cavalry began collecting the harvest from known Royalist estates and areas occupied by the king's army. Corbett recalled that as a result, Gloucester's 'granary was quickly filled'.

In fact, however, Corbett was being characteristically parochial. After almost four weeks of occupation by the swollen Oxford Army, Severn valley agriculture had been badly disrupted. Gloucester's own requirements could be satisfied locally and Essex's men fed for a matter of days but the army's longer-term needs outstripped the area's available resources. Feeding his army during its enforced stay and gathering provisions for the journey home became one of the earl's main preoccupations, and his worries were increased by his lack of money with which to pay for supplies.

Logistics aside, Essex's army was still in reasonable shape. From the muster on Hounslow Heath, it had taken only two weeks to complete the first stage of their mission, and that without fighting a major battle so that combat losses had been light. Though the army will inevitably have suffered from stragglers, desertion and sickness, around 14,500 men were quartered in the villages to the east and north of Gloucester. Foster's account suggests that morale had been boosted by the successes of the campaign so far but that the Trained Band regiments at least were beginning to suffer from homesickness. Some set off for London under their own steam and the Royalists picked up at least one group of fourteen deserters. Corbett described the raising of the siege as 'an imperfect deliverance' because the Londoners 'supposing the work already done, and the date of their commission expired, earnestly contended home-wards'. It may well have been reasons of morale that prompted Essex to make a belated ceremonial entry into Gloucester on 8 September. A parade, the gratitude of the citizens, and free run of the city's ale houses for two nights would be some reward for the army's exertions and compensation for the inevitable absence of pay. No doubt Sergeant Foster spoke for all when he recalled that 'we found very loving respect and entertainment in this city, they being very joyful at our coming'.[5]

Essex too had his mind set on London. Getting his army home in one piece was vital to Parliament's military and political survival. The earl's options were neither plentiful nor attractive. For the moment he was safe within the Severn valley but staying put for any length of time was dangerous because he could expect no reinforcements, his strength would therefore erode relative to the king's army, food would run out and the Londoners would demand to go home. With secure bases at Oxford, Bristol and Worcester, the king would ultimately be able to starve the isolated Parliamentarian army into surrender. Sooner or later, Essex would therefore have to risk a return march. To retrace his route back across the open country of the north Cotswolds would expose the army to the same dangers it had faced on the outward march but magnified because the Royalists were no longer diverted by the siege and intelligence reports were attributing to the king a considerable overall numerical superiority.[6] Two alternative routes presented themselves. The first was the southeasterly direction, through Cirencester to the River Kennet at Marlborough or Hungerford. If the Royalists were not in pursuit, he could march quickly along the valley through Newbury (known to support Parliament) to the safety of Reading's powerful fortifications. As a 1688 map shows that the main road then ran south of the river, the Kennet would provide extra security if the king was nearby.[7] The main disadvantage of this option was the time it would take to cross the south Cotswolds and the equally open Wiltshire downland to the south-east.

A second alternative was to strike north into the midlands, either to seek battle in advantageous circumstances or to outmanoeuvre the Royalists in a rerun of the Edgehill campaign of the previous autumn. This approach would exploit Parliamentarian garrisons at Warwick and Coventry, and pose a threat to the key Royalist base at Worcester. The best route lay up the valley of the River Avon from Tewkesbury through Pershore and Evesham to Warwick. If Essex could cross to the west bank and keep the Royalists on the east bank, it should be possible to avoid a battle in unfavourable circumstances, but he would have to seize the bridges at Pershore and Evesham before Rupert could move his cavalry to screen them. In either case, the earl enjoyed a paradoxical advantage from the tightness of the pocket in which he found himself. Short interior lines of communication meant that he should be able to move his army rapidly from one side of the pocket to the other and, with the kind of imagination for which he was not renowned, create opportunities for feints and deception in the race for home.

How far Essex's strategy for this race was premeditated and how far it was extemporised as he went along is difficult to say. Although his predicament was hardly unexpected and a prudent general would have thought through the choices before he left Kingston, there is some evidence that at key points he also acted upon impulse. It is even less clear whether and how far Essex involved his senior officers in strategic planning. The council of war seems to have been meeting during this period[8] but Essex's autocratic tendencies and the absence of other high ranking officers with a past or future track record of strategic vision suggest that responsibility for planning lay primarily, perhaps even exclusively, with him.

IV

In the popular myth of the siege of Gloucester, King Charles is found sitting on a stone by the road as his army toils up the Cotswold scarp: 'One of the young princes, weary of their present life, asked him when they should go home – "I have no home to go to", replied the disconsolate king'. Yet any objective analysis of his military prospects would have presented a far brighter picture. Parliament's bold strategy had proved the king's generals right and his queen wrong. The investment of Gloucester had acted as bait for two of Parliament's most valuable military assets, Essex's field army and a sizeable proportion of the hitherto untouchable strategic reserve formed by the London Trained Bands. This was the army the king would have faced in front of London, entrenched and well supplied, with the capital's defences at its back. Instead, the earl had delivered it into the midst of the largest concentration of forces the Royalists had managed to assemble since Edgehill, in a tiny pocket surrounded by hostile fortresses and patrolled by Prince Rupert's cavalry. Although the Royalists had no enthusiasm for a battle on the earl's terms among the enclosed country of the Severn valley, they could look forward with confidence to combat in favourable circumstances when the Parliamentarians eventually emerged.[9]

At the beginning of August, the king had possessed an army but no coherent strategy. A month later, he had been presented with a strategy and the challenge of ensuring that his army was still capable of meeting it. The most authoritative source for the Royalists' strength at this stage of the campaign is the letter of 12 September from Sir Edward Nicholas to the Venetians. Nicholas' aim was to reassure the Venetians that the king was confident of victory and he therefore had no reason to underplay the size of the Royalist army; but the Venetians were well-informed observers who would discount unconvincing exaggeration, so his figures of 'over 6,000 horse and 9,000 foot' are likely to be at least a broad approximation of the truth. They ring true for the cavalry, who had been reinforced by Vavasour, Capel and Hopton, and suffered no more than nominal losses during the ineffectual harassment of Essex's advance. The equation for the infantry is more complicated but an analysis of the attrition and additions discussed above tends again to support Sir Edward's figures.

King Charles had gathered over 12,000 foot around Gloucester and although Parliamentarian claims overstated casualties during the siege, there can be no doubt that they suffered significant losses. *Mercurius Aulicus* conceded that 120 Royalists had been killed throughout the operation. That total is consistent with the detailed figures contained in the anonymous Royalist account of the first stage of the siege, which seems not to have been written for propaganda purposes (eg sixteen men killed during the two trench raids on 16 and 18 August). Much more significant was the total of incapacitated soldiers. A Royalist list forwarded to London by Colonel Harvey gave 900 sick and wounded; one of Luke's spies reported 400 casualties being evacuated to Bristol; a further 300 sick men were carried from Sudeley to Cirencester on 9 September. A conservative estimate of 1,200 soldiers dead, wounded or unwell is probably close to the truth. Because Rupert's cavalry were less involved in the skirmishing and quartered away from the main camp, the vast majority would have come from the infantry. Moreover, Parliamentarian intelligence reports suggest that desertion had been a continuing drain on the army's marching strength. Given the state of the Oxford infantry's morale, the frustrations attendant on a prolonged and unsuccessful operation, and the opportunities a siege presented for soldiers to absent themselves, it would be surprising if the army had not lost another 800 men (about thirty per day) by the time Essex's relief force appeared. A reduction of 2,000 men by 8 September is therefore a reasonable estimate for the effects of the siege on the king's strength. Since the Worcester garrison would be unavailable for field operations and some of Lord Herbert's Welsh levies were still without weapons, Nicholas' figure of 9,000 marching infantrymen is again as close as one can get today.[10]

With an army of 9,000 foot and 6,000 horse, the Royalists had a thousand fewer infantrymen than Essex but outnumbered him by three-to-two in cavalry, while the arrival of the latest artillery train from Oxford gave them broad equivalence in field guns. Further reinforcements were on their way. Lord Capel was preparing to send the 700 men of the Prince of Wales' Foot plus 1,000 cavalry and dragoons, and Vavasour's remaining men at Brampton Bryan had been ordered to raise their investment of Lady Harley's castle.[11] Parliamentarian spies returned from the Royalist camp with evidence of renewed self-confidence. On 8 September news of Prince Maurice's capture of

Exeter was circulated 'for which there hath been great joy' (especially among the Welsh soldiers 'who understood not English' and thought that the Earl of Essex had been taken!).

In fact, however, raising the siege had been a severe blow to the already shaky spirits of the Oxford Army. Lord Sunderland summed up the prevailing mood in a letter to his wife:

> I am afraid our setting down before Gloucester has hindered us from making an end to the war this year which nothing could keep us from doing if we had a month's more time which we lost there.

Hyde later noted 'the indisposition that possessed the whole army upon the relief of the town' and 'the licence which many officers and soldiers took' by disappearing from the army, permanently or temporarily, during this period. Parliamentarian intelligence agreed: they 'deal so roughly with their own men that yesterday they hanged a carter and a Welshman for running away'. To combat desertion, Royalist authorities in Worcestershire were instructed to detain and return 'straggling soldiers' and those suspected of committing 'disorders ... to the prejudice of the county'.

The cavalry vented their frustrations on the local population. In part this was officially sanctioned activity to gather food and money for the Royalist army and to deprive the enemy of the same resources. On 9 September a spy reported that

> they make such slaughter of sheep that tis thought they kill 3,000 each night, which [are] rather spoiled than eaten. They took 160 weathers the last night from one of their own side and got up all the horses they can come at.

Other incidents again smack more of freelance extortion. Two days later, a detachment of cavalry responded to 'an affront from a carrier of Tetbury' by threatening to pillage his home town and had to be bought off at a cost of £300. Near Tewkesbury, three troops of cavalry were reported to be seizing horses and then selling them back to their owners. One of Luke's spies was himself detained and taken to Sudeley, where he was able to convince his captors of his innocence and was released, but not before his horse and money were stolen. Nor were the infantry blameless. In Worcestershire, a Royalist sympathiser wrote that looting by the Prince of Wales' Regiment cost the county more than the legitimate bill for feeding the field army.

Private venture criminality aside, the indications are that logistic supply was undertaken relatively efficiently during this phase of the campaign. On 11 September, royal warrants were sent out from Sudeley to each surrounding thirty acre 'yardland' to provide bread and cheese, and this seems to have been repeated on a daily basis. The move northwards meant that greater use could also be made of solidly royalist Worcestershire for food, quarters and money. Sir John Colepeper and John Ashburnham were despatched to Worcester to demand loans of £7,000 from the County Commissioners to meet one week's pay for the Royalist infantry. The Commissioners pleaded poverty and offered £2,000, thereby beginning a process of haggling that was still unresolved when the army left the county. Less ambitiously, on 12 September the commissioners were ordered to produce fifty pounds each of bread and cheese plus transport to haul it to the army. Meanwhile, a convoy system was regularly bringing in food and other supplies from further afield. Forty cartloads of beer, bread and cheese arrived from Cirencester on 10 September and another twenty loads of cheese two days later.

Powder stocks were also replenished. Between 27 August and 10 September, the magazine (now at Sudeley) received 110 barrels from Oxford and Bristol. Lord Percy was able to send supplies to Berkeley Castle and Hereford and still retain 100 barrels, five times the amount used during the fighting at Edgehill. To prepare for the mobile battle to come, the three mortars were to be returned to Oxford. Despite reports of wrecked wagons littering the roads around Sudeley, there is no hint from Royalist sources that they were short of transport for such a campaign. Parliamentarian intelligence later described a train of 500 wagons trundling along in the army's wake.[12]

Meanwhile, Royalist leadership was in flux. Forth had manifestly failed at Gloucester, Wilmot and Rupert had hardly been more successful on the Cotswolds, and the evidence for the next phase of operations suggests that the king now took a more prominent role at Forth's expense. That was not a recipe for sound strategic or tactical decision-making in a fast moving environment. Below the top level of command, other important changes took place during this period. Notwithstanding the scorn heaped by *Mercurius Aulicus* on repeated claims that Sir Jacob Astley had been killed, the veteran Major General of Foot had been wounded early in the siege and played little part in the subsequent campaign, so his injury may have been more incapacitating than Royalist propaganda would admit. Of the infantry brigade commanders, Sir Ralph Dutton and Colonel Henry Wentworth disappeared from view, probably because of illness (Wentworth died the following year), and Forth does not seem to have commanded a brigade after the siege ended. The records suggest that the thirty or so infantry regiments were redistributed among five brigades under two professional soldiers imported temporarily into the Oxford Army, Vavasour and Sir Nicholas Byron (Sir John's uncle, who was serving as Lord Capel's Colonel-General in Cheshire and probably came south with one of the batches of reinforcements), and three Oxford Army colonels, John Belasyse (who had recovered from his injury at Bristol), Sir Gilbert Gerard and Conyers Darcy. In addition, a new detachment of 1,200 commanded musketeers was formed under Lieutenant Colonel George Lisle, an experienced dragoon officer. This was a response to the paucity of dragoons and the failure at Stow, where cavalry alone proved unable to halt Essex's advance. Although it is impossible to say for certain from where the musketeers were drawn, it is likely that they were the second batch of reinforcements from Bristol, who are not otherwise referred to in subsequent operations but were claimed by Hopton to have fought well at Newbury.[13]

Of the cavalry commanders, Sir Arthur Aston was a beneficiary of Oxford's disease-ridden summer. The Governor, Sir William Pennyman, had died of illness in late August and Aston replaced him, apparently because the queen asked to have a Catholic near at hand. Though there is no firm evidence for the appointment of a successor as Major General of Horse at this stage, it is probable that Robert Dormer, Earl of Carnarvon, took Aston's place. Even Royalist hagiographies admitted that he was 'extremely wild in his youth', finishing one supper at sea with the promise that 'by God's blood he would have three whores'. A political opponent of the king who switched sides when war came, he raised a cavalry regiment and impressed both for his military skills and his clemency; at Cirencester, while Sir John Byron hacked down the escaping garrison, Carnarvon did his best to take them prisoner. Sent into Dorset after the capture of Bristol, Carnarvon took Dorchester and Weymouth by negotiation but fell out with Maurice when Royalist infantry broke the terms of his agreements and plundered the towns. Most contemporary accounts of Newbury suggest he had a command role, implicitly in charge of one of the five Oxford Army cavalry brigades, and he had the experience to take over as Major General, although that would have added to the dysfunctionality of the command chain since Rupert is unlikely to have welcomed a senior officer who was at loggerheads with his brother.[14] Nonetheless, despite continued questions over its morale and cohesion, the Royalist army was in a reasonable condition to fight an early battle, and the king and his generals seem to have been keen to force the issue quickly.

V

Essex set out his immediate priorities in a letter to Parliament belatedly reporting on the success of the first stage of his mission. For all his prickly pride, the earl was not prone to boasting and his account of the relief of Gloucester was short and understated:

> I shall not trouble you with the details of our march; you shall, God willing, hear that more at large hereafter ... [u]pon Tuesday in the evening, the king's forces, seeing us approach, raised their siege before Gloucester, whither it pleased God we came very seasonably.

He then outlined Massey's urgent requirements: £8–10,000 to pay the garrison, one thousand reinforcements and, as a sting in the tail for his political adversary, the speedy despatch of Sir William Waller back to the provinces where, in Essex's view, he clearly belonged. Turning to his own position, the earl was his usual pessimistic self: the army was

> in such extreme necessity for want of pay, (being now in an enemy's country, and at this time within four or five miles of the king's army, where no provisions can be had but for ready money,) and so little hopes I have of a supply from you, that unless we can presently fight, I must be immediately necessitated to draw into some other place, which be nearer supplies, and have more free intercourse with London.

This was not a true picture of his situation. Essex had to give his soldiers and public opinion in London the impression that he was seeking out the enemy, but the facts suggest that he was doing all he could to evade the Royalists during this period. By the time the letter was signed on 10 September the earl had moved his army north to new quarters at Tewkesbury, at the confluence of the rivers Severn and Avon.

The redeployment took place without incident during 10 September. Essex's motives were clear. His first duty to his soldiers was to ensure that they were fed. Gloucester's inshire could not satisfy those needs, and Tewkesbury was an attractive base because it was protected on two sides by wide rivers (the Avon was bridged but the Severn was not) and was adjacent to areas actively sympathetic to the king that he could plunder without scruples. Essex's first step was to milk Tewkesbury itself. The town suffered the perennial problem of a frontier community, changing sides regularly as the military balance shifted and paying a tithe to each successive occupying army. On this occasion, the earl demanded one-twentieth of Tewkesbury's estate to offset the costs of its neighbour's relief. Thereafter, southern Herefordshire became the main target since the king could not prevent its systematic sacking without splitting his army and risking defeat in detail. To get there, Essex built a bridge of boats across the Severn using his army's bridging train, which, by coincidence, had been marooned in Gloucester since the Edgehill campaign. The Parliamentarian cavalry were no less brutal with Parliament's enemies than the king's cavalry were with his. At Castle Morton, 'on three several days, three several companies came to visit Master Bartlet's house ... without they plunder him of eight horses, and within, whatever they found, they made clean work'. To protect the raiding parties from Royalist interference, a strong body of cavalry advanced north to Upton, the first bridging point above Tewkesbury, where their presence was reported on 11 September.

Moving to Tewkesbury was, however, more than an exercise in logistic re-supply. The town was at the base of the northerly route from Gloucester to London, following the River Avon through the Vale of Evesham to Warwick. If the king did not respond quickly, there might be the opportunity to outmarch the Royalists up the valley, threaten Worcester and advance even further into the midlands. Building the bridge of boats across the Severn, the plundering raids into Herefordshire and the positioning of cavalry at Upton could all be interpreted as the opening stages of such a plan, and suggested that Essex had ruled out retracing his steps through the north Cotswolds or taking the southerly route to the River Kennet and Reading. Yet with hindsight, moving to Tewkesbury presented a new opportunity as well. If Essex could persuade his enemies that he was indeed about to charge northwards, and thereby cause them to shift their forces along a similar axis, a rapid change of direction might wrong foot them sufficiently for him to gain a substantial lead in a race southeast to the Kennet valley. To succeed, Essex would have to convince the Royalist command that he was pinned down on the banks of the Severn, and then persuade them to conform to a northward feint while retaining his own army in sufficiently close formation that it could perform a quick about face and bolt towards Cirencester and beyond before Rupert's cavalry could react. A deliberate feint was a complex manoeuvre, and this interpretation may give Essex too much credit for foresight and vision. But there is much evidence to support it.

Not only would a covert overnight reverse march have required detailed pre-planning to succeed, most contemporary Parliamentarian sources agreed that the move northwards was a feint. A London soldier, known by the initials TV, explained that the bridge of boats and the advance to Upton were intended to 'cause the enemy to draw all his forces together' for the defence of Worcester, adding with evident pleasure that 'the fools were cozened'. Sergeant Foster agreed that the bridge was constructed 'as if our intention had been to march with our army over there to Worcester' and Robert Codrington described Essex's objective as 'to amuse the enemy, and to cause them to draw part of their forces that way'. The Royalists clearly believed that the earl had deliberately duped them. A letter by Lord Digby, which became the authorised Royalist version of this stage of the campaign, describes Essex as 'amusing' them with his advance to Tewkesbury and Upton, and Hyde too implied that the Parliamentarian aim was to divert attention northwards.

Sir Samuel Luke's intelligence priorities, reflected in the disposition of his agents, also give support to the thesis. His absolute priority was the location of the king's forces and, when they deployed, their direction of march. Only when it was incontrovertible that the Royalist centre of gravity had shifted into the Vale of Evesham and towards Worcester did the Parliamentarians make their move. In addition, however, Luke's spies kept a close eye on Cirencester. They had already noted that the Royalists were quartering in places 'where they may easily be surprised' and from 12 September Essex was receiving daily reports from Cirencester, all indicating that the town was not strongly garrisoned. It seems therefore that the earl had evolved a strategy for re-supplying his army and at the same time creating an opportunity for them to escape from the Gloucester pocket without a pitched battle. But that strategy depended fundamentally on persuading the Royalists to abandon their Sudeley base and follow him northwards, away from his eventual route towards Cirencester, the River Kennet and Newbury.[15]

VI

At Sudeley, news of the earl's advance to Tewkesbury was analysed during the night of 10 September. The consensus was that the Parliamentarians were short of food and aiming for an early escape towards Warwick or Worcester. At noon on 11 September, Rupert and an advance guard of 1,000 cavalry galloped into Evesham, where he peremptorily cancelled the town's fair, while other detachments were reportedly scouting near Cheltenham and Tewkesbury. Behind them, the infantry and the artillery train were prepared for immediate departure. One of Luke's spies counted 132 infantry colours, nineteen cannon and two mortars (the latter useless in open combat and destined for Oxford). It was almost ten miles from Sudeley to Evesham and having descended from the Cotswolds, the bulk of the army spent that night spread out from Bredon Hill to Evesham, where the king himself quartered. Rupert and his cavalry were three miles further on, heading towards Worcester.

Worcester itself was in a state of panic. Strongly royalist in sentiment, it was an important military base controlling communications between Oxford and the key recruiting grounds in Wales and the marches, and along the Severn. Earlier in the year it had seen off a half-hearted attack by Waller but Essex's full army was a different matter, especially if it proved to be determined and desperate enough to launch an immediate assault. Moreover, most of the garrison had been ordered out to join the siege at Gloucester and appear to have been retained with the Oxford Army; two days before, a Parliamentarian spy had identified only 500 men and a handful of guns still in the city. Other intelligence reports talked of hastily issued orders to impress all able-bodied men, and to bring in arms and provisions. Nor was Worcester the sole victim of nervous uncertainty. Vavasour's detachment from Brampton Bryan was sent scuttling back to Hereford in case of attack.

The crisis soon passed. Rupert delivered 2,000 reinforcements to Worcester on 12 September and a further 700 infantry (the Prince of Wales' Regiment) plus 1,000 cavalry and dragoons were shortly to arrive from Capel to secure the city from surprise attack. The prince therefore returned to Evesham, where the army had congregated, and when Essex did not advance, Royalist thoughts turned to how to force him to fight. Though Tewkesbury was safe behind its river barriers, the cavalry detachment five miles upstream at Upton was potentially vulnerable to envelopment. Late on 12 September, the Oxford Army began to advance. The plan was to move overnight from Evesham to Pershore, the first bridge across the Avon above Tewkesbury. To mislead enemy spies, Worcester appears to have been the designated destination but the Royalists would instead march under cover of darkness on 13 September southwest to Ripple Field, open ground between Upton and Tewkesbury where Prince Maurice had defeated Waller in a skirmish in April. Here they hoped to trap the Upton cavalry and oblige Essex to fight to save them or abandon them to their fate. A second force must in parallel have been moving down from Worcester to prevent the Upton cavalry from simply withdrawing down the west bank of the Severn.

To succeed, the plan required Essex to believe that he was not under direct threat. However, Luke's spies followed the Royalist movements and provided same-day reports to the Earl. They did indeed pass on the misinformation that the Oxford Army was bound for Worcester but one of them had gleaned a vital scoop. During 13 September, Edward Roston returned to Tewkesbury to report that there were 1,000 Royalist soldiers within three miles of the town and 'a great party of our horse which lie at Upton which they intend to fall upon this night, and to get betwixt them and our army'. This was priceless intelligence and it was acted upon swiftly. Essex sent out a force to cover the retreat of the Upton cavalry and then withdrawn them all across the strongly fortified Avon bridge. Lord Sunderland described how

> we advanced with all possible speed; upon which he [Essex] retired with the body of his army to Tewkesbury, where, by the advantage of the bridge, he was able to make good his quarter, with 500 men, against 20,000.

It had been a close thing. According to Sunderland, the Royalists had been within two hours of cutting off Essex's cavalry detachment from the rest of the army.

On the morning of 14 September, as Royalist regiments retraced their footsteps to Pershore, a council of war was convened to consider future strategy. Sunderland summed up the outcome for his wife. Because Essex's position at Tewkesbury was unassailable and the earl would not engage in battle

> we should endeavour to force him to it by cutting off his provisions; for which purpose, the best way was for the body of our army to go back to Evesham, and for our horse to distress him.

In Sunderland's judgement, there was now 'no probability of fighting very suddenly', so he 'and many others' had decided to leave the army 'for a few days'. Sunderland himself rode off for a long weekend at his father-in-law's house in Oxford.[16]

Safely back at Tewkesbury, Essex can only have been delighted by his good fortune as further intelligence reports came in over the following twenty-four hours. Whatever his prior strategy, he was now being presented with a golden opportunity to break out from the Severn valley. The Royalist army was withdrawing, first to Pershore and then in the evening yet further back to Evesham. With his enemies spread over an almost twenty mile front from Broadway to Worcester, there could hardly be a better time for the earl to strike south. He did not prevaricate: Parliament's army would begin its return march to London on the night of 14–15 September. Cheltenham was the initial goal, an eight-mile march past Royalist cavalry patrols. *Mercurius Aulicus* was inevitably dismissive: 'never army marched with so great haste, disorder and fear, as if every man in his army had run a race with his fellow, no drum beating, nor trumpet sounding'. Speed and silence were essential but the success of this preliminary stage of the operation suggests that it was carried out with considerable skill and discipline.

Last minute preparations were, however, disrupted by Prince Rupert in person. At Oxington, a small village east of Tewkesbury, Sir James Ramsey's cavalry regiment had mustered from its quarters once darkness fell and was drawn up ready to move out when a detachment of thirty Royalists appeared. They were scouting ahead of a much larger raiding party under the prince himself and had not expected to find their intended victims on full alert. Apparently undeterred by the presence of Ramsey's whole regiment, the Royalists crossed a deep ditch in front of the village and fired their carbines and pistols into the rear of the Parliamentarian cavalry. *Mercurius Aulicus* recorded that the volley created 'such noise and clamour, that the affrighted rebels (though five troops of horse) betook themselves unto their heels in a great confusion'. The Royalists claimed to have killed fourteen and captured twenty-five prisoners and fifty horses, and Foster admitted that 'they slew many of our men, and took many others prisoners'. Although Ramsey's troopers reformed and joined the Parliamentarian column, Foster's account suggests that their experience was unnerving for the whole army.[17] Much more important, however, was the potential impact of the raid on the evacuation from Tewkesbury. Had Rupert realised that a move was in progress? If so, Essex could expect the Royalist cavalry to be close behind him when the morning came. The second decisive phase of the campaign was underway with no clear indication which side held the advantage.

Chapter Ten

'No orders were given out for the manner of our fighting'

I

Duelling was strictly forbidden in the king's armies. So of course were many other misdemeanours such as pillaging and extortion where the Articles of War were routinely ignored. It was, nonetheless, unusual for one of the king's cavalry colonels to kill a fellow officer on active service and an instance could not be ignored, no matter how mitigating the circumstances. On the morning of 15 September, Colonel Sir Nicholas Crispe fought and killed Sir James Enyon in his quarters at Rous Lench, north of Evesham. Enyon seems to have brought the tragedy upon himself. If Crispe would not fight him, he threatened to 'pistol him against the wall'. When they met, 'many passes Sir James made at him [before Crispe] . . . happened to run him through'. The two knights were apparently friends and Sir Nicholas is said to have mourned his victim for the remainder of his life. For King Charles at Evesham, the outcome of the duel was an untimely distraction. Sir Nicholas' newly raised cavalry regiment could be taken over by another officer but his fortune and enthusiasm for the Royalist cause were irreplaceable.

According to one account, the duel had been fought over stolen horses. Enyon had demanded that Crispe parade his regiment to prove that his men were not the thieves.[1] In fact, however, Sir Nicholas' regiment had been elsewhere when the duel took place. As part of the blockade of the Parliamentarian army in north Gloucestershire, less experienced cavalry units were being used to provide escorts for food and other supply convoys, a mundane yet essential role (three days earlier, at Newnham, a detachment of Massey's garrison had seized match, wine and other stores en route from Bristol to Hereford). On the evening of 15 September, Crispe's regiment and that of Colonel Richard Spencer, together about 400 strong, brought a large food convoy into Cirencester, which was being used as a way station between Bristol and the Oxford army at Sudeley and Evesham. Guards were posted, the horses were stabled, and the officers and men settled down to a decent night's rest.

At one o'clock in the morning of 16 September, the two regiments received a rude and unexpected awakening. The advance guard of the Earl of Essex's army, believed by the Royalists to be penned-in twenty-five miles away in the Severn valley, had arrived instead in the midst of the Cotswold Hills. Their capture of Cirencester was carried out quickly and stealthily. First a ring of cavalry was deployed silently around the town. Next, a party of horsemen under Major Robert Hammond, commander of the earl's own troop, swiftly despatched one of the guard posts. Then an assault force of commanded infantrymen stormed into the town with orders that 'if any man presumed to look out or stir, we were commanded to shoot them, or knock them down'. Surprise was complete and resistance minimal. There was a brief exchange of musket fire at one of the other guard posts, during which Parliamentarian Sir Robert Pye was shot in the arm, and some confused skirmishing as the Royalists were routed from their beds, but most of the raw cavalrymen surrendered without a fight. They were dragged to the market place and held in the parish church. A few others escaped towards Highworth carrying lurid stories that 150 of their comrades had been slaughtered as they slept.

Although Sir Edward Hyde blamed 'the negligence of the officers (a common and fatal crime throughout the war, on the king's part)', it is hard with hindsight to be too critical of them for failing to keep a proper guard. By the standards of the period, Essex's army had been two days march away. His men had moved almost twenty-five miles from Tewkesbury in a little over twenty-four hours, up and across the steep Cotswold scarp. This was an extraordinary achievement, not least because of the size of the artillery train accompanying them, and it speaks much for the earl's ability to motivate his soldiers in a crisis, manage a large army, and think and act rapidly when the need arose. The official Parliamentarian account suggests that the earl decided to strike for Cirencester, and thereby double the distance to be covered in this single march, only during the course of that day. His original aim had been to spend the night at Cheltenham, eight miles from Tewkesbury and only fourteen or so miles from the main Royalist concentration around Evesham and Pershore. Yet

> upon advertisement that a body of the enemy's were then in Cirencester (which were reported to be Prince Maurice's forces) and there laid in great store of provision for their army (our want of necessaries and victual still continuing, and miserably increasing upon us) his Excellency made a long march with the vanguard of the army, to fall upon them.

Although Sir Samuel Luke's journal for 15 September is uncharacteristically sketchy, recording simply the comings and goings of his agents, Essex had certainly been receiving regular intelligence reports from Cirencester. It is unlikely that he would have attacked had he believed that Maurice's army was indeed present but the lightly guarded food convoy was too good an opportunity to miss, and its capture amply justified the long and tiring march.[2]

The Parliamentarian army spent the rest of the night and the first part of the following day at Cirencester. Bread, cheese and other supplies from the Royalist convoy (described variously as comprising between twenty-seven and forty wagons) were distributed and the soldiers were able to snatch a few hours sleep. The prisoners were roped together in pairs with match and would be dragged off towards Newbury, together with six standards, as the army's first spoils of war. Under interrogation some said that the two regiments had been destined for operations in Kent, which may well have been the intention earlier in the summer, but the war had since moved on and it seems unlikely that the king's generals were at this stage planning to dissipate their strength by sending half-trained raiding parties into Parliamentarian territory.

During the day, Luke's spies brought Essex reassuring news about the inevitable Royalist pursuit. One had been at Evesham between seven and eight that morning, when 'the king was there and intended not to stir all this day'. Another had heard 'of no forces stirring that way nearer than Evesham, Charlton and Stow'. It was also now raining, which would make it even more difficult for the Royalists to catch up. Nevertheless, the earl took no chances and his army marched a further six miles that afternoon, to spend the night of 16–17 September in Cricklade and the surrounding villages. The London Trained Band regiments chased ten cartloads of sick or wounded Royalists, presumably recuperating after Gloucester, from Latton and took their quarters to shelter from the weather. Not all of the Parliamentarians were eager to return home quickly. Some preferred to stay behind at Cirencester where there was looted food and drink, and shelter, and the Royalists were still many miles behind.[3]

II

There was no doubt that the earl had flat-footed his enemies and gained a head start in the final stage of his campaign, the race back to London. He had been fortunate that Prince Rupert's raid on Oxington on the evening of 14 September had neither detected nor disrupted the initial stage of the withdrawal. In all other respects, his handling of the march had been exemplary, and the intelligence reports indicating that as late as the morning of 16 September the king had still not discovered his departure suggested that Parliament's army might even enjoy an undisturbed return march.

Unfortunately for Essex, the intelligence reports were wrong, though not by a great deal. The circumstances surrounding the Royalist reaction to Essex's night-time disengagement are difficult to disentangle. They were clearly the subject of acrimony during and after the event, although King Charles' involvement inevitably distorted the surviving accounts. One fact is, however, undisputed: it took twenty-four hours for the Royalist command to accept that the earl and his army had indeed disappeared. Hyde again placed the blame squarely with the Royalist cavalry. They were

> always less patient of duty and ill accommodation than they should be;
> and at this time, partly with weariness, and partly with the indisposition
> that possessed the whole army upon the relief of [Gloucester] ... were less
> vigilant towards the motion of the enemy.

It was therefore twenty-four hours before the king learnt which way Essex had gone. There was certainly confusion about Essex's whereabouts. A week later, Lord Digby wrote that the earl was able 'with great silence, secrecy, and strange diligence' to capture Cirencester 'before we could get any certain notice of his motions'.

Although poor intelligence plagued Royalist generals throughout the Civil War, in this case there is evidence that the fault lay not with the cavalry for failing to provide information but with the king and his senior advisers for refusing to believe it. Sir John Byron later complained 'that had Prince Rupert been pleased to credit my intelligence, the advantage which Essex gained might have been prevented'. Since Byron was commanding one of the Royalist cavalry brigades, it can be inferred from this that his men detected the Parliamentarian army but Rupert, his superior officer, did not act upon the information. By contrast, Prince Rupert's Diary suggests that the prince obtained intelligence 'that Essex was marching' from his raid on Oxington, yet the king 'believed himself better informed' and ignored it. Meanwhile, Rupert was assembling his cavalry brigades on Broadway Down, five miles southeast of Evesham, and waiting orders to begin the chase. Gathering the dispersed cavalry regiments and planning the pursuit must have taken a good part of the day, not least because many of the officers seem to have followed the Earl of Sunderland's example and taken impromptu leave. But when night fell on 15 September, with Essex still strung out between Cheltenham and Cirencester, no instructions had arrived. Deeply frustrated, the prince rode through the darkness to the king's quarters where he discovered his uncle playing cards in front of the fire with Lord Percy, while Lord Forth looked on. Rupert is unlikely to have been subtle in these circumstances. He urged immediate pursuit. Forth and Percy, who had evidently discounted the intelligence until now, counselled caution. Rupert at last reasserted himself as he had not done since the council of war at Bristol, and his uncle capitulated. Rupert and the cavalry would leave at once, Lieutenant Colonel George Lisle would follow as soon as possible with 1,000 commanded musketeers and the rest of the army would set out the next morning.

The four Royalist accounts are not necessarily incompatible. From Byron's perspective, Rupert should have confronted the king much earlier. In practice, however, it would have taken some hours to gather the cavalry near Broadway and Rupert probably assumed that the king's approval was a formality. When it did not arrive, he would have been understandably reluctant to leave his men in case a messenger appeared in his absence. Only the prospect of a further twelve hours overnight delay convinced him that his personal intervention was needed. Digby was a senior member of the king's staff, drawing a discreet veil over the whole unfortunate incident, while Hyde presumably decided that it was politic to avoid any hint that the king was responsible for one of the critical Royalist command blunders of the war.[4]

Although the Royalist cavalry were soon on their way, the damage caused by the self-imposed delay was immense. Detailed timings are obscure but the fact that Rupert was able to assemble the bulk of his cavalry well before sunset on 15 September suggests that had the king authorised an early pursuit, they would have been able to intercept Essex during the afternoon of 16 September, shortly after he left Cirencester and still in open countryside. As it was, Rupert can hardly have started south before Essex reached Cirencester, and with rain reducing mobility, he had no prospect of catching up with the Parliamentarian army. He would instead have to cut them off before they reached the security of a major garrison. Reading was the earl's obvious goal. Rupert's only advantage was that to avoid the Oxford garrison the Parliamentarians had to skirt well to the east and south whereas the Royalist army could take a more direct route. If by doing so they could deploy themselves across the earl's line of march, it was still possible that the Royalists could make their numerical superiority tell in open battle.

Rupert had with him around 5,000 cavalry; Lisle's 1,000 musketeers, probably accompanied by a small artillery train (four six-pounders had been prepared for this task), were trailing behind but well ahead of the rest of the Royalist army. Their route lay almost due south from Broadway to Northleach and then southeast towards Newbury. The prince had undoubtedly been galvanised by Essex's escape and he must have pushed his men on at a rapid pace. They rode throughout the day on 16 September and then, while Essex's regiments slept in and around Cricklade, through the following night. It rained. Men and horses fell out of the column and were left to their own devices to catch up. Rupert was at his best as a leader in these circumstances, moving at speed to take opponents off balance. In this case, however, his efforts would be wasted if the Royalist infantry were not being marched in his wake with equal urgency.

Despite the collective lassitude of previous days, King Charles and his generals had been belatedly infected by Rupert's energy. Hyde attributed their vigorous response to the king himself and suggested that he was angry at the 'supine negligence' of those he had trusted, presumably including Forth and Percy. But Forth's experience would be essential if the infantry were to get under way quickly, regain contact with Essex and then be in a state to fight a decisive battle before the Parliamentarians could reach the security of the Reading garrison. Percy too would have a vital part to play in ensuring that the artillery arrived in time and, even more importantly, that the ammunition train kept up with the rest of the army.

Digby recorded that the march began on the morning of 16 September but Parliamentarian intelligence reported that the king, his forces and 500 wagons did not leave Evesham until the evening. The latter timing is more likely. Gathering the infantry regiments from quarters across the Vale of Evesham will have been a prolonged exercise. Some of the more remote units were given orders to follow separately. Sir William Vavasour's brigade appears to have lagged behind, perhaps because they had been quartered on the west bank of the River Avon, beyond Pershore. The Prince of Wales' Foot marched from Worcester east towards Banbury and Oxford, to join the main force near Newbury. Other units did not follow at all. Colonel Samuel Sandys was later accused of having remained behind with his regiment 'contrary to his Majesty's orders for him to march in Sir William Vavasour's Brigade'. Orders were also sent to Oxford for reinforcements from the Thames valley garrisons to join the king on his march and, in all probability, for Sunderland and other absentees to do likewise.

The infantry marched through the night of 16–17 September to reach their former camp at Sudeley Castle at about eight o'clock in the morning. They had covered eight miles but their exertions were only just beginning. After a muster, a Parliamentarian spy saw them setting off again 'towards Oxford'. In fact, their route was rather further to the west, towards Northleach. King Charles joined them at Sudeley after a few hours snatched sleep at Snowshill Manor and then rode with them the ten miles to Northleach, which he reached during the late morning. Here the king and his commanders reviewed the army's progress over dinner. Their original plan had been to quarter that night at Burford, but that would put them some way north of the most direct line of march to Newbury and Royalist scouts reported that supplies were more plentiful four miles further southeast at Alvescot. At midday, the king's decision to press on to Alvescot was set down in a letter to Prince Rupert, explaining that the army would thereby 'save three or four miles march'. The decision to quarter at Alvescot meant that the Oxford Army infantry would have slogged through the autumn rain for thirty miles in about twenty-four hours, a feat comparable to that achieved by the Earl of Essex in taking Cirencester. There does, however, seem to have been a significant difference between the two forced marches. The inevitable stragglers aside, Essex had kept his army and its supply train together but contemporary accounts show that on the Royalist side King Charles, Forth and Percy were unable to do so.

Further ahead, Rupert had chosen to divide his forces in an effort to harry and delay the Parliamentarians. His main body pressed on southeastwards through Fairford and Lechlade towards Stanford-in-the-Vale, where he planned to give them a much-needed night's rest. But the experienced Colonel Urry was sent with 1,000 cavalry to follow Essex's steps. During the morning of 17 September he stormed into Cirencester and took prisoner forty Parliamentarian stragglers. When one of Luke's scouts arrived with the news, Sergeant Foster of the Red Regiment was unsympathetic: men 'who stayed behind drinking and neglecting to march with their colours . . . are not much to be pitied'.

By late afternoon, a report from Urry that Essex 'was no so far out of reach as was feared', and perhaps 'not much further than Cricklade', had reached Rupert at Stanford-in-the-Vale. Within three hours, the king at Alvescot had been briefed by letter from the prince. It is clear from the surviving correspondence between them that Rupert was now in the driving seat. At eight in the evening, Digby signed a reply on the king's behalf seeking urgent guidance on how the main army should proceed on the following day. If the intelligence picture remained favourable, 'His Majesty's desire' was that Rupert should 'send speedily your opinion which way, and to what place it will be fit for the king to march with his army tomorrow'. Seen from Alvescott, 'we conceive that Wantage will be the aptest place: but in this His Majesty conceives he is to be governed wholly by directions from Your Highness'.

Rupert was best placed to take these decisions but he was not given a clear picture of the condition of the main force to help him do so. Digby wrote that the army was 'all, except stragglers, well up hither to Alvescot', which was at best wildly optimistic. Moreover, in a postscript, Digby added: 'I am commanded to add, that you should consider to allow the foot here as much rest as can well be without losing the opportunity'. Rupert was rightly sceptical about the state of the infantry. By one in the morning, the king had received another message, asking for details and suggesting a plan of campaign. This time, the Duke of Richmond replied. He confirmed that the king 'is loath to weary the foot after so great a march' but admitted that many of them had fallen out and been left behind. In addition, Vavasour's brigade had not arrived, although it was expected that day together with the Prince of Wales' Regiment, which had spent the previous night at Warmington, over twenty-five miles to the north. More importantly, however, Richmond confirmed that Rupert's proposals for coordinating the Royalist campaign: 'I have let the king see what you writ who approves all in it, and will accordingly perform his part, only desires to have certain knowledge when Essex moved or shall move from Cricklade, that if his Majesty's army can come time enough . . . he will take up his quarter this night at, or about, Wantage, so to reach Newbury as you propose'. Forth had been marginalized; the king would 'acquaint my Lord General' with the new plan.

No matter how hard the king pushed the infantry, Rupert did not believe that they would reach Newbury before the Parliamentarian army. Perhaps he had been sufficiently startled by the dash to Cirencester to reappraise the normally pedestrian earl. His plan therefore required the cavalry to intercept and delay Essex, a task they had signally failed to achieve around Stow-on-the-Wold during the advance from London. On the morning of 18 September, Rupert led his tired regiments southwest from Stanford-in-the-Vale, past the ancient white horse below the Ridgeway and up onto the Wiltshire Downs. His scouts must have been in contact with the Parliamentarians, and he will have known that their pace had slowed since Cirencester. They had spent that night in and around Swindon and now had to cross sixteen miles of open down-land to reach the relative safety of the River Kennet at Hungerford, during which they would for the last time be vulnerable to the Royalist cavalry. Ideally, the Royalists would hope to catch Essex with his men spread out in line of march on Aldbourne Chase, where there was little natural or man-made cover. Lisle's musketeers were now well behind but Urry had rejoined the prince after Cirencester and was now sent ahead with 1,000 men. Behind them, the main body of Royalist cavalry streamed across the downland, a stiff ride of some twelve miles. Arriving on the Chase in early afternoon, they found Essex's army still strung out on open ground, well short of Aldbourne village. The advantage he had seized between Tewkesbury and Cirencester had somehow been lost in the subsequent three days, and the earl again faced the prospect of one of Rupert's trademark cavalry actions, and perhaps even the threat that the king's infantry would soon appear as well.[5]

III

Essex has been consistently criticised for his leisurely pace during 16–18 September. The consensus has been that he frittered away an unchallengeable lead over his Royalist pursuers, reverting to stolid type when what were needed were more dashes of the kind that had won him Cirencester. In fact, however, the picture is rather more complicated. On the one hand, the earl and his commanders may well have been unduly complacent. Intelligence reporting continued to reassure. Although news of Urry's recapture of Cirencester arrived during 17 September, Luke's spy reported that the attackers were only four troops strong and had carried their prisoners back to Sudeley Castle; that the Royalist army was heading towards Oxford; and that the king was spending the following night at Stow-on-the-Wold. This suggested that Charles had given up the campaign or was hoping to intercept the Parliamentarians rather further to the east, in which case Essex could hope to fight on much more favourable terms as a report from Faringdon suggested that Sir William Waller had advanced towards Reading to cover the Lord General's withdrawal.

Unfortunately, this intelligence was entirely incorrect. The king was fourteen miles further on at Alvescot, a substantial part of his army was even closer, and Waller's troops were sitting impotently at Staines and Windsor. But Luke's spies had been right about Cirencester and conventional wisdom would have been that the gap between the two armies was too great for them to be overtaken. The official Parliamentarian account reinforces the impression of complacency, describing how on 17 September the army marched only five miles from Cricklade to Swindon where, it being Sunday, a sermon was preached; so 'the reader may observe what long marches we made to avoid fighting with the enemy'. This responded to Royalist allegations that the Parliamentarians had been frightened to give battle, though the real reason for the delay was more prosaic. Despite the capture of the supply train at Cirencester, Essex's men were still hungry and the earl was as usual concerned to ensure their welfare. Newbury, the next friendly town, was still three day's march away. Sergeant Foster recalled not the sermon but that 'this day we drove along with our army about one thousand sheep and sixty head of cattle, which were taken from malignants and papists in the country for the maintenance of our army: eighty-seven sheep was allotted for our red regiment'.

Rustling livestock took time. Nonetheless, a modern map shows that the army moved rather further than contemporary accounts suggest. Foster's regiment made almost twelve miles from Latton to the village of Chiseldon, south of Swindon, an average day's march. The bulk of the army had a rather shorter journey from Cricklade to Swindon and thus had time to celebrate the Sabbath. But according to Foster, it was a 'very cold and frosty night' and Essex cannot have wanted his army to camp on the exposed downland further south. In the absence of intelligence of Royalists closer than Cirencester, it therefore made sense to quarter as many soldiers as possible in Swindon and the surrounding villages. The London brigade again missed out. Foster thought Chiseldon 'a poor village . . . where we could get no accommodation either for meat or drink, but what we brought with us in our snapsacks: most of us quartered in the open field'. But the bulk of Essex's soldiers should have had a relatively comfortable night.

Next morning, Monday 18 September, the Parliamentarian army wound its way up onto the downs between Swindon and Hungerford. With an artillery train, supply wagons and a flock of a thousand sheep, this cannot have been a rapid ascent. As during the first march across the Cotswolds, those regiments at the front of the column moved more quickly than the main force so that the army became dangerously extended. Had Essex been concerned about the possibility of attack in such unfavourable terrain, he would in all probability have kept the army tightly bunched. It must therefore have been an unwelcome shock when 'news was brought to the Lord General, that the enemy was coming upon us with a great body of horse'. Whether he had dawdled or not, the harsh fact was that Prince Rupert had caught up and thereby regained the initiative.[6]

IV

From Swindon, there had been four possible routes for Essex to reach the security of the Kennet Valley. The first, south past Chiseldon and then down the Og valley to Marlborough, reached the Kennet soonest yet was by far the longest march, twenty miles to Hungerford along the external sides of an isosceles triangle. Marlborough was also used as a quarter by the Royalists and may have been garrisoned (if so, Luke should have known since he had despatched one of his spies there on the previous day).[7] Essex therefore dismissed it.

The three alternative routes took the earl's army along the triangle's hypotenuse, southeast over the downs between Marlborough and Lambourn, through the village of Aldbourne, and finally along a valley to meet the Kennet near Hungerford. All three were shorter marches of around fifteen miles and the bridge at Hungerford was only lightly guarded. For Essex, the question was how best to cross the exposed downland before Aldbourne. The most northerly route, east past Wanborough and Callas Hill, then southeast along a Roman road between Hinton Downs and Sugar Hill, was nearest to the Royalists, provided no protection from Rupert's cavalry and obliged the Trained Bands to retrace their steps from Chiseldon. A better choice would have been to climb the downs between Callas and Beacon Hills, and make for Aldbourne along a wide dry valley between Sugar Hill and Aldbourne Warren, where the landscape was still open but Rupert was marginally farther away and Sugar Hill offered a potentially defensible position. More attractive again was the most southerly route, south past Chiseldon then east across Aldbourne Chase, a 1,400-acre deer park dotted with woodland and bordered by rabbit warrens. According to the earliest detailed maps (eg Andrews and Dury, 1773, William Stanley's Ordnance Survey drawing surveyed in 1818), the Chase covered the high ground south of a dry valley that ran west to east from beneath the crest of the downs, through the hamlet of Snap to Aldbourne village. To the north was Aldbourne Warren, which conveniently shielded the Snap valley from prying eyes.

All but one of the contemporary accounts point to Essex using the most southerly route across Aldbourne Chase, which involved the shortest march across the open downs and made tactical sense since it allowed the earl to pick up the London brigade at Chiseldon. The strongest evidence for this option is Foster's description of the position when the Royalists appeared: 'our whole army being in a deep valley, and the enemy upon the hills on our left flank'. Even a city dweller like Foster would not have considered the broad dry valleys to the north to be worth commenting upon and visibility from the hills on either side is good, making hidden movement of the kind that took place during the action almost impossible. The Snap to Aldbourne valley has an entirely different feel. It is far narrower and both slopes are steep. It meanders in an extended S-bend and visibility within the valley and even from the hills is often extremely limited. An army caught in the valley bottom would feel very threatened by cavalry on the hills above. If those cavalry had infantry to support them, it would be hard to force a passage, yet the steepness of the slopes and the tightness of the terrain would make it difficult for cavalry on their own to exploit their apparent advantage. *Mercurius Aulicus* gave a similar description to Foster, reporting that the Parliamentarians were found in a 'bottom'.[8]

Essex had therefore marched his army from Swindon south past Chiseldon and then east across the top edge of Aldbourne Chase into the Snap valley. His scouts should have given some warning of the approaching Royalists but most of his men were still spread out in a long winding column along the valley bottom when the first of Rupert's cavalry appeared above them on Aldbourne Warren, the spur running from Upper Upham down past the Giant's Grave tumulus that forms the northern slope of the valley. According to *Mercurius Aulicus*, the prince 'with the whole body of horse' discovered the Parliamentarian army at about three in the afternoon. Prince Rupert's Diary recorded that Essex's cavalry rearguard was two to three miles adrift from the main body. Estimates of the Royalists' strength varied considerably. The Parliamentarians reported from 5,000 to 8,000, Digby 3,000 only. The latter is probably an underestimate but some of the 5,000 or so cavalrymen that had begun the march will have fallen out and the remainder will have been tired after almost three days of hot, and often damp, pursuit. Of Rupert's brigade commanders, Wilmot, Sir John Byron and Charles Gerard were certainly present, together with Urry, who had to all intents been acting in that role.[9]

In the valley below the Royalist advance guard, Essex had drawn up his men in some form of battle order but they were still too widely dispersed to support each other properly. One wing of cavalry under Sir Philip Stapleton was at the head of the column, perhaps as far away as Aldbourne itself. Most of the infantry deployed along a low ridge running almost east-west along the valley floor, where they were joined by the artillery train. Some light guns were hastily prepared to provide support. They had no benefits from the terrain, which was unenclosed arable land or sheep pasture. The rest of the cavalry, under Colonel John Middleton, formed the rearguard and were 'somewhat distant' from the main body, probably escorting the baggage train.

Having brought Essex to bay, what were Prince Rupert's intentions? Sir Edward Hyde had no doubt:

> to get between London and the enemy before they should be able to get out of those enclosed deep countries, in which they were engaged between narrow lanes, and to entertain them with skirmishes till the whole army should come up.

In fact, however, it is clear from the correspondence between Rupert and the king that the infantry and artillery were at the time marching directly towards Newbury. This was therefore a delaying operation to allow the king to block the Kennet valley. But the form it took became a matter of dispute between those involved. Sir John Byron alleged that Rupert failed to fully brief his subordinate commanders:

> notwithstanding the necessity there was of fighting (at least if they persisted in their marching to London and we in ours of preventing them) yet no orders were given out for the manner of our fighting and how the army should be embattled as usually is done on the like occasions.

Byron implies that Rupert prevaricated and thereby lost the chance to inflict a major reverse on the Parliamentarian army:

> we were placed that we had it in our power both to charge their horse in flank and at the same time to have sent another party to engage their artillery, yet that fair occasion was omitted, and the enemy allowed to join all their forces together.

Prince Rupert's Diary places the blame elsewhere, explaining that Rupert had deployed his forces in preparation for an attack when a cabal of senior officers including Wilmot, Digby and the queen's favourite, Colonel Henry Jermyn 'importuned the prince not to fight'. Rupert was enraged and while the generals argued on their hilltop, the Parliamentarian horse and foot combined in the valley below and the opportunity was indeed lost.[10]

Neither interpretation tells the full story. Despite Byron's criticism, other contemporary accounts show that the prince's opening move was decisive enough. Noting that some at least of Middleton's rearguard was still isolated from the main body, Rupert sent Urry with 1,000 cavalrymen to circle around to the west to take them in the flank. How far Middleton's men were from the security of Essex's infantry and artillery is unclear. According to *Mercurius Aulicus* they were on the far side of a 'village', probably a reference to Snap, a substantial medieval settlement reduced in the seventeenth century to a single row of cottages. In that case, Middleton was still perhaps half a mile or more from the rest of the army.

Urry was able to outflank the rearguard without being observed. He could have used any one of a number of ridges to hide his progress from the opposite slopes, where Middleton's troopers were slowly shepherding the baggage towards the safety of the infantry. Middleton had five regiments with him, well over a thousand men, but 200 or so were at the very rear of the column, standing on another ridge. This was probably Colonel James Sheffield's Regiment. Their attention was presumably focused on the main Royalist formation so that they did not see Urry's detachment until too late and were quickly overwhelmed by a savage surprise charge. As the Royalist cavalry poured along the valley, firing pistols and carbines as they came, disorder spread through the Parliamentarian rearguard. Some of the baggage train was abandoned. Two ammunition carts overturned and by one account exploded. The Royalists claimed to have killed forty or fifty and captured two officers. Even the official Parliamentarian report conceded that 'the enemy pursuing hotly both on rear and flank, our retreat was not without some confusion and loss'. Sheffield's Regiment lost a standard and took no further part in the day's events.[11]

Urry could not charge the entire Parliamentarian army with 1,000 cavalrymen. He was already coming under ineffective fire from the light guns deployed among the infantry. But from the opposite hillside, it seemed that his surprise attack had so unnerved Essex's whole army that Rupert was tempted to bring the rest of his force down into the valley to mount a full attack. Perhaps this was Byron's idea, which was why he was piqued when it was not followed. Digby explained, however, that at that moment news arrived that 'our foot, was beyond expectation, advanced within six or seven miles of us'. This 'imposed upon his Highness prudence' and it was decided to wait for these reinforcements to arrive the next day before seeking battle. Meanwhile, the Royalist cavalry would continue to 'hinder their march'. Taken at face value, Digby's explanation appears implausible. As discussed above, on 18 September the main body of Royalist infantry was well to the east, trudging from Alvescot towards Newbury; King Charles was at Farringdon for dinner and Wantage for supper, at no time nearer than twelve miles from Aldbourne. Even if diverted, the Royalist infantry would not arrive until late on the following day. A more credible explanation is that the reinforcements were Lisle's musketeers, who should certainly have arrived by the next morning. If Rupert could keep Essex pinned down overnight in the steep-sided valley bottom, 1,000 musketeers would improve substantially his ability to harass the Parliamentarians throughout the following day, thereby increasing the likelihood that the king would then win the race to Newbury. This is probably when Digby, Wilmot and Jermyn urged caution and the Parliamentarians were able to regroup.

Whatever the reason, Rupert decided not to press home Urry's advantage. There was some skirmishing between dismounted dragoons, and the prince and his advisers may have expected that this and the continuing threat of cavalry attack would be sufficient to deter Essex from attempting to disengage. They were wrong. Digby wrote that they 'had not stood long, when we discovered that the enemy prepared for a retreat, and by degrees drew away their baggage first, then their foot, leaving their horse at a good distance from them'. Middleton had rallied his regiments and they now covered a slow withdrawal. Although disengagement in these circumstances was a difficult and risky operation, the Parliamentarians had noted that the Royalists had no infantry present. Rupert had shown on the Cotswolds that he was unwilling to commit his cavalry alone against the pike walls and musket volleys of formed infantry brigades. The valley's southern slope is relatively steep. Though the artillery was scrambled up it, the rustled sheep and cattle were abandoned, together with three cartloads of ammunition and fourteen carrying wheat or other foodstuff. When the infantry reached the top, they deployed again to cover the rest of the baggage train and wait for Middleton's cavalry to rejoin them. They were now little more than a mile from Aldbourne village and the ground would become increasingly enclosed as they descended towards it from the Chase.

As at Stow-on-the-Wold, Essex seemed to have faced down and evaded the Royalist cavalry. This time, however, Rupert decided not to stand idly by. According to Digby, his initial inclination was to launch a full-scale attack before the Parliamentarian army could follow their baggage train into the lanes in front of the village. But dusk was falling and the Parliamentarian withdrawal was happening so slowly that the prince chose instead to try to provoke Middleton's rearguard, which was still in the valley, into fighting rather than retreating. These tactics smack of another compromise between the combative prince and his more cautious senior officers so it is not surprising that Rupert turned yet again to the likeminded Urry. Across the valley, some of Middleton's force had already started to make their way up the slope. With about 500 commanded men, Urry moved forward to engage the remaining regiments before they too could withdraw. To tempt Middleton to fight not flee, Rupert gave Urry little immediate support. Two regiments only followed him down onto the valley floor. Nonetheless, for the second time that day, Urry carried all before him, at least to begin with, putting the tail end of the Parliamentarian rearguard 'into the like disorder'.

The ploy succeeded in drawing Middleton back into the valley. At the head of his own regiment and three attached troops, together probably similar in strength to Urry's force, he counterattacked the Royalists with unusual effectiveness. His men will have been charging downhill and in tight order, whereas the Royalist had lost their formation in the first clash. As Urry was pressed back down the slope, the two supporting Royalist regiments should have intervened but Digby admitted that they did not do 'their part as well as they ought' and Urry was 'forced to make somewhat a disorderly retreat'. Middleton's troopers now turned on the two supporting Royalist regiments, probably part of Gerard's northern brigade, who were also routed. Digby commented ruefully that while Rupert's aim had been to tempt the Parliamentarian cavalry to engage, they had done so 'with a little too much encouragement'.[12]

Nevertheless, the prince persisted with his plan. Rather than commit his full strength, which would have obliged Middleton to retreat, he ordered a third detachment forward into the valley. The Queen's Regiment of Horse was the largest regiment in Gerard's brigade, with as many as 500 officers and men, including mercenaries and French volunteers. At its head rode Jermyn, newly ennobled at the queen's request as Baron Jermyn of St Edmundsbury, with Digby and the Marquis de Vieuville, a young French nobleman, at his side. In their own minds, they were the elite of the Royalist horse. By the time that the Queen's Regiment had made its way down the slope into the valley, Middleton's men had reformed. When the Royalists attacked, they were received not by a counter charge but by an old-fashioned volley of pistols and carbines. Digby wrote with approval of the unusual steadiness of the Parliamentarian cavalry who waited until the Royalists were within ten yards before firing, and in particular of the remarkable composure of their commander, presumably Middleton, who peered at the Royalist commanders in turn before deciding

> to discharge his pistol, as it were by election at the Lord Digby's head, but without any more hurt (saving only the burning of his face) than he himself received by my Lord Jermyn's sword, who (upon the Lord Digby's pistol missing fire) ran him with it into the back; but he [Middleton] was as much beholden there to his armour, as the Lord Digby to his headpiece.

Past precedent suggested that the momentum of the attacking Royalists would sweep away the static Parliamentarians, but as the Queen's Regiment drove into Middleton's men they were themselves charged in the flank or rear. Colonel Richard Norton led his own regiment and that of Colonel Edmund Harvey into the mêlée. The Parliamentarian rearguard was becoming increasingly embroiled as Rupert intended, yet they were also fighting with unexpected vigour. Jermyn's regiment recoiled from the surprise assault, 'the greatest part of it shifting for themselves'. The officers, at the head of their troops and already hacking and slashing at Middleton's front ranks, were suddenly deserted and isolated. Unable to retreat and with his arm shattered by a pistol ball, Jermyn showed great presence of mind by leading his officers through Middleton's Regiment, which had been disrupted by the initial impact of the Royalist charge, past a body of Parliamentarian infantry and around the edge of the action back to their own lines. He had, however, lost de Vieuville who had been hit three times, in the chest, shoulder and face, although reports published in London suggested that he was actually killed by a blow from a pole-axe when he tried to escape from a lieutenant who had captured him. Stunned and blinded by the pistol shot to his helmet, Digby too was taken prisoner.[13]

Essex's rearguard were now completely committed, and the earl had sent a party of dragoons and musketeers from his own regiment back into the valley to support them (they were the infantry that Jermyn evaded), and recalled the rest of his cavalry. Urry, Gerard and Jermyn having been defeated in detail, Rupert led his own brigade, probably 1,000 or so strong, down the steep slope in an effort to regain the initiative. Even now, the despised Parliamentarian cavalry stood their ground. Grey's and Meldrum's regiments, supported by the musketeers, saw off the first Royalist charge but the prince reformed his men and at the second attempt broke the Parliamentarian line and sent them retreating back towards the main body. From the hilltop, Foster thought that the cavalrymen 'performed with as brave courage and valour as ever men did'. Digby was

> fortunately received out of the middle of a regiment of the enemy by a brave charge, which Prince Rupert in person made upon them with his one Troop, wherein His Highness' horse was shot in the head under him.

Rupert had to accept that his men could achieve no more. The Parliamentarian cavalry had reformed on the slope under the guns of the infantry brigades where the Royalist horse had no hope of following. Moreover, Middleton's rearguard had been reinforced by Sir Philip Stapleton with the remainder of Essex's cavalry regiments, together with the Trained Band and Auxiliary Regiments, so that Rupert was clearly outmatched. With night falling, the prince withdrew to his original position on the far side of the valley. Skirmishing between dragoons continued for an hour or so, but the main action was over.

The Parliamentarians claimed to have inflicted heavy losses, and to have captured up to sixty prisoners, including a lieutenant colonel and four other officers, but they also admitted two or three of their own captains killed, numerous other officers injured and 'some common soldiers slain'. A Parliamentarian soldier told a London newspaper that about 100 from both sides had been killed. Essex's biographer, Codrington, later estimated a combined total of 80 dead and more than 80 wounded. The Royalists were especially concerned about de Vieuville, who was believed at first to have been taken prisoner, but Hyde later acknowledged that many other officers had been wounded.

Aldbourne Chase had been a hectic cavalry skirmish of the kind at which Rupert usually excelled. On this occasion, however, Essex and the Parliamentarian horse had taken the tactical honours. Byron's sarcastic comment that no action was taken until the enemy had joined their forces together, after which 'we very courageously charged them' is justifiable criticism of the action as a whole. Yet Rupert's mistake was not to do too little, but to attempt too much. His unexpected appearance imposed delay on the Parliamentarian march; Urry's original charge was sufficient to persuade Essex to abandon seventeen wagons and one thousand hobbled sheep; a full-scale attack during the afternoon could perhaps have inflicted further damage. But once the prince had accepted, however reluctantly, the advice of Wilmot and Digby not to provoke a major battle, the evening's skirmishing had done little more than further tire and frustrate his own men, and boost the morale of the Parliamentarian cavalry.

V

Under cover of darkness, Essex's army withdrew to the relative security of Aldbourne village. Prince Rupert quartered his men in the open, around Lambourn, four miles to the north-east. From here, the Royalist cavalry could strike at Essex as he marched to Hungerford the next day or push on towards Newbury. Rupert did not, however, remain with them. The journal of his marches shows that he spent the night riding over the downs to and from Wantage for a conference with the king, who was spending the night at Sir George Wilmot's house.

Despite the tactical disappointment at Aldbourne Chase, Rupert had achieved his objective and the strategic balance had shifted towards the Royalists. Their infantry had covered another fourteen miles from Alvescot to Wantage during 18 September and were now only the same distance again short of Newbury. Meanwhile, Essex at Aldbourne was no closer and shadowed by the Royalist cavalry. The equation was simple. If the Royalists reached Newbury first, they could cross the River Kennet, block the road to Reading and force Essex to give battle. If the earl proved to be faster, then he would reach Reading unmolested and the campaign would be over. But thanks to the delay imposed by Rupert's cavalry, the king was winning the race and Rupert would be able to tilt the odds even further the next day by resuming his harassment of the Parliamentarian column and slowing their march to Hungerford.[14] Not everyone agreed. According to Prince Rupert's Diary, when the prince desired 'ye army might march', Forth advised against it but was again overruled. Relations between the elderly Scot and the young German were evidently at an increasingly low ebb.

After the meeting, King Charles retired to bed but his nephew was soon back in the saddle. His ride will have been difficult and unpleasant. The weather had again deteriorated: 'it was a night of much rain' recalled Sergeant Foster. As a result, Rupert's scouts once more failed to detect the earl marching his army away from immediate danger. Though Essex's men were 'much distressed for want of sleep; as also for all other sustenance', to remain was to risk the appearance of the king's full army the next day.

Essex's overnight march from Aldbourne to Hungerford does not rate with his marathon approach to and seizure of Cirencester. It was, nonetheless, a considerable achievement in its own right. Infantry, cavalry and guns, together with the increasingly depleted supply train, tramped through darkness, mud and rain. 'We were wet to the skin' grumbled Foster. The advance guard had six miles to travel to secure the bridge over the River Kennet at Hungerford. Once beyond the river, it would be much more difficult for the Royalists to harass the remainder of the march to Reading and they would be only ten miles from Newbury. Stapleton's cavalry wing now took over as rearguard but they were untroubled. The weather shielded the Parliamentarian column from any of Rupert's scouts enthusiastic enough to brave the conditions and hid their approach from a small Royalist detachment at Hungerford. As at Cirencester, the town was taken completely by surprise. One Royalist was killed in the scuffle and twenty-five were captured. Having seized the bridge, the army succumbed to its exhaustion. The Red Regiment was one of a number of units, presumably forming the rearguard, which took shelter in the cottages of Chilton Foliat, still a mile or more from Hungerford itself on the north bank of the river. Their confidence that Rupert was not in pursuit was justified. Although *Mercurius Aulicus* mocked the rapidity of the Parliamentarian withdrawal, the prince can only have been livid to discover that, in his absence, Essex had succeeded in another professionally executed disengagement. Digby only hints at the implications, stating simply that 'the enemy ... by the next morning was stolen away as far as Hungerford'. But the truth was that Essex's night march had yet again transformed the strategic picture.

Rupert's dash to Aldbourne Chase had delayed Essex's progress by about half a day. Now, a matter of hours later, Essex had slipped away, reached the Kennet valley and taken control of the bridge at Hungerford. His army was shaken and dispersed but no longer in immediate danger. By taking advantage of the weather to cover his departure from Aldbourne, he had made up lost ground and regained the initiative. Back at Lambourn, there could be no time for recriminations. As his tired and damp troopers broke camp on the morning of 19 September, Rupert sent a message to the king explaining the new position and confirming that they should still aim to join their forces at Newbury that night. Then he put himself at the head of his men and set off 'with all possible expedition' towards the rendezvous.[15]

Chapter Eleven
'Exceeding long and quick marches'

I

On the early morning of 19 September, the Oxford Army was spread over the countryside south-west of Oxford in four or five widely dispersed formations. At Lambourn, Prince Rupert was rousing his cavalry regiments in the open fields in the knowledge that the Earl of Essex had disappeared into the rain-swept night and was in all likelihood at Hungerford. Somewhere nearby was Lieutenant Colonel George Lisle and however many of the 1,000 musketeers had stayed on their feet in Rupert's wake. Eight miles away at Wantage, King Charles and the Earl of Forth were with the vanguard of a loose column of infantry regiments, guns and supply wagons that trailed back towards the Cotswold Hills. Among the rear markers was Sir William Vavasour's brigade, which had been expected to catch up the previous day but was unlikely yet to have made up the extra distance from its original quarters on the west bank of the River Severn. Nor was it likely that the Prince of Wales' Regiment, marching from Worcester, had yet caught up.

Smaller parties of reinforcements from the already depleted garrisons of Oxford and its satellites were also moving south; Colonel Blagge's Regiment at Wallingford seems to have detached more than 200 men. Officers who had taken untimely leave from the army at Evesham, such as the Earl of Sunderland, were hurrying to rejoin their units. Sunderland wrote a short letter to his wife complaining light-heartedly that 'I have so great a cold that I do nothing but sneeze and mine eyes do nothing but water'. At Bristol, Sir Ralph Hopton received orders from the king to come at once to Newbury with as many men as he could spare. Only two days previously, he had written to Prince Rupert complaining of shortages of men, arms and money but in a matter of hours, Hopton gathered 700 infantry, 400 cavalry and a train of packhorses loaded with ammunition, and was on his way.

No summary can fully describe the chaotic reality on the ground. Cumulative demoralisation, the rapid and unexpected departure from Evesham, the appalling weather and the rate of march over three days would have tested the best organised of early-modern military structures, let alone the Oxford Army. Horses were lame, food short or non-existent, men left behind, lost or deserted. Without paved roads, the rain transformed the army's path to a mud bath, and turned the task of moving artillery and supplies into a nightmare. While Colonel John Belasyse wrote simply that to intercept Essex the army had 'performed ... a quick march to Newbury' and Hyde noted the 'exceeding long and quick marches', Lieutenant John Gwyn of Lloyd's Regiment of Foot remembered that we made such great haste in pursuit of Essex's army that there was an account given of fifteen hundred foot quite tired and spent, not possible to come up to their colours before we engaged the enemy.

For most of his comrades, the worst part was that 'we were like to drop down every step we made with want of sleep'. The number of stragglers is the most persuasive testimony to the state of the army, especially the infantry. Hyde estimated that more than 2,000 men had been lost since Gloucester, although some had disappeared before the race to Newbury began.

Forth and the king therefore deserve credit for keeping a body of infantry of any size in being and on the move. Royalist accounts predictably emphasised the king's role but Parliamentarian intelligence also reported that during 19 September he had 'marched six miles on foot . . . to encourage his soldiers'. Credit too should be given to the much-maligned Lord Percy. Despite the conditions, the artillery train was largely intact and in touch with the main body. In practice, however, King Charles and the infantry were not going to decide the race to Newbury. Only Rupert and the cavalry could do that. Though the weather seems to have eased that morning and the eleven-mile ride down the Lambourn valley was rather less demanding then previous exertions, Rupert and his commanders knew that Essex's cavalry were only ten miles from Hungerford. If the campaign was to be resolved by a confrontation at Newbury's bridge over the Kennet, Essex was likely to get there first and to be able to concentrate his army quickest. He would therefore win.[1]

The reality proved to be very different. When Rupert's advance guard clattered into Newbury, probably in the late morning, they found the town un-garrisoned and the bridge undefended. There were Parliamentarian soldiers present but they were quartermasters sent ahead by Essex to arrange food and shelter. Rupert's cavalry captured some and sent the rest scampering out of the town to report the ill tidings to the earl, who was evidently still some way to the west. That the Royalists had achieved complete surprise was attested by the first report received in London: 'Several clothiers, who came from Wiltshire' told Parliament that 'the king's forces having notice [of Essex's impending arrival in Newbury] . . . wheeled about that way, and got into the town unexpectedly before Parliament's army'. A plausible local tradition described Newbury's Parliamentarian sympathisers working throughout the previous night to prepare food for Essex's army only to have it seized by the king's equally famished soldiers. The king may himself have been one of the first to take advantage of this unforeseen windfall. According to the detailed record of his movements, on 19 September he had 'Dinner in the field Newbury'. As the Royalist cavalry regiments poured into Newbury's streets, to be followed by Lisle's musketeers and eventually by the first infantry regiments, Rupert sent scouts along the Kennet Valley to establish Essex's precise whereabouts. The presence of the earl's quartermasters confirmed that he had planned to pass through Newbury rather than further south. For Rupert and the king, the key question now was how long they had to assemble their forces before he finally appeared.[2]

II

Two miles to the west, between the villages of Hampstead Marshall and Enborne, the Parliamentarian army was brought to a sudden and unexpected halt by the appearance of the fleeing quartermasters. Although contemporary accounts take the setback in their stride, this was a disaster of the greatest magnitude. The Royalists had somehow outpaced them and in so doing had rendered valueless Essex's masterly feint and reverse march to Cirencester, and the four days relentless tramping through the sodden countryside of Gloucestershire, Wiltshire and Berkshire.

Essex's failure to reach Newbury on 19 September is perhaps the most tantalising question of the entire campaign. The earl should now have been safe behind the Kennet while his soldiers feasted at the tables of Newbury's Roundheads. Instead, he was confronted by the inevitability of the pitched battle that he had sought to avoid. The criticism that Essex received as a result had a major influence on his subsequent reputation and helped create a lasting impression of sluggish, mediocre generalship. Parliamentarian reports skate over the events but *Mercurius Aulicus* set the tone that history has followed. After 'wandering to Hungerford', which took until six o'clock in the morning, the Parliamentarians 'conceived such a necessity of haste that, allowing only some hours halt to the soldiers, they advanced presently towards Newbury'. In other words, Essex dawdled and his men slept while Rupert and his cavaliers rode. Does this explanation stand up to scrutiny? Most accounts criticise Essex for failing to march a mere nine miles in a day. But Rupert reached Newbury early enough for the king to have dinner (the equivalent of lunch today) there. The issue is not therefore whether Essex should have pushed his army more quickly but why he did not send cavalry and dragoons ahead to secure the bridge.

The starting point is Essex's situation when he reached Hungerford early that morning. There is no reason to doubt *Mercurius Aulicus*' assertion that the army did not arrive until six o'clock. The march from Aldbourne, six miles in darkness and appalling weather, is unlikely to have taken less than three or four hours, and the artillery and supply train would have taken even longer. Moreover, as Foster admitted, a significant proportion of the army had taken shelter still some two miles before Hungerford. In the absence of surviving reports from Luke's scouts, we cannot know whether the earl had accurate intelligence of the Royalist cavalry. But his willingness to leave a substantial proportion of his infantry to the north of Hungerford and the protection of the River Kennet suggests that he was aware that they were no longer an immediate threat.[3]

Rupert did, however, leave behind a token presence in the form of a trumpeter, who appeared at the earl's headquarters while it was still at Hungerford. His mission was to request that Royalist doctors should be allowed access to treat the young French nobleman, the Marquis de Vieuville. Whether the trumpeter was in earnest or seeking intelligence is impossible to say for certain but the political stir caused by the Frenchman's death suggests that the motives were, in part at least, genuine. Sergeant Foster, who had seen the corpse, recalled grimly that the trumpeter 'came too late: for the marquis was past their cure'. But Essex agreed to release the body if the Royalists sent men to collect it. Foster added that the 'death of this marquis hath much enraged the enemy, being one whom they did highly esteem'. That was an understatement. *Mercurius Aulicus* accused the Parliamentarians of murdering him in cold blood. Rumours circulated that Essex had demanded three hundred pieces of gold for the body. Three years later, the earl's biographer was at pains to show that the marquis had been killed legitimately while trying to escape his captors but did not attempt to refute the charge that a ransom had been paid. In addition to genuine distress at the loss of an aristocrat in apparently questionable circumstances, there was an element of diplomatic anger in the Royalist response, switching the blame for the death of a senior member of the French nobility from the English king to the king's enemies.

Essex and his senior officers had little time to linger on negotiations with the Royalist trumpeter. To take advantage of his army's night march, he needed to get them on the move again quickly towards Newbury, the next crossing point over the River Kennet. It was unlikely that the king would risk a confrontation further to the east, close to the Parliamentarian garrison of Reading and with the possibility that Waller's new army would appear at his rear. Provided that he could forestall the Royalists from seizing Newbury's bridge, the earl could for the first time be confident of achieving his campaign objectives. Crossing to the south bank of the Kennet was no disadvantage since, unlike the eighteenth century coach road that superseded it, the main route between the bridges at Hungerford and Newbury ran there. It was, however, a rather longer journey than is generally recognised, ten miles as the crow flies yet twelve miles following the road around the edge of Hamstead deer park, a similar distance to Rupert's ride from Lambourn.

Newbury itself was, like Gloucester, a cloth town and inclined politically to Parliament. It therefore promised a chance to feed and quarter the army in relative comfort. Food was undoubtedly a problem after the losses on Aldbourne Chase and, according to Codrington, Hungerford and the surrounding area had been left 'destitute of provision' by marauding Royalists. Essex prepared to take full advantage of this opportunity. Two days later, the Wiltshire clothiers reported to Parliament that 'the Town of Newbury having intelligence' of the earl's 'advancing that way, had provided great store of provisions and other necessaries for both horse and men, for the entertainment of his army'. The unfortunate quartermasters followed to supervise the preparations.[4]

Not surprisingly, there is no suggestion from Parliamentarian sources that the earl's army was unduly dilatory in getting underway that morning. Indeed, the fact that they had assembled from their various quarters and marched, with their cumbersome artillery and baggage, ten miles along a waterlogged heavy clay river valley by the time that the quartermasters appeared with news of Rupert's seizure of Newbury implies that there was in fact little delay. So why did the earl not take the elementary precaution of detaching one of his cavalry commanders, Stapleton or Middleton, to forestall Rupert's coup de main? This is the key question at the heart of Essex's failure on 19 September. Only a matter of months before, he had prevented the king from relieving Reading by taking and holding Caversham bridge. Two thousand cavalry and dragoons posted at Newbury could similarly have stopped any Royalist attempt to force a passage over that bridge, and if the quartermasters could reach Newbury before Rupert, so could the cavalry.

Overconfidence is one possible answer. Having again seen off the Royalist cavalry, Essex may have felt that he had nothing to fear so long as he kept his army in tight formation. But that state of mind would be understandable only if his scouts were telling him that the Royalist army had given up the chase. A more plausible reason, consistent with Essex's personality and military record, is over-caution. There is no evidence that he was able to break down the bridge at Hungerford behind the army. He could not therefore be confident that Rupert would not follow and resume his delaying tactics on the south bank of the Kennet. If the Royalist infantry were coming up, the Parliamentarian army could find itself penned in with its back to the river, able to defend itself in the enclosed valley bottom but once again vulnerable to being starved into surrender. Only by keeping all of his cavalry to hand could Essex be sure of preventing Rupert from inflicting such a potentially fatal delay. This explanation also presumes faulty intelligence, this time on Rupert's location. Yet it runs counter to the earl's behaviour earlier in the day, when he seems to have been confident that Rupert was not in pursuit.

There is another possibility that is consistent with the intelligence picture built up by Sir Samuel Luke over the preceding days. Since the raising of the siege of Gloucester, a recurring theme in his agents' reports had been rumours that Prince Maurice was marching back from the south-west to reinforce the Oxford Army. On 11 September, the Prince and his army had been reported at Cirencester; on 12 September, he was on his way towards Bristol at the head of 4,000 Cornishmen flushed with victory after their capture of Exeter; by the next day, he had reached Bath and his army had grown to include some of the queen's forces. Or, alternatively, Exeter was still holding out but the prince had raised the siege and was indeed at Bath with his entire army. From 14 September, the reporting ceased but that was because Luke was concentrating on the tactical picture and his spies were no longer travelling as far afield. However, TV, who took part in the capture of Cirencester on 16 September, had heard that Maurice and 2,000 horse were in that town, and that the assault had succeeded because the attackers were mistaken for Maurice's men.

The truth was that Maurice had taken Exeter on 7 September and then moved further westwards towards Dartmouth. On 19 September, he was at Totnes. Yet for Essex, the prince and his Cornishmen were a very real threat that he could not ignore. Six days ago, two separate reports had placed them at Bath. Since then, Luke had lost track of their movements. From Essex's perspective, it was therefore entirely possible that Maurice was hovering somewhere to the south, waiting to strike at his flank as he marched east along the Kennet. Some of his soldiers clearly believed that Maurice was an immediate threat; TV told his employer that Maurice's infantry had joined forces with the king before the battle. Furthermore, the earl would not have been alone in worrying about a Royalist army on his southern flank. On 20 September, presumably as the result of similar rumours, Parliament received an urgent request for reinforcements to prevent a Royalist thrust into Hampshire. Nervousness about the dangers posed by Rupert's cavalry and his brother's Western Army are therefore the most plausible explanations for Essex's failure to send an advance guard to make Newbury secure. He can be acquitted of *Mercurius Aulicus'* allegation of undue sluggishness although not, with hindsight, of unnecessary caution. In the circumstances, perhaps the right conclusion is that Prince Rupert won the race for Newbury rather than that the earl of Essex lost it.[5]

III

There was a second intelligence failure on 19 September, this time in Luke's immediate tactical reporting. As news that the Royalists had occupied Newbury spread through the Parliamentarian army, the earl was again obliged to reconsider his options. Scouts were sent to establish the strength of the Royalist position. From them, according to Codrington, Essex understood

> that the whole army of the king were at hand, and that they had not only possessed themselves of Newbury, but that they had made themselves masters of all advantages that could be desired, for the disposing of battle.

The Parliamentarian official account took the same line:

> when we approached within two miles of the town, we might discover the enemy's forces upon a hill; their whole army, having prevented us, were gotten to Newbury and possessed the town.

In fact, the scouts should have reported that the Oxford Army had not yet concentrated and was in no condition to fight a pitched battle. Indeed, it is probable that only the cavalry and Lisle's musketeers were present for most of the day. Although the king must have ridden ahead to reach Newbury in time to eat dinner, most of his exhausted infantry had at least a thirteen mile march from Wantage and cannot have arrived much before late afternoon. The artillery and supply trains will have appeared later still. Meanwhile, Rupert was confronted by the entire Parliamentarian army, with its advance guard drawn up only two miles away. From the low hills to the south-east of Newbury, his scouts will have seen the Parliamentarian column snaking back up the Kennet valley. If the earl continued his advance, it would be impossible for the cavalry to confront infantry and artillery for any length of time. Lisle's musketeers might hold the bridge but a bold general would gather his forces into tight formation, brush the Royalists aside and continue along the south bank of the Kennet towards Reading.

Rupert's response appears to have been to bluff. Exaggerating the size of your army was an acknowledged part of a good commander's repertoire. Earlier in the year, Waller had won the battle of Highnam by persuading a Royalist army that they were heavily outnumbered by his small force. Now the prince sent cavalry and musketeers a mile or so westwards to occupy the flood plain between the Kennet and the Wash Common plateau that ran south towards the parallel valley of the River Enborne. While Lisle's musketeers occupied the enclosures on either side of the lane towards Enborne village, the bulk of the cavalry were drawn up behind them on the open ground of Newbury West Field in front of the town. Parties were also sent up onto the high ground where they were clearly visible to the Parliamentarians. This was a strong defensive position and the display of readiness was sufficient to fool Essex's scouts. Their assessments and the narrowness of the lane along which his troops would have to pass were evidently enough to persuade the earl that discretion was the better part of valour.

Given the intelligence available to him, Essex's caution was understandable. While he might have been able to brush the Royalist cavalry aside, the full Royalist army that he believed to be deployed in front of him could only be defeated by a formal attack, and it was now too late in the day to deploy the Parliamentarian regiments and mount a decisive assault. A half-hearted effort was made to push forward along the Newbury road. Major General Philip Skippon led a forlorn hope of musketeers to skirmish with Lisle's men in the valley bottom, and desultory fighting continued 'without effect, till night did separate them'. Well before then, Essex had abandoned any hope of further progress that day. So concerned was he by the parties of cavalry on the high ground that he ordered Skippon back to take command of the army's flank defences. By that time, the opportunity to brush the Royalists aside had been lost as the king's infantry and artillery began to march across Newbury bridge and out through the town to join the cavalry. From a distance at least, the tired and hungry soldiers will have made an impressive sight. Codrington recalled that the Royalist 'main body ...

were resolute and ready to receive our forces'. Whether they would have been willing or able to fight that evening is questionable but in the event their presence alone was sufficient.[6]

IV

Leaving the forlorn hope to give warning of any Royalist advance, the Parliamentarian army withdrew behind the ditches and hedges of Hamstead Park, two-and-a-half miles west of Newbury, and prepared for yet another night in open fields. Sergeant Foster summed up their position in by now familiar terms:

> we had no provision but what little everyone had in his snapsack. We had now marched many days and nights with little food, or any sustenance, and little sleep ... had not the Lord himself been on our side, they had swallowed us up quick.

Codrington later painted a picture of an army keen to come to grips with the enemy on the following day, 'impatient of the sloth of darkness, and wishing for the morning's light, to exercise their valour', and this became a central feature of the Parliamentarian myth; the army was 'full of courage and in no way disheartened at their hard service'. But Foster's contemporary account emphasises the desperation of their position, facing an enemy with 'all advantages they could desire' and reliant on divine intervention for victory. For the common soldier, it must have seemed that, however hard they marched, the cavaliers were always one step ahead of them.

Parliamentarian propaganda contrasted the calm determination of Essex's army with Royalist over-confidence for the coming battle. In fact, however, the king and his generals were far from certain that there would be a battle at all. Throughout the campaign, Essex had demonstrated an unexpected ability to escape from apparently unpromising situations, and in particular to avoid combat on unfavourable terms. Once it became clear that the earl did not intend to fight that day, a Royalist council of war met to decide how best to exploit the Oxford Army's successful pursuit. In addition to the king, the key figures were Rupert, Forth and Percy. Digby explained that their primary concern was to 'prevent their further evading us'; the Royalist infantry were in no condition for another hard march and another Parliamentarian sidestep to the south would reduce the king to delaying actions by the cavalry of the kind that had already proved unsuccessful. The focus was therefore on ensuring that the Royalists were ready to move at short notice if Essex tried to disengage. Hyde later suggested that the council also considered the option of taking the offensive and forcing Essex to give battle but all agreed that the king

> seemed to be possessed of all advantages to be desired ... So it was conceived, that it was in the king's power, whether he would fight or no, and therefore that he might compel them to notable disadvantages, who must make their way through, or starve; and this was so fully understood, that it was resolved overnight, not to engage in battle, but upon such grounds as should give an assurance of victory.

Rupert's Diary suggests that even the prince was in favour of remaining on the defensive, at least until Lord Percy's ammunition train had arrived.

Reluctance to resort to battle had been a consistent feature of the king's strategy since Bristol. In this instance, it also made practical sense to the military professionals. If Essex could be prevented from a further sidestep south and then eastwards, the Royalists were indeed in a strong position that would only improve over time. Since the earl's army was encamped between two rivers (the Kennet to the north and the Enborne to the south) and would be vulnerable to attack if he tried to cross either, the danger of another attempted evasion was a short term one. Once the Oxford Army had assembled and recovered from its exertions, it should be able to checkmate Essex in all circumstances except a withdrawal due westwards – where he had nowhere to go but back to Gloucester. By holding the road to Reading and the high ground to the south of Newbury, the Royalists could remain on the defensive and force Essex to attack or starve. Although this was a repetition of the strategy used without success in the Severn valley, geography now favoured the king. The pocket occupied by the Parliamentarians was much smaller; the rivers hindered Parliamentarian rather than Royalist movement; Essex had no base such as Gloucester into which he could withdraw; and the main Royalist magazine at Oxford was only a day's ride away.

The council of war's decision is therefore entirely explicable in the circumstances. Unlike Gloucester, it was not the result of a timid reluctance to risk casualties. King Charles and his generals were agreed that because of the terrain and the state of the Royalist army, it was better to allow Essex the initiative and respond to his movements than to force a battle prematurely. If they could survive the next few hours in contact with the Parliamentarians and without the lottery of an unplanned battle, things could only get better. So while scouts and cavalry patrols kept the camp at Hamstead under observation, and officers stood ready to marshal their men if word came that Essex was on the move, most of the Oxford Army took advantage of the food seized in Newbury before collapsing for a few hours exhausted sleep in the open ground south and west of the town. For his part, the king favoured a Mr Cox of Newbury with his unexpected presence for supper and a bed for the night.[7]

Chapter Twelve
'A hill called Big's-hill, near to Newbury'

I

According to local tradition in the nineteenth century, Essex spent the night of 19–20 September in a cottage at Bigg's Hill, almost 2,500 yards to the south of road on which his army had been marching towards Newbury. Although recycled in some recent descriptions of the battle, the story is supported by no contemporary evidence and is one of many myths that can be traced to a fascinating but misleading history and battlefield plan published by local antiquarian Walter Money in 1881. Money knew the area intimately and collected countless stories about the fighting but his effort to relate written evidence to landscape was fundamentally flawed. By relying unduly on tradition and the ground as it was in his time, not in 1643, Money concluded that Essex mounted his assault on a very wide front with the main thrust in the south. Unfortunately, he persuaded S.R.Gardiner of his thesis, which became the basis for the description of the battle in the classic *History of the Great Civil War* and of most subsequent accounts until Alfred Burne re-examined the area in 1950. Burne's analysis gave more prominence to events at the northern end of the battlefield and has been followed by many writers since then, yet uncritical acceptance of Money's theory that the Parliamentarian centre of gravity was to the south has continued to undermine attempts to produce a coherent evidence-based narrative of the overall battle.[1]

Because my interpretation contradicts Money's thesis and the many versions of the battle based upon it, I have set out the evidence in some detail. A few discrepancies are difficult to resolve but, taken overall, the written and landscape evidence can be interpreted to produce a plausible version of the battle that explains most of the individual events described by the participants.

Sources

A dozen more or less reliable eyewitness records have survived. The Parliamentarian official account, which even Royalists seem to have accepted as largely accurate, was said to have been written collectively by a number of Essex's colonels. Three identifiable Parliamentarian soldiers saw the battle from the front line: Sergeant Foster; another Trained Bandsman, from the Blue Regiment, who wrote a shorter version for the newspaper *Certain Informations*; and a published letter by TV, who seems to have been an infantryman in Essex's regiment. Essex's biographer, Robert Codrington, may have served as a volunteer but he lifted some aspects out of context from second-hand sources. A final apparently first-hand description in *Mercurius Britanicus* covers many of the same events but also records two incidents that do not tally with other evidence. Other Parliamentarian accounts drew on these primary sources and added fresh anecdotes plus propaganda disinformation.

For the Royalists, the official record was a letter written for publication shortly after the battle and attributed, in my view convincingly, to Lord Digby. No-one has yet produced a credible theory for the authorship of the detailed post-Restoration notes forming the so-called Prince Rupert's Diary, but they clearly rely on eyewitness evidence. The most comprehensive personal account from the Royalist side was produced four years after the event by Sir John Byron as background for Hyde's *History of the Rebellion*, though he was by then a bitter man with scores to settle. Colonel John Belasyse left an uncharacteristically terse description of the battle in his *Memoirs*, perhaps because his brigade was strongly criticised after the battle, and Welsh lieutenant John Gwyn included a colourful section in his own recollections. *Mercurius Aulicus* published a version of Digby's letter plus anecdotes, polemic and propaganda, and further stories appeared in Restoration histories such as Lloyd's 1668 *Memoirs*.

There is in addition an anonymous account written by the Royalist officer who commanded the forlorn hope deployed overnight to give early warning of Essex's movements and thereafter played an important part in the early stages of the fighting. Among the tantalising clues to his identity are his tone, which suggests a man seeking vindication; his willingness to take on the least attractive jobs (such as picket duty); his description of being snubbed by Sir John Byron and Sir Lewis Kirke when searching for a replacement horse, but then receiving spare mounts from Major Daniel of the Prince of Wales Regiment and Captain Sheldon of Prince Maurice's Regiment; and, later in the battle, his frustration that his request for orders from the king went unanswered. An officer who would have prompted these contrasting responses was Colonel Richard Feilding, the professional soldier who had fallen into disgrace for surrendering Reading prematurely in April, and escaped a death sentence only by the intervention of Rupert, Maurice and the Prince of Wales. Although he does not reappear formally in the Royalist command structure until early 1644, one of Luke's spies reported a Colonel Feilding taking reinforcements from Oxford to Gloucester in late August; and Lloyd later recalled that though the Colonel 'suffered something in reputation about Reading', he 'recover[ed] it at Newbury ... where he stirred not an inch'. Richard Feilding was an experienced officer trying hard to rebuild his career. It seems an unlikely coincidence that the author of the anonymous account was treated poorly by those who would have been loath to forgive Feilding for the loss of Reading, and treated well by partisans of those who had taken his side during the court martial. If the evidence is not conclusive, and Professor Wanklyn has recently suggested an alternative identification, it is in my opinion strong enough to attribute authorship of the letter to Feilding on a provisional basis.[2]

These contemporary descriptions need to be compared with the map record of the area, which fell within the Berkshire parishes of Newbury and Enborne. Walter Money would not have had the benefit of the new generation of detailed Ordnance Survey maps, which started to appear only in 1881, the year in which his book was published, though he does seem to have used early nineteenth-century sources such as tithe maps and the parish enclosure maps produced for Enborne in 1815, Newbury in 1849 and Wash Common in 1858. While generally accurate, they present a picture of the battlefield after the expansion of Newbury, the grubbing out of many hedgerows, and the construction of a new road system and canals such as the Kennet and Avon, and need therefore to be compared with earlier sources.[3]

The best picture of the pre-industrial terrain comes from three main sources produced during the period 1755–1810. Technically most proficient is the first Ordnance Survey drawing, surveyed anonymously in 1808 to a scale of two-inches-to-the-mile, with the rolling landscape meticulously picked out in a delicate hatching. The second, earlier, source is John Rocque's 1761 two-inch-to-the-mile map of Berkshire, an invaluable starting point for the landscape prior to nineteenth century enclosure, giving terrain features, the road system, and a simplified interpretation of field boundaries and buildings. It seems to have formed the basis for a less detailed map of the Newbury district produced by John Willis in 1768. Evidence for actual field boundaries and buildings is contained in the third main source, a collection of large-scale eighteenth century surveys in the Berkshire Record Office, supported by an analysis of the process of enclosure in the county published by the Berkshire Record Society in 2000.

Most important is a five-inch-to-the-mile survey of the manor of Enborne, in which the majority of actual fighting took place. Surveyed by Matthias Baker in 1775, it depicts an almost entirely enclosed landscape of small irregular fields with an average size of under five acres. The Berkshire Record Society analysis concludes that Enborne was already heavily enclosed in 1600 and that the field pattern is indicative of ancient enclosure. Examination of Baker's work alongside tithe, enclosure and Ordnance Survey maps shows how this pattern changed gradually over the following century and comparison with Rocque's 1761 map shows how the latter simplified the late-eighteenth century field pattern (where Rocque divides an area of the northern battlefield measuring an eighth of a square mile into five fields, Baker shows and names fifteen fields). However, Baker and Rocque agree on the size and shape of the five open areas comprising 20 per cent of Enborne parish, which were not enclosed until the early nineteenth century; the course of the River Kennet before canalisation; and, for the most part, the network of lanes and paths in the area.

There is no equivalent single representation of Newbury parish but other eighteenth century maps help to fill in the gaps. The Berkshire Record Society assesses that perhaps only 25 per cent of the land was enclosed in 1600. Immediately south of the town were two large open arable areas known as East and West Fields. Though Rocque suggests that by 1761 they had been largely enclosed, a twenty-inches-to-the-mile 1757 map of land owned by St Bartholomew's Hospital, surveyed by Andrew Northcroft, shows that West Field still came right up to the Enborne Parish boundary between the Kennet and Wash Common plateau. To the south, however, a 1777 plan of the estate of Mr Henry Grace, surveyed by Josiah Ballard to the same scale, shows that enclosures covered the northern slope of Wash Common. Both of these surveys are consistent with the early nineteenth century enclosure maps. Further south again, Rocque's 1761 map, that by Willis of 1768 and the 1809 Ordnance Survey drawing provide a coherent picture of Wash Common, though one surprisingly at variance with interpretations of the battle from Money onwards which ignore the forked stream they show running in a pronounced gulley north-south through the bottom half of the plateau.[4]

Other maps add useful detail. Johannes Jansen's 1646 study of Hampshire and Berkshire seems to show the only bridges over the Rivers Kennet and Enborne at the time, while one-inch-to-the-mile maps of Hampshire by Isaac Taylor in 1759 and

Thomas Milne in 1791 record the fords and bridges over the River Enborne.[5] Despite the inevitable gaps, we have a considerable body of evidence from which to construct a picture of the ground over which the battle was fought on 20 September.

Landscape

That battlefield can be divided into three sections: starting in the west, high ground around and south of Enborne village; in the centre, an area of undulating lower ground; then Wash Common plateau sloping gradually down towards Newbury in the north-east corner. The town straddled the River Kennet, which flowed west-to-east, with the River Enborne following a parallel course some 3,500 yards to the south. As night fell on 19 September, Essex's army was strung out on the high ground running south from Enborne village, while the Oxford Army blocked their advance towards Newbury in the Kennet valley and, according to Parliamentarian scouts, on Wash Common plateau.

A defining feature of the battlefield was the constraint it imposed on movement outside the sleeve of land between the two rivers. The Kennet is a major tributary of the Thames which, before canalisation, meandered between a belt of marsh and water-meadows. The only bridges on Jansen's 1646 map were at Hungerford, Newbury and much further east at Padworth. Rocque's 1761 map identifies no other bridges or fords in the area of the fighting and describes the river's northern bank above Hamstead Park as Benham Marsh. However, Baker's 1775 map shows three small crossing points in Enborne parish, which could be bridges or fords, two about 800 yards northwest of Enborne village and another 1,000 yards or so further east. It is impossible to say whether they were in use in 1643 though there is a reference by Digby to a 'pass on our right hand near the river', which is consistent with the third of them. Nonetheless, for large-scale military purposes, the Kennet was impassable except by the bridge at Newbury; and the adjacent belt of water-meadows, although narrower south of the river than to the north, would still have been poor going for cavalry and artillery, and perhaps even for infantry in formation. Baker's map shows the Hungerford to Newbury road passing within 350 yards of the river at one point, and it may be that the recent prolonged heavy rain had already turned the fields on either side to mud.[6]

Two miles to the south, the River Enborne (called the Auburn[7] in the seventeenth century and the En Brook by Money) is a smaller tributary of the Kennet, which it eventually joins some nine miles east of Newbury. The Enborne's valley is steeper and narrower than the Kennet but not so as to prevent movement; Baker and Isaac Taylor's 1759 map of Hampshire both show numerous fords between Holt and Wash Commons, although an army using them would be extremely vulnerable to attack. In Money's day, the Andover road crossed the river over a bridge at the southern end of Wash Common and Baker shows a bridge in about that spot in 1775, but it had not been built in 1643. Neither Rocque's 1761 map nor that by Taylor produced two years earlier portray a bridge, although Taylor shows a ford in the same area labelled as 'Sheepwash or Monk's Hill', and Jansen in 1646 has no bridges over the Enborne until Knight Bridge (the main road south, three miles east of the battlefield). Travellers from Newbury south-west towards Andover would probably have used the ford at Enborne Row, identified on later maps as part of the old Andover road.

Turning to the three sectors of the battlefield between the two rivers, and starting in the west, a stretch of high ground ran roughly south from the Kennet valley through

Enborne village. At its northern end, between the road from Hungerford and the river, was Hamstead deer park, a series of rolling hills rising to almost 400 feet, bounded by a pale or ditch and surmounted by a house owned by Lord William Craven, a prominent Royalist known best for his romantic attachment to Rupert's mother, the Queen of Bohemia.[8] At the park's eastern edge was a substantial area of woodland known as Enborne Copse, to the south of which was Enborne village, clustered around St Michael's church on the edge of the high ground facing along the road towards Newbury. Further south again, the ground was heavily enclosed and sloped gradually away before rising up again to an area of open land overlooking the River Enborne, described by Baker as Holt Common and by Rocque as Red Hill Common.

East of the high ground was the expanse of low-lying undulating farmland that formed the core of Enborne parish, and across which one of the armies would have to march to get to grips with the other. Drained by streams running north into the Kennet, this rolling landscape is still covered with fields and patches of woodland but, according to Baker's 1775 survey, the density of enclosure was then much higher. Wash Common and Hamstead park aside, the only significant pieces of unenclosed ground were Crockham Heath, about 800 yards south of Enborne village, and Skinner's Green, just over 1,000 yards to the east, at the foot of the northwestern spur of Wash Common; neither measured more than 400 yards in any direction. Otherwise the ground between Enborne village and Wash Common was not conducive to drawing up or moving troops, especially cavalry. The Baker and Rocque maps suggest that many of the hedgerows bordering the enclosures were tall and thick. There were also the streams to cross, and after the recent prolonged spells of rain, it would be hard to move guns and wagons through the heavy clay soil, even using the few available lanes and paths.

Baker and Rocque show only three routes running east-west between the Kennet and Enborne rivers. The main road from Hungerford to Newbury had to bypass Hamstead deer park to the south, after which it forked with the main northern road skirting the eastern boundary of the park through Enborne village and then along the Kennet valley to Newbury (known on the earliest maps and today as the Enborne Road). The second lane ran east along the edge of Crockham Heath and up onto Wash Common (this was called Crockham Heath Road in the early nineteenth century, but the western end is now part of Skinner's Green Lane and the eastern end is called Wheatlands Lane). Two further lanes linked the fork's two prongs, one between Crockham Heath and Enborne village (known today as Church Lane), the other through Skinner's Green (and called Skinner's Green Lane), from where two more lanes (both now disappeared) ran east towards Newbury.

To the south, the final major east-west route (known as Enborne Street Road in the nineteenth century) followed a low, narrow ridge that ran along the north bank of the River Enborne from Holt Common to the Wash plateau. For 1,000 yards or so, Baker and Rocque show the ridge to have been covered by a dense pattern of small enclosures, at the end of which was the small house described by Money as Bigg's Cottage and, to the north, a hillock he called Bigg's Hill. Bigg's Cottage stood opposite the south-western boundary of the large expanse of heathland that covered the rest of the southern ridge up to the Wash Common plateau. Most battlefield plans from Money onwards do not portray this area as open ground, but both Rocque and Baker have it running for some 1,200 yards up onto the plateau (they describe this as Trundle Hill), and to a depth of up to 400 yards, sloping down to the River Enborne.

Wash Common and the Kennet valley to the north would dominate the coming events. Seen from the Hungerford to Newbury road, the northern and western slopes of the Wash Common plateau form a distinct crest, rising from the valley floor just south of the road and then falling away more gradually towards the River Enborne. The plateau's western slopes are steep in parts, especially towards the north where it reaches a height of 410 feet. Baker, Rocque and contemporary accounts agree that these slopes were also heavily enclosed and dotted with small copses. Although not obvious from a distance, the crest is indented. Most significantly, the highest point, the spur which juts out to the northwest, from some angles resembles a round hill. Identification of this spur with the feature described as the 'round hill' mentioned in contemporary accounts was the work of Alfred Burne writing in the mid-twentieth century. This is not a contentious point. No credible alternatives overlook the Kennet valley in the way that eyewitnesses such as Digby describe.

In the 1640s, the central and southern part of the Wash Common plateau was common land, straddling the Enborne-Newbury parish boundary and stretching north from the River Enborne for about a mile and to a depth of some 1,000 yards. Although modern interpretations of the battlefield all describe it as flat, open heathland and therefore good cavalry country, the evidence is rather different. As recently as 1561 'the Wash' had been heavily wooded (a survey counted 350 timber trees plus lopped and pollarded trees and saplings). By 1623, when the mayor of Newbury was looking for wood to rebuild the town's bridge, the big trees had gone[9] and there is no mention of vegetation of any kind in contemporary accounts of the battle. Nor is there any suggestion that the ground over which fighting took place was anything but flat. In fact, however, only the northern end of the plateau was flat; the rest sloped gently down to the Enborne valley. More importantly, as mentioned above, a stream ran in a deep gulley southwards down the centre of the common into the River Enborne. It was noted as a significant feature by Rocque in 1761, Willis in 1768 and all Ordnance Survey maps thereafter (not by Baker because it is just inside the Newbury parish boundary). Although Money includes the gulley but not the stream on his battlefield plan, and Gardiner has both on his map, neither considers their impact and no subsequent account that I have found even mentions them.

The gulley, which started about 500 yards of the common's northern boundary, was steep sided and is today up to sixty feet deep. Two smaller tributary streams joined it from the west. In 1643, less than a century after the area was described as wooded, it would not be surprising if the gully's slopes were still covered with undergrowth. Even without such vegetation, the stream's potential as a constraint on movement and combat, especially cavalry charges, can be judged from the 1858 Enclosure award for Wash Common which records that all three arms of the then canalised 'public watercourse' were five feet deep, seven feet wide at the top and two feet wide at the bottom. As late as 1810, the first one-inch-to-the-mile Ordnance Survey map shows that not a single track crossed the stream, instead either skirting the gulley to the north or following the higher ground from north to south, and the stream was still marked on the successor map in the 1920s.

If the gulley was indeed difficult or even impossible to traverse, that would explain some of the oddities of Royalist tactics on 20 September, including their failure to exploit their numerical superiority in cavalry on the common or to outflank the main Parliamentarian positions. Why then was such a potentially important feature ignored in contemporary accounts? Digby provides a clue. He called the open ground where, from the Royalist perspective, the Parliamentarians were drawn up at the outset of the battle, and where the cavalry action took place, 'a little heath'. This can only be Wash Common yet the full extent of the common land, including the southern spur towards Bigg's cottage, is over a mile long and between half and one mile wide. If, however, the open heath itself covered only the flat ground extending 500 yards from the common's northern edge, and not the area to the south in and on either side of the gulley, that would fit Digby's description and provide a plausible reason why the gulley and stream were not mentioned: quite simply, they were not part of the 'little heath' on which the battle was fought and, from the perspective of the combatants, therefore irrelevant to its outcome.

This interpretation is supported by a close examination of the names used to describe the common land and its various component parts. The central and southern part of the plateau has since the battle been called either Newbury Wash, or Wash, Enborne or Newbury Common, almost interchangeably, and treated as a single entity running from the northern edge of the plateau down to the River Enborne, including the westward extension down Trundle Hill to Bigg's cottage. Baker's map uses this approach, describing all of the open ground that fell within Enborne parish as Wash Common. By contrast, Rocque's earlier map makes a clear distinction between Newbury Wash at the northern end of the plateau and Enborne Common, the westward extension at the southern end. The western arm of the stream and gulley appears to form the dividing line between them. That distinction was still apparent on the first Ordnance Survey maps around 1810 but was lost later in the nineteenth century so that when Money wrote and the new generation of Ordnance Survey maps appeared in the 1880s the whole area was known as Wash Common.

Finally, it is striking that the battle's only eyewitnesses to attach a name to the 'little heath', the Parliamentarian soldier identified as TV, described it as 'a place called Newbury common'. My conclusion is therefore that in 1643 there were two separate areas of open heathland on Wash Common and its southwestern spur: Newbury Wash or Common to the north and Enborne Common to the southwest. They were linked by a stretch of open ground running between the western edge of the plateau and the gulley. The gulley itself was impassable to troops in formation and appeared to eye-witnesses to be separate from either heath. Limiting the fighting to Newbury Common in this way helps explain a number of other anomalies, including why Sergeant Foster and his Blue Regiment comrade both reported being on the Parliamentarian army's right flank when it is clear from the evidence that they spent most of the day towards the northern end of the plateau.[10]

Aside from the gulley and stream, the only significant feature on the Wash Common plateau was a cluster of three tumuli to the north, the largest of which was recorded as 120 feet in diameter and nine feet high. Money thought they were Civil War grave pits but modern archaeology has confirmed their prehistoric origins. Contemporary accounts mention at least one building on or adjacent to the Common's northern end and Baker's 1775 map suggests that they could have been where Wash Farm now stands, at what was then the Common's north-west corner, and further east on its northern fringe.

The plateau was criss-crossed by trackways and paths connecting to a number of lanes. Baker and Rocque agree on the pattern a century or so after the battle. Three lanes ascended the plateau from the west: Enborne Street Lane ran from Holt Common and entered Enborne Common opposite Bigg's Cottage; Wheatlands Lane led from Crockham Heath up a fairly steep slope between enclosures and woodland and entered the Common about 300 yards from its northern boundary; and Cope Hall Lane led from Skinner's Green through tall, thick hedgerows up the steeper north-west face of Round Hill to the Common's north-western edge. Newbury was linked to the Common by Wash Lane, later the road to Andover, which ran south-west from the town up a gentle incline onto the Common where the Falkland Memorial now stands, and an almost parallel route further to the west which Money called Dark Lane. Both Rocque and Baker show it winding up the plateau's northern slope from the Newbury-Hungerford road and crossing two other lanes running west-east from Skinner's Green before entering the Common 600 yards west of the Memorial. Only part of it exists today, petering out in the middle of a field. Burne identified an alternative Dark Lane, now a public footpath following the Newbury-Enborne parish boundary, but it does not appear on the eighteenth century maps and is almost certainly a more recent development. Two lanes led east from the plateau, one described on Rocque's map as Monkey Lane (now shortened to Monks Lane) towards Greenham Common, the other (now a footpath) south-east to a ford over the Enborne at Newtown.

North of the common, the Wash Common plateau sloped gradually down towards the Kennet through another indented and heavily enclosed landscape, with a much more extensive and tighter field pattern than survived into the nineteenth century; Byron described 'a little hill full of enclosures'. Baker's 1775 map and that by Ballard from two years later suggest that many of these fields, including on Round Hill, were surrounded by thick hedgerows; as discussed earlier, those closest to the Kennet were water meadows.[11] In the Kennet valley between the plateau and Newbury was the old-style open arable ground known as West Field, which will have presented a very different aspect from the tightly packed enclosures to the west, with no obstacles to drawing up troops in the conventional manner. The same was true of East Field, a second area of open ground due south of the town.

Newbury itself lay a mile and a half to the northeast of Wash Common, straddling the River Kennet and lacking even the rudimentary medieval defences that had helped to protect Gloucester. The powerful walls of Donnington Castle, north of the Kennet covering the road to Oxford and visible from the battlefield, were too far away to exert direct influence on the fighting. Newbury's population was smaller than Gloucester but it shared the same Puritan sympathies and also owed its prosperity to cloth. Most of its citizens would not have relished the presence of their king or, more especially, his army. Having been secured by the Royalists, Newbury's main military value now was as a base with access across the Kennet to the magazine at Oxford.

Money's thesis

Before leaving the battlefield, the arguments surrounding Walter Money's interpretation of the ground need to be examined. Money's thesis was based on three main planks, beginning with the local tradition that Essex spent the night of 19–20 September in Bigg's cottage, 'situated at the foot of Bigg's Hill ... on the borders of what was formerly Enborne Heath or Down, and in about the centre of Essex's position'. Its position on the lane running along the north bank of the River Enborne was, Money argued, on Essex's route from Hungerford. Because Money also thought that the Parliamentarian artillery and baggage trains were placed in Hamstead park north of Enborne village, he concluded that Essex's overnight camp was spread over a front of almost 3,000 yards from the park to Bigg's cottage, and that the next morning his regiments were drawn up in battle order on the same ground. With Essex based at the right of this line, it made sense to Money that the battle started on the right with an advance from the cottage up onto Wash Common, and that most of the day's fighting took place on the southern half of the battlefield. To support this view, he quoted the official Parliamentarian account ('by break of day order was given for our march to a hill called Big's-hill, near to Newbury, and the only convenient place for us to gain, that we might with better security force our passage') and Hyde's account ('Essex had, with excellent conduct, drawn out his army in battalia, upon a hill called Bigg's Hill, less than a mile of the town').[12]

Money's assertions are, however, demonstrably incorrect. Essex was not advancing south-east from Hungerford and Kintbury, and then along the north bank of the River Enborne past Bigg's cottage, to march around Newbury as Money's theory would demand; he was instead heading towards Newbury through Enborne village and then along the Kennet valley. Every contemporary record of the evening's skirmishing puts it on this more northerly axis; the official account, Foster and Codrington are explicit that the intention was to march to Newbury; and Essex had ordered provisions from Parliamentarian supporters in the town. Moreover, even if Money's theory about a route bypassing Newbury to the south were correct, the pre-industrial road pattern would have taken Essex from Kintbury and Hamstead Marshall across Crockham Heath, onto the Wash Common plateau along Wheatlands Lane, and then towards Greenham Common via Monkey Lane. To pass Bigg's cottage would require an unnecessary diversion and place the Parliamentarian army at the wrong end of Wash Common where no lanes led to the east and the north-south gulley would have impeded progress.

Having been stopped in their tracks around Enborne village, did Essex's army then disperse over a wide front as Money suggests? There is no evidence for their doing so. Foster recalled that having reached 'a village called Embry, about a mile and half from Nubury ... our whole army quartered in the open field'; other Parliamentarian eyewitnesses agreed the approximate distance from Newbury and that the night was spent in the open. Digby described how the Parliamentarians had retreated into 'certain hedges and fastnesses' and placed their baggage train 'upon a hillside under a wood near Hamstead, fenced by hedges and ditches inaccessible'. Given the enemy's close proximity, Essex's perennial fear of the king's cavalry and continuing concern about Maurice's presence to the rear, it is improbable that the earl would march them 2,000 yards forward from the relative security of Hamstead Park to sleep in penny packets among the enclosures around Bigg's cottage, on the extreme southern flank of the battlefield. The evidence suggests instead that the Parliamentarian camp was on high ground covering the eastern edge of Hamstead Park and the adjoining fields. Even without an additional forward march, it will have taken the army many hours to assemble in and around the park; the column must have been about five miles long so when the vanguard was halted at Enborne village, the rearguard had barely reached Kintbury.[13]

Nor is it at all likely that the Parliamentarian army drew up as Money proposed on the following morning, in battle order over the same 3,000 yard front. That tallies neither with the official account's narrative nor with Digby's description of the deployment as it appeared to the Royalists. Moreover, Baker's 1775 map of Enborne manor shows that except on Crockham Heath, where some units may well have assembled, the ground was far too enclosed to draw up an army for offensive action (Money's plan conveniently ignores all field boundaries in this part of the battlefield).

The final issue is the role played by the so-called Bigg's Hill. Although not marked on any maps that I can find, it is a fair assumption that the hillock north of Bigg's cottage now occupied by Boame's and Hill farms was associated at some stage with the name Biggs. Baker identifies the cottage and three small enclosures to the west as 'Bigg's'; the Enborne Parish Records show people with the surname Biggs living in the parish between 1670 and 1718; and Margaret Gelling has traced use of the word Biggs in relation to the Enborne landscape back to 1547. But Money misinterpreted the evidence relating to the hill. To recap, the official account says that 'by break of day order was given for our march to a hill called Big's-hill'. So there is no suggestion that the army camped there. The hillock is, however, immediately to the south of the lane along which the right wing of Parliamentarian cavalry would have passed to advance from Hamstead park and Crockham Heath to Wash Common. It is therefore entirely possible that part of the army was ordered to advance towards Bigg's Hill. The official account adds that 'Big's-hill' was 'the only convenient place for us to gain, that we might with better security force our passage'. Yet seen from the west, the hillock is an insignificant feature compared to the Wash Common plateau behind it and its occupation would have conveyed no military advantage. Indeed, the official account is the only eyewitness record to use the term 'Big's-hill' for the high ground seized by Essex at the opening of the battle. Most call it simply 'the hill'. Digby described it as 'a round hill', Byron 'a little hill full of enclosures' and 'Feilding' as 'ye hill upon our left hand'. Hyde's use of Bigg's Hill probably reflects his use of the official account as one of his sources.

Most telling of all, the official account states that 'Big's-hill' was 'near to Newbury' and Hyde agrees that it was less than a mile from the town. Other contemporaries all give the site of the battle as only a mile or so from Newbury and overlooking the Royalists' overnight position in the Kennet valley. Digby, for example, stated explicitly that from the 'round hill ... a battery would command all the plain before Newbury'. Money's Bigg's Hill is almost three miles from the town and in no sense does it overlook the Kennet valley. Even allowing for the use by some writers of non-statute miles, the discrepancy is just too great to be credible. I have set out the evidence that contradicts Money in detail because it produces fundamental differences between this analysis of the Battle of Newbury and not only Money's version but all those which have been based upon it.[14]

II

Contrary to tradition, Essex will have spent the night of 19–20 September among his regiments in Hamstead Park agreeing plans for the following day with his council of war. It is unlikely that the council gave serious consideration to options other than offering battle on the morning of 20 September. As an experienced professional soldier, Skippon will have had no illusions about the army's dire position; Stapleton's reputation for rash advice makes it unlikely that he counselled caution; Luke had a similar reputation for hot-headedness and, as chief logistician, Merrick will have known better than anyone what would happen to the army if they were penned into their present position. Some writers have attributed a degree of fatalism to the decision to fight and to the way in which Essex subsequently managed the battle. This is unsubstantiated and unfair. He had achieved his first objective and relieved Gloucester, and then done his best to bring Parliament's army back to London in one piece. But his scouts now told him that, against reasonable expectations, the king had brought his infantry hotfoot from the Severn valley to reinforce the cavalry and the terrain now conferred substantial advantages on the Royalist commanders. If the Oxford Army held Newbury and the high ground from Round Hill through Wash Common in strength, it would be extremely difficult for the earl to dislodge them. If Essex stayed put, his army would starve. Yet if he tried yet again to march away, encumbered by guns and ammunition, there was a real danger that his army would be caught on unfavourable ground, perhaps crossing one or other of the rivers to north and south, defeated in detail and destroyed.

Though usually a cautious general, Essex was not afraid to give battle if that was the sensible course, and the odds now were unlikely to improve. The Royalists were close to their main base and would quickly recover from their forced march, while his intelligence suggested that Prince Maurice's Western Army might shortly materialise to his rear. If, however, Essex could seize the initiative, and thereby optimise his strengths and the king's weaknesses, he might (with God's help) force his way through to Reading or at least achieve the kind of bloody stalemate that had enabled him to avoid defeat at Edgehill. Better that than the disaster that had befallen Sir William Waller at Roundway Down; and perhaps Waller might then come to his support, trapping the exhausted Royalists between them.

The main features of Essex's battle plan can be reconstructed from contemporary accounts. As so often before, the earl's first concern was to negate the influence of the Royalist cavalry by fighting the battle as far as possible on enclosed ground, where his infantry could shelter from cavalry attacks behind hedges and ditches, and where the king would be obliged to rely on his own infantry to dislodge them. In such a fight, Essex could be confident of the quality of his infantry regiments compared to those of the Royalists, which his intelligence had been describing in disparaging terms throughout the campaign. Although the Parliamentarian camp at Hamstead would have satisfied this criterion, there was little chance that the king would sacrifice his army in attacking it. If Essex did not take the offensive, the Royalist cavalry would simply blockade and starve them into surrender. Another alternative was to continue the previous evening's advance on a narrow front along the Kennet valley, but the Royalist infantry would then have been on the defensive in favourable terrain; and the king would have been able to attack or bombard Essex's right flank from the Wash Common plateau to the south.

Wash Common plateau was the key to Essex's dilemma. Luke's scouts could tell the council of war that on the northern and western slopes – including on Round Hill, the most northerly spur that dominated the Kennet valley – the ground was tightly enclosed by an irregular grid of small fields surrounded by thick hedgerows. If Essex could gain control of Round Hill, he would outflank the Royalist defence of the valley and his artillery could make Newbury Common untenable to Rupert's cavalry regiments. At best, the king would have to withdraw leaving the road to Reading open. At worst, he would be forced to take the offensive to drive Essex's guns and infantry from the high ground in circumstances broadly favourable to defence. Unfortunately, however, the high ground appeared to be occupied by Royalist troops and, according to some reports, artillery. Essex had therefore to presume that his attack would be opposed and might conceivably fail. His response was to divide the Parliamentarian army into the traditional three components: the vanguard would assault Round Hill;

behind it, the main force would advance to reinforce their success or cover their retreat; finally, a rearguard would protect the artillery and supply trains, and provide a secure base to which the army could retreat if the plan did not succeed. So the army would not be drawn up in battle order but would advance in column and deploy sequentially according to evolving circumstances.

Attacking in column was not unusual; Hopton had done so recently against defended hilltop positions at Stratton and Lansdown. But the plan's implementation would depend in large part on the success of the initial attack. Essex therefore called upon the experienced Scots professionals, Harry Barclay and James Holburn, to conduct it. Their six regiments were reinforced by Essex's own infantry regiment and accompanied by light field guns plus a pair of 9-pounder demi-culverins. The earl himself would lead the attack. This had symbolic value but, if the attack succeeded, it would also place him at the centre of the fighting with probably the best view of the rest of the battlefield; should the attack fail, he would also be well positioned to organise the retreat. Once on the high ground, Essex's infantrymen would be vulnerable to counterattack by Royalist cavalry, so they were supported by a strong wing of cavalry under Sir Philip Stapleton, based on the regiments which had not been engaged at Aldbourne Chase. Behind Essex's vanguard, the bulk of the army would advance under Skippon's command. It comprised ten infantry regiments in three brigades, the second wing of cavalry under Colonel Middleton and the artillery train. A reserve and rearguard would consist of three of the London Trained Band regiments. Skippon's role would be especially important. If the Captain General could not control the battle from Round Hill, it would be up to Skippon to do so from the flanks and rear.[15]

No fully authoritative figures survive for the fighting strength of Essex's army on the eve of the battle. Royalists were still uncertain of its true size, apparently confused by their assessment of the forces confronted at Aldbourne Chase, which Lord Digby had described as comprising only 2,000 cavalry and 5,000 infantry. By contrast, later accounts tended to attribute Essex roughly the same total at Newbury as at the outset of the campaign, 14,000–15,000 men. Neither is plausible in the circumstances. Perhaps the most likely figure is that of 13,000 reported to the Venetians immediately after the battle. This would represent attrition of about thirteen per cent since the army assembled, reflecting cumulative combat losses in skirmishing and the action on Aldbourne Chase, desertion and the continuing impact of disease. A proportionate reduction from the numbers at the opening of the campaign postulated in Chapter Seven would produce a fighting strength of just over 9,000 infantry, and almost 4,000 cavalry and dragoons.

The breakdown in table 4 shows that the two infantry brigades in the vanguard were both smaller than a single regiment's theoretical establishment. This would leave the Royalists with the impression that the initial attack was mounted by only three regiments. More importantly, their numerical weakness restricted the ground that the vanguard could control. Formed up at 'order' and in standard six-deep formation, the seven regiments would together cover a front of less than 600 yards. Two of the three infantry brigades in Skippon's second wave were no stronger. The other four regiments allocated to Skippon were nominally brigaded under Colonel Randall Mainwaring but in practice employed individually. Two were London Auxiliaries and therefore substantially bigger than Essex's own units, as were the three remaining Trained Band regiments held in reserve, each covering a frontage of about 175 yards. Although both cavalry wings comprised six regiments, Stapleton's vanguard had been reinforced and appears to have been significantly stronger than that of Middleton, which had been in the thick of the previous day's fighting on Aldbourne Chase. Cavalry frontages are more complicated to assess because they could use a variety of different formations (one or two lines, three or six ranks, regiments or squadrons) but the maximum likely frontage for Stapleton's wing, deployed in a single line of six ranks, would be 700 yards and 400 yards for Middleton's men.

Table 4:   *Parliamentarian infantry and cavalry organisation at Newbury*

Brigade	Infantry Regiments	Strength
Vanguard		
Barclay	Barclay, Holmstead, Tyrell.	1,050
Holburn	Holburn, Langham, Thompson.	800
	Essex	650
Mainguard		
Skippon	Brooks, Bulstrode, Skippon.	1,050
Robartes	Constable, Martin, Robartes.	750
Mainwaring	Mainwaring, Springate, Blue and Red Auxiliaries.	2,400
Rearguard	Blue and Red Trained Bands, Orange Auxiliaries.	2,300

Wing	Cavalry Regiments	Strength
Stapleton	Essex's Lifeguard, Essex, Dalbeir, Goodwin, Harvey, Norton, Ramsey, 3 commanded troops, 2 or 3 troops of dragoons.	2,600
Middleton	Behr, Denbigh, Groby, Meldrum, Middleton, Sheffield.	1,400

Despite leaving three large guns at Gloucester, the army was still plentifully supplied with artillery, with around forty pieces in total and no indication of ammunition shortages. Drakes and other light guns were deployed liberally among the infantry brigades; Robartes' brigade had four or five, some regiments had one or two in direct support and four were allocated to a forlorn hope. Two demi-culverins accompanied the vanguard but most of the heavier guns were grouped together at the rear in the artillery train. At least five later formed a battery on Newbury Common. The continued presence of a large artillery train makes the earl's dash for Cirencester all the more remarkable and his subsequent much slower pace less inexplicable.

Morale is more difficult to assess. There can have been few illusions among officers or men about the army's prospects. Reading and safety were only a day or so away but they believed that the Royalists had seized the hills in front of them; they probably believed that the Royalist army was as at least as large as their own; they had repeatedly frustrated Prince Rupert's feared cavalry but had yet to face them in pitched battle; and, as ever, they were exhausted and hungry. Sergeant Foster explained that they 'had now marched many days and nights with little food, or any sustenance, and little sleep'. If God was on their side, it was perhaps time for Him to make his preferences known and felt. To encourage Him to make the right decision, Essex made 'religion' the army's field word to facilitate identification on the battlefield. More practically, he also ordered his soldiers to strip 'branches of furze and broom' from the hedgerows to wear in their hats 'for distinction-sake, to be known by one another from their adversaries'.[16]

III

Artillery and ammunition stocks apart, the official Parliamentarian account contains an almost comprehensive description of Essex's order of battle. For the Royalists, the position is precisely the reverse. We know what guns the king had brought with him to Newbury and the broad state of Lord Percy's magazine yet the rest of the picture is more a matter of conjecture. Most subsequent descriptions of the battle state that the two sides were evenly balanced with about 14,000 soldiers each. The Venetians reported 13,000 per side but were almost certainly reflecting Parliamentarian assessments which tended to overestimate the enemy's strength. By contrast, we have seen that Royalist intelligence had underestimated the size of Essex's army throughout the campaign. This uncertainty was compounded by the nature of the fighting at Newbury. Neither side was drawn up in plain sight of the other to allow experienced soldiers an opportunity to gauge their opponents' full strength, before or during the battle. Indeed, the attitude of the Royalist council of war on the evening of 19 September, worried more that Essex would again evade them than about the outcome of a battle, suggests that their common perception was that they enjoyed a significant superiority.

The evidence is, however, that they were wrong. Those detailed figures that have survived from the Royalist side suggest that the active strength of the Oxford Army on 19–20 September had fallen substantially since the siege of Gloucester had been raised and was now rather smaller than the Parliamentarian army facing it across the Berkshire countryside. Hyde wrote that infantry numbers had fallen by 'above two thousand' as a result of desertion and attrition during the march to Newbury. Sir John Byron, who may have provided that figure, agreed. Lieutenant Gwyn recalled in his memoirs that 1,500 soldiers had not reached the battlefield in time. Moreover, some units that had fought at Gloucester were no longer with the army, including Lord Capel's midlands regiments which remained at Worcester, and Lord Rivers' Regiment had been kept north of the Kennet to occupy Donnington Castle and protect the army's rear. Against that, the Prince of Wales Regiment and detachments hastily summoned from the garrisons of Abingdon and Wallingford were welcome last minute reinforcements. When the siege ended, the Royalist infantry had totalled around 9,000. At Newbury, a figure of 7,500 is more likely, perhaps lower still in the front line because some soldiers were 'sick and not able to march', either through exhaustion or illness, forty-one in Sir Gilbert Gerard's brigade alone.[17]

Gerard commanded one of five brigades of very different sizes, drawn from almost forty infantry regiments. The breakdown at figure 5, which comes from a wide range of contemporary sources and modern research, suggests that the brigades of Gerard and Colonel John Belasyse contained the majority of the regiments that had marched with Rupert to Bristol two months previously, reinforced primarily from the Thames valley and Bristol garrisons. Since Lisle's commanded musketeers seem to have been detached from the Bristol reinforcements, Belasyse's eleven regiments would not have been much more than 1,800 strong, with more pikemen than musketeers, while Sir Gilbert Gerard's brigade can be deduced to have comprised six regiments with a combined strength of about 1,000. A third brigade, probably the largest with up to 2,000 men, was commanded by Sir Nicholas Byron and included the King's Lifeguard, a composite regiment from the Oxford garrison under Charles Gerard's lieutenant colonel, Edward Villiers, and the newly arrived Prince of Wales Regiment. As discussed previously, a fourth brigade had until at least 7 September been led by Colonel Conyers Darcy, who was mentioned in contemporary Royalist accounts as one of the senior officers involved in the day's fighting, so it is reasonable to conclude that he was still leading the rump of the queen's northern infantry, four regiments with around 800 men. The fifth brigade, formed by the Welsh and marcher soldiers of Sir William Vavasour, comprised five regiments, probably no more than 1,000 strong. Finally, it is clear that Lieutenant Colonel George Lisle's musketeers were still operating as an independent formation, though by now reduced to around 900 men. Frontages would have ranged from 170 yards for Darcy's brigade to around 420 yards for that of Sir Nicholas Byron.

Table 5:   *Royalist infantry organisation at Newbury*

Brigade[18]	Regiments[19]	Strength
Belasyse	Marching units: J Astley, Bolle, Dutton, Herbert, Owen (plus Rivers in Donnington Castle). Garrison units: B Astley, Belasyse, Prince Maurice, Washington (all Bristol); Dyve (Abingdon); Blagge (Wallingford).	1,800
G Gerard	Marching units: G Gerard, Lloyd, Molyneux, Stradling. Thames valley units: Northampton, Vaughan.	1,000
N Byron	Marching units: Grandison (ex-Fitton), Lord General. Thames valley units: King's Lifeguard. Oxford garrison: composite regiment (drawn from C Gerard, Pennyman, Percy, Pinchbeck and Queen's Lifeguard). Midlands: Prince of Wales, Sandys.	2,000
Darcy	Thames valley units: Blackwell, Darcy, Eure, Tyldesley.	800
Vavasour	South Wales and Marcher units: five regiments, perhaps Bassett, Mansell, Price, Vavasour, Williams.	1,000
Lisle	Commanded musketeers	900
Total		7,500

The cavalry had suffered a similar level of attrition. Still 6,000 or so strong after Gloucester, the subsequent stalemate had encouraged the Earl of Sunderland and many others to take impromptu leave and not all will have been able to catch up with the army, even if they wanted to. Thereafter, two regiments had been destroyed at Cirencester, losing 400 men, and others had stayed behind at Worcester, including that of Colonel Sandys. Byron later claimed that as many cavalrymen had 'been lost by the way' as the 2,000 foot. Even if that was an exaggeration, Hyde's estimate that Rupert had fewer than 5,000 cavalrymen with him at the beginning of the march from the Severn valley is plausible and suggests that by the time they reached Newbury, after a hard ride and the skirmish at Aldbourne Chase, a figure closer to 4,500 is a realistic total.[20]

Like the infantry, the Royalist cavalrymen were still divided into five brigades. Those of Sir John Byron and Colonel Charles Gerard were well established, and had clear regional affiliations, in the midlands and north respectively. Evidence for Lord Carnarvon's appointment in place of Aston has been considered earlier, and it is likely that his brigade was based around the west country regiments with whom he had served before and after Bristol, including Vavasour's cavalry. The two remaining brigades, commanded by Rupert and Wilmot, comprised the core of the pre-Edgehill regiments, including Prince Maurice's Regiment, hotfoot from Bristol. Additionally, according to Belasyse, his infantry brigade had been supplemented by a single cavalry unit, probably that of Sir Charles Lucas, and the king was as usual protected by his Lifeguard. All five brigades were probably 800–1,000 strong, the usual size of Royalist cavalry formations at this stage of the war, and each therefore covered a frontage of over 500 yards when drawn up in squadrons of three ranks.

Table 6:   *Royalist cavalry organisation at Newbury*

Brigade	Regiments[21]	Strength
Rupert	Prince Maurice, Percy, Prince of Wales, Prince Rupert.	
Wilmot	G Digby, Lord General, Northampton, Wilmot.	
C Gerard	Dalton, Eure, C Gerard, Molyneux, Queen's Lifeguard, Tyldesley.	All
J Byron	T Aston, J Byron, J Digby, Morgan.	c.800–1,000
Carnarvon	Andover, A Aston, Carnarvon, Chandos, Pye, Vaughan, Vavasour.	
Others	King's Lifeguard, Lucas.	

Hard evidence for the Royalist artillery comes from the Ordnance Papers, which contain an order sent from Newbury to Oxford on 20 September to provide twenty round shot 'for the pieces of cannon which we have here'. In response, Sir John Heydon despatched 380 cannon balls in a proportion that shows that Lord Percy had hauled with the army an artillery train of nineteen guns comprising the two 24-pounder demi-cannon and two 15-pounder culverins, three 12-pounders, seven 6-pounders, a 5-pounder saker and four 3-pounders. Other pieces (including mortars) had been returned to Oxford or local commanders. As to munitions, the Ordnance Papers show that since withdrawing from Gloucester, Percy had built up a stock of over 100 barrels of powder, and Digby agreed that the train had carried around this amount with it from Sudeley Castle. On the basis of usage at Edgehill, when only twenty barrels were expended, Percy could be forgiven for thinking that the army's needs had been provided for. He should have been equally confident about supplies of cannon balls. Almost 1,100 were received between 23 August and 1 September from Bristol, Oxford and Soudley, and the final stages of the siege do not appear to have made great inroads into these stocks; moreover, the ten smaller field guns sent from Oxford in early September had been deployed with thirty round shot and ten case shot apiece.[22]

Royalists command arrangements remain opaque. There are no suggestions in contemporary accounts that Lord Forth played the major role in controlling the battle. A reference to orders given by 'my Lord Lieut-General' has been attributed to Forth but from the context is more likely to have come from Wilmot as Lieutenant General of Horse. According to some contemporary accounts, Forth spent the battle charging with the main body of Royalist cavalry, which does not suggest that his was the controlling hand on the Royalist side. The most likely alternative candidate was of course Rupert, who was certainly the most active Royalist general, appearing throughout the day across the battlefield. His influence was considerable at the tactical level but he too seems not to have been exercising overall control. The unusually frequent invocation of decisions taken by the council of war may imply that the king was involved more closely than normal in tactical decision-making, perhaps as part of a de facto triumvirate with his nephew and senior general. Further down the command chain, Wilmot played an influential role in drawing up the Royalist cavalry; and Belasyse's memoirs placed Sir

Jacob Astley on the battlefield while Parliamentarian newspapers as usual claimed that he had been killed in the fighting, but although Sir Jacob had recovered from the wound sustained at Gloucester (he was shortly appointed governor of Reading), his influence also appears to have been limited.

The nature of the terrain and the fighting would create additional confusion in the chain of decision making. With only primitive communications and no central staff, the command structure would be difficult to sustain in prolonged and dispersed fighting. Officers such as Digby and Sir Lewis Kirke were used to pass orders and messages around the battlefield, but Royalist accounts suggest that for much of the day, senior commanders were not in control of events. In consequence, the initiative often passed down the command chain to brigade and regimental commanders or even more junior officers. Here, the composition of the Oxford Army became a critically important factor. Among the cavalry officers was a high proportion of young, aristocratic amateur soldiers such as Viscount Andover, Lord Chandos and the Earl of Northampton who were socially superior to many of their senior officers and, at the end of a frustrating campaign, determined to destroy the rebel army that seemed to be all that stood between their king and a crushing military victory. Hyde recalled 'the precipitate courage of some young officers who had good commands, and who unhappily always undervalued the courage of the enemy'. This mood, and the ability or otherwise of the Royalist chain of command to control it, would have a major impact on the outcome of the battle.

The morale of the Royalist rank and file, especially the infantry, would prove to be equally influential. Cohesion had been poor from the outset. At Gloucester, their mood had become bleaker as the siege progressed. Since then, Hyde judged that desertion had been one of the main causes of the dramatic decline in the strength of the infantry. A succession of hard marches in appalling weather with little sustenance cannot have improved the picture. From the Parliamentarian side, Codrington later imagined the Royalist army 'incapable of sleep, their enemy being so nigh . . . [as they] thought upon the melancholy element of which they were composed'. But Lieutenant Gwyn's recollection that the worst aspect of the previous days marching 'in most men's opinion . . . [was that] we were like to drop down every step we made with want of sleep' makes it more likely that the soldiers simply collapsed into exhausted stupor.[23] It was not fear or melancholy that depressed their spirits but physical tiredness and war-weariness at the end of a long campaigning season.

To sum up, the traditional picture of Newbury as a battle between two evenly matched armies is incorrect. The evidence suggests that Essex had 13,000 men and forty guns against the king's 12,000 men and nineteen guns. Significantly, the Royalist superiority in cavalry, which many writers from the Venetian Secretary onwards judged to have offset their weakness in infantry, was not as great as generally believed: Rupert with 4,500 or so men had an advantage of well under a thousand over the earl's force of approaching 4,000 cavalrymen and dragoons. By contrast, Essex's advantage in infantry (9,000 against 7,500) was substantial, especially when reinforced by the much larger number of light field guns deployed in their support. Firepower was the key. On an enclosed battlefield, cavalry and pikemen took a back seat compared to muskets and artillery. Two-thirds of Parliament's infantrymen were armed with matchlock muskets but only half of the king's were similarly equipped, which meant that at the outset Essex enjoyed a numerical superiority of 6,000 to under 4,000 musketeers, a better than three-to-two advantage in the crucial battle-winning weapon.

Chapter Thirteen
'Let us fall upon them'

Unlike the better known Civil War battles of Edgehill, Marston Moor and Naseby, there are no near-contemporary maps of the fight at Newbury on 20 September 1643. Both sides will have had generic battle plans, but this was not to be a day for the text book; nor did events follow the popular conception of English Civil War combat. The ground was hilly and partly enclosed; neither side was drawn up at the outset in the approved manner with infantry in the centre and cavalry on the flanks; the fighting was not short, sharp or decisive; and the outcome was ambiguous and disputed. Although the two sides had camped less than three miles apart and each had known broadly where the other was when night fell, Newbury was not so much a set-piece engagement as a confused encounter battle over which neither set of commanders exercised effective control. To bring some form to this chaos, I have therefore divided the battlefield into three sections: the Kennet valley in the north, the slopes of Round Hill in the centre and Newbury Common to the south.

Both sides' plans are clear enough. As in the Severn valley, King Charles and his council of war had decided to wait upon events while Essex had developed a bold plan and was preparing to seize the initiative. The success or failure of his attempt to take and hold the high ground south-west of Newbury would dictate the course of the battle and perhaps its final outcome. But Essex's implementation of his plan and the Royalist reaction to it were to become the subject of heated disagreement between the two sides and the cause of considerable confusion among historians of the battle.

Round Hill, early morning[1]
At the Parliamentarian camp on the high ground in and around Hamstead Park, Essex's army was roused and assembled well before dawn. If all the stories circulating after the battle were true, it had been a busy night. One described a formal challenge issued by the king, others an attempt on the earl's life by an old woman, who was at the same time a Royalist agent, invulnerable to pistol fire and the harbinger of a Parliamentarian victory. According to one of the first reports published in London, Essex decided on his plan only after Royalist artillery opened fire from Newbury Common and he had gone 'from regiment to regiment ... [putting] the question of a battle unto them'. Vicar's *Parliamentary Chronicle* had the earl warning his men that the enemy had all the advantages before they shouted out in reply: 'Let us fall upon them! We will, by God's assistance, beat them from them all'. Though Essex would not have wanted to send a noisy warning of impending movement to any Royalist scouts, he

would certainly have sought to motivate and inspire the cold, tired and hungry men in the vanguard that he was about to lead personally to storm the high ground away in the darkness to the east.

With the benefit of hindsight, Parliament's partisans agreed that the army's morale was high that morning. Codrington recalled that the army was 'impatient of the sloth of darkness, and wishing for the morning's light, to exercise their valour'. Sergeant Foster wrote that he and his comrades advanced 'with most cheerful and courageous spirits'. Though this was primarily propaganda, the soldiers were at least dry. It had not rained during the night and did not do so throughout the coming day. This would also make movement easier for both sides, but especially for the Parliamentarian artillery train, which would have to drag the heavy guns across country and then to the top of a steep slope before they could be brought into action.

Dawn broke shortly before six o'clock. By this time, the vanguard was advancing towards the round hill at the northwestern edge of the Wash Common plateau which formed 'the only convenient place for us to gain, that we might with better security force our passage'. Essex led the column of seven infantry regiments, his own regiment first, followed by Barclay's brigade and then Holburn's. In addition to light guns, they had with them a pair of 9-pounder demi-culverins. Sir Philip Stapleton and his wing of cavalry were to accompany them onto the plateau. Presuming that Essex had continued to follow the conventional tactic of rotating his cavalry formations daily between the vanguard and rearguard while on the march, Stapleton's five regiments would have been at the back of the column during the previous day and therefore camped some way south of Enborne village. That would have enabled them to advance through Crockham Heath, past Bigg's Hill and onto the open ground of Newbury Common along Wheatlands Lane, the only route to fit contemporary descriptions of the battle.[2] It is, however, unlikely that Stapleton's men pushed up the slope until the infantry had secured the crest and when they did so only two regiments were initially involved, which suggests that their preparations and advance had not gone smoothly. Meanwhile, to the north, the forlorn hope of musketeers deployed across the Enborne Road provided early warning against any Royalist patrols scouting along the Kennet valley.

From Hamstead Park to the foot of Round Hill was a distance of 2,500 yards, an hour's march for the Parliamentarian infantry in the semi-darkness. It cannot have been an easy beginning to the day. The heavy clay soil was sodden from the recent rain, there was a stream to cross and the ground was heavily enclosed with few convenient paths. Regiments would not have kept their order in these circumstances so Skinner's Green, the open land at the foot of Round Hill, gave them a welcome chance to reform before the final attack. Essex is unlikely to have envisaged storming the hill in the dark but he will have wanted to give the Royalists whom he believed to be occupying it as little warning as possible. From the official account it is evident that, even at this late stage, the Parliamentarians thought that they were advancing against a defended position: Essex attacked only when 'he perceived that the enemy's forces had possessed themselves of that hill'; Codrington thought that the full Royalist army, including artillery, had been formed up on the brow of the hill to meet them; other Parliamentarian reports agreed: as dawn broke, Essex found the Royalists 'set in battalia upon a place called Newbury common'; 'by day break, the enemy's foot were come to the hill'; 'we advanced towards the enemy, who were prepared for us'.

Since there were no indications that his advance had yet been detected and it was essential not to allow the king time to reinforce the Royalist defences, Essex cast caution to the winds and from Skinner's Green led his seven infantry regiments storming up the north-west slope of Round Hill. The earl's own tawny coated regiment was at the front, at least 650 strong and commanded by Lieutenant Colonel Joseph Bamfield. Recruited mainly from the county of Essex, it had performed well at Edgehill, spearheaded the capture of Cirencester and supported the cavalry counterattack at Aldbourne Chase. Given the tightly packed small fields covering the hillside, an attack could only be mounted with the desired momentum along Cope Hall Lane, which was bounded by earth banks surmounted by hedgerows and recorded in the Enborne enclosure award as thirty feet wide. Hopton's Cornish infantry had undertaken successful attacks in similar circumstances at Stratton and at Lansdown, when the pikes had advanced up the road with parties of musketeers moving from hedge to hedge on either side. A phalanx of sixteen-foot pikes at close order, perhaps ten wide and twenty deep, spurred on by Essex and his officers, adrenalin and (very probably) alcohol, would have been difficult for any defenders to halt in the morning half light, especially with the element of surprise favouring the attackers and musketeers firing volleys from the hedgerows.

The attack was a complete success. According to the official account, Essex 'charged so fiercely that he beat [the Royalists] from the hill'. TV, who seems to have been serving in Essex's Regiment and was therefore at the head of the column, described how they 'drew up towards them, [and] fell on them pell-mell'. Soon after sunrise on 20 September, the earl was in undisputed possession of Round Hill and the northwestern side of Newbury Common with infantry and artillery, and had therefore secured his initial objective. But this opening phase of the battle poses a number of important questions. There is no mention of casualties to either attackers or defenders. Parliamentarian accounts implied that the Royalist defenders abandoned their positions and ran away, although they do not explain what happened to the Royalist guns which they claimed had already been deployed. By contrast, the Royalists asserted later that Round Hill and the rest of the high ground running south from the Kennet valley was unoccupied when Essex seized it. The circumstances of Essex's capture of Round Hill subsequently provoked a bitter war of words in the competing London and Oxford newspapers. Both sides' arguments have a ring of conviction but although Essex and his partisans seem to have been genuine in their belief that they had assaulted and captured a defended position, the facts suggest that the Royalist version was closer to the truth. In other words, the king and his generals had been caught napping.

Sir John Byron was in no doubt that there had been a blunder:

> Here another error was committed, and a most gross and absurd one, in not viewing the ground, though we had day enough to have done it, and not possessing ourselves of those hills above the town by which the enemy was necessarily to march the next day to Reading.

Lord Digby accepted that the Royalists had erred in failing to occupy 'a round hill not suspected nor observed by us the night before, from whence a battery would command all the plain before Newbury, where the king's army stood'. Both comments were made by senior officers who should have been aware of the facts. But a third contemporary account makes clear that, contrary to the views of Byron and Digby, action had actually been taken the previous evening to secure the vital high ground. According to the anonymous officer who was probably Colonel Richard Feilding, after the Parliamentarian advance towards Newbury had been halted, Prince Rupert 'commanded me to advance with [a detachment of cavalry] to the hill upon our left hand, from whence we sent out parties all night, which gave His Highness satisfactory intelligence'. The presence of these patrols would explain why Essex thought the high ground had been occupied by the Royalists. If, however, 'Feilding' was there, why did his patrols fail to observe Essex's approach march? For it is equally clear from this account that 'Feilding' and Rupert did not become aware that Essex had seized Round Hill until they attempted to occupy it themselves, a little later that morning.

'Feilding's' men could have been deployed in the wrong place, asleep or simply inattentive. Royalist scouts had proved notoriously ineffective throughout the campaign and were now expecting Essex to withdraw rather than advance. Nonetheless, not to maintain a watch on what was the most direct route for Essex to have taken to mount a surprise attack on the main Royalist camp around Newbury itself would have been an extraordinary oversight. From 'Feilding's' own version of events, the most likely reason is that as the senior officer on the Wash Common plateau, he had returned to Newbury before dawn to brief Prince Rupert and perhaps the Royalist council of war. When he left the plateau, Essex's vanguard was still invisible in the darkness. It therefore seems most likely that the patrols, exhausted after four days pursuit and a night on high alert, subsequently relaxed their guard knowing that the king's army would soon be deploying. So while 'Feilding' briefed the Royalist commanders, Essex led his regiments up Round Hill, scattering the patrols; and in their elation at reaching the crest alive, the Parliamentarians believed that their irresistible charge had swept away an invisible enemy.

Gaining a foothold on the high ground was one thing, keeping it entirely another. The earl had only 2,500 infantrymen with him and their frontage, drawn up in Dutch-style battalions of 300 to 500 in the standard six-deep formation, would have stretched for no more than 600 yards. This was sufficient to do little more than secure the top of Round Hill and the northwestern end of Newbury Common. The two demi-culverins were sited close to the end of Cope Hall Lane from where they commanded not only the Common but the floor of the Kennet Valley, which was well within their range for indirect fire. Contemporary accounts suggest that Essex's Regiment was at the right of the short Parliamentarian line on the northwest fringe of Newbury Common, with Colonel Harry Barclay's brigade to their north, on either side of the hedges lining the Common's edge, and Colonel James Holburn's brigade at the top of the northeastern slope of Round Hill, with an excellent view towards Newbury.

All of this was as yet unsuspected by the king and his generals. Their strategy left Essex to take the initiative but they had presumed that he would not do so, or at least not quickly. That is not to say that the Royalist camp was inactive. As Essex advanced towards Round Hill, tired soldiers were being marshalled on East and West Fields, the large areas of open arable ground to the south of Newbury. As they assembled, they were given the field word 'Queen Mary' for battlefield identification. The likely plan at this stage was for some of the cavalry to deploy on the left, on Newbury Common; for Lieutenant Colonel George Lisle's commanded musketeers to hold the enclosures to the north of the Common; and for the rest of the cavalry and infantry to block the road to Newbury itself. This would have been an entirely sensible way to force Essex to either attack on unfavourable terms, take the risk of being caught on the march during another attempted disengagement across one or other of the rivers, or wait to be starved into surrender.

Rupert was his usual energetic self. He agreed with the Royalist strategy and was now at the forefront of putting it into effect. His first priority was to occupy Round Hill. As dawn broke, he took the 900 or so commanded musketeers, led by Lisle and the experienced Lord Wentworth, together with his own Lifeguard and a party of cavalry under 'Colonel Feilding' and Major Paul Smith of Lord Wilmot's Regiment, to seize the high ground. From Newbury, they will have marched south-west up the gentle slope towards Round Hill following the lane that runs conveniently from West Field to the Common just to the east of Round Hill (Money's Dark Lane). They had no advance warning that the Parliamentarians had got there first. According to 'Feilding', 'I drew the party into a close that contained a considerable part of the hill, then we discovered the enemy and there began the service'. This measured description of an initial exchange of musket fire does not do justice to the importance of the incident. For Rupert, the unexpected appearance of a substantial body of the enemy on the high ground above Newbury will have been as devastating a blow as Essex had suffered by the prince's occupation of Newbury the previous day. It undermined completely the king's strategy for the battle. Leaving 'Feilding' and Lisle to skirmish with the enemy on the hill, he returned to Newbury to help direct the Royalist response.

Kennet valley, early morning[3]

The Royalist council of war reconvened at once to digest the implications of Rupert's unwelcome discovery. Byron's account, describing the failure to secure Round Hill as 'a most gross and absurd' error, suggests that the meeting was acrimonious. The arguments in favour of caution that had dominated discussion the evening before had certainly been discredited. Whatever the state of the Oxford Army and its magazine, Essex had transformed the tactical picture and reinforced the case of those who urged decisive action to smash his army. Digby's letter of 22 September gave the official version of why the king now decided to give battle at Newbury. The Royalists had expected Essex to try to evade them overnight but when dawn broke

> we discovered them settled in the most advantageous way imaginable of receiving us ... their foot, their horse, and their cannon planted with much skill, not only for molesting us, and preserving themselves, but even for temptation to us to assail them.

Digby then described the Parliamentarian order of battle:

> having lodged their baggage and principal reserve both of horse and foot upon a hillside under a wood near Hamstead, fenced by hedges and ditches inaccessible...and having disposed another principal part of their strength betwixt that and a place called Enborne, in strong hedges, and houses, with apt batteries on both sides, for bravadoes sake, or to invite us, they had drawn out into battalia into a little heath on the south side of Enborne three bodies of foot both lined and flanked with strong bodies of horse and under favour of cannon.

This is clear eyewitness evidence. Either Digby had seen the Parliamentarian army himself or he talked to someone who had. It is also an accurate portrayal of Essex's deployment as it would have appeared not to Rupert but from the Wash Common plateau shortly after the storming of Round Hill. The three bodies of foot tally with the two brigades and one large regiment in the vanguard, supported by the first echelon of Stapleton's cavalry and the pair of demi-culverins. As discussed previously, the 'little heath' could only have been Newbury Common, and Digby goes on to explain that from the heath the Parliamentarian vanguard controlled 'a round hill ... from whence a battery would command the plain before Newbury'. Behind them, Skippon was marshalling the main part of the army in and around Enborne village and the baggage train, escorted by Middleton's cavalry, was still gathered in Hamstead Park.

According to Digby, it was in part the presence of what seemed to be an exposed fraction of Essex's army on the Common that decided Royalist tactics. The vanguard, 'a little Battalia' well ahead of the rest of the army, presented the 'tempting prospect' that they should be able to defeat it and gain control of the Wash plateau without great difficulty. But there was also, as at Gloucester, a matter of honour. The council persuaded itself that the Oxford Army deployed in West Field was now so vulnerable to artillery on Round Hill that

> unless we possessed ourselves of that hill, there was no holding that field, but the king must have retreated with his army thence, the dishonour of which, I believe you will easily consent ought to outweigh the hazard of attempting them.

Byron agreed:

> the enemy ... had brought up two small field pieces and was bringing up more, whereby they would both have secured their march on Reading (the highway was lying hard by) and withal so annoyed our army which was drawn up in the bottom ... that it would have been impossible for us to have kept the ground.

The council decided, apparently unanimously, to divide the Oxford Army into three main formations to recapture Round Hill and then defeat the rest of Essex's forces. Their battle plan can be deduced from the army's subsequent deployments. Sir William Vavasour's infantry brigade would remain in the Kennet valley to prevent a dash for Newbury and to threaten the Parliamentarian left flank, supported almost certainly by artillery and, at the outset, some cavalry, probably Rupert's brigade which did not appear on Newbury Common until later in the day. The task of pushing the Parliamentarian vanguard from Round Hill, where Lisle's 900 commanded musketeers were already in action, was given to the two Byrons: Sir Nicholas in charge of two brigades of infantry, his own and that of Colonel Conyers Darcy; and his nephew, the acerbic Sir John, with two regiments from his cavalry brigade 'in case the enemy's horse should advance towards them'. Both were trusted commanders with a powerful force of about 3,300 foot and 500 horse at their disposal. The remainder of the Oxford Army would deploy to their left on Newbury Common, the cavalry brigades of Wilmot, Carnarvon and Charles Gerard, plus the remainder of Sir John Byron's brigade, together some 3,000 strong, alongside the infantry brigades of Colonels John Belasyse and Sir Gilbert Gerard, 2,200 men in total supported by a powerful artillery battery.[4]

Newbury Common was the focal point of the Royalist plan; Lord Forth was here and Rupert would be for much of the day. And the plan made sense. Once the Common had been cleared and Round Hill secured, the Royalists could use their cavalry brigades to envelope Essex's right flank and drive his army back against the River Kennet. If this left hook were successful, the Parliamentarians would then have little choice but to surrender or starve. Alternatively, with the high ground under their control, the Royalists could revert to their previous cautious approach and wait for Essex to make the next move. Either way, speed was now of the essence. The less time Essex had to reinforce his vanguard, the easier it would be to dislodge him.

Round Hill, early morning[5]

Given the physical condition of the Oxford Army, it is unlikely that its response was uniformly rapid or enthusiastic. At one extreme, local tradition in Newbury recalled Lord Carnarvon riding through the town 'with his sword drawn and jocosely taking measure of a gate (through which he proposed bringing Essex as a prisoner) to know whether it was wide enough for the Parliament General's [cuckold's] horns'. At the other is the romantic story of Lord Falkland, weary of war and despairing of the future, dressing himself carefully in a clean shirt before seeking death on the battlefield. From the evidence of their performance in combat, morale among the infantry regiments was at best variable. They do not seem to have moved quickly into position. But most of the Royalist cavalrymen probably shared Carnarvon's view that the battle was already as good as won, and the two freshest brigades, Wilmot's and Carnarvon's, appear to have reached Newbury Common very early in the day.

Fighting had, however, already started in the fields on the northeastern slope of Round Hill. Lisle's musketeers clearly did their best to evict Essex's vanguard, which was acknowledged by the Parliamentarian official history to have been 'hotly charged'. But the two sides are unlikely to have come to close quarters. Lisle's 900 men were heavily outnumbered. The seven Parliamentarian regiments on Round Hill together comprised around 2,500 officers and men, of whom two-thirds will have been musketeers; and, unlike the Royalists, Essex already had field guns deployed in support.

This first stage of the fighting was a prolonged musketry dual along the enclosed north-east slope of Round Hill, with the Parliamentarians enjoying the advantage of position, firing down hill into the Royalist ranks. At this point, only one of the Parliamentarian brigades seems to have been directly engaged (probably Holburn's), which would explain why Lisle's men were able to maintain the exchange. But from 'Feilding's' account it is clear that the Parliamentarians eventually began to gain the upper hand, for the Royalist musketeers pulled back and 'Feilding's' detachment of cavalry came under intense musket and artillery fire instead. His own horse was hit in the shoulder. With his men falling around him, 'Feilding' drew the party through a hedge into the next field, leaving Lisle's musketeers without support. Not surprisingly, the musketeers cried out for the cavalry to return. 'Feilding' therefore 'returned to the first mentioned close and was very slowly followed by reason of the straitness of the passage' but eventually gathered enough of his men to mount a charge against the Parliamentarian infantry. He could see about 1,000 Parliamentarians and a light gun drawn up on the far side of the field. The charge was not a success:

as I was charging my horse was shot again in the breast and faltered with me, for that, I being out of hopes to do other service than to lose myself, I gave orders to the party in these very words in Major Smith's hearing – 'Fall on, my Masters! For I must go change my horse.

By the time 'Feilding' had found a replacement mount (not an easy task because of his unpopularity with much of the army – both Sir John Byron and Sir Lewis Kirke refused his pleas for assistance) and made his way back to Round Hill, he found the remains of his party, about forty strong, skulking at the bottom of the slope. When he tried to lead them back into the attack they told him that Wilmot personally had ordered them to stay where they were. With the failure of the cavalry charge, the Royalist musketeers also retreated. Lisle was wounded during the day, probably during this engagement, and it may be that with the loss of his leadership, his men could no longer be persuaded to stand. Whatever the cause, their withdrawal left Essex once again in undisputed control of Round Hill.

Newbury Common, morning[6]

On Newbury Common, the Royalist cavalry regiments pouring out of the lane from Newbury town were marshalled by Lord Wilmot, the king's Lieutenant General of Horse. As he had demonstrated at Roundway Down, Wilmot was an experienced and able cavalry officer and he deployed the regiments at Newbury 'with so strict an eye upon all advantages and opportunities'. This care was necessary because, as discussed in the previous chapter, Wash Common plateau was bisected by a gulley and stream which effectively limited the ground suitable for cavalry action to the 500 yards or so forming Newbury Common, and even here the three tumuli at the northern end would disrupt a charge. A single brigade of 900 cavalrymen, drawn up in two lines each three ranks deep in the Royalists' preferred manner, would have covered a frontage of 250 yards and it was the norm for brigades to form up in more than one division with gaps between them. Lloyd's *Memoirs* record that despite the lack of space, Wilmot followed this approach, placing the brigades 'that one Troop might be ... assistant to another, and no part stand naked or fail in the singleness of its own strength, but that one may second another from first to last'. Nevertheless, no matter how skilfully Wilmot placed his men, the reality was that there was simply not enough room on the Common for upwards of three Royalist cavalry brigades to deploy in a way that would enable them to take advantage of their numerical superiority.[7]

At the outset, Wilmot seems to have had with him the two brigades not directly involved at Aldbourne Chase, his own and that of Lord Carnarvon, but in the clear ground between the tumuli and the gulley, he would have found it difficult to field more than one brigade at a time, with 150 men in the front rank. If he advanced a second brigade between the tumuli, their cohesion would have been disrupted and they would have been exposed to fire from Essex's infantry regiment and the demi-culverins. If he tried to push them across the gulley, the disruption would have been even greater. This limitation on the numbers that the Royalists could engage at any one time would have a significant impact on the early stages of the cavalry battle.

Though there were Royalist cavalry on Newbury Common before the Parliamentarian horse began to arrive from Wheatlands Lane, they did not seek to prevent the deployment. The leading two regiments of Sir Philip Stapleton's right wing were those of

Essex and Colonel John Dalbeir. Stapleton commanded the Earl's regiment, eight troops including the Lifeguard, two wearing the full armour of cuirassiers; Dalbeir's was rather smaller, probably five troops only, but with a substantial leavening of experienced Dutch and Walloon mercenaries; and their combined strength was equivalent to a Royalist brigade, near to nine hundred men. Once on the Common, they deployed to the south of Essex's infantry, where they were seen by Digby or his informant. There is no direct evidence for the initial formation of the Parliamentarian cavalry. At Edgehill, they had deployed six deep in the Dutch style, the optimum defensive formation for using pistols and carbines, firing by rank to break the enemy's momentum before following up with a charge, and it is probable that this is the approach adopted by Stapleton, advised by the veteran Dutchman Dalbeir; that would have given the two regiments deployed side-by-side a similar combined frontage to a Royalist brigade, about 250 yards.

By the time Stapleton and Dalbeir had deployed their regiments, the Royalists too had completed their preparations and according to the official account were drawn up on the eastern side of the common in 'several great bodies'. The road to Reading was therefore securely blocked. Essex's army was believed to be smaller than the king's, and Digby had reported that most of it had not yet advanced. Moreover, Newbury Common was not large enough to maximise the Royalists' advantage in cavalry. So why attack now?

Digby conceded that the Royalists were 'tempted' by a quick and easy victory. Hyde was blunter:

> by the precipitate courage of some young officers, who had good commands, and who unhappily always undervalued the courage of the enemy, strong parties became successively so far engaged, that the king was compelled to put the whole to the hazard of a battle.

Lloyd identified three youngish aristocratic officers as leading the cavalry at Newbury: Carnarvon, who was said to have displayed 'too much heat' at Edgehill; the Earl of Northampton, described as 'the true heir of his father's valour'; and Lord Chandos, apparently criticised after the event yet defended by the king on the grounds that 'his errors are safe'. Carnarvon had certainly demonstrated in the western campaign that he was a vigorous commander and may have led a lobby by the frustrated nobility to take the initiative and reassert the natural supremacy of the king's horse after the disappointments of Stow, Gloucester and Aldbourne Chase. Wilmot had previously been accused of lacking fighting spirit and is unlikely to have put up too much resistance. He did, however, give strict orders that the attack should not be carried from the open common into the enclosures on its western slopes.

Not for the first time, the Royalist attack miscarried. If, as is likely, it was carried out by Carnarvon's brigade, this would have been for many their first taste of pitched battle. Carnarvon's own regiment were veterans of Edgehill and later west country engagements but the others had little combat experience. According to the Parliamentarian official account

> part of them advanced immediately, and charged our horse, whom we so well received (giving no fire till we joined close with them) that the enemy

was wholly routed, and pursued with much execution near to the place where their whole body of horse stood.

Though Dalbeir and Muster Master Copley, one of Essex's troop commanders, were wounded, the Parliamentarian tactic of meeting an attack with pistol and carbine fire rather than at the charge proved successful. Bristol's former governor, Nathaniel Fiennes, had demonstrated the approach in the skirmish at Powick Bridge when his troop had held their fire until the noses of the Royalist horses almost touched those of his own front rank, shattering the enemy with the first volley of their carbines; and Middleton had used it effectively at Aldbourne Chase. Now, on a narrow front, with the tumuli to disrupt the Royalist advance and Essex's Regiment of Foot protecting Stapleton's left flank, a Royalist charge had once again been smashed. Stapleton's men, the cream of Essex's cavalry, were probably better trained and undoubtedly better equipped, but their static defensive tactics could only have worked if the Royalists were advancing tentatively rather than at a good trot as Rupert advocated.[8]

Stapleton was not an experienced soldier but he evidently kept his two regiments under tight control because by the time that the Royalists were able to mount another charge, his men had withdrawn, reformed and were ready to receive them. At this stage, the remainder of Stapleton's wing was arriving but they had not yet had time to deploy. A second Royalist brigade, probably Wilmot's, 'with all possible haste advanced again upon Sir Philip; but received no better entertainment than before, being again routed by him'. Stapleton's tactics were identical because the official Parliamentarian account explained that after these two attacks, his regiment had 'spent both their pistols'. Wilmot's brigade was made up of experienced regiments, which shows that the topography of the Common gave the Parliamentarian cavalrymen and their obsolete tactics an unusual advantage.

As at Aldbourne, the Royalist horse had become embroiled in unfavourable circumstances against an enemy they held in contempt. Moreover, the balance of forces on Newbury Common had shifted against them. In the first two clashes, both sides had been numerically matched whereas now a further four regiments (those of Sir James Ramsey and Colonels Goodwin, Harvey and Norton), plus the three unattached troops under Sir Samuel Luke, had reinforced Stapleton, bringing him to almost 2,500 men. In addition, unseen by the Royalists, two companies of Parliamentarian dragoons had deployed behind the cavalry to protect the entrance to Wheatlands Lane and secure their retreat. Both sides needed time to marshal their men. Stapleton was able to deploy all six regiments and to push out a forlorn hope under Captain Draper of Essex's Regiment to disrupt the attackers. Given the limited space available, he must now have arranged his regiments in at least two lines.

What followed was a pitched cavalry battle across Newbury Common in which, with the benefit of hindsight, the Royalists took victory for granted. Digby said simply that the action was 'quickly ended' with 'the total routing of their horse'. Hyde wrote that

> [the] king's horse, with a kind of contempt of the enemy, charged with a wonderful boldness, upon all grounds of inequality; and were far too hard for the troops of the other side, that they routed them in most places, till they left the greatest part of their foot without any guard at all of horse.

The fight was, however, a hard one. According to the Parliamentarian official account, all of the Royalist cavalry were engaged: 'the enemy with their whole body charged upon them bravely, and were as well received'. But those Parliamentarian regiments which had been involved in the first two actions had been unable to reload their pistols and the implication is that this time the Royalist onslaught was met not with shot but with a countercharge.

Most significantly, the third Royalist attack was much better handled than its predecessors. Rupert may himself have led the charge since he is identified by one source as being confronted by Stapleton, whose pistol then misfired[9], but the credit for the victory was widely given to Colonel Charles Gerard. According to Prince Rupert's Diary, it was Gerard who was responsible for 'beating Essex's right wing of horse off of the heath' while Sir Philip Warwick recalled that 'Gerard appeared eminent'. The implication is that it was Gerard's northern brigade who provided the momentum that previous attacks had lacked and it may well have been the Queen's Regiment, with its high proportion of French mercenaries, that formed the spearhead since a Parliamentarian report complained that 'this front of horse with which they charge, are most of other nations'. Furthermore, for the first time the Royalists were able to hit the Parliamentarian cavalry both from the front and at least one of their flanks. Either a party had made its way across the gulley and stream or, more likely, a brigade was sent forward between the tumuli, under the guns of Essex's Foot. Although they would have had little room in which to accelerate, any attack from a flank conferred a substantial tactical advantage. Thereafter, as both sides lost their formation and the fight became a confused melee, the Royalists' numerical superiority began to tell. The official account explained that

> Sir Philip Stapleton was here charged both in front and flank ... and was so encompassed, that the enemy and ours, were all mixed together, and in this confusion many were slain on both sides, and our men at last were forced towards the lane's end where they first came in.

This was the kind of cut and thrust close–quarter combat at which the cavaliers excelled and it now gave them belated control of Newbury Common. Stapleton's regiments were scattered and in retreat. Not all can have sought refuge in Wheatlands Lane as the official account suggests but the enclosures at the edge of the common provided similar protection from pursuit by the now equally disorganised Royalists. And at the entrance to the lane, the carbines of the two dragoon companies of Captains Abercromby and Shibborne took considerable toll of those Royalists who followed too closely; those 'that entered the lane with ours were most of them slain'. Essex's infantry, standing to the north of the lane, acted as an additional deterrent and the Royalists therefore pulled back to regroup.

Stapleton's regiments had once again performed well in the circumstances, defeated only at the third attempt. However, not everyone on the Parliamentarian side shared this view. One of the first messengers to reach London reported dismissively that the cavalry 'being drawn up in front of [Essex's] army, after some slight skirmishing lost their ground, whereupon they wheeled about and retreated to the rear of the army'. A later newspaper account argued defensively that Stapleton's wing had lost many lives because his men were tired from repeated charges while the Royalists were able to throw in fresh troops. From the surviving evidence, some of the Parliamentarian cavalry regiments did indeed suffer heavy casualties. According to the official account, in the decisive third charge only three captains, Robert Hammond and Charles Fleetwood from Essex's Regiment and Charles Pym from Dalbeir's Regiment, plus a cornet, were wounded, but Captain Francis St Barbe of Norton's Regiment and Captain Peter Ware of Ramsey's are also known from other sources to have been killed at Newbury. So, over the morning's fighting, Stapleton's six regiments had seven troop commanders killed or injured. Although muster records are similarly incomplete, a number of troops suffered significant losses among their other ranks: for example, in Essex's regiment, Copley's fell from sixty-eight troopers in August to thirty-seven in October. Worst hit was Dalbeir's Regiment, which had fought in all three charges. Its colonel and another troop commander had been hurt, at least two out of five troops took significant losses (over thirty troopers apiece disappeared from the pay records) and the regiment's major, George Ulrick, became a noisy dissenter from Parliament's subsequent campaign to paint the battle as an unalloyed triumph.[10]

Royalist casualties are more difficult to assess. Most of their cavalry losses, especially among the officers and aristocratic volunteers, happened later in the day. It is, however, likely that among the Royalist dead in the entrance to Wheatlands Lane was Henry Bertie, whose father the Earl of Lindsey had been killed at Edgehill. Parliamentarian newspapers later alleged that he was offered but refused quarter. The most prominent casualty was lost after the actual fighting had ended. According to Hyde, Lord Carnarvon was 'coming carelessly back by some of the scattered troopers, [and] was, by one of them who knew him, run through the body with a sword; of which he died within an hour'. Other accounts gave slightly different versions while agreeing that the earl was caught unawares while rallying from a charge. The Earl of Northampton appears to have taken over temporarily as brigade commander.

Though this had not been a blood bath on either side, there could be no doubt about the outcome: Prince Rupert now controlled Newbury Common. His victory had, however, taken more time and effort than the Royalists would have expected. This reflected the difficulty of bringing their numerical superiority to bear in a constrained space, the overconfidence that led them to mount the first two attacks with too few men, and the initial effectiveness of the Parliamentarians' firepower-based tactics. The question now was how quickly the Royalist commanders could reform their regiments to exploit this hard won success.

Kennet valley: morning[11]

At the northern end of the spreading battlefield, in the Kennet valley where the Royalists had expected Essex to attack and therefore first deployed their army, the bulk of King Charles' forces had now been called away to retake the Wash Common plateau and it seemed that both sides had decided to remain on the defensive. The king himself was, however, still on this flank. He had placed his standard on a hillock in a large enclosure to the south of the Hungerford to Newbury road, well positioned to control a battle in the valley but dangerously remote from the battle's new centres of gravity if he planned to take an active role in its direction. Worse still, his position was visible to Essex's troops at the top of Round Hill and well within range of their artillery. TV, the soldier serving in the Earl's vanguard, explained that the king 'stood all the day upon a hill hard by, in sight of us, and beheld all'. Digby complained that 'the king's person was exposed all day to much more hazard of the cannon than was fitting, the rebels employing it very freely wherever by any signs they could discover his presence'. *Mercurius Aulicus* later claimed that the 'Rebels espying from the Hill where many in the field stood bare-headed in a part of our Army, made above forty great shot at the place', suggesting that the king was their real target. That seems improbable but the Royalist forces in the Kennet valley would certainly have presented an attractive target for indirect fire from the hill.[12]

Vavasour's five Welsh and marcher infantry regiments had been chosen to remain in the valley to prevent an attack up the Hungerford to Newbury road, supported by Rupert's cavalry brigade. However, during the early stages of the battle, they moved from a defensive posture onto the attack. The king's presence may have had something to do with this, together with the cannon balls being lobbed at the Royalist line by the two demi-culverins on Round Hill. Although no more than 1,000 or so strong, Vavasour's brigade was rather larger than the Parliamentarian forlorn hope left there the previous evening under Major Fortescue of Bulstrode's Regiment, even after Skippon reinforced them with 300 musketeers from the Trained Bands' Red Regiment. Fortescue was also given four small guns, which he deployed to cover the road. It is unclear precisely were this position was but it is unlikely to have been much further east than the junction between the Enborne Road and Skinner's Green Lane, which ran south-north below the Wash Common escarpment. Otherwise they would have been uncomfortably close to the Royalists' overnight camp on the open ground in front of Newbury (and to the hillock on which the king had positioned himself).

The ground to the south of the River Kennet was tightly enclosed and therefore better for defence than attack. Nevertheless, it is clear that during the morning Vavasour, an experienced and ambitious officer, mounted a serious attempt to dislodge the forlorn hope. Parliament's official account recorded that 'the enemy came up so close, that they took away a limber of one of our pieces, but it was with loss of many of their lives'. Though Sergeant Foster's company commander, Captain George Mosse, was shot in the back, the Royalists do seem to have come off rather worse. Vavasour's brigade reported three officers and forty-five soldiers wounded during the day, and most were likely to have been sustained in this action. Interestingly, this is the only direct evidence of the Royalist infantry closing with the enemy in a defended position, and even here their success was evidently both limited and temporary. For most of the rest of the day, both sides were content to trade long range musket fire along the valley hedgerows.

Round Hill: morning[13]

The battle had now spread over a front of around 2,000 yards. Such was the nature of the ground that even without the smoke of cannon and muskets, it was impossible for combatants to see very far beyond their immediate vicinity. This in turn makes it extremely difficult to attach precise timings to specific events.[14] For example, Digby wrote that the fighting began at seven o'clock, but he gives no indication of when the Parliamentarian cavalry was forced from Newbury Common. Nevertheless, given the time it would take to reform brigades after three separate charges, one can safely assume that the next stage in the fight for Round Hill in what was now the centre of the battlefield took place in parallel with the cavalry charges described earlier.

With the withdrawal of Lisle's musketeers and 'Feilding's' party of horse, the task of driving Essex's regiments from the enclosures on Round Hill fell to the two Colonels

Byron, John leading the cavalry and Nicholas the infantry. Sir John's account is detailed and for the most part corresponds with the less comprehensive Parliamentarian versions. Rupert had ordered him to take two regiments from his cavalry brigade, his own and Sir Thomas Aston's, to support Lisle's musketeers in case the Parliamentarians used cavalry against them. From Baker's 1775 map, it seems certain that Sir John and his two regiments would have followed the musketeers up Dark Lane and then near the top of the hill formed up in a pair of larger fields to the left of the lane, where the ground was already flat and they would have been hidden from sight by hedgerows and deep banks.

It was not, however, cavalry that were needed at this stage but more infantry to regain the momentum lost when Lisle's men fell back, and to root out the Parliamentarian foot from the tight enclosures northeast of Round Hill. Sir John Byron recalled that 'my uncle Byron, who commanded the first tertia, instantly came up with part of the regiment of guards and Sir Michael Woodhouse's and [Charles] Gerard's regiments of foot, commanded by his Lieut-Col. Ned Villiers'. This was a powerful force: the King's Lifeguard, the Prince of Wales Regiment of which Woodhouse was colonel and Charles Gerard's composite unit drawn from the Oxford garrison were among the largest in the army (Woodhouse's had started the march to Newbury 700 strong); and many among the Lifeguards and Gerard's men had fought at Edgehill. Edward Villiers was younger brother of Lord Grandison, whose life was now ebbing away in Oxford, and a similarly promising young officer. Looking again at the 1775 map, it is likely that this advance element of Sir Nicholas Byron's brigade followed the cavalry up Dark Lane but that they then deployed to the right of Lisle's musketeers by taking a fork that led west along the lower slope of Round Hill towards Skinner's Green. That would have outflanked Holburn's brigade which was still confronting Lisle's men further up the hill, created a salient between the Parliamentarian positions in the valley and on the plateau, and given Sir John Byron's cavalry a platform from which to start rolling up the Parliamentarian line.

Unfortunately for the Royalists, their attack did not come as a surprise. With the Earl of Essex planted on Round Hill, Major General Philip Skippon had come forward to consult. He had already ordered the artillery train and the main guard infantry, a total of ten regiments, to advance from where Digby had seen them near Enborne village. The question now was where best to employ them and from the top of Round Hill the answer quickly became obvious. Parliament's official account described how, looking 'towards Newbury, [Skippon] perceived a great strength of the enemy both horse and foot in diverse great bodies advancing directly towards the way which all our train was of necessity to march'. These bodies can only have been the two Byrons and their men moving to reinforce Lisle and outflank Round Hill. The implication is that the Parliamentarian guns and infantry were planned to assemble at the base of the hill on Skinner's Green. Whether on his own initiative or in concert with Essex, the vastly experienced Skippon responded rapidly and decisively. His own brigade of three regiments plus Sir William Springate's and the Red Auxiliaries were pushed up Round Hill to reinforce the earl. In parallel, Lord Robartes' brigade and Colonel Mainwaring's Regiment were ordered to occupy the fields east of Skinner's Green to block the advance of Sir Nicholas Byron's infantry.

Robartes' brigade was extremely weak, the three regiments together amounting to only some 750 pikemen and musketeers, and Robartes himself had no pre-war military experience. But all three units, Constable's bluecoats, Martin's greycoats and Robartes' own redcoats, had fought well at Edgehill, and, on their left, Mainwaring's London regiment fielded another 500 or more men. Moreover, Skippon had reinforced Robartes with four or five small artillery pieces that his soldiers were able to bring forward and deploy before the Royalist infantry appeared. It must have been a close run thing but the Parliamentarians were in place 'just where the enemy advanced'.

The brunt of the Royalist attack fell on Robartes' brigade. Although the Parliamentarian official account reported simply that the three regiments 'gave them so warm an entertainment that they ran shamefully; and my Lord Robartes possessed the ground which the enemy came first up unto', this was evidently a very sharp fight. Although Robartes had only 500 musketeers in his brigade, they and the light guns (which will have been firing case shot, metal or wooden boxes of musket balls) were unusually effective in inflicting casualties. Sir John Byron conceded that 'the service grew so hot, that in a very short time, of twelve ensigns that marched up with my Lord Gerard's regiment, eleven were brought off the field hurt, and Ned Villiers shot through the shoulder'. Byron's recollection is confirmed by the contemporary list of Royalist casualties which recorded that by the end of the day, Gerard's composite regiment had lost sixteen officers, seven sergeants and seventy-eight soldiers wounded, including nine ensigns. These were the highest casualty figures for any single Royalist regiment, and although some may have been incurred later on, Byron clearly thought this was a particularly bloody combat. The Prince of Wales Regiment, which also suffered heavily during the battle, may have taken casualties at this time as well. By contrast, the only mention of Parliamentarian losses is that Robartes' lieutenant colonel was shot in the face. Sergeant Foster described how the reserve Trained Band regiments rushed forward to support Robartes' brigade but they were not needed at this stage.

Since there is no suggestion that the two sides closed to push of pike, it seems most likely that Robartes' musketeers and light artillery outgunned Villiers' men and inflicted the casualties at relatively long range, probably beyond 100 yards. Perhaps the high proportion of ensigns and other officers on Gerard's casualty list reflected their attempts to lead from the front, pushing through hedgerows under fire. Whatever the cause, the result was that the Royalist advance came to a sudden stop, their infantry falling back in confusion and calling to Sir John Byron's cavalry for help. What followed was one of the decisive phases of the battle, recounted in detail by Byron some years later. He made the events sound breathlessly immediate, thereby conflating the timetable, and his description suggests that he mounted three charges against the same Parliamentarian regiments, those that had brought Gerard's advance to such an abrupt halt. From the Parliamentarian accounts, however, it seems that Byron engaged a number of different units, with varying degrees of success. In the confusion of a bitter fight from hedge to hedge, none of this should be at all surprising.

Indeed, Byron's first task was to discover where the enemy was and then to find a way to get his cavalrymen close enough to them to mount an attack. He therefore 'advanced with the two regiments I had, and commanded them to halt while I went to view the ground, and to see what way there was to that place where the enemy's foot was drawn up'. However, the field in which he found the Parliamentarian infantry was 'enclosed with a high quick hedge and no passage into it, but by a narrow gap through which but one horse at a time could go and that not without difficulty'. The Parliamentarians were drawn up 'near the hedge', supported by a pair of light guns. Byron's party included Lord Falkland, who was riding as a volunteer and, according to some stories, deep in depression either over the lack of a political solution to the war or, more scurrilously, following the death of his mistress 'whom he loved above all other creatures'.[15] Hyde, a close friend, denied any hint of depression or suicide, though Byron's regiment was an odd choice for an unmilitary politician such as Falkland to serve in. The black–coated midlanders had a justifiable reputation for brutality, won in February at the storming of Cirencester, and Byron himself had complained about their indiscipline after the fall of Bristol. Having discovered the gap in the hedge, Sir John was giving orders for it to be widened to allow his men better access when the Parliamentarian infantry opened fire:

> my horse was shot in the throat with a musket ball and his bit broken in his mouth so that I was forced to call for another horse, in the meantime my Lord Falkland (more gallantly than advisedly) spurred his horse through the gap, where both he and his horse were immediately killed.

This was a political calamity for the moderate Royalists but of no military significance. No effort was made even to recover Falkland's body. Pioneers hacked down the hedge to create a wider passage while Byron found himself another horse and brought up his regiment.

This part of the battle was almost certainly fought over the three relatively large enclosures which, according to Baker's 1775 map, covered most of the northeastern slope of Round Hill and the spur itself up to Cope Hall Lane. They are the only fields big enough for Parliamentarian infantry brigades or Royalist cavalry regiments to deploy and the only ones with a layout that tallies with both Byron's narrative and the Parliamentarian official account. Byron had assembled his regiment behind the expanded gap in the hedgerow, with his own troop at its head. They would have to pass through the gap and either reform under fire or charge the enemy in column. Either way, with the Parliamentarians standing within musket shot of the gap, it was an unattractive choice. Byron led the attack. The Parliamentarian official account suggests that the brigade lined up in the field to receive him was Holburn's, 800 strong with pikes flanked by wings of musketeers. According to Byron, they

> entertained us with a great salvo of musket shot, and discharged their two drakes upon us laden with case shot, which killed some and hurt many of my men, so that we were forced to wheel off and could not meet them at that charge.

This was evidently not a rolling fusillade by single rank but one or two volleys, fired by three ranks at a time in what was called the Swedish fashion. With such an easy target, the Parliamentarian musketeers and gunners again inflicted unusually heavy casualties. But Byron was a capable regimental commander and he managed to rally his men, while the second regiment of Sir Thomas Aston filed through the gap in the hedge to join them.

While the Royalists regrouped, the Parliamentarians withdrew their guns, and when Byron and Aston led their men forward, they were able to 'beat [the infantry] to the end of the close, where they faced us again'. This was not, however, a rout but a disciplined withdrawal. With the hedge at their backs, Holburn's brigade unleashed 'another volley of shot upon us, when Sir Thomas Aston's horse was killed under him, and withal kept us off so with their pikes we could not break them, but were forced to wheel off again'.

Byron reformed his battered regiments for a second time and Holburn's brigade pulled back 'into another little close' and made 'haste to recover a lane which was very near unto it'. From the 1775 Baker map, this can only have been the top end of Cope Hall Lane, between the crest of Round Hill and the common. Though to Byron the Parliamentarian infantry appeared to be in retreat, the official account explained that Essex had in fact chosen this moment to relieve his tired vanguard with fresh units. Holburn's brigade and that of Barclay on its right 'had been four hours upon very hot service'. They were to be replaced in the front line by Skippon's brigade, Springate's Regiment and the Red Auxiliary Regiment, which had probably been held centrally on Skinner's Green, and by Mainwaring's Regiment, which was sidestepped up Round Hill from the left flank of Robartes' brigade. The plan seems to have been that the Red Auxiliaries would relieve Essex's Regiment on Wash Common with Skippon's brigade on their left, then Mainwaring's Regiment, Robarte's brigade and Springate's Regiment in line along the slopes of Round Hill. Essex presumably thought that Byron's cavalry had shot their bolt and that this was a good time to feed in the fresh troops. He was mistaken.

Colonel Randall Mainwaring's London regiment took over the ground held so successfully by Holburn's brigade, flanked by one of the other newly arrived regiments. Although numerically strong compared to most of Essex's regiments and a regular unit, Mainwaring's redcoats had seen little active service beyond suppressing the recent Kent uprising and keeping order in the capital. Parliament's official account admitted that 'it fortuned that this regiment was no sooner brought on, but they were over-charged with two great bodies of horse and foot so that they were forced to retreat and lose the ground' which the vanguard had captured and held. Byron's version tallies with this: 'I rallied the horse again, and charged them a third time, and then utterly routed them'. Whether the assault was carried out with greater determination or the nerves of the less experienced replacement Parliamentarian infantry failed in the face of the advancing cavaliers, this was a potentially decisive breakthrough for the Royalists. The disintegration of Mainwaring's Regiment seems to have carried away some at least of Skippon's neighbouring brigade; Skippon's own regiment lost two light artillery pieces and Sir William Brook's another. These units probably rallied in due course but for the moment they were incapable of stemming the Royalist advance. If Sir John Byron's cavalry and Sir Nicholas Byron's infantry brigade, which was evidently following closely behind, could drive across Cope Hall Lane, they would control Round Hill and force Essex to retreat from Newbury Common or risk being taken in the rear. After two months of successive frustrations, King Charles had been presented with his very last chance of a strategic victory in 1643. The king's army was within half a dozen small fields of destroying Parliament's main bulwark; it was perhaps the tipping point of the First Civil War.

Chapter Fourteen
'Our foot played the jades'

Round Hill, late morning and afternoon[1]

Sir John Byron's troopers hacked down the fleeing Parliamentarian pikemen and musketeers of Colonel Mainwaring's Regiment without pity. Even without their reputation for brutality, Byron's Midlanders had seen too many of their comrades slain in the fight among the enclosures on Round Hill to give quarter in the heat of battle. In seventeenth century combat, the heaviest losses were sustained during routs such as this and, according to Sir John, his cavaliers 'had not left a man of them unkilled, but that the hedges were so high the horse could not pursue them'. Yet the hedgerows would not delay for long the infantry regiments of Sir John's uncle Nicholas, which were following behind the Royalist cavalry, and would then be in the rear of the Parliamentarian right flank on Newbury Common.

Most historians underestimate the extent of the Byrons' advance and the consequent vulnerability of Essex's position.[2] Their battlefield plans have the Parliamentarian line running north from Newbury Common to the Kennet valley roughly along the line of Dark Lane and therefore imply that the Royalists failed to penetrate as far as Round Hill. That contradicts sources from both sides which put the morning's early fighting firmly on the slopes of Round Hill and make clear that the Byrons' advance pushed significantly further. Moreover, Sir John Byron's testimony shows that his cavalrymen crossed at least two fields during the advance before coming to a lane, which he twice refers to as the scene of his main clash with the Parliamentarian infantry. *Mercurius Aulicus*' report of Sir Thomas Aston's part in this stage of the battle also places it on a lane along which the Parliamentarians were able to counterattack. The only lanes that could conceivably be in the Byrons' path are Dark Lane and Cope Hall Lane, and Dark Lane is too far to the east of Round Hill to fit the descriptions. Only Cope Hall Lane, the route of Essex's original assault, is consistent with contemporary accounts and landscape evidence. It runs along the spur from Newbury Common to Round Hill and even today the banks on either side are steep, and the hedgerows tall and dense. If the Royalists gained control of it, they could roll up Essex's regiments on the common from the flank or advance southwards to cut them off from the rest of his army.

Neither Essex nor Major General Philip Skippon was present as Mainwaring's men streamed back through the hedgerows. Without their leadership, panic could quite easily have gripped the infantry regiments on either side of the gap created by the Royalist cavalry; at Edgehill, a brigade of Essex's foot had bolted simply at the sight of a Royalist attack. Here, at least two neighbouring regiments, Skippon's and Brook's, had lost their guns and were also in retreat. With the entire Parliamentarian battle line in jeopardy, an immediate response was essential to seal off Byron's breach.

In the fields on the south-west side of Cope Hall Lane, the seven infantry regiments of Essex's vanguard were resting after their first four hours of battle. Their withdrawal had facilitated the Royalist breakthrough and it would not have been surprising had Mainwaring's rout infected them too. Fortunately for Parliament, their brigade commanders, Scotsmen Harry Barclay and James Holburn, were professionals who had served on the continent. Their regiments had performed creditably at the siege of Reading and their acknowledged competence had presumably led to their appointment as brigade commanders for the march to Gloucester. Now their experience was at a premium. As for their men, casualties had not yet been especially heavy and the seven regiments would still have numbered close to 2,500 all ranks; but though they were regulars, few were veterans. Only Essex's own regiment had been at Edgehill; another, Tyrell's Buckinghamshire greencoats, had missed the battle; the rest, led by Barclay, Holburn, and Colonels Holmstead, Langham and Thomson, had been raised during the subsequent winter and spring, and lacked battlefield experience.

Both brigade commanders quickly formed their tired men into ranks and the musketeers prepared their matchlocks. Although Sir John Byron wrote simply that 'a great body of their own foot advanced toward the lane', at which the Royalists chose to consolidate their gains, it is evident from other sources that there was rather more to it than that. Parliament's official account explained that

> Colonel Holburn perceiving [the Royalist horse and foot advancing] with his brigade gave the enemy a round salvo, and instantly his own and Colonel Barclay's brigades and His Excellency's regiment again advancing beat back the enemy.

These were well-established infantry tactics, volleys fired three ranks at a time followed by an advance to push of pikes. Since the Royalists' cohesion would already have been disrupted by the hedgerows, it is unlikely that they waited for the attack to hit home. Even if they did so, the Parliamentarians' momentum would have soon pushed them back to the lane. *Mercurius Aulicus* conceded that it was this fierce defence which brought the Byrons' attack to a stop: 'yet though they lost the hill they kept the hedges all the forenoon' and from the shelter of the hedgerows their musketeers 'much annoyed both our foot and horse'.

Despite subsequent Parliamentarian claims to have recaptured their original position, the battle line in fact stabilised along Cope Hall Lane. Sir Nicholas Byron's musketeers defended the hedgerows, supported by blocks of pikemen and, further back, Sir John Byron's battered cavalry. However, Essex and Skippon were not yet content to accept this stalemate. According to Sir John, the 'enemy drew up fresh supplies to regain the ground again, but to my uncle's good conduct (who that day did extraordinary service) was entirely beaten off'. The Royalist position was akin to a small salient in the Parliamentarian line because Essex's men still controlled the top of Cope Hall Lane where it entered the common and could use the bottom of the lane to attack the Royalists from the flank. *Mercurius Aulicus* described how

> a fresh supply of near 200 musketeers advancing up a lane to have surprised our pikes and colours, by that gallant resolute charge made by Sir Thomas

Aston with his own troop (through a double quick-set hedge) those poachers were dislodged, their fresh supply routed, and fled before him in such haste, that though his horse was shot in the entrance of the lane, and drew him by the leg amongst them, they had not the civility to help him up, but let him walk away on foot.

Notwithstanding Aston's counter-attack, it took Prince Rupert in person with a 'fresh relief of foot' to regain control of the lane. Rupert pops up whenever there is a Royalist crisis, suggesting that whatever the formal command structure, it was the prince who was in practice galvanising his uncle's army.

Though Holburn and Barclay could not evict the Royalists from their position on Cope Hall Lane, they had prevented a local crisis turning into a catastrophe for Essex's army. Stalemate was better than rout, and they still controlled the south-western half of Round Hill. Lord Digby described this phase of the battle, which he believed had lasted for a total of six hours, as 'the hottest dispute that hath been seen'. Thereafter, skirmishing continued among the hedgerows along the lane. Despite the losses suffered at the beginning of his advance, Sir Nicholas Byron still had the better part of two infantry brigades (his own and Darcy's) plus Lisle's musketeers, 3,000–3,500 men, deployed in a semi-circular line between Newbury Common and the northern slopes of Round Hill. At around three o'clock they were reinforced by two artillery pieces and they could still call on Sir John Byron's cavalry in an emergency. But half of the Royalist infantry were pikemen and therefore of little value among tight enclosures except to hold cavalry at bay. Instead, musketeers were needed to wear down the enemy's resistance and beat them gradually back from hedge to hedge, and in this respect the Royalists were heavily outnumbered. Essex had fourteen or fifteen infantry regiments opposing the two Byrons on Round Hill, around 4,500 men, two thirds of whom were musketeers who could deploy along the hedgerows two or three deep in open order (two yards between each man), and maintain a steady fire whenever the Royalists came within range. Now that the situation had stabilised, they would be difficult to dislodge.

To prevent a repetition of Sir John Byron's breakthrough, the earl also reinforced this central section of his position with the second wing of cavalry, 1,400 men under Colonel John Middleton. Most descriptions of the battle have placed these six regiments on the extreme left of the Parliamentarian line, covering the Hungerford to Newbury road in the Kennet Valley. This reflects Parliament's official account which stated that the 'left wing of our horse commanded by Colonel Middleton, and the right wing of the enemy's horse, could not be engaged but in small parties by reason of the hedges' and the assumption, following Money, that Essex's army was drawn up in orthodox formation with cavalry on both flanks. Prince Rupert's brigade spent some of the morning in the valley covering the approach to Newbury but there is no evidence that they undertook any offensive action and by the afternoon they had joined the vast majority of the Royalist cavalry on Newbury Common. For most of the day the Royalist right wing of cavalry was formed by Sir John Byron's two regiments, fighting among the hedges referred to by the Parliamentarian account. Lloyd's *Memoirs* described how 'valiantly and warily' Sir John Byron 'led the king's horse at the first Newbury fight, when Col. Middleton protested that there was no dealing with Byron, who would give no advantage', and Middleton is hardly likely to have said this unless his regiments were directly engaged with Sir John's cavaliers. The greater part of

Middleton's wing was probably drawn up on Skinner's Green, from where they could quickly counter any cavalry threat in the Kennet valley and push squadrons forward to join the skirmishing on the slopes of Round Hill.[3]

Kennet valley, afternoon[4]

Major General Philip Skippon was controlling the disposition of the Parliamentarian main guard and reserve. Although Round Hill was his primary focus, he was sufficiently concerned about the attack by Sir William Vavasour's infantry brigade along the Newbury to Hungerford road to send the Blue Auxiliary Regiment to reinforce the forlorn hope among the hedgerows. From the Parliamentarian official account, it appears that their musketeers were being rotated into forward positions, probably in groups of fifty or so, to wear down Vavasour's five regiments which, despite reinforcement by a detachment of the King's Lifeguard of Foot, had proportionately fewer musketeers and would have been at a disadvantage in skirmishing of this kind. But the Auxiliaries also made an attempt to push the Royalists out of their position because Digby noted an attack 'made by them from their grand reserve upon a pass on our right hand near the river possessed by the King's Lifeguards, in which they were repulsed'. As a result, the officer I believe to be Colonel Richard Feilding was ordered by Sir Lewis Kirke, one of the king's staff officers, to 'look to ye pass by the river side which the enemy was then endeavouring to gain'. 'Feilding' recalled that 'when I came to ye place I found Sir William Vavasour there with his brigade, which I conceived sufficiently secured that place'. Here too, the battle had reached a stalemate and by four o'clock Essex was considering redeploying 200 of the Red Regiment musketeers to reinforce the firing line on Round Hill.

Newbury Common, afternoon[5]

From the Royalist perspective, that left Newbury Common as the only possible site for a decisive attack to break the Earl of Essex's army. Sir Philip Stapleton's cavalry wing having retreated into the enclosures on the western edge of the common, the next step was to deal with the Parliamentarian infantry and artillery deployed at the north-west corner of the common. Since the Royalist cavalry needed time to reform, this task was given to the two infantry brigades of Colonel John Belasyse and Sir Gilbert Gerard, some 2,800 strong and supported by a battery of eight guns.

Because the Royalist cavalry had arrived first on the common, the infantry would have to deploy in whatever space was left. From Parliamentarian accounts it is evident that the Royalist artillery battery was sited opposite the entry to Wheatlands Lane, next to the southernmost tumulus from where it would have had a clear field of fire towards Essex's infantry regiments at the common's north-western edge. The two Royalist infantry brigades would therefore have deployed between the battery and the north of the common, a distance of only 300 yards with the biggest of the tumuli to their front. According to Belasyse's memoirs, his brigade formed the vanguard so it would have arrived first and been drawn up on the left, behind the large tumulus. That tallies with the recollections of Lieutenant John Gwyn of Colonel Charles Lloyd's Regiment, which formed part of Sir Gilbert Gerard's brigade and was standing at the very edge of Newbury Common to the right of Belasyse's brigade. We have no description of the formation adopted by the two brigades but if, as at Edgehill, they used the so-called Swedish brigade of four battalia deployed in a diamond pattern, both would have been able to deploy in combat formation despite the limited space. Behind them was a cavalry unit which a Parliamentarian believed was placed there to stop the Royalist infantry from running away, a tactic used previously by Rupert at the storming of Cirencester.

On the other side of Newbury Common, the Red Auxiliaries were protecting the two demi-culverins at the north-western edge of the common and Essex's own regiment moved up to join them once Round Hill had been made secure. Until the Royalist cavalry regrouped, the odds were not unduly stacked against the earl's infantry. If the two Royalist brigades were prepared to close to push of pike with their enemy, then weight of numbers would probably tell; if, however, they relied on firepower, the higher proportion of pikemen in Royalist regiments meant that they would have little or no advantage, at least until Lord Percy's artillery train arrived.

As discussed previously, the Royalists' most experienced infantry general, Sir Jacob Astley, seems to have been in overall charge of the two brigades on the common. If so, this was not his most glorious day. The king's foot were undoubtedly tired but they were also gun-shy. Paradoxically, among the seventeen regiments represented here were some of the most experienced and battle-hardened in the Oxford Army; nine had fought at Edgehill and ten had stormed the walls at Bristol. Yet these same soldiers had been humiliated at Reading, mutinous at Culham and again after the fall of Bristol, and frustrated in front of Gloucester, and all of the evidence suggests that on Newbury Common their officers were unable to lead or bully them to charge Essex's less experienced but better motivated troops. Lieutenant Gwyn subsequently pretended that 'we beat the enemy ... from the town's end to the top of the hill by the heath' but the reality was reflected in Colonel Belasyse's usually garrulous memoirs, which is uncharacteristically silent about his brigade's contribution to the battle. Questioning the performance of the Royalist infantry is not a matter of hindsight. Two days later, Lord Digby was quite prepared to make his criticism public: the action on Newbury Common 'was done merely by our horse, for (to say truth) our foot having found a hillock in the heath that sheltered them from the enemy's cannon, would not be drawn a foot from thence'. The hillock was undoubtedly the largest of the tumuli, a key feature on the otherwise open common. A few years further on and Sir John Byron was even more scathing: 'had not our foot [on the Common] played the poltroons extremely that day, we in all probability had set a period to the war'.

That is not to say that the Royalist infantry refused to budge at all. Casualty returns in the contemporary list of 'hurt soldiers of Newbury' demonstrate that Sir Gilbert Gerard's brigade lost more than thirty officers and 200 men killed or wounded. Figures for Belasyse's brigade are less comprehensive, apparently excluding fatalities and officers, yet record that the twelve regiments between them suffered 139 wounded men. Some will have been suffered later in the day but Parliamentarian accounts show that the two Royalist brigades did at the outset engage with Essex's infantry, though in a prolonged exchange of musket fire, not a close-quarter attack. Once again, however, the Royalists had fewer musketeers and were out-gunned, and after a time some of them used the tumuli as cover from the rolling Parliamentarian volleys and cannon fire, from where their officers could not persuade them to re-enter the fighting.

From Essex's perspective, this was only a temporary relief. Once Prince Rupert's cavalry had reformed, it would be impossible to maintain a hold on Newbury Common without substantial reinforcements, especially as the Royalists were building their battery of eight guns to support an eventual all-out assault. This was in effect the earl's last throw of the dice. Round Hill had sucked in three-quarters of his twenty infantry regiments. Another was holding the Kennet Valley and the Orange Auxiliaries seem to have formed a rearguard to protect the baggage train. That left the Red and Blue Trained Band Regiments. Because the former had previously sent 300 musketeers to reinforce the forlorn hope in the valley, they together consisted of only 1,300 well trained and equipped but still largely inexperienced soldiers, drawn for the most part from the City of London wards of Tower Street, Potsoken, Aldgate, Billingsgate, Bridge, Candlewick, Wallbrook, Dowgate, Vintry, Cordwayner, Cheape, Bread Street and Queenhithe.[6] Late in the morning, the two regiments were ordered forward to the Common, to be joined by five of the heavier guns which had not been distributed among the infantry regiments. As usual, Skippon supervised the advance of the foot while Sir John Merrick brought up the artillery. Sergeant Foster makes clear that when the Red Regiment eventually arrived on the Common, the Royalist artillery battery was already in place supported by 'a great body of horse and foot'. This was not a remote threat. Foster and his comrades would form up 'far less than twice musket shot from them' and would therefore be extremely vulnerable as they marched onto the open ground. Deploying the guns would be a particular challenge. Surprisingly, however, there is no mention of any concerted Royalist opposition at this stage.

The reason was that Essex used his cavalry to distract the Royalists' attention at the most critical time. Sir Philip Stapleton's wing had reformed and now mounted a two-pronged sortie onto the common, probably from Wheatlands Lane. One detachment swung north towards the two Royalist infantry brigades. Lieutenant Gwyn's memoirs make clear that the attack took place between the tumuli and the Common's edge, a distance of only 150 yards or so. Such a frontage would have limited the attackers to ranks of no more than eighty to ninety men. The normal cavalry formation of two lines each of three ranks would therefore have been around 500 strong. Stapleton's troopers posed the same kind of threat to the two Royalist infantry brigades as Sir John Byron's cavalrymen had to Mainwaring's Regiment, and were almost as successful. Gwyn's account has generally been quoted because of its picaresque description of the lieutenant vaulting across a hedge to save his company colours:

> a wing of Essex his horse moving gently towards us, made us leave our execution upon the enemy, and retreat into the next field, where were several gaps to get into it, but not direct in my way; yet, with the colours in my hand, I jumped over hedge and ditch, or I had died by a multitude of hands.

What this actually shows is the disintegration of part of Sir Gilbert Gerard's brigade as the Parliamentarian cavalry advanced towards them.

A rout was averted because not all of the Royalists followed Gwyn to the relative safety of the fields bordering Newbury Common. Lined up behind the infantry was the cavalry regiment commanded by Sir Charles Lucas. His potted biography in Lloyd's *Memoirs* describes an episode during the battle that makes sense only in the context of this particular stage in the fighting. A professional soldier with continental experience, Lucas had interspersed his squadrons with blocks of musketeers, presumably from Gerard's brigade. With support from a light gun, he met the advancing Parliamentarian cavalry not with a counter charge but in the same manner that Stapleton had blunted the early Royalist attacks, with firepower. Lucas, according to Lloyd maintained with one regiment well disposed and lined with musketeers, and a drake, with small shot against the gross of Essex his army, the leading man of which he pistolled himself in the head of his troop, giving close fire himself, and commanding others to do the like.

To Lucas and his men, it would have appeared that they were facing a major Parliamentarian thrust because the Trained Band regiments were at this moment filing out onto the Common. Although Lucas himself was reported to have suffered multiple injuries, the Parliamentarian horse did not press home their attack. They had done their job effectively.

Further south, the second detachment of Stapleton's cavalry emerged onto the common to cover the attack on Gerard's infantry brigade and the arrival of the Red and Blue Trained Band Regiments, who advanced from Skinner's Green along Wheatlands Lane. The Blue Regiment soldier complained that when they arrived on the right wing of the army 'we were flanked with horse, who being charged by the enemy wheeled off and left us'. Disappointing though this was to the Trained Bands, there would have been no benefit in a one-sided cavalry encounter at that point. Most importantly, the balance of forces on the Common had shifted significantly in favour of the Parliamentarians.

Essex seems to have used Barclay's brigade, deployed in the fields beyond the Common's northwestern boundary, as a pivot between the line along Round Hill and his forces on the Common itself. To their right, at the entrance of Cope Hall Lane, stood the pair of demi-culverins, flanked by the Red Auxiliaries and the earl's own regiment. Next, on either side of Wheatlands Lane, was the rump of the Red Regiment and the Blue Regiment, strongest of all of the Trained Band units. To Sergeant Foster, it appeared that the two Trained Band regiments now stood exposed 'in open campania upon the right wing of the whole army'. His comrade from the Blue Regiment agreed: they 'made the right wing of our army'. In fact, although Stapleton's cavalry regiments had withdrawn once again into the fields bordering the common's western edge, they formed an invisible presence and protection that the Royalist generals could not ignore. Altogether, Essex now had close to 3,500 infantry and 2,500 cavalry on or around Newbury Common.

Forth, Rupert and Wilmot thus faced a difficult challenge. In the wake of the morning's fighting, they could call upon only 2,500 or so demoralised infantrymen and probably no more than 4,000 cavalry, plus the eight gun artillery battery. Moreover, the limited space available meant that the Royalists were again unable to use their superiority in horse to best effect. The four Parliamentarian infantry regiments on the Common, some 2,500 men in total, would have had a combined frontage of about 550 yards and could form an unbroken line along its full length. With their own infantry now occupying the common's northern end but unwilling to advance to contact, the Royalists were obliged to consider mounting cavalry attacks directly against the muskets, pikes and supporting guns of the Trained Band regiments on Essex's southern flank. This was an unappetising prospect even for the king's self confident cavaliers, especially with Stapleton's cavalry lurking in the wings, and may explain why, for much of the afternoon, there is no sense of urgency, coordination or strategy about the Royalist efforts. Rupert's absence for some of the time, leading reinforcements to stabilise the line on Round Hill, could have been a contributory factor, together with the arrival on the common of the casualty-averse king. Whatever the reasons, the

Royalists resorted instead to using artillery to erode the Trained Bands' cohesion, exhibiting recognition of the tactical limitations of cavalry against unbroken infantry formations which would have profound consequences for the day's outcome.

What followed was a one-sided and ultimately unsuccessful artillery barrage. Not that the Royalist artillery was completely ineffective. Hyde later wrote that 'during the whole day, no use was made of the king's cannon' but he was mistaken. Foster, who stood directly in front of their barrels, explained that from a distance of less than two musket shots (200–300 yards), 'they began their battery against us with their great guns', probably comprising the bigger pieces used at Gloucester (the two 24-pounder demi-cannons, two 15-pounder culverins and two 12-pounders, plus a pair of 6-pounders), all firing round shot.[7] It was unusual for artillery to be given the opportunity for sustained fire against infantry in the open field. Most battles opened with the exchange of a shot or two but the soldiers then tended to close with each other before too much damage was done. In this case, however, Foster recalled that the 'enemy's cannon did play most against the Red Regiment of trained bands, they did some execution amongst us at the first, and were somewhat dreadful when men's bowels and brains flew in our faces'. This was no exaggeration. Next morning, Lieutenant Gwyn saw 'upon the heath ... a whole file of men, six deep, with their heads all struck off with one cannon shot of ours'.

For half an hour, the Royalist guns fired without reply. Foster complained that when at last the Red Regiment's light cannon appeared 'our gunner dealt very ill with us, delaying to come up to us'. Major Tucker, who commanded the regiment, took control and 'fired one piece of ordnance against the enemy' but 'aiming to give fire the second time, was shot in the head with a cannon bullet from the enemy'. The horse ridden by Captain Lieutenant Thomas Juxon, a volunteer from the Green Regiment, was hit in the forehead by another cannon ball and galloped uncontrollably into the Royalist lines where it collapsed, leaving Juxon mortally wounded. Despite such losses, Foster wrote proudly: 'blessed be God that gave us courage, so that we kept our ground, and after a while feared them not'. This was a great tribute to the Trained Bands' stoicism under fire and to their cohesion despite the loss of their commanding officer. It is, however, striking that most of the Parliamentarian casualties inflicted by artillery fire were hit in the head; the Blue Regiment soldier claimed scornfully that in four hours bombardment they 'did us no harm, only the shot broke our pikes'. Lord Percy had done well to get his artillery train to the battlefield but in the heat of combat his gunners appear to have laid their guns on too high a trajectory.

Although the Blue Regiment, standing at the extreme south of the Parliamentarian line, was not under such heavy artillery fire as Foster's comrades, it was the obvious target for a probe by the Royalist cavalry. Foster watched as

> [t]wo regiments of the king's horse which stood upon their right flank afar off, came fiercely upon them, and charged them two or three times, but were beat back with their musketeers, who gave them a most desperate charge, and made them fly.

Robert Codrington, whose version of the battle is often confused and contradictory, nevertheless gave a vivid description of these attacks which has the flavour of an eyewitness account: the two regiments

with a fierce charge, saluted the Blue Regiment of the London Trained
Bands, who gallantly discharged upon them, and did beat them back; but
they, being no whit daunted at it, wheeled about, and on a sudden charged
them; our musketeers did again discharge, and that with so much violence
and success, that they sent them now, not wheeling, but reeling from them:
and yet, for all that, they made a third assault, and coming in full squadrons,
they did the utmost of their endeavour to break through our ranks; but
a cloud of bullets came at once so thick from our muskets, and made such a
havoc amongst them, both of men and horse, that, in a fear, full of confused
speed, they did fly before us.

This was the kind of fighting the London volunteers had practiced before the war, a
solid phalanx of pike and shot standing on open ground, facing and defeating a cavalry
charge.

When the Blue Regiment did not break, the Royalists turned to subterfuge.
Recognising that in the smoke and confusion of battle there was little to distinguish
friend from foe, a regiment of Royalist horse copied their enemy's field sign, a green
branch worn on their hats, and advanced slowly towards the Blue Regiment's lines
shouting that they were friends and urging the infantrymen not to fire. Foster saw
simply that the Blue Regiment's musketeers 'let fly at them, and made many of them
and their horses tumble, making them fly with a vengeance'. Yet the Blue Regiment
soldier conceded that the ruse had almost worked. The cavaliers reached the
Parliamentarians' pike heads and their protestations were convincing 'which made us
not know what to do'. Finally, one of the Blue Regiment's captains broke the stalemate
and ordered the wavering musketeers to fire 'which they did all at once, which made
the enemy run away, and killed many of them, with some small loss to our own side'.

Finally, the Trained Bands received an invaluable reinforcement in the shape of a
battery of their own heavy guns. Covered by the Blue and Red Regiments, Sir John
Merrick brought up and sited five cannon opposite the Royalist guns and cavalry. The
official account paid tribute to Merrick's 'skill and care'. He had served on the
continent and, after commanding an infantry regiment during the Edgehill campaign,
had taken command of the artillery train in place of the late Earl of Peterborough
(father to the current earl who was riding as a volunteer with the king's cavalry).
Merrick's main target was the king's cavalry, some of whom were protecting the
Royalist battery and standing closer to the Parliamentarian guns than would usually
have been the case, and the Parliamentarian gunners proved to be better at their
business than Lord Percy's men.

Whereas Foster and his Blue Regiment comrade were ultimately dismissive of the
Royalist guns, the Parliamentarian battery clearly inflicted significant casualties. The
first messenger to reach London described how 'he saw the Lord General's gross
ordnance fired upon the cavaliers, which made such lanes amongst them, that many
of them fell to the ground'. Hyde acknowledged that Essex's guns 'did very great
execution on the king's party'. Among the dead were the Earl of Sunderland, riding
with the King's Lifeguard and 'taken away by a cannon bullet'; Colonel Thomas
Morgan, one of Sir John Byron's regimental commanders, killed by another cannon
ball; and Lieutenant Colonel Thomas Eure, serving in Charles Gerard's brigade. The
infantry were also targeted. Colonel Belasyse 'escaped a dangerous shot ... from a
cannon bullet, which killed his horse under him and tore part of his breeches'. The two

demi-culverins at the other end of the Parliamentarian line on Newbury Common were no less effective. According to the official account, a party of Royalist musketeers had occupied a house on the northern edge of the Common (the only building mentioned on the battlefield) from where they 'pelted' some of Barclay's men standing in the enclosures facing Sir Nicholas Byron's enclave on Cope Hall Lane. Skippon, who like Rupert was riding across the battlefield from crisis to crisis, ordered the demi-culverins 'to bestow eight or ten . . . shot upon the enemy', which evidently removed the problem.

The Royalist lines, afternoon.[8]

As artillery and musketeers duelled along the front, from the Kennet Valley through Round Hill to Newbury Common, it became apparent to the king and his generals that they faced not only the prospect of stalemate, which was strategically acceptable, but of logistic disaster, which was not. Essex's army, although unsupplied with ammunition since leaving Aylesbury on 29 August, showed no sign of running out of powder or shot. By contrast, the Royalists were rapidly exhausting their stocks. *Mercurius Aulicus* admitted later that 'we were (to tell you the truth) in great difficulty for cannon shot' and told a story of one cannon being loaded with a tailor's smoothing iron instead. Sir John Byron wrote angrily about a 'want of powder'. Parliamentarian officers reported that 'before half the fight was over their powder and shot was so far spent that they were not able to answer us one shot for three'. Digby explained that the Royalist army had started the day with over 100 barrels of powder, eighty 'more than had served the turn at Edgehill', but the battle was lasting longer and the way in which it was being fought was producing an unexpectedly high rate of expenditure.

At some time during the afternoon, the Royalist commanders were forced to address this unpalatable development. The only practical option was to send to the magazine at Oxford for more supplies, which meant a twenty-six mile ride, finding and mobilising the stocks and wagons to carry them, and then bringing the convoy back to Newbury, the equivalent of two days stiff march by seventeenth century standards. It is difficult to avoid the conclusion that the king's generals, and Lord Percy in particular, had delayed the decision for too long. Nonetheless, an order was signed by the king requiring Sir John Heydon 'immediately upon sight hereof to send unto us fifty barrels of powder with match and bullet proportionable. And for ye pieces of cannon which we have here twenty shot round'. When the message arrived in Oxford, between seven and eight that evening, it was actioned quickly by Secretary Nicholas and Heydon but it was three o'clock the following morning before a convoy of thirteen wagons carrying 380 iron round shot, fifty barrels of powder, and two tons each of match and musket shot was on its way south.

Newbury Common, afternoon[9]

On Newbury Common, the fighting was reaching a climax. The Red and Blue Regiments, supported by Merrick's guns, had held the Royalists at bay for three hours. Sergeant Foster commented grimly that 'our ordnance did very good execution upon them: for we stood at so near a distance upon a plain field, that we could not lightly miss one another'. Eventually, however, the pressure told and the Trained Bands sought cover from the artillery, either spontaneously or as the result of an orderly shift of position. The cover they wanted was offered by the biggest of the tumuli which stood a little to their left. Royalist infantry from the brigades of Belasyse and Sir

Gilbert Gerard had been sheltering passively behind it since the morning, but both they and the Trained Bands were now desperate enough to come to close quarters to secure this unique protection. According to Foster,

> our Red Regiment joined to the Blue . . . [and] gained the advantage of a little hill, which we maintained against the enemy half an hour: two regiments of the enemy's foot fought against us all this while to gain the hill, but could not.

However, when the Royalist foot withdrew, the Trained Bands were quickly confronted by a much more dangerous threat. By advancing to the cover of the tumulus, the Red and Blue Regiments had moved away from their supporting guns, broken the Parliamentarian line and made themselves extremely vulnerable to another cavalry attack. And this time, Rupert was in command. According to Prince Rupert's Diary, which implies that the attack was only necessary because Belasyse's infantrymen still 'would not march', Rupert had with him his own troop of lifeguards (generally held to be about 140 strong) plus Wilmot's regiment (355 strong the previous December) with the Lieutenant General of Horse in person at its head. Foster's account suggests that they were divided into two squadrons and since the space available between the tumulus and the western edge of the Common was little more than 150 yards, it would have been impossible to charge with more than eighty or so men in each squadron's three ranks.

Nonetheless, even with such small numbers, Rupert again made the difference. Wilmot's regiment and the prince's troop quickly overran the Parliamentarian artillery battery, where some of them dismounted and started to harness up the cannon to drag them away. The rest carried on towards the Trained Band infantry. Caught on open ground and vulnerable to attack from front and flanks, the two regiments might have been expected to disintegrate. Instead, their peacetime training asserted itself. Foster recorded that two bodies of the Royalist cavalry 'came fiercely upon us, and so surrounded us, that we were forced to charge upon them in the front and rear, and both flanks'. In other words, the Red and Blue Regiments formed the kind of squares popularly associated with British soldiers of later centuries, and poured musket fire into Rupert's horsemen while keeping them at a distance with their pikes. The 'hollow-square girdled with shot', formed by interior ranks of standing pikemen and exterior ranks of musketeers, crouching or kneeling under the pikes, was a standard defence against cavalry in contemporary manuals but to form one in these circumstances, rapidly and with the enemy advancing, was another testimony to the quality of the Londoners' training and cohesion.[10]

Even Hyde paid them a fulsome tribute:

> [The] London Trained Bands and Auxiliary regiments, (of whose inexperience of danger, or any kind of service, beyond the easy practice of their postures in the Artillery Garden, men had till then too cheap an estimation) behaved themselves to wonder; and were, in truth, the preservation of that army that day. For they stood as a bulwark and rampart to defend the rest; and . . . kept their ground so steadily, that, though Prince Rupert himself led the choice horse to charge them, and endured their storm of small shot, he could make no impression upon their stand of pikes, but was forced to wheel about

Digby too accepted that the Parliamentarian foot remained unbroken and 'showed themselves like good men' although he claimed that the Royalists succeeded in dragging one of the cannon back to their own lines. On the Parliamentarian side Foster recorded that 'we made a great slaughter among them, and forced them to retreat'. Royalist casualties were undoubtedly heavy. In the confined space between the Common's edge and the tumulus, the cavalrymen were especially vulnerable to even the slow rate of fire of matchlock muskets. Prince Rupert's Diary recorded that his troop suffered thirty casualties in this action alone, which suggests that Wilmot's Regiment may have lost another seventy-five men. Wilmot himself was unhorsed and the Earl of Cleveland 'knocked down'.

Rupert pulled his cavalrymen back to regroup and, according to the Diary, took command of a pair of cannon: 'his hi[ghness] caused some shot to be made at ye enemy, whereupon they retired into the hedges'. The implication is that although the prince's cavalry attack had not driven the Parliamentarians from the common, their morale had been shattered by it. Once again, however, the truth was not quite as simple. It was in fact the much maligned Royalist infantry who demonstrated sufficient initiative to exploit Rupert's charge. Foster admitted that 'the two regiments of the enemy's foot in this time gained the hill, and came upon us before we could well recover ourselves, that we were glad to retreat a little way into the field'. Square formations worked against cavalry but they were highly vulnerable to infantry, whether musketeers or pikemen, and as the men of Belasyse's and Gerard's brigades attacked around the tumuli, the Red and Blue Regiments evidently broke and sought shelter behind the hedges at the western side of the Common.

Essex's army faced another crisis moment. This time it was the earl himself who stemmed the tide. He had been prominent throughout the battle in organising and leading the forces on Newbury Common, 'present in all places of danger'. Like King Charles, he was inevitably a target but refused to take a low profile on the battlefield. Codrington wrote that 'in the heat and tempest of the fight, some friends of his did advise him to leave off his white hat, because it rendered him an object too remarkable to the enemy'; the earl apparently refused saying 'it is not the hat, but the heart; the hat is not capable either of fear or honour'. Fighting the battle from Newbury Common was not an abdication of responsibility as some writers have suggested but the kind of bold personal leadership for which other generals are celebrated. Middle-aged, physically unprepossessing and mocked by his enemies as a cuckold, Essex was genuinely popular with his troops because he looked after their welfare and shared their risks in the battle line. Throughout the campaign, he had led from the front and his army had responded. The same was true now on Newbury Common.

Despite Foster's underplaying of the Trained Bands' retreat, it is clear from another Parliamentarian account, in the newspaper *Mercurius Civicus*, that the two regiments had been severely mauled by the Royalist infantry: 'the enemy had broken through them and almost routed them, so that many of the Trained Bands ... were ready to fly and turn their backs to the enemy'. Essex had no reserves left. If the Londoners bolted, his army could – and probably would – disintegrate. He therefore rode among them, using

> many excellent encouragements to persuade them not to fly or stir from their
> ground, wishing them to remember what the cause was they fought for,
> that it was for the Protestant religion, and for the glory of God, and for the

liberties of them and their posterity: that they should not be discouraged though some of their fellow soldiers lay dead at their feet, for that their retreat would much animate the other party, and they would by that means soon rout the whole army.

The earl's personal intervention succeeded. Before the Royalists could regroup and resume their attack, the Red and Blue Regiments 'were so animated, that they charged upon the enemy with more resolution than ever, and His Excellency having rallied them together, led them on again in the face of the enemy'. Foster agreed that when the Trained Bands had rallied and been put 'into their former posture' of lines rather than squares, they 'came on again'. The Parliamentarian line had been restored, though only at 'great danger and hazard' to Essex personally. As the Trained Bands advanced 'a cannon bullet of about four and twenty pound weight grazed on the ground about a yard from him, and cast up the earth upon his Excellency and diverse others that were near unto him'. Had Essex been killed at this point, his army could yet again have been defeated.

Kennet valley to Newbury Common, late afternoon to evening[11]

Nonetheless, from the king's point of view, even with the earl in command the battle was by no means lost. Essex had to reach Reading to save his army and as the afternoon turned to evening he was as far as ever from achieving that aim. The Royalists had failed to destroy the earl's forces or even throw them back from the Wash Common plateau but neither had the Parliamentarians come close to making any kind of breakthrough. At best, they had avoided tactical defeat while still facing strategic disaster. With hindsight, perhaps the most important aspect of the battle's final phase was that it was happening at all. Musket and artillery fire continued along the whole front, using powder and shot which Lord Percy's supply train could neither afford to lose nor replace.

On the slopes of Round Hill the stalemate continued into the evening, although both sides tried to retake the local initiative. Major Butler led Essex's Regiment and a reinforcement of 200 musketeers across Cope Hall Lane to recover the three guns lost when Sir John Byron's cavalry chased off Skippon's and Brook's regiments. Then, at about four o'clock, 600 Royalist musketeers from the brigades of Belasyse and Sir Gilbert Gerard, supported by dragoons, were seen advancing through the fields to the north of Newbury Common towards Round Hill. These were the right tactics but a further and now unnecessary expenditure of ammunition. As it was, a detachment of the Red Auxiliary Regiment came to the assistance of Barclay and Holburn's battered brigades, and according to the official account together they 'beat the enemy off, who else had done us great mischief'. Despite this final repulse, both Royalists and Parliamentarians felt that they had had the better of the day on Round Hill. To Digby, it was clear that the enemy had held the ground, been ejected and then tried but failed to recapture it. By contrast, Parliament's official account was equally certain that Essex had 'beat them from the hill, and kept it (rather gaining than losing ground) the whole day'.

On Newbury Common, the fighting seems to have died down earlier than elsewhere. After Essex rallied the Trained Bands, there are no references to attacks by either side. The Royalist guns were probably out of ammunition, the infantry exhausted and cowed, and the cavalry chastened by their failure to break the Trained Bands. To the Blue Regiment soldier, it seemed that the 'enemy's foot were so shattered that they were fain to be kept up by their horse'. On the other side of the Common, the Parliamentarian artillery resumed its steady battering of the exposed Royalist cavalry, who were obliged to remain in place until the eight gun battery could be removed. Prince Rupert's Diary noted that Essex's cannon 'did a great deal of mischief, especially to [Rupert's own] Regiment, which was then newly come up to him'. Otherwise the Parliamentarians will have been content with the status quo and unwilling to provoke more attacks. Indeed, Royalist accounts suggest that some or even all of Essex's infantry were now deployed not in the open but behind the hedgerows on the common's western fringe. For the moment, their main problem was hunger and thirst; 'during the whole day our soldiers could not get a drop of water to drink' wrote Parliament's historian, John Vicars. Sergeant Foster agreed:

> we were in great distress for water, or any accommodation to refresh our poor soldiers ... we were right glad to drink in the same water where our horses did drink, wandering up and down to seek for it.

A London newspaper reported that one soldier had paid ten shillings for a quart of water. But there are no indications that the soldiers were deserting their posts in large numbers.

Though the sun set at around six o'clock, desultory skirmishing continued for some time. Digby wrote that the fighting ended an hour later. One of the London newspapers described a sally by 'a great body' of Royalist cavalry on Newbury Common which was interpreted as an attack on Essex's baggage train, although it appears in fact to have covered the withdrawal of the eight artillery pieces from what would have been an even more exposed position once night fell. According to Parliament's official account, firing continued in the Kennet Valley and on Round Hill until ten o'clock, 'about which time the enemy gave a good round salvo upon Colonel Barclay, and Colonel Holburn's posts'. Whatever the exact time, the battle had lasted for well over twelve hours. Both sides were exhausted and had suffered an unprecedented outpouring of blood, from aristocrats and commoners alike.

Royalist lines, evening[12]

During this time King Charles, who had been appalled by the losses suffered by the aristocracy and gentry at Bristol, had watched horrified as rebel cannon and muskets scythed through the flower of England's nobility on Newbury Common. This is not twenty-first century hindsight. Sir Edward Hyde, the king's devoted servant, wrote bitterly that

> the loss on the king's side was in weight much more considerable and penetrating; for whilst some obscure, unheard of colonel or officer was missing on the enemy's side, and some citizen's wife bewailed the loss of her husband, there were, on the other, above twenty officers of the field, and persons of honour, and public name, slain upon the place, and more of the same quality hurt.

Wilmot's adjutant, Sir Richard Bulstrode, recalled that 'we staked there pearls against pebbles, and lost some men there of great consideration'.

How far the king's aversion to casualties among his friends and court influenced the discussion in the Royalist council of war held that night is impossible to say. It must, however, have affected the mood. Not surprisingly, Lord Digby did not mention it in purporting to give a comprehensive account of the factors under consideration, claiming instead that because the Royalist army was 'extremely tired' and their scouts were reporting that most of Essex's men had retreated, it was decided to withdraw the cavalry across the River Kennet and the infantry into Newbury 'principally to refresh them, and to enable them for the next day's pursuit'. But he also admitted that the withdrawal was in part 'to make a bridge to a flying enemy, lest indeed too great a despair of retreat might have made them opiniate a second fight in that disadvantageous place'. Hyde gave a similar explanation:

> though the number of slain was not so great as, in so hot a day, might have been looked for, yet very many officers and gentlemen were hurt; so that they rather chose to take advantage of the enemy's motion, than to charge them again upon the old ground.

If Digby's account is accurate, the Royalist scouts were once again providing faulty intelligence, for the Parliamentarians had not withdrawn. In practice, however, the key factor was the Royalists' shortage of ammunition. According to Digby, they had at most powder for another half day's sustained combat only, and the resupply from Oxford was not expected until noon at the earliest. Prince Rupert's Diary suggests that only ten barrels remained. Lack of powder was evidently used internally as the principle reason for pulling back into Newbury though Sir John Byron thought this was a 'foolish and knavish' excuse for abandoning the hard-won battlefield to a defeated enemy. In his view, the fault lay once again with the Royalist infantry on Newbury Common: when

> intelligence was brought us of the great fright they were in, many of them stealing from their arms in the darkness of the night, we ... quitted all our advantages, and about 12 o'clock at night drew off all our men as if we had been the beaten party.

Parliamentarian spies corroborated Byron's criticism. On 22 September, one reported from villages near Wallingford that he had found 'some of the king's foot ... which ran away from the fight at Newbury'; another 200 infantrymen arrived in Wallingford itself without officers, having 'straggled from their colours'. Near Oxford, a second spy heard that 'many of the [Royalist] foot ran from the fight to their several quarters before it ended'. Byron believed that 'our foot played the jades', yet he also felt that withdrawal was an unnecessary overreaction and blamed the army's commanders for 'another very great error'.

Since the king was present, the decision to abandon the battlefield was taken on his ultimate authority, but Prince Rupert's Diary claimed that it was not a unanimous choice: 'the prince's advice was to keep where they were'. This is yet another example of Rupert's limited influence in the face of the risk-averse Oxford Army establishment. The withdrawal was conducted quietly for the Parliamentarians seem to have been completely unaware that it had taken place and the exhausted Royalist army will at least have been able to snatch a few hours sleep. But Byron's analysis was right. By abandoning the Wash Common plateau, King Charles had brought the battle of Newbury to an end and thereby opened the road for the Earl of Essex to leave the trap between the two rivers into which he had been drawn and from which there was no other escape. Whatever the Royalists' reasons for breaking off the fighting, from today's perspective it appears as nothing less than a monumental collapse of nerve.

Chapter Fifteen

'They knocked out their brains with the butt-ends of their muskets'

I

Despite their exhaustion, both armies made recovery of casualties a priority. This was easier on Newbury Common where the Royalist withdrawal to the eastern edge enabled soldiers to move freely among the bodies. Captain Lieutenant Juxon was found alive though mortally injured where his horse had fallen. But there was also much looting. Foster noted the next morning that one hundred bodies lay 'stripped naked in that field where our two regiments stood'. A London newspaper claimed that 'there were diverse fine and rich crucifixes found about the dead, whom we pillaged'. The confused nature of the fighting meant that the fate of many remained unknown. Prince Rupert sent a note to Essex asking 'whether he have the Viscount Falkland, Capt. Bertie, and Sergt-Major Wilshire prisoners, or whether he have their dead bodies, and if he have, that liberty may be granted to their servants to fetch them away'. Falkland and Bertie, the Earl of Lindsey's brother, were both lying dead on the battlefield. John Aubrey described the discovery of Falkland's body the following morning 'stripped, trod upon, and mangled ... [It] could only be identified by one who waited upon him in his chamber, by a certain mole his lordship had upon his neck'.

Lord Digby's letter of 22 September provides a near contemporaneous account of known losses among the Royalists' senior ranks. In addition to Falkland and Bertie, Carnarvon, Sunderland, Colonel Thomas Morgan and Lieutenant Colonel Edward Feilding were dead; seven colonels or lieutenant colonels (Andover, Darcy, Thomas Eure, Charles Gerard, Lisle, Lucas and Edward Villiers), the Earls of Carlisle and Peterborough, and a clutch of other aristocratic volunteers, had been wounded. From other sources, it appears that Sir Anthony Mansell, Colonel Thomas Dalton and Lieutenant Colonel Haughton were also killed, and Lord Wentworth and Colonel Thomas Pinchbeck wounded. Eure and Pinchbeck died later of their injuries. Though Digby claimed that overall losses were only half those of the Parliamentarians, the evidence is that the contrary was true.

The Royalist list of 'hurt soldiers', a working document rather than propaganda which covers most of the infantry formations, shows that on the south bank of the River Kennet, Vavasour's brigade had three officers and forty-five 'common soldiers' sufficiently badly wounded to be taken to Bristol to be treated; the King's Lifeguard, which reinforced them, had twenty-nine ordinary soldiers injured. On the slopes of Round Hill, Sir Nicholas Byron's brigade reported that twenty-nine officers and 252 men had been wounded; while on Newbury Common, Sir Gilbert Gerard's brigade had nine officers and 100 soldiers 'slain' and twenty-two officers and 116 soldiers 'shot', and Belasyse's brigade recorded 139 soldiers, though no officers, wounded. These figures are undoubtedly incomplete (it is unlikely that Belasyse's eleven regiments sustained not a single casualty among their officers). Nonetheless, presuming that the proportion of dead to wounded sustained by Gerard's brigade was the norm across the battlefield, they show a very high percentage of losses; on Round Hill, Sir Nicholas Byron would have suffered 500 dead and wounded or twenty-five per cent of his brigade's strength, and Gerard a similar proportion on Newbury Common.

Although few contemporary details survive of the casualties to Darcy's infantry brigade or Lisle's commanded musketeers, both commanders had been wounded, together with Lisle's co-commander Lord Wentworth and one of Darcy's regimental colonels, Thomas Pinchbeck; and as many as five captains were killed or mortally wounded. Neither formation was subject to the mauling inflicted on Sir Nicholas Byron's regiments, but they were fighting for many hours among the same hedgerows and it is improbable that their casualty rate was proportionately much less than half that of their neighbours. If so, Darcy's 800 men and Lisle's 900 are together likely to have lost around 200 of their number killed or wounded. Altogether, this analysis suggests that the Royalist infantry suffered casualties in the region of 1,300 men, including more than 550 fatalities.

Losses to the Royalist cavalry proved to be one of the battle's enduring controversies. King Charles was again shocked by the carnage inflicted on the country's aristocracy and Hyde suggested that the casualties were suffered disproportionately by officers and blue-blooded volunteers: 'though the number of the slain was not as great, as, in so hot a day, might have been looked for, yet very many officers and gentlemen were hurt', including more than twenty field officers or noble volunteers 'slain upon the place', most of them riding with the cavalry. But the sole near-contemporary estimate of unit casualties paints a rather different picture. According to Prince Rupert's Diary, the prince lost 300 men from his regiment that day, including thirty from his own troop, presumably from Parliamentarian artillery and Trained Band muskets. Even if the early clashes with Stapleton's cavalry produced relatively few casualties, the later attacks by Rupert and Wilmot, and the stand-off in front of Merrick's guns, appear to have caused losses beyond the aristocratic elite. Assuming these figures were for dead and wounded (if they were for fatalities only, they were truly horrific), the total number of casualties among the 4,000 or so Royalist horsemen on the Common was probably in the region of 500. In addition, Sir John Byron later claimed that in fighting among the enclosures on Round Hill, terrain entirely unsuitable for horsemen, 'I lost near upon a hundred horse and men out of my regiment', in which case Rupert's five brigades together lost around 600 dead and injured, and the king's overall casualty bill was close to 2,000 men.[1]

Arguments about Royalist losses began almost at once and continued throughout the autumn. Foster thought they had lost four times as many as his own army, including seventy 'chief commanders'. TV estimated 500 Royalist bodies on the battlefield but had heard of sixty cartloads of dead and wounded taken into Newbury. Within a couple of days, one of Luke's spies reported that the king had lost 2,000 slain. Another agent brought detailed figures from Oxford: 'Parliament's forces lost 1,000 men and the king 800, whereof 200 were commanders and gentlemen of quality'. London newspapers gave figures ranging from 1,260 to 3,000, and suggested a ten-to-one rate of exchange in Parliament's favour. The Venetian Secretary reported 4,000 dead on both sides. *Mercurius Aulicus* lampooned Parliamentarian claims but was uncharacteristically reticent about the actual figures. When the dust of controversy had settled, Colonel John Belasyse admitted that the battle 'cost us dear by the loss of about 1,000 men', which, given the poor rate of recovery from gunshot wounds, is probably near to the truth.[2]

There is less evidence for Essex's losses. The only recorded death among the Parliamentarian infantry in the Kennet valley was Foster's captain, George Mosse, but since the fighting here was more equal than elsewhere on the battlefield, it is unlikely that their losses were many fewer than Vavasour's reinforced brigade, perhaps around 120 men dead and wounded. On Round Hill, pay warrants suggest that Robartes' brigade lost relatively fewer casualties than other regiments, strengthening the impression that after they brought the Royalist advance on Skinner's Green to a halt, they faced little active opposition for the rest of the day. Although TV recalled that 'the fight was long and terrible ... such crying there was for surgeons as never the like was heard', only three men from his company had been killed in a full day's fighting. TV's regimental commander, Lieutenant Colonel Joseph Bamfield, was dead; Robartes' lieutenant colonel, William Hunter, had been shot in the face; and Sir William Springate was said to have lain for nights injured on the field in Robartes' coach, sustained by 'candied citron and biscuits'. Yet aside from the rout of Mainwaring's regiment and its neighbours, there had been little hand-to-hand combat; no attacks were launched in the face of intense musket fire and artillery; and the Royalists had been outgunned during the prolonged musketry exchanges among the hedgerows. It is therefore unlikely that total Parliamentarian infantry casualties on Round Hill exceeded fifty per cent of the comparative Royalist losses, or some 350 dead and wounded.

Trained Band losses became another propaganda issue. Major Tucker and five captains were either dead or mortally wounded[3], yet *Mercurius Aulicus* ridiculed Parliamentarian claims that no more than 100 soldiers had been killed. Foster, keen to emphasise the contribution made by his comrades, wrote that 'we lost about sixty or seventy men in our red regiment ... besides wounded men, we having the hottest charge from the enemy's cannon of any regiment in the army'. If that were true, it would be consistent for the Blue Regiment, which was larger but not subject to the same intensity of artillery bombardment, to have suffered losses of up to fifty dead to make a total of about 120. So *Mercurius Aulicus* was right to be sceptical of this figure as the total for all five London volunteer regiments, but if the Parliamentarians were referring specifically, and undoubtedly disingenuously, to the two Trained Band regiments proper, they may well have been broadly accurate, in which case their total figure of dead and wounded would have been about 300.

The strongest support for a relatively low number of Trained Band casualties comes, paradoxically, from attempts by *Mercurius Aulicus* to paint a blacker picture. Having argued at the beginning of the campaign that London newspapers were exaggerating the size of Essex's army, it seized on reports of the earl re-entering the capital on 28 September with 3,300 men to claim that if the earlier figures had been accurate, he had suffered much heavier losses than Parliament was prepared to admit. It is, however, clear that the 3,300 men brought into London on 28 September were the five Trained Band and Auxiliary regiments, which means that of the 4,400 or so pikemen and musketeers that marched to Gloucester (excluding Mainwaring's regulars), 1,100 were now absent. Taking account of pre- and post-battle attrition, and the 300 men lost by the Red and Blue Regiments, the Blue Auxiliaries on Newbury Common and the Red Auxiliaries in the Kennet Valley would have sustained about 150–200 casualties between them, a figure consistent with comparative units.

Politics mixed with propaganda. Once back in London, Stapleton was criticised for losing too many of his cavalrymen. There is some evidence for this. Three troops involved in the fighting on Newbury Common show significant falls in muster strength after the campaign compared to July or August; two troop commanders were killed (Captains Ware and St Barbe), and five wounded (Colonel Dalbeir, Muster Master Copley and Captains Fleetwood, Hammond and Charles Pym). Nonetheless, given that the Parliamentarian cavalry were not required to face prolonged artillery or musket fire, it would be surprising if the total losses, including Middleton's wing, exceeded 200 dead and injured.

Taken overall, this analysis suggests that Essex lost 1,000 or so casualties, around 450 of whom had been killed. This is consistent with Whitelock's total of 500 Parliamentarian deaths, which is the most plausible seventeenth century assessment, and about fifty per cent of the Royalist total, the inverse proportion to Digby's claim. Though not the rate of exchange argued by Parliamentarians, it still reflected the tactical advantage won by Essex at the beginning of the day and maintained by his soldiers thereafter.[4] Yet it was not of itself sufficiently decisive to justify confidence on the Parliamentarian side that they had gained more than a stay of execution. For all the successes gained by Essex's soldiers, they had failed to defeat the Royalists and the road to Reading still appeared blocked, which meant that the king had won.

In their own minds, however, it was the Royalists who had been defeated. Despite Rupert's arguments, King Charles and his generals used exhaustion and a shortage of powder to justify an unnecessary retreat from a battlefield where their soldiers had won a clear strategic victory, and where they could next day have stood on the defensive with little danger of defeat. On Newbury Common, the Royalist cavalry retained their numerical and tactical superiority, while among the hedgerows of Round Hill and the Kennet valley it would be as difficult for Skippon's infantrymen to make progress on 21 September as it had been for the king's the previous day. Ammunition was short, yet by Digby's account there was enough for half a day's fighting and the resupply convoy from Oxford was expected at noon. And though the Royalist foot were undoubtedly tired and demoralised, and some were drifting away, the king and his officers should between them have been able to stem the tide.

They do not seem even to have tried. Essex had gambled, kept his nerve and avoided defeat. Charles played safe, but lost both his nerve and the battle. This was the culmination of a campaign of lost opportunities and, once again, a decisive factor in the king's miscalculations seems to have been his sentimental squeamishness at the loss of England's young nobility. With 'above twenty officers of the field, and persons of honour, and public name' dead, and as many others wounded, he was unwilling to order their brothers and cousins to charge yet again into battle on the morrow. As at Gloucester, this aversion to aristocratic casualties led directly to military failure and, from the Royalist point of view, condemned his cause to defeat and his country to another decade of civil war.

If this seems too harsh a judgement on the king and his commanders, it should be considered in the light of what his opponents were expecting to happen when dawn broke on 21 September. The Parliamentarian official account makes it clear that Essex expected the battle to resume, and on unfavourable terms:

> the enemy both horse and foot stood in good order on the further side of the green, where we expected their stay till next morning, and ... they were working (as was reported) to place their cannon, to make use of them against us when day should break; against which supposed encounter we encouraged our soldiers before hand, and resolved by God's help the next day to force our way through them or die.

Sergeant Foster and the other Parliamentarian eyewitnesses confirm that although they considered themselves to have remained in possession of the ground on which the battle had been fought, the Royalists still held the eastern side of Newbury Common and were skirmishing in the hedgerows on Round Hill well after sunset. There is no sense in these contemporary reports that the battle had yet been decided.[5]

II

It did not rain overnight but neither was there shelter, water or food for the Parliamentarian soldiers. Most seem to have slept where their units had ended the day, although Colonel Middleton's cavalry wing advanced into the Kennet Valley, presumably to guard against a surprise attack. Each regiment had its share of wounded, without anaesthetic and with few trained surgeons to treat them. Some of the injuries were hardly treatable; Robert Maddock, a cloth-worker turned Trained Band soldier from the parish of All Hallows the Less, had seen his leg shot off by a cannon ball; Henry Delves, a dyer from the same parish, had both legs smashed by another cannon shot. Essex characteristically spent the night amongst his men. Once again, their officers roused them before dawn and drew them up for battle. Luke's scouts should already have given Essex the news that the Royalists had pulled back but, for the majority, it will have come as a welcome surprise and overdue evidence of God's favour to find as the sky lightened that Newbury Common was empty and the road to Reading open.

The army's battle-order was now closer to the text-book norm. Middleton's cavalry had reinforced the left flank, and the infantry occupied the north slopes and peak of Round Hill, and the top half of Newbury Common, supported on the right by Sir Philip Stapleton's cavalry wing. But this formation was essentially defensive and would not see them through to Reading. For one thing, the Royalists still held Newbury and the Parliamentarian left wing would have to side-step to the south to avoid them. More importantly, the first leg of the route to Reading crossed open ground, Newbury, Greenham and then Crookham Commons, where the army would be as vulnerable to Rupert's cavalry as they had been on the march to Gloucester across the Cotswold Hills. There was no alternative. Essex was still trapped within the sleeve formed by the Rivers Kennet and Enborne. To ford the Enborne would not only disorder the army and offer the king a final chance of victory, but take them south, away from the safety of Reading. Yet beyond Newbury, the next safe bridging point over the Kennet was ten miles away, beyond the three commons at Padworth.

Essex therefore reverted to the tactics used to keep Rupert at bay around Stow-on-the-Wold and Aldbourne Chase. He drew the army into a tight formation on Newbury Common so that the massed infantry regiments could deploy rapidly to offset the

Royalists' advantage in cavalry, and to protect the artillery and baggage train, now carrying hundreds of wounded from the previous day's fighting. This will have taken some hours. According to *Mercurius Aulicus*, barrels of musket and pistol balls, together with surgeons' chests, were left behind, presumably to make room for the casualties. Some heavy carriages were also abandoned, either in haste or to quicken the rate of march. In the meantime, the soldiers already on the Common started to bury their dead comrades (in 'wells, ponds and pits ... and sundry places with arms and legs sticking out' sniped *Mercurius Aulicus*), counted the Royalist corpses and exchanged rumours with pro-Parliament townsfolk from Newbury.

By ten o'clock, the concentration had been completed and the Royalists had still not reappeared so the earl ordered his army to begin a slow march east across Newbury Common. After a single cannon shot had been fired as a token of their victory, Stapleton's horse led the way, with the London brigade towards the back of the column, and a rearguard of four of Middleton's cavalry regiments and a detachment of commanded musketeers under Colonel Barclay. Written instructions were left behind for the rector and churchwardens of the parish of Enborne to complete the task of interring the dead.[6]

III

In Newbury, the Royalist army were in disarray. Some at least had had roofs over their heads, and food and drink to revive them, the cavalry north of the Kennet and the infantry to the south. Most of the wounded had been brought in from the battlefield in cartloads and should have had shelter before the nightmare journey north to Oxford or west to Bristol. But there is little evidence for Lord Digby's contention that the army was preparing 'for the next day's pursuit'. Indeed, it is difficult to discern what the Royalist plans actually were.

Warburton describes Rupert cobbling together a column of cavalry and musketeers, and leaving before dawn to set an ambush ahead of Essex's line of march. That he was in the saddle all night and intended to surprise the Parliamentarians before they reached Reading is supported by Prince Rupert's Diary. Hyde agreed that Rupert shadowed Essex towards Reading and ambushed his army but implied that he should have acted earlier: Rupert 'suffered him, without interruption or disturbance, to pass'. The most detailed, and most contemporary, Royalist version, in *Mercurius Aulicus*, states however that it was Lord Wilmot, supported by the Earl of Northampton, who commanded the initial Royalist pursuit with 'a great fresh body of our horse'.

What seems most likely is that, as Rupert's deputy, Wilmot was given the task of covering the Royalist withdrawal from the battlefield with his own cavalry brigade and that of Lord Carnarvon, now under Northampton, and then of keeping the Parliamentarians under surveillance. Meanwhile Rupert was preparing the largest force possible to follow Essex and attack him if circumstances allowed. Whether this was more than a token final fling is impossible to say. When Essex's column began to move across Newbury Common, Wilmot shadowed them to the north, moving out of sight along the Kennet Valley. Royalist dragoons 'at a great distance shot from several hedges' but, according to the Parliamentarian official account, 'troubled us not', although the threat from the Royalist cavalry was such that once Essex reached Greenham Common, 'a long heath' two miles from his starting point, he 'drew up the whole army several times' to forestall an attack.

The probable reason for the Royalists' unwillingness to do more than harass Essex at long range is that Wilmot had no infantry with him. *Mercurius Aulicus* explained that Wilmot and Northampton 'desired part of the foot to march up to them, which accordingly was ordered, and instantly put in execution'. But Hyde makes clear that fewer than 1,000 commanded musketeers were sent, almost certainly Lisle's detachment, which had followed close on the heels of the cavalry from the Severn valley to Aldbourne and then to Newbury, and fought as well as any among the hedgerows of Round Hill. Rupert seems to have brought up the reinforcements but although the Parliamentarians assessed that their pursuers comprised most of the Royalist horse and 800 musketeers, the balance of forces still favoured Essex; indeed, this was almost an exact re-run of the actions in the Cotswolds during his outward march and there is no basis for Hyde's grumbling that Rupert should have been readier to attack. Had he done so on Greenham Common or the adjacent Crookham Common, Essex's infantry and guns would have had time to form up and beat off the cavaliers with little difficulty.

Rupert can instead be justifiably criticised for not recognising that the campaign was over and for seeking one final opportunity to bloody the retreating Parliamentarians instead of shepherding his battered regiments back to Oxford. It would not be surprising if, after the previous day's bloody stalemate, he too had been infected by the cumulative frustrations of a summer that had promised and delivered much yet ultimately fallen far short of his uncle's expectations. Warburton is wrong to describe what took place as a pre-planned ambush. It bears a far greater resemblance to the misjudged final charges on Aldbourne Chase, when Rupert became embroiled unnecessarily in an action he could not win.[7]

IV

Essex had by late afternoon conducted a cautious stop-start march of about five miles from the western edge of Newbury Common across Greenham and then Crookham Commons. At about four o'clock, the column left the open heathland and, protected by the rearguard, began to enter a narrow lane flanked by fields and hedgerows. It was here that the Royalists struck. Once again, the various accounts do not agree on precisely where the action took place. Walter Money located it between the villages of Aldermaston and Padworth. The earl's only feasible route certainly took the army past the village of Brimpton and across the River Enborne to the village of Aldermaston, from where it was only two miles from the next bridge on the Kennet at Padworth. Money's choice is based on a detailed report published in the London news sheet *Mercurius Britanicus* for 19–26 September, in which the narrow lane was said to be 'near Sir Humphrey Forster's house'. Forster was a Royalist supporter who owned Aldermaston Park, southeast of the village, where he had built a new house in 1636. Two roads ran east from Aldermaston village towards Padworth, and the most southerly passed along the edge of Forster's estate.

Subsequent accounts have largely followed Money's lead. In fact, however, the majority of contemporary descriptions do not support it. *Mercurius Aulicus* located the fighting 'about three miles from Newbury towards Reading', which would put it not beyond Aldermaston but at the eastern end of Crookham Common. Foster described it as 'about a mile and half from a village called Aldermaston' which would place the action near Brimpton, the village closest to Crookham Common. Another reference in *Mercurius Britanicus*, overlooked by Money, related that Essex had marched six or seven miles before the Royalists attacked. While Aldermaston is nine miles from the Newbury battlefield, Brimpton is only six miles or so distant, yet still close enough to Forster's house to locate the events for *Mercurius Britanicus* readers. More importantly, most descriptions agree that the Royalist attack took place at the end of a heath or common. Aldermaston Parish was not heavily enclosed in the seventeenth century but neither did it contain significant areas of common land. The same was true of the parishes to the west, Wasing and Brimpton, through which the Parliamentarians had to march. Only Greenham and Crookham Commons tally with the contemporary accounts.[8]

According to the earliest surviving local maps, including Rocque's 1761 survey of Berkshire and the first detailed Ordnance Survey drawing on the Kingsclere sheet produced by Charles Budgen in 1808[9], Crookham Common narrowed down almost to a point at its eastern end, from where a lane led first to Brimpton and then across the River Enborne to Aldermaston; and the greater part of the land north and east of the Common had been enclosed. As Essex's army reached the end of the open ground, it was therefore funnelled into the lane. The artillery and baggage trains in particular will have had to move in single file through Brimpton and across the Enborne. There was a bridge here, at Shalford, in the mid-eighteenth century but whether the crossing point was a bridge or a ford, it will have delayed the advance. If Rupert wanted a place to ambush the Parliamentarians, this was it. The head of the extended column was probably well across the river before the rearguard could leave the common and vulnerable to cavalry attack along its entire length.

Most accounts of the action come from the Parliamentarian side and there is no indication from any of the sources as to what provoked it. *Mercurius Aulicus* reported simply that

> the last blow was given to the rebels ... in which Prince Rupert (who had three horses shot under him) giving them a fierce charge in their rear, two of their horse regiments were routed and chased into their foot, we doing good execution upon them for a farewell.

Rupert's initial attack was undoubtedly effective. Middleton in fact had four cavalry regiments drawn up to protect the lane's entrance on the eastern edge of Crookham Common, his own and those of Colonels Meldrum and Sheffield, and Lord Grey, close to 1,000 strong. Although these regiments had seen little action at Newbury, they had been shaken at Aldbourne Chase and were still lacking in confidence. According to one Parliamentarian report, Middleton's regiments countercharged before being forced to retreat but the official account noted simply that the Royalist attack 'caused our horse then in the rear to make a very disorderly and confused retreat'. TV complained of 'the base cowardice of our horse ... that upon a weak assault of the enemy they ran away'; and his comrade in the Blue Regiment, near the rear of the column, agreed that the cavalry 'ran away, and did not fire at all'.

Sergeant Foster, who was also close to the action, gave the most graphic description:

> our horse which brought up our rear, durst not stand to charge the enemy, but fled, running into the narrow lane, routed our own foot, trampling many

of them under their horse feet, crying out to them, 'Away, away, every man shift for his life, you are all dead men'; which caused a most strange confusion amongst us.

Barclay's 600 commanded musketeers were broken by the panicking cavalrymen, some throwing away their weapons and joining the headlong flight up the lane. Foster watched in horror as fear engulfed the baggage train: 'many of our wagons were overthrown and broken; others cut their traces and horse harness, and run away with their horses, leaving their wagons and carriages behind them'. Sir Samuel Luke lost not just his wagon and horses but his personal papers, including his commission as scoutmaster. Behind the routing Parliamentarian cavalry came Rupert's men, who 'fell on with great eagerness and resolution', while Lisle's musketeers advanced through the fields alongside the lane and opened fire at the Trained Band regiments from the cover of hedgerows.

For a second time in two days, the cohesion of the Red and Blue Regiments was tested in the most extreme circumstances. The Blue Regiment soldier recalled that when some of the Parliamentarian foot bolted, 'the rest of us, seeing we were lost if we did not stand to it, got our drake up into the lane, and fired it upon them, and so beat them away'. This was not a solo effort. According to Robert Codrington, ten drake light guns were used to stem the Royalist attack. They seem to have been mounted on three wooden platforms and fired case-shot. The lane was 'so crowded with the enemy, that the execution which the drakes performed was very violent, for it did beat down both horse and man, and in the midst of the lane, made a new lane amongst them'. Prince Rupert's Diary suggests that the Prince tried to keep his troopers away from the Parliamentarian foot but Codrington described how the Royalist cavalry 'adventured on the mouth of our ordnance, and on the jaws of death', capturing two of the gun platforms as they did so. Before they could overrun the third, sixty Parliamentarian musketeers led by Middleton, who had dismounted and joined the infantry when his cavalry regiments fled, rushed forward to protect the gunner and his three assistants.

Other Trained Band musketeers clambered through and over the hedges into the fields, where they formed up and advanced against Lisle's infantrymen. This first attack was beaten back, but 'on the second charge . . . they forced the enemy's foot, who lined the hedges, to betake themselves unto their heels'. Having cleared the flanks, the musketeers began to pour musket fire through the hedgerows into the Royalist cavalry in the lane, killing some 'like dogs' and forcing the rest to retreat 'with as much confusion over the heath as they did us before'. They also recaptured the two drakes before the Royalists could drag them away. This was a bitter, bad tempered skirmish. Foster admitted that when a few Royalists tried to surrender, 'our men were so enraged at them that they knocked out their brains with the butt-ends of their muskets'. The chaos was compounded when one of the powder wagons, which had overturned during the rout of the baggage train, exploded, killing two Parliamentarians and burning seven others.

Whether Rupert withdrew his men or they were repulsed as the Parliamentarian accounts claimed, it is clear that the Trained Bands believed that they had won another victory. Foster thought over 100 Royalists had been killed; Codrington agreed. Foster's Blue Regiment comrade reported 120 Royalist dead including a colonel, plus eighty horses, and only seventeen Parliamentarian other ranks. Royalist sources were silent about their casualties though Prince Rupert's Diary conceded that Parliamentarian musketeers behind the hedgerows had savaged a squadron of attacking cavalry under Major Legge. Rupert's personal involvement, leading the attack and losing three horses as a result, added to his reputation as a fighter but suggests that his heart was ruling his head. Far from a Royalist success, the action between Crookham Common and Brimpton was a bloody and unnecessary postscript to the king's failure at Newbury.[10]

V

Most of the Parliamentarian column would have been unaffected by the fighting at the rear but for those directly involved, it had been a traumatic end to the campaign. Not surprisingly, the rearguard withdrew towards Aldermaston as quickly as possible, leaving behind the wrecked baggage wagons. The whole army seems now to have cast caution to the winds. From Crookham Common through Aldermaston to the crossing of the River Kennet at Padworth, and then on to the next sizeable village, Theale, was eight miles. Yet Foster makes clear that even the rearguard covered that distance in no more than four hours, arriving at Theale around ten in the evening. Either Essex had decided that the Royalists no longer posed any threat to his extended column or, more likely, his men determined the pace themselves and were desperate to put the river between themselves and Rupert's cavaliers. Theale was only four miles from the Parliamentarian garrison at Reading and some food seems to have been provided for the exhausted soldiers, although Foster makes no reference to it. For most, a roof over their heads will have been the best they could expect, and the majority will have had to sleep in the open once again. Next day, Friday 22 September, the earl's army was drawn up and marched to Reading where, Foster recorded with relief, 'we refreshed our soldiers after our hard service and wearisome marchings'. Essex himself composed a letter to Parliament describing his victory and, as usual, detailing his army's urgent needs.[11]

Back at Newbury, the king's army was if anything in an even worse state. Once the Parliamentarians had marched away during the late morning of 21 September, it was the Royalists' turn to scour the battlefield for their dead. This was when Lord Falkland's body was discovered and Lieutenant Gwyn noted the file of six Parliamentarian soldiers decapitated by a single cannon ball. Newbury Common was littered with the detritus of war. In addition to abandoned wagons and supplies, Essex was rumoured to have buried some of his artillery as well as his army's dead. *Mercurius Aulicus* noted that members of King Charles' own troop tried to clear a deep well of bodies, and pulled up eight or nine 'but left off the rest as not able to endure the noisomeness of the employment'. Their motives may not have been humanitarian. The buff coats of the more affluent Trained Band soldiers were especially prized by the Oxford Army infantry.

In Newbury itself lay more than a thousand Royalist injured soldiers, the majority with gunshot wounds and therefore at particular risk of infection and death. In London, it was reported that King Charles 'desired to see the wounded, which, some say, having viewed, he went sadly away'. Following Essex's example, the king issued instructions for the local authorities to take care of the casualties of both sides, but added that when they had recovered, rebels as well as Royalists should be sent to Oxford. Earlier in the year, in response to an officers' petition, a military hospital had been set up at Yarnton, north of the city. That will have been the destination of many of the injured, although those from Vavasour's western regiments faced a longer journey back to Bristol. During the day, a first convoy of thirty cart loads was reported to have left for Oxford. A second convoy followed two days later. As with the Parliamentarian wounded, jolting slowly back towards London, their suffering will have been almost unimaginable. In a letter dated 25 September, Sir Henry Anderson wrote that the 'sight of so many brought to Oxford, some dead, some wounded, since the battle, would make any true English heart bleed'. But these were only the most seriously injured. As one of Luke's spies reported, many of the walking wounded had to shift for themselves, so that 'a great number of sick, maimed and other soldiers have been for these three days straggling from the army to their several quarters'.

After the forced march from Evesham and a day of pitched battle, both fit and wounded urgently needed sustenance. As usual, the answer was a mixture of commerce and coercion. On 22 September, while Essex moved east from Theale, 'all of the country about Reading, Wallingford and Abingdon carried in great store of provision ... to His Majesty'. That night, the unfortunate people of Theale paid a heavy price for Essex's decision to bivouac with them when 1,000 Royalist horse appeared and plundered the village of whatever the Parliamentarians had left them. Other reports spoke of Royalist cavalry pillaging 'all the country about Newbury and within four miles of Reading'.

Rupert's return from his harrying of Essex's rearguard with another batch of casualties will only have heightened the Royalists' gloom. Lord Digby's hastily written official account of the campaign, signed at Newbury on 22 September, was evidently intended to counter any impression that the campaign and battle had not been a resounding victory. It even acknowledged that critics already existed in the king's own camp. The letter was needed because there was as much danger of some Royalists 'charging the conduct of His Majesty's designs with rashness and imprudence, as of the Rebels perverting the truth of the success of His Armies'. From Parliamentarian intelligence reports, it is however clear that the battle was generally being seen as a reverse for the king. Within the Royalists' heartland around Oxford, the extent of losses among the aristocracy was already widely known, as was the poor performance of the infantry and the army's overall 'very sad condition'. When during the night of 21–22 September a messenger found Hopton at Marlborough with another 1,200 reinforcements from the seemingly inexhaustible Bristol garrison, it was to deliver 'news of the unfortunate issue' of the battle. It is therefore striking that while his army began to march back towards Oxford, the king lingered in Newbury for three nights and two full days after the fighting had ended. He was certainly concerned for the wounded. One of Luke's spies heard that he himself was ill. But the most likely reason for the delay is that he wanted to prepare the political ground in Oxford for a triumphal return. For both sides, the final stage of the campaign would be a propaganda battle, bloodless yet no less bitter than what had gone before.[12]

Chapter Sixteen
'A stop to the career of the king's good success'

I

To be effective, propaganda requires a minimum of facts to interpret or distort. The strategic geography of Essex's relief of Gloucester and subsequent return march meant that his political masters in London were for the most part in the dark about his progress. Although rumours that the Royalists had raised the siege started to arrive in London on 7 September, Parliament's leaders had not learned for sure that Gloucester had been saved until Essex's first despatches arrived on 14 September, delivered by a boy messenger. The Venetian Secretary, briefed by letter from Royalist Secretary Nicholas, thought that the king still held the whip hand but acknowledged that the good news had boosted morale among Parliament's leaders: 'With matters in this state they do not lose heart here'.

Meeting on 15 September, the House of Commons listened first to the earl's letter of 10 September, giving a brief account of his march from Aynho to Gloucester, the state of the garrison and a request for its reinforcement, and then to one from Colonel Massey of 11 September setting out his urgent needs. MPs' relief was such that they were prepared to agree almost everything: Massey would be rewarded with £1,000 and promotion; the garrison's back-pay plus an extra month's bonus, £4,000 in total, would be paid immediately; 1,000 foot and some troops of horse would be sent to reinforce Massey; letters of thanks would be sent to Essex, Massey, Mayor Wise and the Gloucester townsmen; and a public thanksgiving would be held throughout London on the following Sunday. In this unusual spirit of generosity, they even granted £20 to the messenger-boy. Finally, to reassure the families and friends of London soldiers, an up-beat letter from an officer in Colonel Harvey's cavalry regiment was rushed into print. Three days later, another letter arrived from Essex reporting the capture of Cirencester. After that, the curtain descended once more on his movements.

Once Essex had started his march south from Tewkesbury on 15 September, Massey characteristically filled the information gap with a second letter to Parliament containing an expanded list of requirements. By drawing the Royalists southwards, Essex opened the route from Gloucester to London and it took a deputation only two or three days to slip around the north of Oxford, reaching the capital by 19 September. Major Constance Ferrer was the leader and spokesman, accompanied by Captains White and the younger Pury. When Ferrer addressed the Commons on 19 September, he wanted more money to pay the garrison's arrears (£8,000 according to *Mercurius Aulicus*) and more troops, including 400 of the Earl of Stamford's men from Exeter, which had surrendered to Prince Maurice on 7 September. Though the Commons rapidly agreed to Ferrer's requests, and ordered the confiscation of £6,000-worth of property from two Royalist landowners to pay for them, delivering these promises would inevitably take time, not least because Gloucester would now have to take its place among Parliament's pressing priorities.

Meanwhile, the prospect of Essex's army being bottled up in Gloucester had pushed Sir William Waller firmly back into the limelight, either to march to the earl's rescue or defend London if the Royalists were victorious in the west. From Gloucester, Essex wanted Waller 'speedily sent down into these parts, which is the only means to preserve those friends you have here'. The Venetians were sceptical about Waller's reputation and motives: 'he has no wish to see his enemy Essex successful'. Parliament was more concerned about the size of his under-strength army. On 12 September the Commons directed that Waller should be reinforced by 5,000 foot impressed in London and the south-east, and 3,400 of the Earl of Manchester's newly recruited horse and dragoons. More immediate reinforcements came from the pool of London units, one regiment of cavalry and three or four from the Trained Bands, but when Waller marched west to Staines and Windsor on 21 September, the Venetians estimated that he went with fewer than 6,000 men.[1]

By that time, however, the silence from Essex had again been broken. During the night of 20–21 September, while the Earl's army tended its wounded on the Newbury battlefield, a first messenger arrived in London. He had left the Parliamentarian lines at eight in the morning and could say only that their artillery had opened fire and inflicted casualties. Early on 21 September, London's Committee for the Militia ordered that biscuits, cheese and other food be sent to sustain Essex's men, although with no evidence of the battle's outcome, this was largely a political gesture. Indeed, when a second messenger appeared later in the day, his report was even more ambiguous. While the guns had done great execution and the London Auxiliaries had fought well, the cavalry had retreated after only 'some slight skirmish', and the battle was still undecided. As late as 22 September, the news sheet *Certaine Informations* was prepared only to speculate that if 'yesterday's news prove true ... the Cavaliers' army was as good as defeated at Newbury'.

Later that day, hard news finally arrived and the Parliamentarian propaganda machine swung into action. The best surviving indication of how this occurred comes from *Mercurius Aulicus*, which immediately went onto the offensive to ridicule Parliament's message. Politically, London's focus had moved on to the Solemn League and Covenant and the prospect of intervention by a Scottish army, while John Pym, Parliament's consummate political manipulator, was increasingly debilitated by cancer. But Pym knew better than anyone the risks Parliament had run and the debt it owed to Essex for preserving the army and, though weak, he was still engaged. Given the strong sense of stage management in the way in which news of Newbury and Essex's return was handled, this was probably Pym's last hurrah.

Indeed, it was unlikely to have been a coincidence that the officer nominated by Essex to carry his report to Parliament was John Pym's soldier-son, Charles, an MP with fresh wounds from the cavalry action on Newbury Common. Charles Pym brought news of a hard-fought battle of attrition, the king having suffered disproportionate losses as Essex forced his way through to Reading. *Mercurius Aulicus* mocked the Commons' efforts to make this account the only authorised version of the battle, and the London news books were indeed quickly flooded with other eyewitness testimonies, but they all served to reinforce the impression that Newbury and the campaign as a whole had been Essex's victory. The Commons certainly treated it as such. They set aside Sunday 24 September to give thanks for the 'good success of the Lord General's army' and appointed a committee of both Lords and Commons to 'acquaint his Excellency what value and esteem the Houses set upon the great service done by the blessing of God upon the conduct of his Excellency and the valour of the army'. The committee was also tasked to assure Essex that his requests for men, money and supplies would of course be met.[2]

Having set the stage in London, the next step was to fill it. To foreclose the possibility that the king would repeat the strategy of the previous year with a march on the capital, Essex did not bring his exhausted army back from Reading until sure that the campaign was truly over. Only on 24 September was it clear from Sir Samuel Luke's agents that the Royalist army was withdrawing to Oxford. Meanwhile, the soldiers ate, drank and slept, and Essex took stock. The London Trained Bands had performed beyond expectations but having achieved their objective by relieving Gloucester they would now have to be demobilised. Morale and clothing aside, that left his army in little better shape than earlier in the summer. What had changed was the threat posed by the Royalists. With the campaigning season coming to a close, London was no longer in any immediate danger and Essex could therefore begin to prepare for the winter. In the short term, the army would regroup on Windsor.

Sunday 24 September was a day of celebration in London and for the soldiers at Reading, where they 'gave public thanks for the great victory'. Next morning, the army marched out for the last time together. Essex was accompanied by the Parliamentary committee, keen to bathe in his new reflected glory. The Trained Bands advanced to Maidenhead where they quartered for the night; Essex led his regular regiments, the artillery train and, it was claimed, 500 Royalist prisoners further on to Windsor. That day in London, 112 MPs signed the Solemn League and Covenant at St Margaret's church, an act of religious commitment by some, a pragmatic recognition of military weakness and political necessity by others. The Venetians noted fears that the treaty and the intervention of a large Scottish army would buy 'a more painful slavery, instead of liberty', so the imminent return of Essex and London's Trained Band heroes was even more timely than ever.

At this point, the sense of orchestration is very evident. Foster wrote that on 26 September 'we advanced from Maidenhead about four o'clock in the morning, having some intention of marching to London that night, but came no farther than Brentford, where we stayed the next night also, being a fast day'. More likely, Pym and Essex wanted to draw out the celebrations and allow the Earl to milk the political benefits of success before the Trained Bands stole the limelight. Meanwhile, seven other Trained Band regiments were mustered at Finsbury Fields, reinforcing the impression of Parliament's military might. While Foster and his comrades dallied at Brentford, Essex rode in triumph from Windsor into London, to his home at Essex House. Parliament rushed to pay him court. The Lords passed a motion that they should go 'to give his Lordship thanks ... for his great service done to this Kingdom'; the Commons followed suit, commending his 'incomparable conduct and courage'. Bulstrode Whitelocke recalled how they congratulated the General his safe return to them. The Lord Mayor and Aldermen of London waited in their scarlet gowns upon the General, and highly complemented him, as the protector and defender of their lives and fortunes, and of their wives and children.

Essex can rarely have enjoyed a more agreeable afternoon.

Two days later, on Thursday 28 September, the theatre of victory reached its climax. Londoners' expectations had been manipulated to fever pitch by the calculated delay. Now their husbands, fathers, friends and sons were marching proudly back from what they were being told was Parliament's greatest victory of the war. All five Trained Band and Auxiliary regiments, 3,300 strong, together with Harvey's cavalry paraded from Brentford to the City, with green branches in their hats as they had worn at Newbury. The Venetian Secretary described them 'all crowned with laurel' and Foster concluded his account of the campaign: 'the Lord Mayor together with the aldermen of the City met us at Temple Bar, and entertained us joyfully: many thousands bidding us welcome home, and blessing God for our safe return'. At Finsbury Field, Essex reviewed the five Regiments and formally dismissed them from service. As the militiamen, apprentices and volunteers dispersed, he rode back to Westminster to accept further praise from the House of Lords. Here the theatre was even more pronounced as the earl entered the chamber with six colours captured, he said, at Cirencester and Newbury, tangible evidence of his success.

Not everyone was convinced. *Mercurius Aulicus* reported that George Ulrick, Colonel Dalbier's major, had been arrested for saying 'openly in the streets, that the king's army had much worsted His Excellency's ... killing two for one'. *Aulicus* also alleged, implausibly, that Essex had press-ganged 'poor shepherds and labourers' to march with the army to hide the number of casualties suffered and the Venetians told a similar story of London militiamen creeping out the night before the Trained Bands' return to make up their depleted numbers. More credibly *Aulicus* argued that the flags paraded in the Lords all came from the capture of Cirencester and demonstrated nothing about the outcome at Newbury. Essex's return was nonetheless a spectacular success. On 6 October, the Venetian Secretary reported that the earl 'moves in a halo of glory here, having recovered his reputation by the relief of Gloucester and vindicated himself with the citizens of London, who had reviled him'.[3]

Parliament's propaganda barrage kept up throughout October and beyond. On 2 October, Sergeant Foster's account was published. Five days later, the official version, *A True Relation of the Late Expedition of His Excellency, Robert Earl of Essex for the Relief of Gloucester, with the Description of the Fight at Newbury* was authorised by the House of Commons. London's news books added detail and claims, some credible, others outlandish but, a few mild criticisms aside, all trumpeted Essex's success and the contribution of the capital's valiant Trained Bands.[4]

Yet by painting Newbury as an unqualified victory, Parliament created a new set of dangers for itself. So convincing was the propaganda message that some Parliamentarian leaders began to believe it. If the king had been comprehensively defeated and his infantry decimated, surely now was the time to march on Oxford and finish the war before Scottish intervention became necessary? On 29 September, the weekly Venetian despatch talked authoritatively of meetings between Parliament's political leadership, Essex and Waller to consider besieging Oxford, which was seen by the politicians to be 'the best way of finishing the business, as the thoroughly wearied citizens desire'.

Though the Venetians cynically thought that the generals were reluctant to force the war to a conclusion because that would 'see the end of their honours and advantages', Essex is more likely to have been using the possibility of a thrust against Oxford as a bargaining chip in the new round of funding negotiations with his parsimonious paymasters. According to *Mercurius Civicus*, he had returned to London to treat with Parliament over the army's condition and would only consider marching against Oxford if his demands for supplies and reinforcements were met. In practice, another autumn campaign was never an option. Gloucester and Newbury had restored the earl's reputation and Parliamentarian morale, but Essex knew that Oxford was too ambitious a goal before winter with the forces he had available.

Although militarily too weak to confront King Charles for a third time that year, Essex was now strong enough politically to bring his rival Waller to heel. Sir William's inability to meet his recruiting targets, to which Essex's partisans in London, especially on the Committee of the Militia, had contributed, and his perceived reluctance to march west during the crisis had lowered his political stock. The earl's triumphant return further eclipsed both Waller and his backers at Westminster, and he was quickly able to claw back the primacy in Parliament's military affairs he had been forced to share only a few short weeks before. On 3 October, Essex complained to the House of Lords about 'the great inconvenience that is by the quartering of Sir William Waller's forces within his army' and suggested that unless those forces were put under his command 'some inconvenience will soon happen'. Four day's later, after Waller's supporters had tried to resist, Essex threatened to resign and leave the country unless Sir William surrendered his independent commission. No-one was prepared to call the bluff, both Lords and Commons caved in, and Waller had little choice but to follow suit, returning his commission to the Speaker on 9 October. Pym manufactured a face-saving formula, Essex was publicly magnanimous and an impression of unity was restored but everyone knew that Sir William Waller had been humiliated.[5]

II

King Charles returned to Oxford on Saturday 23 September with the spoils of victory. But aside from a collection of captured colours, a handful of prisoners, and three cannon of uncertain size and origin, the spoils were as elusive as victory had proved to be. The king's propagandists did their best. There was a service of solemn thanksgiving 'for the safety of His Majesty's Sacred Person'. The queen wrote to the Marquis of Newcastle admitting that 'we have lost a quantity of honest men'; but claiming a clear Royalist victory in which the northern regiments had played an important part. Lord Digby's 'Letter from the Army to a Noble Lord' was published on or around 25 September to give the Royalists' authorised version of the campaign. *Mercurius Aulicus* gamely rehearsed the same story but was more convincing in mocking Parliament's inflated claims than in arguing the king's. On 7 October, it listed thirty-five allegedly false assertions or contradictions in its rival London news books, most relating to Newbury, from casualties ('this is the fourth time you printed Sir Jacob Astley dead') to captured booty (two thousand pistols and many crucifixes) and bizarre stories of Royalist witches. For those living in and around Oxford, the state of the Royalist army gave the lie to propaganda claims of battlefield success. From the grieving widows and stricken sons of the nobility to the cart-loads of wounded pikemen and musketeers, the evidence of failure was everywhere. Some units had been broken, either by casualties or the loss of their colonels. Luke's spies painted a dismal picture of much of the rest of the army. For days, great numbers of soldiers, wounded and unwounded, often without officers, were reported slowly making their way back to their garrisons. At Abingdon, the men of Sir Lewis Dyve's Foot were complaining about their losses and threatening to desert 'for fear they should be used in the like kind' as at Newbury.

Moreover, while Essex had marched his regiments home in one piece, Charles, Forth and Rupert now presided over the dismemberment of a large proportion of their army. In part, this was an inevitable consequence of the hurried gathering together of so many local units in front of Gloucester. Once the king had conceded the campaign, they were of greater value helping to extend Royalist control at home than in Oxford. Sir William Vavasour departed with his regiments to confront Massey in the Severn valley and Lord Chandos joined him to protect his castle at Sudeley. Colonel Richard Herbert's Regiment and the Prince of Wales' foot, whose commander, Lieutenant Colonel Woodhouse, had been knighted after the battle, marched off to reinforce Lord Capel in the west midlands. To control the road from London to the west, Lieutenant Colonel Boys was commissioned to hold Donnington Castle, on the north bank of the Kennet overlooking Newbury, with Lord Rivers' Regiment of Foot and Sir Robert Howard's Dragoons.[6]

In the short term, however, the king's strategic position was by no means unfavourable. Newcastle remained unchallenged in the north, Maurice was mopping up Parliament's outposts in the west, Vavasour would soon blockade Massey at Gloucester and there were signs that the Parliamentarians were about to abandon their hard-won garrison on the Thames at Reading. Hyde recalled that, despite Gloucester and Newbury, 'the parliament was in so much a worse state than they were in the spring'. At a council of war held at Oriel College in Oxford on 29 September, King Charles and his advisers were evidently keen to retain this momentum, returning once again to the strategy of attacking London by strangulation. A winter blockade could undermine morale, prevent Parliament from raising money to finance the Scottish intervention and weaken Essex's army for the next year's campaign. Thereafter, pressure would be applied along the Thames valley, by a new army under Lord Hopton in the south and by Rupert operating against supply lines to the north of the capital. Plans to take the war into Kent were also revived. The Venetians were either briefed or Royalist security was even laxer than usual because only a week after the council the Secretary in London was reporting to his masters on this renewed emphasis on London.

For a while, things went well. In early October the Parliamentarian garrison pulled out of Reading, and Astley reoccupied it with a 3,500-strong garrison. There was talk of Essex and Waller combining to retake it before more prudent counsels prevailed. Sir Lewis Dyve captured Newport Pagnell, Rupert moved to Towcester in support and Hopton began building his army at Bristol. But Hopton was pre-empted when Waller at last advanced westwards to besiege Basing House in Hampshire. Although Hopton eventually shepherded Waller's larger army back to Farnham and captured Arundel Castle, London spent the winter unthreatened from the south. Rupert's initiative ended in a farce of the king's creation. In late October, Essex moved to throw Dyve out of Newport Pagnell. Reinforcements were delayed while Charles and his advisers worried about precedence among potential commanders; supplies were not sent because no wagons were available; and Dyve was sent ambiguous orders which he took to mean that he should withdraw. The surviving correspondence concludes with a grovelling apology to Rupert from Sir Edward Nicholas on behalf of the king:

> What was done by Sir Lewis Dyve, was done, as appears, upon Sir Frederick Cornwallis's mistake of His Majesty's directions, whereof His Majesty is sensible, and will for the future be more careful by whom he conveys his orders.

The *Journal of Prince Rupert's Marches* lamented that 'the mistake about Newport Pagnell ... spoiled all'.[7]

Royalist incompetence at the routine business of ordering and supplying war was exacerbated by an explosion of factionalism in the court and the army. Disagreements were founded less on the fundamentals of policy as in London than on the means used to achieve common ends (Hyde repeatedly complained about the brutality of the professional soldiers, especially Rupert), personalities and individual ambition. Factionalism was hardly new but the influence of the queen, strong-minded and an inveterate schemer, and the appointment of her ally Lord Digby to replace Falkland as Secretary of State combined with bitter recriminations over who was to blame for Essex's escape to create a debilitating atmosphere of intrigue and animosity.

Despite Hyde's distaste for the king's generals, there is no reason to question his picture of autumn in Oxford:

> nothing but dejection of mind, discontent, and secret mutiny in the army, anger and jealousy among the officers, every one accusing another of want of courage and conduct in the actions of the field; and they who were not of the army, blaming them for all their several failings and gross oversights ... [and] the temper of the court was no better than that of the army.

If there was any doubt about which side had really won the campaign, the contrast between the renewed sense of unity in London, no matter how temporary, and this internecine warfare in Oxford should have settled it.

Hyde recorded the arguments in detail. The strategy decided at Bristol had been flawed. Even the officers who had been there and supported it disclaimed the whole design, blaming the abrasive Colepeper for taking them to Gloucester instead of London. At Gloucester, the siege was said to have been mishandled: the city 'might have been taken in half the time they were before it, if it had been skilfully gone about'. This barb was presumably directed at Lord Forth. Rupert's partisans blamed Wilmot for 'not engaging the Earl of Essex in all the march over so open a country' and questioned the Lieutenant General's courage. Rupert himself was criticised for allowing Essex

> after all the horse was joined, to march down a long steep hill into the vale of Gloucester, without any disturbance; and that the whole army, when it was found necessary to quit the siege, had not been brought to fight in that vale, and at some distance from the town, when the king's men were fresh, and the other side tired with so long a march.

At Newbury, younger commanders had attacked prematurely and the artillery had been ineffectual. Sir John Byron's later criticisms of Rupert's reluctance to press home his perceived advantage at Aldbourne Chase and of the overall handling of the battle of Newbury, especially Lord Percy's logistic failure, were presumably also circulating. Percy appears to have fallen out with Rupert at around this time, which suggests that the prince too was critical of his handling of the campaign's logistic support. Despite Hyde's bias against Rupert, the growing hostility to the prince at court and his general absence from Oxford suggests that it was an accurate reflection of the mood among large sections of opinion in the capital.

King Charles was 'much troubled' by the temper of both court and army. Hyde tactfully excluded his monarch from any share of the blame but it would be surprising if the king's reliance on militarily inexperienced courtiers, his tendency to take the advice of the last speaker, the growing influence of the queen and his unwillingness to risk casualties were not the subject of private criticism. However the blame was divided, one of the most important consequences of Gloucester and Newbury was the creation of a deep and enduring fissure in the king's army, not between amateurs and professionals but between the camp party based around Rupert and the ultra-Royalist court party revolving around the queen's favourites. With Falkland gone, the Scots casting an increasingly long shadow, culminating in an invasion of northern England, and the prospect of a negotiated settlement more remote than ever, moderates such as Hyde saw their influence in decline. Whether King Charles could heal the rift would be a critical factor in the success or failure of next year's campaign.[8]

III

For many soldiers on both sides who had survived the heat of combat, Pym's gamble and King Charles' response eventually proved fatal. Few survived gunshot wounds and disease was rampant. Only a few names and dates are known. Among them in London were the maimed Trained Band soldiers Robert Maddock and Henry Delves, who had lost one and two legs respectively to cannon balls, and were buried on 28 September and 11 October. John Salway, one of Essex's lifeguards, lingered until January. Royalist Colonel Thomas Dalton died in Andover on 2 November of the wounds he sustained on Newbury Common, Colonel Thomas Pinchbeck in Oxford on 22 January the following year of those suffered on Round Hill. Although the level of casualties bore no comparison to the continental bloodbaths of the Thirty Years War, they evidently had a significant impact on political perceptions in London. Perhaps because so many of the soldiers wounded at Newbury were respectable citizens of the Trained Band, a special tax of £4,000 per month was levied from November 1643 to provide an allowance of up to four shillings a week for those disabled in the service of Parliament.[9]

For those still fighting, the rest of the year proved to be an anti-climax. Both sides could now only batten down for the winter and prepare for the inevitable widening of the war in 1644. South of London, the armies of Hopton and Waller bickered along a line of garrisons running from Farnham to Southampton and Arundel. In the Thames valley, Astley fortified Reading while the Parliamentarians blocked the road east at Windsor. Much of the king's field army was in garrison in Oxford, Abingdon and Wallingford. Further north, Royalist cavalry raided through the Chiltern Hills and harassed Essex's main quarters in Newport Pagnell, Aylesbury and St Albans.

The Oxford Army diaspora continued in November with the detachment of Sir John Byron, newly raised to the peerage, to Chester to build a new force from troops arriving from Ireland. A couple of months later, Colonels Belasyse and Lucas were sent still further north to join the Marquis of Newcastle's fight against the long awaited Scottish invasion. Meanwhile, troop numbers fell as disease continued to ravage both sides and lack of pay encouraged desertion. Neither King Charles nor the Earl of Essex would ever command such large armies again. By December, muster returns for Essex's infantry regiments had dropped by seventy per cent; the strength of Astley's Reading infantry brigade had fallen by one-third by the spring. It was a difficult and demoralising winter for king and Parliament alike.

What though of the catalyst for the campaign, the City of Gloucester? On 15 September the Commons recommended that Essex should promote Colonel Massey to 'some place of honour and profit'. Massey was ambitious and increasingly at odds with the local committees over money. He responded to Parliament's 'gaudy letter of kindness and value' by asking for an immediate change of post. This was not what the Commons had intended and on 7 October they urged Essex to 'continue Colonel Massey as Governor of Gloucester, and that the gentlemen of the county would take care that the post should be worth his service and employment'. No more than fine words but they were enough to keep Massey in Gloucester.

Militarily, Massey and his garrison benefited briefly from the disappearance of both Royalist and Parliamentarian field armies towards Newbury. He was able to raise money and an attempt to neutralise the Royalist base at Berkeley Castle was thwarted only by Hopton's fortuitous return from the Oriel College council of war. But by the end of the month, Gloucester was once again under increasingly close blockade. To the north, Vavasour occupied Tewkesbury; to the east were Chandos' stronghold at Sudeley and a new garrison at Beverstone Castle; to the south were Berkeley and Bristol; while to the west, Sir John Winter declared for the king and controlled the Forest of Dean. Massey was heavily outnumbered, Ferrer had failed to bring supplies, money or men from London and his soldiers were grumbling about their arrears of pay. John Corbett thought that the Royalists planned 'not to leave one strong house unguarded, both to enlarge their own quarters, and to stop our markets and contributions'. The county gentry were mostly hostile and the elder Thomas Pury, who had played such a key role in stiffening the city's resolve in the summer, had returned to London.

Massey not only kept up his letters of complaint to Parliament but launched sorties against Beverstone, Newnham and Tewkesbury, where Vavasour's unpaid Welsh infantry fled, and put his own garrisons into Frampton and Prestbury. This was active defence on a grander scale than during the siege yet it could not hide the fact that Gloucester was, more than at any time since the fighting had started, an isolated Parliamentarian island in a Royalist sea. Moreover, it was an island which was contributing little to the wider war. Vavasour's forces were small, diverted few resources from the king's main efforts elsewhere and could be quickly summoned to reinforce the Oxford Army. Except for the north-south route up and down the River Severn, Royalist trade and soldiers could by-pass Gloucester without great inconvenience. As a result of the siege, the garrison's exploits had propaganda value for Parliament but in truth it could do little more than sustain itself. Gloucester's rapid return to strategic irrelevance underlines the extraordinary nature of the gamble taken by Parliament to save it from capture in August 1643.[10]

IV

Militarily and politically, Parliament's position at the beginning of October 1643 was demonstrably far stronger than in late July. With hindsight, the capture of Bristol was the high tide of King Charles' war, his best and only chance of ending the conflict on his own terms. Hyde conceded as much by reflecting that Massey had given

> a stop to the career of the king's good success, and from his pertinacious defence . . . the Parliament had time to recover their broken forces, and more broken spirits; and may acknowledge to this rise the greatness to which they afterwards aspired.

If the months of July and August 1643 were indeed the tipping point of the Civil War, what can we draw from a detailed reconstruction of events to add to Hyde's succinct explanation of the reasons why?

Though Sergeant Foster and contemporaries on both sides gave generous credit to the Almighty for their successes, God's traditional support for the big battalions was tempered by an unusual preference for the numerical underdog. Even after sending Maurice back to the west, King Charles was able to gather the largest army he would ever command for operations against Gloucester, putting around 18,000 men in the field. But his generals were unable to manufacture circumstances in which that theoretical advantage could be brought effectively to bear. Neither on the Cotswolds, in the Severn valley nor at Newbury was Essex forced to fight except when the Parliamentarians enjoyed a local superiority in numbers. This failure to concentrate force at the right place and the right time was finally decisive at Newbury where the Royalists' superiority evaporated to the extent that they found themselves out-numbered by around 1,000 men. By contrast, Essex and Pym built a 15,000-strong relief army from unpromising beginnings and the earl then conserved his forces successfully throughout the campaign. Equally important were the structural differences between the armies. The Royalist shortage of musketeers, which put them at a real disadvantage in the enclosures south of Newbury, was in part an unavoidable consequence of supply constraints but it also reflected an overinvestment in cavalry that absorbed disproportionate resources, limited strategic and tactical options, and unbalanced the Oxford Army on the battlefield. While Essex compensated for his much lamented paucity of cavalry by tactical ingenuity and firepower, Rupert's brigades of horse failed to live up to their fearsome reputation and were repeatedly driven off by massed infantry formations and their supporting artillery.[11]

Quality counted most with the infantry. Man-for-man and regiment-for-regiment, the Royalist infantry were outperformed. Massey's garrison soldiers won the honours in the siege-line skirmishing around Gloucester; Essex's men retained a higher level of cohesion during the march to Newbury; and the Oxford Army infantry were rightly criticised for their gun-shyness on Newbury Common. Essex's officers were more professional and proved better able to maintain morale and effectiveness under pressure. And the London Trained Bands, untried yet well trained and socially cohesive, defied expectations by standing firm against infantry, artillery and cavalry alike. A similar disparity is evident in the relative professionalism of the Royalist and Parliamentarian artillery. The failure of the Royalist guns at Gloucester was the consequence of unsuitable equipment and inadequate ammunition supplies, while the evidence suggests that at Newbury they were handled poorly as well. Essex, who had been mocked for his insistence on marching with such a large train, proved his detractors wrong by deploying field guns to keep the Royalist cavalry at arms length on the Cotswolds and at Aldbourne Chase, and then to batter their horse and foot to a standstill at Newbury. In no other Civil War battle did artillery play such a critical role.

Sir John Merrick's achievement in ensuring that Essex could fight at Newbury with, apparently, no concerns about ammunition was one of the main factors in the Parliamentarian success. Despite its deep financial crisis, money could be raised quickly when there was the political will to do so in London, and logistic support was an unheralded strength of Parliament's military organisation.[12] The earl had, however, taken a conscious risk by requiring his army to live off the land for their food. While this undoubtedly increased their mobility, Essex's efforts to provide for his men, whether altruistic or prompted by fear of declining morale, contributed to the slow rate of progress from Cirencester to Newbury, and therefore to the unfavourable terms on which the battle was fought. As for the Royalists, it is received wisdom that logistic inadequacies were one of the main reasons for their failures at both Gloucester and Newbury, but the evidence suggests that though Lord Percy could conceivably be blamed for not preparing an adequate supply of artillery ammunition in advance of the campaign, he and his subordinates responded well to the king's changes in strategy, fed the army around Gloucester, made the best use of limited stocks of gunpowder and successfully mobilised different sources to manufacture cannon balls. As for the powder shortage on 20 September, Newbury was not the battle the Royalist generals had planned or expected, and the 100 barrels of powder carried from the Severn valley would have sufficed in almost every other contingency. The decision to send to Oxford for re-supply should of course have been taken earlier but the withdrawal from the battlefield was ultimately a failure of nerve rather than logistics.[13]

That failure of nerve was in part a product of the inadequate intelligence received by the Royalist generals at every stage in the campaign. At Bristol, their intelligence under-estimated the capacity and determination of Gloucester and its leaders to resist; throughout the campaign they based decisions on faulty assessments of Parliament's military strength; in the Severn valley, their tactical intelligence failed repeatedly; their scouts allowed Essex to disappear into the night for a second time after Aldbourne Chase; and at Newbury the Parliamentarians were able to seize Round Hill, and the initiative, unopposed despite the deployment of patrols on the Wash Common plateau. To be fair, Sir Samuel Luke's network of agents had some equally poor material to their credit, including their failure to warn the army of Rupert's advance to Aldbourne Chase; their misleading reporting of Prince Maurice's whereabouts which seems to have caused the snail-like progress from Hungerford; and the unduly pessimistic picture painted of Royalist strength in front of Newbury later that day. On the other hand, Luke also provided a mass of accurate information from Oxford, the camps at Gloucester and Sudeley, and garrisons across central England. One of his men had provided real-time reporting of Rupert's movements after Stow. Another delivered the snippet that saved Essex's army from envelopment north of Tewksbury. Others had reconnoitred Cirencester and kept the Oxford Army under close surveillance during the hazardous disengagement from the Severn valley. It may be that Scoutmaster General Neale's Royalist intelligence apparatus enjoyed similar successes which are not apparent today. If not, this was another major disparity between the two sides.[14]

Throughout the campaign, the abiding sense is that Parliament's military machine was quite simply more competent and professional than its Royalist equivalent. Despite the strong element of mythology, Massey's achievement was as significant as Parliament's propagandists argued. Pury's political support and determination was invaluable but it was Massey who led the defence, and it was his tactical nous and motivational skills that gained the garrison a moral ascendancy over their besiegers and kept Gloucester in Parliament's hands.[15] By the same token, Essex's brigade and regimental commanders performed with greater spirit and effectiveness than their Royalist counterparts during the marches to and from Gloucester and on the battlefield. Although Stapleton, Ramsey and Middleton did not lead the cavalry to victory, they repeatedly prevented Rupert from exploiting the Royalists' qualitative and quantitative advantages. It was, however, the Parliamentarian infantry and their officers who won the campaign for Essex. From the outset around Stow, regiments stood firm when they might have been expected to disintegrate and in combat their leaders were able to rally them after even the most brutal tactical reverses. At the time, the Trained Bands' courage on Newbury Common received most notice yet the resilience of the rearguards at Aldbourne Chase and Greenham Common, together with the success of Robartes' regiments in blunting the Royalist advance on the northern slope of Round Hill, was equally praiseworthy. Most significant of all was the response of Colonels Barclay and Holburn to the potentially battle-winning breakthrough by Sir John Byron on Round Hill itself. The usual reaction of tired troops to panic amongst neighbouring units and the threat of being over-run by cavalry was to join the rout, but Barclay and Holburn successfully reformed their men whose rolling musket fire then smashed the king's last real hope of victory.

Similar professionalism was shown by Parliament's senior commanders. Skippon has received due, perhaps even excessive, credit for his contribution, especially at Newbury where he undoubtedly played a key role in marshalling the main and rear guards to frustrate Royalist efforts to envelop Round Hill. Though not Essex's first choice for the post, the earl evidently trusted and worked well with his deputy, and used his gritty leadership skills to the full. It is, however, to Essex himself that the greatest plaudits should be reserved. History has tended to focus more on his strategic failures in 1642 and 1644, when he should arguably have twice won the war for Parliament, yet it is equally true that in the early autumn of 1643 it was the success of his strategy, high risk gamble though it seems with hindsight, that preserved the fragile political coalition in London and re-energised support for the war. Once aroused by Pym from the lethargy which engulfed him for most of the summer, Essex's preparations were characteristically thorough and his handling of the campaign, though far from flawless, stood head and shoulders above the Royalist command. He can justifiably be criticised for putting the Trained Bands at unnecessary risk at Oddington, for allowing Rupert to catch him at Aldbourne Chase, and for undue caution in the advance from Hungerford and in front of Newbury on 19 September. On the other hand, his approach march across the Cotswolds was for the most part a masterly case study in combined arms tactics to neutralise the Royalist cavalry; his feint north and subsequent disengagement from the Severn valley was one of the best examples of operational deception and rapid movement of the war; and his tactics and leadership at Newbury exploited the ground, his army's strengths and his opponents weaknesses to snatch victory in the most unpromising of circumstances. 'Old Robin' was a soldier's general, most comfortable in the front line with a half-pike. But he was also a highly professional builder, organiser, equipper and motivator of armies; and in this campaign he demonstrated, for some of the time at least, genuine strategic vision and tactical flair.

Essex's achievements were amplified by his enemies' incompetence. Tactically and strategically, the Oxford Army's leadership proved incapable of transcending the weaknesses endemic in its structure, equipment and morale. Compared to the Parliamentarian officer corps, Royalist colonels lacked professionalism and failed to inspire their men when it really mattered. Among brigade commanders or their equivalent, only Charles Gerard, the serial turncoat Urry and perhaps the two Byrons seem to have displayed more than routine competence, and many did not meet even that poor standard. Belasyse's inability to move his infantrymen from the cover of the Newbury Common tumulus stands in stark contrast to the Trained Bands' resilience in the face of cavalry attack and artillery fire.[16] Further up the command chain, Wilmot's tentative handling of the cavalry was the antithesis of his victory at Roundway Down and Astley had no discernable influence on events after his injury at Gloucester.

At each stage in the campaign, there is evidence of growing dissension within the Royalist leadership. The Bristol council of war set the tone with its factionalism and incoherent strategic thinking. At Gloucester, the king's refusal to risk casualties constrained his generals, sacrificed the momentum of the early summer and condemned the army to weeks of morale-sapping inactivity. Forth conducted siege operations competently enough but appears little more than a cipher for the king's increasingly pro-active involvement in strategic decisions. Whether or not he had been ordered to avoid combat during the Parliamentarian relief march, once the siege was raised Rupert played a much more active leadership role. Yet he seems to have done so in opposition to a strategic consensus formed around Forth, Percy and the king himself, and his influence over his uncle and Royalist decision-making was often surprisingly limited. The farce surrounding contradictory intelligence reports of Essex's counter-march to Cirencester; the squabble between Rupert and an aristocratic cabal at Aldbourne Chase; the clear sense in Prince Rupert's Diary that he was at odds with Forth over the march to Newbury; and his unhappiness over the decision to withdraw overnight on 20–21 September all demonstrate the prince's good judgement (he was right in at least three of these cases), the growing tendency of well-born officers to challenge that judgement and, as at Bristol, the king's willingness to overrule his nephew on vital strategic issues. Rupert's inspirational leadership won the race to Newbury and flamed across the battlefield but without his immediate presence the Royalists lacked drive and initiative, and nobody else from the king downwards was able to galvanise the army to anything like the same extent.[17]

It is hard not to conclude that, as in so many things, Charles I was the author of his own tragedy and that the die was cast once he decided to join the army at Bristol. As he had shown earlier in the year, the king could not resist interfering in military decision making, his judgement remained poor and his advisers were unable or unwilling to contest the royal will. Had he remained in Oxford, it is improbable that such an unsatisfactory strategy would have evolved or that casualty and risk aversion would have been so decisive in campaign decision making. The withdrawal from Newbury Common was especially, though not uniquely, damaging to the Royalist cause. This subordination of military expertise to the prejudices of an amateur strategist and tactician exemplifies the relative lack of professionalism in key aspects of the Royalist war-making machinery. Essex may have been pedestrian but he was competent, most of his officers knew their business, and John Pym protected him from political meddling in strictly military matters; Rupert was touched by genius yet neither he nor solid soldiers like Forth could overcome the influence of factionalism and a weak absolute monarch.

That contrast in political contexts is a key aspect of the campaign. Both King Charles and 'King Pym' stood at the head of loose coalitions combining profoundly different war aims. In London, the political battle was bloody and public, and gave an impression of continuous discord and fundamental weakness. There was truth in this perception but Pym (who was perhaps the first Englishman of non-noble blood to qualify for the description of war leader) was able to outmanoeuvre his enemies and impose a strategy, based on Scottish intervention and enforced Presbyterianism, which widened the war, ruled out political compromise and ensured that Parliament would eventually triumph. Since Massey's defence of Gloucester and Essex's campaign made all of this possible, it is difficult to exaggerate their importance as contributory factors to Parliament's ultimate success. More immediately, Massey and Essex together frustrated the king's political agenda for exploiting the Royalists' run of military victories. The difference was that whereas Pym was able to gain temporary acquiescence to his strategy, reinforced by Essex's successful campaign, which gave Parliament a prospect of battlefield success in 1644, Charles was unable to impose or otherwise create a consensus among his supporters, and the aftermath of Newbury both increased these divisions and weakened the Royalists' war-making potential for the following year. Rupert's 'promotion' to build his own army in the west midlands can be seen as much a result of his impotence in strategic decision making and isolation on the council of war as Charles' wish to reward his nephew with an independent command. That the Oxford schisms took place largely behind closed doors and were shrouded by common loyalty to the king should not obscure their debilitating impact on the Royalist war effort, nor the profound consequences of the military failures in front of Gloucester and on the hills south of Newbury.

The Earl of Manchester summed up the campaign's ultimate significance more than a year later when the soldiers of king and Parliament confronted each other yet again across the Newbury countryside. In November 1644, a Parliamentarian council of war debated whether to fight or allow the Royalists to march away unscathed. Oliver Cromwell argued that they should seek to defeat the king in battle before he could receive reinforcements from France. Manchester disagreed:

> in fighting we venture all to nothing. If we fight a hundred times and beat him ninety-nine times, he will be king still. But if he beat us but once, or the last time, we shall be hanged, we shall lose our estates, and our posterities be undone.[18]

In late 1644, Manchester was being unduly pessimistic about the risks of defeat. In September 1643, however, Parliament's position was as Manchester described. Pym and Essex had been prepared to fight, perhaps recklessly so, and King Charles had the capability to defeat his opponents in battle. In the Severn valley and then at Newbury, Essex could have lost the Civil War in a single day's fighting. Never again would that be the case. By depriving Charles of military victory and bringing his own army back to London, the earl ensured that the revolution to which he was ambiguously attached would eventually take his monarch's head.

V

I offer some final thoughts.[19] First, it is striking how, in 1643, leadership of the English Civil War had been internationalised. The majority of King Charles' most influential commanders were Scots (Forth, Urry), Germans (Rupert, Maurice) or English mercenaries (Astley, Aston). Less obvious is the outlander presence throughout Parliament's army. The cavalry in particular had been colonised by German and Dutch (Behr and Dalbier) or Scottish (Middleton and Ramsey) colonels. Among the infantry, the Scots professionals Barclay and Holburn were given brigades over the heads of their English counterparts. Parliament's reliance on imported military expertise was so contentious politically that contemporary propaganda had consistently to emphasise their loyalty and effectiveness, and the key role played by Essex's Scottish colonels in particular was later air-brushed from the record. All sides subsequently conspired to emphasise the Englishness of the campaign. Its heroes were Gloucester's defenders, 'conservators of the parliament of England', and the Trained Bands, eventually pictured setting out from London in a stirring Victorian painting on the wall of the Peers' Corridor in the Palace of Westminster. But the reality is that English democracy owes much to a handful of mercenary officers from north of the border.[20]

This rewriting of history's inconvenient passages has a remarkably up-to-date feel. Indeed, though drawing comparisons between eras is usually misleading, many elements of the campaign have a similarly contemporary ring: the political spin in London and Oxford; orchestrated political protest and violence; barbed media gossip about celebrity sex lives (Essex the cuckold, hen-pecked Waller and Henrietta Maria the serial adulteress); discord between politicians and generals; high-level casualty-aversion; concern about soldiers' morale; failures of intelligence collection and assessment; political squabbling about the army's poor equipment and inadequate funding; English hostility towards foreigners; prisoner abuse; and the inexorable brutalisation of a society at war with itself (even the campaign's pious, respectable urban everyman, Henry Foster was by Greenham Common sanguine about his comrades' new-found preference for taking no prisoners). Sadly, the mindset of religious intolerance and fanaticism also seems less unfamiliar in this century than the last.

As today, the people meeting these challenges in 1643 were neither giants nor pygmies, neither totally incompetent nor invariably inspired. Their failures are often inexplicable without the context. The most expert siege engineer seems incompetent until one discovers that he had been given inadequate artillery and munitions. The boldest cavalry officer appears timid and indecisive unless you know he had orders not to fight. The nimblest general looks leaden-footed if it is no longer apparent that he was misled by false intelligence. Though I have been especially hard in my judgements on King Charles, the circumstances in which his decisions were taken and the divergent advice he was receiving make his choices understandable (and in some cases admirable) even when they were palpably wrong. It is easy to criticise leaders for playing it safe when hindsight tells us that is not the right course, vastly more difficult to embrace bold options when you have direct responsibility and so much depends on the outcome, especially when you also have to preserve the integrity of a disparate political coalition.

All of which puts into stark relief the high-risk gamble adopted by (or thrust upon) John Pym, which not only placed Parliament's army in jeopardy but relied on a demoralised and little-trusted leader to deliver his strategy. Was that inspired or foolhardy? If Essex is judged solely on Edgehill and Lostwithiel, he appears an inadequate general on almost all counts; yet for two months in 1643, he outperformed his enemies (both Royalist and Parliamentarian) in every respect. Was he playing below par in 1642 and 1644, or above par at Gloucester and Newbury? My sense is that context shapes how leaders act and whether they succeed to a much greater extent than we generally accept, and that very few are able to maintain high performance or repeatedly transcend unfavourable circumstances. Had the Royalists not made more and greater mistakes in 1643, Pym's gamble would have failed and the strategic advantages that now make Parliament's eventual victory look well-nigh inevitable would have been dissipated.[21]

In the event, Newbury was Essex's finest hour. It is also one of the most important battlefields in southern Britain and unusual as an example of large scale combat in an enclosed landscape. My interpretation of the terrain and fighting is, I believe, a significant advance on all previous versions. It certainly uses a wider range of sources than preceding writers. But it is inevitably only a partial picture because no-one has, to my knowledge, conducted a comprehensive archaeological survey of any part of the battlefield. It is received wisdom that most of the ground fought over in 1643 was built upon in the twentieth century. If my reading of the landscape and written accounts is correct, the contrary is true. Moreover, I have placed key parts of the fighting on ground that would otherwise be devoid of substantial tell-tale finds of lead shot. I hope that this book will inspire those with the necessary skills and equipment to prove or disprove my theories. I would also be delighted if the evidence I have provided helps stave off the westward advance of urban Newbury across the remainder of the battlefield site. Battlefields are not shrines. They are, however, as important a part of our historical inheritance as any cathedral, stately home or factory, including as untapped sources of evidence for the lives and deaths of thousands of our forbearers. To destroy this inheritance at Newbury without an overwhelming need would be vandalism that would do us no credit in the eyes of posterity.

Notes and References

Chapter One
1 De Gomme, 'Bristol taken', Ede-Borrett, 1988, 1–6; Luke II, 122–3; Warburton, II, 266.
2 De Gomme, op cit., describes the capture of Bristol in detail. See also Slingsby in Ede-Borrett, op cit, 27–8; an anonymous Royalist letter in Warburton, II, 264–5; 'Trial of Colonel Fiennes' in State Trials, IV; Lynch, 'For King and Parliament, 1–104.
3 State Trials, IV, 192, 221, 229, 270; Warburton, II, 264; Clarendon, IV, 149.
4 De Gomme, 13 and 20; Slingsby, 27.
5 De Gomme, 24–25; State Trials, IV, 193; Warburton, II, 265–6, 238.
6 De Gomme, 25; Clarendon, IV, 147–8; Warburton, II, 267.
7 Warburton, II, 268, 167–8; MA, 27 Jul; Clarendon, IV, 148–9, 152; Pythouse Papers, 56–7.
8 Clarendon, IV, 162–9; Hopton, 'Bellum Civile', Wicks, 1988, 59; MA, 1 Aug; Luke II, 127, 129.
9 De Gomme 1, 5–6; Warburton, II, 266 and I, 509; Luke, II, 126.
10 Warburton, I, 497; MA, 1 Aug; Clarendon, IV, 148, 166, 195–6.

Chapter Two
1 Clarendon, IV, 156–162, 171–2, 182–3; MA, 2 Aug; Hopton, 58–60.
2 Although Hyde's description (in Clarendon, IV, 166–177, 194–197, 200–201, 259–262) was written well after the event and reflects the author's prejudices, it is detailed and apparently based on primary documents. He cannot be relied on for the whole story but, using all of the surviving sources together, including Prince Rupert's Diary and contemporary correspondence, it is possible to compile an analysis that explains what took place at Bristol in early August and why. The best modern analysis is by Wanklyn, originally in 'Royalist Strategy in the South of England 1642–44' in Southern History 3, 54–79 and more recently with Jones in 'A Military History of the English Civil War', 109–112.
3 Green, 'Letters', 197–200.
4 Young, 'Edgehill 1642', 180–2; ROP A93, B108, B117; Luke, II, 74, 81, 93, 102.
5 Luke, II, 123–4; State Trials, IV, 259; ROP, I, 199; Reid, 'All the King's Armies', 37; Luke, II, 80, 120; Warburton, II, 222, 225–8; Clarendon, IV, 139; Green, 'Letters', 211, 222.
6 Clarendon, IV, 169, 194; State Trials, IV, 259; ROP, B148, A93.
7 This table reflects my interpretation of all sources, contemporary and modern. It excludes regiments no longer or not yet involved in operations. The evolution of the brigade structure during the campaign is addressed in later chapters. Strength of Rupert's regiments post-Bristol includes recovered typhus victims from Oxford.
8 Stoyle, 'Soldiers and Strangers', chapter 1; Gray, 'Humble Desires of the King's Infantry', ECW N&Q, No 44; 'Pythouse Papers', 12–13; Clarendon, IV, 142; De Gomme, 12–21; Luke, II, 131; Clarendon, IV, 169; Hopton, 58.
9 Warburton, II, 188–192.
10 Young, 'Edgehill', 86–8, 105, 204–14; Luke, II, 120; Stoyle, 'Soldiers and Strangers, 98–99; Adair, 'Hampden', 230; Clarendon, IV, 139; Young, 'Roundway Down', JSAHR, 1953, 127–31; Clarendon, IV, 171; Van Creveld, 'Supplying War', 34; Barratt, 'Cavaliers', 48–53 (although the evidence is that the use of dragoons was already in steep decline); Warburton, II, 262, 276–7 (I disagree with Lynch, 'For King and Parliament', 69–70, who suggests that all 6,000 Oxford cavalry were at Bristol).
11 As for vii above. Brigade structure is addressed in later chapters.
12 This section, including the table, is drawn primarily from contemporary manuals by Eldred, Hexham, Norton and Ward; Duffy, 'Siege Warfare', various; ROP, various; Guilmartin, 'Gunpowder and Galleys', 166–183; Young and Holmes, 'The English Civil War', 48–50; Barratt, 'Cavaliers', 57–63; Firth, 'Cromwell's Army', 394–5; Fassnidge, 3, 'Military Skills', 20–23; Dawson, 'English Civil War Artillery', 'Miniature Wargames', Oct 2005; conversation with G. Foard, Aug 2006 (on caseshot). The complexity is demonstrated by the differences between culverins and cannon, the former longer, thicker, heavier, more expensive and increasingly overshadowed in seventeenth century armies; the different

specifications and performances of iron and brass weapons (iron demi-cannon weighed around 6,000 lb, but Hexham makes clear that modern Dutch brass demi-cannon weighed 4,500 lb and a demi-cannon drake only 2,250 lb); and the chaos surrounding classifications with culverin cannon-balls ranging from 15 to 19 lbs, and culverin gun barrels from 2,000 lb for a drake up to 8,500 lb when reinforced.

13 De Gomme, 5; ROP, B138–139 (De Gomme ignored the mortar and wrongly described the demi-cannon as demi-culverins); ROP, B118, B144, A100; Duffy, "Siege Warfare", 96. Lynch, op cit, 71–2, suggests that a shortage of transport animals limited the size of Rupert's artillery train. There may well have been such a shortage but the ROP show that the main constraint was the types of guns available.

14 This list reflects my re-evaluation of the contemporary sources and differs from most modern summaries. The guns covered are those for which there is evidence of Oxford Army utilisation in 1643. Some were drakes and therefore lighter and less powerful than these specifications. I can find few details for 6- and 3-pounders, and the distinction between 3- and 4-pounders is very blurred, hence I have treated them alike. Gun weights are for brass pieces, which were considerably lighter than their iron equivalents and it is clear that the vast majority in the Oxford Army inventory were of brass. For commonality, I have used ranges given by Ward. Eldred's alternatives, based on actual weapons, suggest that brass gun ranges were longer (culverin 460/2,740 yards, saker 360/2,180 yards, falcon 320/1,920 yards). The numbers for gun crews and towing teams come from actual ROP warrants in 1643 and are significantly lower than for example Barratt, 'Cavaliers', 58. The numbers of guns comprises pieces used by Rupert at Bristol and then Gloucester (but not the pieces captured at Bristol, which were not taken over by the Oxford Army) and those present at Oxford in early August, either in the marching train or in the garrison defences. Those deployed subsequently to join the field army after Gloucester are detailed in brackets. My estimate of the strength of the Oxford garrison artillery reflects the melting down of eight guns in early August to cast three new 6-pounders and the despatch of three guns to Basing House, and tallies with Parliamentarian eye-witness intelligence reports in Luke, II, 141, 143. Key ROP documents are A100, A111, B118, B137–9, B141, B144, B146, B155–6, B159, B163, B168, B171, B175, B183. See also Young, 'Edgehill', 176–7.

15 ROP, A100, B138–9; State Trials, IV, 193, 203, 261; De Gomme, 26; Warburton, II, 278; ROP, B146.

16 Biographical details in this section come primarily from contemporary sources such as Hyde and surviving correspondence, the DNB (old and new editions), and recent biographies such as Carlton on Charles and Kitson on Rupert. References are limited to direct quotations and explanations where I have departed from received opinion.

17 Warburton, II, 189, 223–4, 165–6, 171–2, 174, 176–7, 167–8; Clarendon, IV, 471; Green, 'Letters', 211; Warburton, II, 189.

18 Clarendon, IV, 471–2. Reid, 'All the King's Armies', rightly gives Forth's influence on Royalist operations more credit than it usually receives but in my view he does not attribute sufficient blame to Forth for Royalist failures.

19 Rupert's title comes from a commission dated 23 Sep 1643 quoted in Macray, 'Ruthven Correspondence', 150. Other quotations from Warwick in DNB; Pythouse Papers, 54, 55; Clarendon, III, 270–1.

20 Clarendon, III, 188, 190, 320 and IV, 138, 472, 527; Warburton, II, 74; Pythouse Papers, 54.

21 Clarendon, IV, 28; Wood is from DNB; Clarendon, II, 292 and IV, 473–4, 615; GRO D115.

22 Clarendon, IV, 531; Green, 'Letters', 210–11; Roy, 'Digby', 73; 'Pythouse Papers', 55.

23 For Neale, see Washbourn, 163–72; Aubrey, 'Brief Lives', 220–1. Warwick on Colepeper from DNB; Green, 'Letters', 174; Warburton, II, 222. Ollard, 'Clarendon and his Friends', chapter VII, gives a thoughtful though partial analysis of key relationships at the political and personal level.

24 Luke, II, 123; Clarendon, IV, 170–1; Hopton, 60; 'Vindication of Richard Atkyns', 28. Hamilton's horse and dragoons, raised originally in the south midlands, had been 'utterly broken' before Lansdown, were at Tewkesbury (presumably to recruit) on 6 August and only 50 strong in late September (Hopton, 51; GRO D115 10/10/4; Edgar, 'Hopton', 140).

25 Hutton, 'Royalist War Effort', 114, 65; Warburton, I, 509 and II, 225–7; Dorney, 207. Capel's main force was preparing for an attack on Nantwich – Hutton, 64.

26 Green, 'Letters', 215; Warburton, II, 221; Warwick, 'Memoirs', 242–4. Johnson, 'Adwalton Moor', argues for 5,000 foot and 5,000 horse in June.

27 This categorisation is my own. It does not mean that the participants in the debate necessarily thought of themselves in those terms as I hope I have made clear in the main text.

28 HMC, 12th Report, Appendix IX, 60.

29 Wedgwood, 183.

30 Clarendon, V, 288.

31 Unless otherwise indicated, all the quotations from and references to Hyde during this discussion come from Clarendon, IV, 169–77, 194–7, 200–1, 260.

32 De Gomme, 26; Hopton, 60. Four of the six regiments can be positively identified from references in Hopton and the Royalist Ordnance Papers, B157-9 – Hopton's own and Prince Maurice's from the Western Army, and Prince Rupert's (formerly Lunsford's) and Washington's dragoons from the Oxford Army. Commanded men from all four regiments were placed under Lieutenant Colonel Gilby of

Belasyse's Regiment at Gloucester, which suggests that Belasyse's was also still at Bristol with its injured colonel. The final Bristol regiment was in my view Bernard Astley's (formerly Hertford's from the Western Army), which was under Hopton's command and in or around Bristol at the end of September 1643.

33 Warburton, II, 274; I, 492, 509; GRO D115 (Ernest Baker, who transcribed the letter to Vavasour, thought it was a draft but it is clearly stated to be a copy and Vavasour's letters of 4 and 6 August are undoubtedly replies to it); Dorney, 208–9; ROP, B146; De Gomme, 26; WRO 413/444.

34 Luke, II, 128; Herne's approach is in the Venetian report for 23 Jan 1643 (the most accessible version is 'The English Civil War; A Contemporary Account', Vol 3, 9); the trident strategy is set out by Gardiner, I, 67–8, 197; the subsequent debate is examined by Wanklyn in 'Royalist Strategy', 64–8 and 'A Military History', 92–4; claims of Royalist prisoners are in POffA, 241. Wanklyn's discussion of whether or not there was a pre-existing strategy in some ways misses the point. It is clear from correspondence and intelligence reports that in the summer of 1643 there was a strong lobby in favour of action against London and the expectation on both sides that this was what the king would do. That the strategy was flawed does not mean that it had not been developed or adopted.

35 Sunderland's letter is in Atkin and Laughlin, 171; GRO, D115 (I can identify no alternative explanation for the switch between Grandison's foot and Hamilton's horse, especially as Grandison was recuperating from his Bristol injury and therefore unfit for a mobile campaign); Warmington, 'Civil War, Interregnum and Restoration in Gloucestershire', 49; 'Vindication of Richard Atkyns', 29.

36 Bulstrode, 'Memoirs and Reflections', 94–5; Walker's list is British Library, Harley MSS, 1608, f.118; Warburton, II, 274.

37 Hyde is the source for the attempt to subvert Massey. His account was written after Massey had indeed fallen out with Parliament but he does not show Massey in a particularly flattering light and there is no reason to think that the story is untrue; Dorney, 207–9; Warburton, II, 278. For the reasons why I am so precise about timing, see Chapter Three.

38 Bulstrode, ibid; Warburton, II, 276–7. 'Journal of Prince Rupert's Marches' (EHR, Vol 13, 729–41) does not confirm that the prince left Bristol at this stage but Aston's letter strongly suggests that he had opted out of the forthcoming operation.

39 Warwick, 'Memoirs', 260; the queen's letter to Newcastle is printed in Washbourn, l (in English) and 369 (in the original French).

Chapter Three

1 Corbett, 37–9; MA, June 23, 26. Henry Stephens was the eldest son of Nathaniel, a Gloucestershire MP who was among the most influential Parliamentarian leaders in the County – Warmington, 45.

2 This section relies to a great extent on Clark's 'The Ramoth-Gilead of the good: Urban change and political radicalism at Gloucester 1540–1640', Manning's 'The English People and the English Revolution', Warmington, and Atkin & Laughlin.

3 Corbett, 6–15; Warmington, 24–39; Atkin & Laughlin, 13–43; and Fletcher, 'The Outbreak of the English Civil War'.

4 Corbett, 16–26, and three contemporary pamphlets in Washbourn, 153–185.

5 Corbett, 26–30; Washbourn, 195–7; Clarendon, III, 461–7; Adair, 'Roundhead General', 54–63; Hutton, 'Royalist War Effort', 52–5.

6 Corbett, 30–7; Adair, 63–73; Hutton, 55–8; Warburton, II, 194.

7 I am disagreeing here with the established view which derives in large part from Fiennes in De Gomme, 26; and Corbett, 5, 40. Both are I believe partial and unsubstantiated by subsequent events.

8 Corbett, 37, 42; Dorney, 229.

9 Corbett, 11, 37, 42; Young, 'Edgehill', 246–7; Dorney, 229; Peachey & Turton, 'Old Robin's Foot', 58. Although Stamford's Foot will have started the war with both musketeers and pikemen, there is no evidence of pikemen being retained in significant numbers after it became a garrison unit. Morris, 'Siege of Gloucester' suggests detailed lists of officers (11–16). It is possible that 1,500 is a propaganda figure which understates the actual garrison strength but not by a factor of more than a couple of hundred men.

10 Corbett, 11; Washbourn, xxvi, cxli, 163, 180, 285–324; Morris, ibid, 17; State Trials 1816, IV, 229; ROP, B144.

11 State Trials 1816, IV, 193, 203, 229, 261; Corbett, 42; Dorney, 226.

12 Corbett, especially 42–3, and Dorney; Washbourn, 285–324 (the Backhouse plot) and lvi–lix; Atkin & Laughlin, 44–74, including modern archaeological findings. Speed's 1610 map gives a good impression of the city's layout. Atkin & Laughin, 34, suggest that work on the defences may have been directed by a local mason, Samuel Baldwin.

13 Command arrangements reflect Corbett and Dorney, Warmington, 43–50, and Atkin & Laughlin, 32–7.

14 The Puritan oligarchy is discussed in Clark, 244–73; see also Warmington, 7–39 and Atkin & Laughlin, 13–23.

15 Corbett, 39–42; Gardiner, I, 198; Atkin & Laughlin, 40 (there was a parallel letter jointly from the governor and the civil authorities, asking for help in less emotive terms); Warburton, II, 274 and I, 504.

16 DNB; Washbourn, l–li, clxiv–cixv; Warmington, 27; Atkin & Laughlin, 22–3, 40; Dorney, 227; Clarendon, IV, 225. Corbett's silence about Pury is a reflection of the later appalling state of relations between his hero, Massey, and the local civilian authorities – see Warmington, chapter 3 (although I think he is unduly hard on Massey, here and in the DNB). The timing of Pury's return is based on the reference to him in Massey's letter of 29 July (xv above).

17 Warmington, 48; Corbett, 40–2; Warburton, II, 274.

18 Corbett, 40–1; Gardiner, 198; Dorney, 227; Clarendon, IV, 225.

19 CSPV, 1643, 6; MA,7 Aug; Warburton, II, 280; Warmington, 48; Clarendon, IV, 175–7, 195; Gardiner, 198.

20 Chapter two and Dorney, 208 – Gerard's excuse for a parlay is feeble even by 17th century standards, unless there was an ulterior motive.

Chapter Four

1 Letters quoted in Hexter, 'Reign of King Pym', 130.

2 Hexter, 108–11; CSPV, 1642–3, 297. The best account of Essex's Thames valley campaign is Wanklyn and Jones, 'Military History', chapter VIII. Dils, 'Epidemics, mortality and the Civil War in Berkshire' explains the typhus outbreak.

3 Warburton, II, 202; for Hampden's influence on Essex, see Hexter, 115–6, Snow, 369, and Adair, 'John Hampden'; Tennant, 'Edgehill and Beyond', 108–15, covers the queen's convoy.

4 Snow, 370–2; CJ, 3, 11 July 1643; Essex's 9 July letter is at LJ, 6, 11 July 1643; Hexter, 117–20; CSPV, 1642–3, 300–1.

5 CSPV, 1643–7, 2; Tennant, ibid, 111; Hexter, 121–4; MA, 31 July; Wedgwood, 'King's War', 237.

6 Snow, 373–6; Hexter, 122–4; CJ, 3, 18 July 1643; CSPV, 1642–3, 301.

7 CJ, 3, 27, 29 July, 1 Aug 1643; LJ, 6, 28 July 1643; CSPV, 1643–7, 1–2 and 5; Adair, 'Roundhead General', 98–101. Parliament did not make Waller personally responsible for leading an army to Gloucester as most previous accounts have suggested. The language used refers to reinforcements for the garrison. It was, however, to Waller that they turned as the general responsible for the West.

8 Snow, 300. These pen-pictures are drawn from the DNB, old and new, biographies such as Snow and Adair, and contemporary correspondence.

9 'The wife of this esteemed and beloved commander accuses General Essex to Parliament, who when asked by three messages to approach Oxford to secure Waller against attack there by a diversion, would never listen' (CSPV, 1642–3, 304–5).

10 There is an excellent explanation of the financial background to Parliament's campaign in Scott Wheeler, 'The Making of a World Power', chapters 4–8.

11 I disagree with Gardiner's influential statement in 'History of the Great Civil War', I, 193: 'The King's strategy was thus to be met by counter strategy. Essex, with the main army of the Parliament, was to be opposed to the main army of the King. Waller on the left was to meet the army of Maurice, whilst Manchester was employed to ward off the forward march of Newcastle. The plan had against it the inherent weakness which attaches to all purely defensive measures . . .'. A defensive strategy would have made more sense militarily but it is clear from the evidence that Parliament's strategy was offensive, designed to recapture the West, and that it was adopted before Gloucester was besieged, primarily in response to the loss of Bristol.

12 LJ, 6, 22, 31 July 1643; CJ, 3, same dates; Peachey and Turton, 'Old Robin's Foot', 8–11, 58; Turton, 'Chief Strength of the Army', 15–69; Roberts, 'London & Liberty', 13 suggests the Trained Bands comprised 20,000 foot and two regiments of horse.

13 Hexter, 134–5; Adamson & Folland, 'Sir Harry Vane', 183–203. An important point is that some contemporaries expected the negotiations to bear fruit more quickly than they actually did. Hence Scots intervention was a more immediate prospect in July and August 1643 than it seems with hindsight – eg CSPV, 1643–7, 12, 19, 28.

14 Hexter, 125–8; Adair, 'Roundhead General', 101–2; CSPV, 1643–7, 5.

15 Hexter, 137–44; Snow, 377–80; Adair, 'Roundhead General', 101–2; CJ, 3, 31 July, 1–3 Aug 1643; LJ, 6, 31 July, 2–3 Aug 1643; CSPV, 1643–7, 6, 8.

16 Clarendon, IV, 182–94; Hexter, 142–7. Hexter argues that the threat to Pym was greater from Holland and the peace party than from Martin and the militants. The chronology of events suggests otherwise.

17 Gardiner, I, 183; Clarendon, IV, 208; Hexter, 144–6; Adair, 'Roundhead General', 102–3; Snow, 379; CJ, 3, 4,5,7 August 1643; LJ, 6, 2,5 August 1643; CSPV, 1643–7, 8.

Chapter Five

1 Warburton, II, 276–7; ROP, B149 (according to intelligence received at Gloucester, 2,000 Royalist cavalry were in the area – Dorney, 208); 'Notes and Recollections of Stroud', 218–9; Dorney, 209 (the intelligence was, however, incorrect in placing the king with them); Warburton, II, 280. Firth, 'Cromwell's Army', 108, suggests that the New Model Army managed ten to thirteen miles per day.

2 Washbourn, clxxvi; ROP, B146, 148; 'Journal of Prince Rupert's Marches', EHR , 13, 734; Clarendon, IV, 181 (Hyde's recollection that Forth was not summoned until after a decision to besiege Gloucester had been taken on 10 August is disproved by the Royalist Ordnance Papers, ibid); Hutton, 'Royalist War Effort', 113–4; Luke, II, 132, 134; Warburton, II, 273; Dorney, 209.

3 Dorney, 208–9; Corbett, 41; Atkin & Laughlin, 39; Warburton, II, 274, 276–7.

4 Dorney, 209–11; Corbett, 43–5 ; 'A True Relation of the Manner of the Siege ...' in GN&Q, III, 464–66; 'A Journal of the Siege ...', in Warburton, II, 280–3; Clarendon, IV, 177–81, 223n; MA, 11 Aug.

5 Dorney, 207; ROP, B152–3. The twelve Bristol infantry regiments were J Astley, Bolle, Dutton, Fitton/ Grandison, G Gerard, Herbert, Lloyd, Lord General, Molineux, Owen, Rivers and Stradling. The Oxford detachment comprised Blackwell, Darcy, Eure, Tyldesley, Sandys, H Vaughan and the King's Lifeguard. See xi below for numbers. The two cavalry brigades from Bristol were commanded by Aston and Charles Gerard with (probably) the regiments of A Aston, Andover, Chandos, C Gerard, Hamilton (already at Tewkesbury-GRO D115 10/10/4), G Vaughan, Dalton, Eure, Molyneux, Sandys, Tyldesley and the Queen's, plus R Howard's dragoons. It is unclear which brigade escorted the column from Oxford but it probably included the regiments of Crispe and Spencer.

6 Warburton, II, 280–1; GN&Q, III, 464; Dorney, 209–11; ROP, B152; Washbourn, clvi–clvii; Corbett, 43–4; Clarendon, IV, 178; MA, 11 Aug.

7 Dorney, ibid; Corbett, 43–5; Warburton, II, 281; Clarendon, IV, 178–80, 223n. Jordan later became Mayor of Gloucester. Except for the siege, the only reference I have been able to find to Pudsey is in Pafford, 'Accounts of the Parliamentarian Garrisons of Great Chalfield and Malmesbury 1645–6', from which it appears that Pudsey subsequently served under Nicholas Devereux as a lieutenant colonel. He is therefore likely to have been one of the reformado officers who accompanied Devereux from Berkeley.

8 Clarendon, IV, 180–1, 194–7, 223–4n; Atkin & Laughlin, 13–4; Warwick, 'Memoirs', 242–4, 260–1, 263–5 (much of Warwick's account, produced much later, verges on the incoherent but he is in my view reliable where he is writing from direct personal experience, as here. Warwick's suspicion of King's motives may be personal or reflect more widely held Oxford prejudice).

9 Dorney, 211–3; Corbett, 45; Warburton, II, 280–1 (for Forbes, see also II, 274); Washbourn, clviii, clxiii; Atkin & Laughlin, 65–71; Clarendon, IV, 180; MA, 11 Aug.

10 Dorney, 211; Corbett, 45; Warburton, II, 281; MA, 11, 19, 20 Aug; ROP, B152–3; Luke, II, 133, 135. All sources agree that Astley commanded the eastern approach. For the location of Darcy's brigade, Dorney, 213, says that a captain from Blackwell's, one of the northern units, was killed in front of the East Gate on the following night; ROP, B153 shows that (individual regiments apart) only Darcy's brigade and Dutton's new arrivals needed ammunition on 11 August, and that by 12 August, Forth's, Wentworth's and Dutton's brigades were grouped together for ammunition distribution. Since all sources also agree that the biggest concentration of infantry was that under Forth to the south, it is a reasonable deduction that Darcy's was the brigade quartered with Astley to the east. Dorney attributed Astley's wound and Edward's death to the following night but for Astley I have preferred the Royalist eyewitness version in Warburton, and MA, 19 Aug says that Edwards was lost 'at the first approach'.

11 ROP B 152; GRO, D115. Ammunition issues during the first three days of the siege provide further evidence for the strength of the Royalist infantry. If, as seems likely, the musketeers and dragoons were all given full twelve-shot bandoleers for the opening stage of the operation, at which point ammunition shortages were not the problem they were later to become, their numbers totalled c. 2,600 (13 cwt of powder was issued; 1 cwt represented 2,400 charges or 200 x twelve-shot bandoleers). This is consistent with a major issue for the three brigades quartered with Forth on 12 August, which was probably in preparation for an eventual assault once the walls had been breached, when full bandoleers would again have been needed. That issue of nine hundredweight of powder suggests that there were 1,800 musketeers in the combined brigades of Forth, Wentworth and Dutton, together with the 600 under Darcy and 200 dragoons. I suggested in Chapter Two that musketeers formed about 40% of a regiment's strength. On that basis, the Oxford Army deployed around 6,000 infantry at the beginning of the siege.

12 Dorney, 212; Corbett, 42, 45; Warburton, II, 281; Washbourn, lv, clxxvi; Clarendon, IV, 180.

Chapter Six

1 Duffy, 'Siege Warfare', 58–105, 145–60, 174–85 (though I disagree that lines of circumvallation would have helped the Royalists at Gloucester); Firth, 'Cromwell's Army', 145–81; Carlton, 'Going to the Wars', 154–72; ROP, B138–9, B146, B167.

2 Dorney, 212–3, 207; Corbett, 45–6; ROP, B153; Atkin & Laughlin, 78, 90–3 (this provides an excellent summary of archaeological evidence for the Royalist positions); Washbourn, lx, clxi; Luke, II, 133–4; Warburton, II, 281. Vavasour's force seems to have initially comprised elements of his own infantry regiment and those of Lingen, Price and Williams, plus his own cavalry regiment and that of Pye; later reinforcements included Basset's foot and Lord Herbert's troop of horse. Another 700 men carried on the siege at Brampton Bryan. The Worcester foot probably came from the regiments of Beaumont and Russell, the horse from Russell's regiment (Hutton' 'Royalist War Effort', 112–4, 78–9). The Banbury

contingent was from Northampton's regiment. Capel's army was not called upon at this stage – it was engaged in an unsuccessful attack on Nantwich.

3 Corbett, 45–7, 49–50; Dorney, 212–4 (Corbett, 46 suggests Gray's raid may have been on 13 August but I have preferred Dorney's more contemporary account); Warburton, op cit; WRO 413/444.

4 ROP, B153–4; Dorney, op cit; Luke, II, 138–9; Corbett, ibid; Warburton, op cit.

5 ROP, B154 n218; Luke, II, 135; Dorney, 212, 214; Corbett, 45–6; GRO, D115; and ROP, B158 (Vavasour received his first issue of ammunition from Percy's central magazine on 14 August); Washbourn, clxii–clxiii. According to Lloyd, 'Memoirs', 676, Vavasour's camp was 'the best leaguer Sir J Astley ever saw'.

6 Warburton, op cit; Dorney, 214–5; Corbett, 46–7; De Gomme, 10–11; ROP, B138–9, B146, B152 (although the published Ordnance Papers are a selection and not comprehensive, records for ammunition supply during the siege appear to be complete and certainly add up convincingly. Rates of fire are inherently tricky. Eight to ten rounds an hour seems to be the accepted maximum for bigger guns. Maximum rates are unlikely to have been sustained for long periods but if they were the two cannon would simply have run out of shot more quickly); ROP, A106, 109 (initial deliveries from Soudley did not begin until 26 August).

7 Dorney, 214–5; ROP, B157–9; Hopton, 60 (500 commanded musketeers were sent from Bristol under two captains, which suggests that Gilby was given command only when they reached Gloucester); Warburton, II, 278; Luke, II, 138–9; Warburton, II, 282; Corbett, 46.

8 Warburton, op cit; MA, 16 Aug; Luke, II, 138–9; Sunderland's letter is in Atkin & Laughlin, 171; queen's letter is in Washbourn, 369–70; Clarendon, IV, 196–205, 224n; Percy's letters are in 'Pythouse Papers', 54–6.

9 Percy's letter is in 'Pythouse Papers', 57–8; ROP, B154–5, B158–9; Luke, II, 139; Dorney, 215–6; ROP, C12 (I have accepted Roy's judgement that the letter was signed on 17 rather than 20 August); Corbett, 47.

10 Dorney, 216–7; Corbett, 47–8; GN&Q, III, 465; Warburton, II, 282; MA, 18 Aug; Luke, II, 137–40; ROP, B160, B165 (Pinchbeck was the senior available colonel of the five regiments still in garrison at Oxford and was with the army on 10 September).

11 Luke, II, 139; MA, 18 Aug; Warburton, II, 282; Dorney, 217–8; Corbett, 48; ROP, B159, B139, B146; MA, 20 Aug; Luke, II, 138.

12 Luke, II, 134–6, 138–40, 142, 144; MA, 19, 20 Aug; CSPV, 1643, 12; Clarendon, IV, 142; GRO, D115; Corbett, 53–5; Clarendon, IV, 225–6; Warmington, 'Civil War, Interregnum and Restoration', 49; Dorney, 215, 220, 226; Warburton, II, 283; GN&Q, III, 465; Atkin & Laughlin, 172 (to be fair to Sunderland, he also wrote of "the horrid spectacles and hideous cries of dead and hurt men"), 5, 48–9; Washbourn, lx, clx–clxi; Wedgwood, 'King's War', 246–7.

13 Corbett, 49–50, 53, 55–6; Washbourn, lxii–lxiii, clxiii; Dorney, 222, 224, 226–8; Clarendon, IV, 225; Warmington, 'Civil War',48–50; Atkin & Laughlin, 106–11. Luke's intelligence gathering organisation has often been disparaged but he had agents inside the Royalist camp at Gloucester within a week or so providing detailed military information as well as gossip (eg George Fermer's report of 19 August giving an assessment of Royalist casualties and a breakdown of infantry colours, boats, cannon and carts at the main leaguer – Luke, II, 137–8).

14 Dorney, 218–9; Warburton, II, 282–3; Luke, II, 139–40; MA, 20 Aug; Corbett, 48–9; GN&Q, III, 465; Luke, II, 144; ROP, B161; MA, 24 Aug; Clarendon, IV, 225; Atkin & Laughlin, 172; MA, 23 Aug.

15 ROP, B162, A105–6 (the saker iron shot were either for the six pounders from Oxford or perhaps for Vavasour's guns from Worcester, the calibre of which is unknown); Dorney, 219–21; Washbourn, 370. I have concluded that the iron bars were used by the demi-cannon because of their weight (18 and 22 pounds according to Dorney) and the issue to them of powder but no shot (ROP, B164).

16 'Pythouse Papers', 57–8; Dorney, 219, 221, 225–6; Corbett, 51, 54; Luke, II, 145; for sows, see Duffy, 'Siege Warfare', 145.

17 Dorney, 219–21; Corbett, 51, 53; Washbourn, 274; Warburton, II, 283; Luke, II, 143–4; GN&Q, III, 465–6 (this gives a smaller number of rounds fired but seems to cover the night only); ROP, A105, B164; Luke, II, 146 (this intelligence report suggests that Hatton was directing the demi-cannon with the objective of hitting the garrison's magazine, an extremely difficult target for indirect fire).

18 Warburton, op cit; Atkin & Laughlin, 172; Luke, II, 141–4; Clarendon, IV, 229–30; MA, 26 Aug; ROP, B166; Hopton, 60; GRO, D115; Clarendon, IV, 180; Warburton, II, 286–7.

Chapter Seven

1 CSPV, 1643, 8, 9, 11; MA, 12, 18 Aug; TT E64/13, 65/17; CJ 3, 15 Aug; Adair, 'Roundhead General', 103–4; Hexter, 147; Snow, 381–2.

2 Peachey and Turton, 'Old Robin's Foot', 8–10, 58; Turton, 'Chief Strength of the Army', 15–69. Essex's foot regiments were his own, Barclay, Bulstrode, Constable, Holburn, Holmstead, Langham, Martin, Robartes, Skippon and Tyrrell. Aldrich was at Aylesbury, Venn at Windsor and Stapeley's appears to have been at Chichester. Kent regiments were Brooks and Springate; the London regiments Mainwaring

and Thompson. Essex's cavalry regiments were his own, Behr, Dalbeir, Goodwin, Meldrum, Middleton, Ramsey and Sheffield, plus Balfour which stayed around London. There was also a small number (perhaps only two) of dragoon companies. Estimates of total strength included 5,000 by the Venetians (CSPV, 1643, 2), 4,000 in London newspapers (TT E64/13) and 5,500 plus 3,000 sick by Essex himself (LJ, 6, 31 July).

3 CSPV, 1643, 13, 14, 16; CJ 3, 18 Aug; Snow, 382; MA, 23, 26 Aug; Luke, II, 142. Conscription riots give these events a modern ring.

4 Peachey and Turton, 9; Luke, II, 143; CSPV, 1643,14, 18; Hexter, 142–3; Rushworth, Part III, Vol II, 291–2; LJ, 6, 23 Aug; MA, 23 Aug. The infantry regiments chosen to march with Essex were the Red and Blue Trained Band Regiments; the Red, Blue and Orange Auxiliary Regiments, and Mainwaring's London regulars (the latter was in fact one of the London regiments then in Kent). The Southeastern cavalry regiments were Harvey and Norton; the Midlanders included Grey and Denbigh; and Luke commanded three independent troops at Newbury (POffA seems to refer by name to all regiments involved). For Hertfordshire horses, see MA, 23 Aug.

5 CSPV, 1643, 16; LJ 6, 11 July; Reid, 'All the King's Armies', 174–5.

6 CSPV, 1643, 14, 16; TT E65/33; MA, 26 July, 23 Aug; Peachey and Turton, 8–10; Codrington, 230; POffA, 236.

7 CSPV, ibid; CJ 3, 25, 26 Aug; Adair, 'Roundhead General', 103–5; POffA, ibid.

8 POffA, ibid; Tennant, 'Edgehill and Beyond', 115–9; Foster, 253–4; Peachey and Turton, 9.

9 Corbett, 54; Washbourn, clxviii (the movement of messengers between Bridges and Essex can be traced in Luke, II, 142–3); POffA, 236–7.

10 Clarendon, IV, 230; CSPV, 1643, 18; Washbourn, 275; Warburton, II, 273 (Wilmot's letter); Luke, II, 144 puts the column at 4,000 strong. Wilmot's letter was misdated by Warburton and written not on 3 August but 31 August. None of the facts mentioned by Wilmot make sense on 3 August. Essex was demonstrably not at Chilton north of Thame but at Kingston and his army was certainly not advancing westwards towards Bicester but moving back from Buckinghamshire towards London (see Chapter Four). By contrast, the events described by Wilmot make perfect sense if one assumes that Warburton omitted a '1' when he transcribed the date, or that Wilmot had already made the same mistake. Harvey's column certainly included his own cavalry regiment and Mainwaring's infantry (Foster, 254); Norton had been at Basing House with Harvey in early August (MacLachlan, 'Civil War in Hampshire', 109); and the regiments of Brooks, Springate and Thompson would have shared in the clothing distribution had they already been at Aylesbury (Peachey and Turton, 9).

11 Warburton, ibid; POffA, 236–7; Foster, 254; Washbourn, 275–6, clxix (Preston Bisset is elided as 'Pusset'); MA, 28 Aug; Luke, II, 146.

12 Tennant, 'Edgehill and Beyond', 117–8 (which suggests that Grey had been waiting for three days around Ascott and Whichford, and had 200 men with him together with others quartered in small groups); CSPV, 1643, 18; POffA, 237; Foster, 254–5. POffA says the rendezvous was on Brackley Heath but the only open ground near Brackley, Brackley Field, is north of the town and well out of Essex's way; Foster is clear that the site was 'Bayard's-greene in Oxfordshire, being three miles distant from Brackley, and eight miles from Banbury'.

13 The full Parliamentarian order of battle, based mainly on the POffA, is set out in Chapter Twelve. Strengths come primarily from Foster, 254; Peachey and Turton, 4–11, 58; Turton, 15–69; and contemporary references. Compared to the Royalists, information on individual commanders is sparse, especially on military careers pre-1643. The DNB fills some gaps (eg Skippon, Stapleton, Luke, Mainwaring) but there is very little in any source on key figures such as Barclay and Holburn. Stoyle, 'Soldiers and Strangers', chapters 4–5, is very good on Scottish and continental officers and influence. For Fantom, see Aubrey, 'Brief Lives'.

14 In 1642, Essex had a train of up to forty-six guns (Young, 'Edgehill', 103); in 1644, he lost twelve or thirteen guns during the south-western campaign and surrendered another thirty six plus a mortar and up to 300 barrels of powder at Lostwithiel (Ede-Borrett, 'Lostwithiel', 45). Rushworth says the London reinforcements included eleven cannon and three drakes (Part III, Vol II, 292). See also POffA, Foster and Harvey in Washbourn. Three culverins were left behind in Gloucester (Corbett, 57). The Royalist comparison is based on the artillery trains deployed with Forth (six larger guns, thirty-three carts, 193 horses) and in early September (ten small guns, fourteen carts, sixty-two horses), and assumes Essex had eighteen larger and thirty smaller cannon (ROP, B146, 171).

15 Young, 'Edgehill', 103, 306 (Du Bois); ibid 245–6 and POffA, 247 (Merrick); POffA, 239 and Foster, 56, 258, 259, 260 (hungry soldiers).

16 LJ 6, 22 July; Foster, 255; Washbourn, clxxi. The council of war which signed the letter to Parliament received on 22 July comprised (in order of signature) Tho Grey (conceivably either Lord Grey of Groby or Lord Grey of Wark, although neither was formally part of Essex's army at the time), Jo Holburne, Will Brooke, Lionell Copley, Jo Middleton, Jo Meyricke, Hary Barclay, Phill Skippon, Jo Bulbeir (presumably Dalbeir), Phill Stapleton, Fran Russell, Ed Aldrich, Tho Tyrrill, Sam Luke.

17 POffA, 237; Foster, 254–5; Washbourn, 276.

Chapter Eight

1 Dorney, 221–2, 228; Corbett, 51, 54–5; Luke, II, 143–5; ROP, A107; GN&Q, III, 466; Atkin & Laughlin, 172.
2 ROP, A106, A108, B167; Luke, II, 145; Corbett, 51; Pythouse Papers, 57–8; 'Memoirs of John Gwyn', 51–2; Warburton, II, 286–7.
3 Dorney, 222–4; Corbett, 51–2.
4 CSPV, 1643,16; Dorney, 223–4; Corbett, 51–2; GN&Q, III, 466; ROP, B171, B172; Washbourn, clxx; Luke, II, 145–6.
5 POffA, 237–8; Foster, 255–6; Washbourn, 276, clxix; Luke, II, 146; EHR 13, 1898, 734.
6 Dorney, 224–5; Corbett, 52, 55; ROP, B171–3.
7 POffA, 238–9; Foster, 257–8; Washbourn, 276–7, clxxi; MA, 5 Sep. The detailed geographical attributions are my own, drawing on current large scale maps, the 1828 Ordnance Survey map, Anderson's 1815 Ordnance Survey drawing BL OSD 222,11 accessible on www.collectbritain.co.uk, and Taylor's one-inch-to-the-mile 'Map of the County of Gloucester', completed in 1777 and published in 1786 (GRO 71026/CA12CE). The afternoon action took place following a river crossing three miles beyond Stow (both the Official account and Foster agree on that), probably where the B4068 crosses the River Eye north of Upper Slaughter – on the 1828 Ordnance Survey map it is identified as Eyeford. The most plausible alternative site, the west bank of the Dikler valley behind Upper and Lower Swell, is too close to Stow.
8 Luke, II, 146–7; Hopton, 60–1; Warburton, II, 286–7; Dorney, 225–6; Corbett, 51, 53–4.
9 Foster, 258–9; Washbourn, 277–8; Luke, II, 146–7 (the intelligence report refers to Woolpit Hill, which I have been unable to identify); POffA, 239–40; EHR 13, 1898, 734; Warburton, op cit; Dorney, 225–7; Corbett, 55.
10 Luke, II, 146–7; EHR 13, 1898, 734; Washbourn, clxxvi; 'Military Memoirs of John Gwyn', 52; Hopton, 60.
11 POffA, 239–40; Foster, 258–9; Washbourn, 277–8; Corbett, ibid.

Chapter Nine

1 Clarendon, IV, 230; 'Military Memoirs of John Gwyn', 52; Washbourn, clxxvi, 278; Luke, II, 146–8; ROP, A110; POffA, 239–40; Foster, 260; MA, 8 Sep; Digby, 2; ROP, B171, B176; Warburton, II, 287.
2 Washbourn, clxix–clxxii, lxx–lxxii; CSPV, 1643, 18, 20–1, 23; Luke, II, 147, 150–2; MA, 10 Sep.
3 Dorney, 226–8; Washbourn, lxx (Essex's letter to Parliament confirms that the powder shortage was not simply part of the siege mythology); Clarendon, IV, 225–6, 230; 'Military Memoirs of John Gwyn', ibid; Warburton, II, 286; Corbett, 50–1. For Massey's promotion, see CJ, 3, 1 Aug 43 when he is referred to as lieutenant colonel and CJ, 3, 15 September when he is described as colonel.
4 For effectiveness of Royalist artillery, see Corbett, 47–8, 50–1, 56; Dorney, 214–8, 220–1, 226–7. For Royalist casualties and the garrison's losses, see Corbett, 56; Dorney, 227; Washbourn, 279; Foster, 261. For Royalist risk aversion, see Corbett, 53–4, 56.
5 Foster, 260–2; Luke, II, 146, 152; Corbett, 56–7; Warburton, I, 503; Washbourn, clxx, lxx–lxxi; Clarendon, IV, 231; POffA, 240.
6 Luke's spies consistently reported Royalist strength at 10,000 infantry and 10,000 cavalry, probably the broad figures being bandied about in the Royalist camp – Luke, II, 143, 148–9.
7 18th century maps show the coach road from London to the west running north of the Kennet between Reading and Marlborough but the earliest map I have found with roads marked in any detail, which was published in 1688, demonstrates clearly that from Newbury to Marlborough it ran along the south bank, through Enborne, Hamstead, Kintbury and Hungerford – 'A Mappe of Kent, Southsex, Surrey, Middlesex, Berke and Southampton Shire…', based on Hollar's 1644 'Quartermaster' map with roads added and published by John Garrett, London, 1688 (see www.geog.port.ac.uk).
8 Foster, 262.
9 Washbourn, lxviii; MA, 28 Sep; Digby, 2.
10 Washbourn, 279; Luke, II, 146, 149; MA, 19 and 26 Aug, 9 Sep; Warburton, II, 282; Dorney, 215, 217; Warmington, 'Civil War, Interregnum and Restoration in Gloucestershire', 50; Atkin & Laughlin, 45–6. My estimate of 12,000 foot is based on a 6,000-strong initial deployment, 1,200 under Vavasour, 1,200 from Worcester and Banbury, 500 from Glamorgan, a first reinforcement of 450 from Bristol, 1,000 in two batches from Oxford and a final 2,000 from Bristol (I doubt Lord Herbert's claim to have brought 4,000 foot to the siege).
11 The artillery train certainly comprised two demi-cannon, two culverins, two 12-pounders, seven 6-pounders, a single 5-pounder and four 3-pounders, all brass. On 11 September, one of Luke's spies counted nineteen field guns at Sudeley (Luke, II, 149). Young and Holmes, 'English Civil War', 145, suggests that by Newbury the train had lost two 6-pounders and gained four iron guns, including two 4-pounders. For further reinforcements, see 'Diary of Henry Townshend', II, 127; MA, 15 Sep; Eales, 'Puritans and Roundheads', 169, 172.

12 Luke, II, 147–51, 154; Money, 91–2; Clarendon, IV, 231; 'Diary of Henry Townshend', II, 127–30; ROP, A110, A111; B167, 171, 176, 181; Warburton, II, 287.

13 For Astley's injury, see Dorney, 213; Luke, II, 138; Washbourn, clxviii; MA, 2 Sep, 7 Oct. For Darcy and Vavasour at Sudeley, see ROP, B174. MA, 20 Sep refers to Darcy as one of the 'chief officers' wounded at Newbury and there is no indication that he had lost his command in the interim. For Belasyse, see Money, 97; Belasyse, 383. For Sir Nicholas Byron, see J. Byron in Money, 51. For Gerard, see 'Hurt souldiers', JSAHR 1939, 30–1. Reid, 'All the King's Armies', 60, 67, says that Lisle's detachment took part in Rupert's operations around Stow but I have been unable to find an earlier reference to them than 7 September (ROP, B174), and there are no contemporary descriptions of infantry at Stow. For the link between Lisle's detachment and the Bristol garrison, see Hopton, 60–1.

14 For Pennyman's death and replacement by Aston, see Toynbee and Young, 'Strangers in Oxford', 23. For Carnarvon, see DNB and Lloyd's 'Memoirs', 370. The king may have felt the need to compensate him for Maurice's alleged abrasiveness.

15 Washbourn, lxx–lxxi; POffA, 240; Foster, 261–2; TT E69/2; Morris, 'Siege of Gloucester', 16; Sherwood, 'Civil Strife in the Midlands', 85–6; Luke, II, 149–53; 'Diary of Henry Townshend', II, 27; Codrington, 230; Digby, 2; Clarendon, IV, 231; MA, 15 Sep.

16 Digby, 2; Luke, II, 148–53 (the king may also have been with the advance guard); EHR 13, 1898, 734; 'Diary of Henry Townshend', ibid ("our own Country soldiers Horse and foot being in his Majesty's Army"); Hutton, 'Royalist War Effort', 114; Washbourn, clxxvi; Money, 91. For the composition of reinforcements sent to Worcester, see Luke, II, 151; MA, 15 Sep; 'Diary of Henry Townshend', ibid.

17 Luke, ibid; Washbourn, ibid; POffA, 240; MA, 15 Sep; Foster, 261–2. Oxington was not an isolated incident. Royalist raiding continued throughout Essex's stay in north Gloucestershire (Luke, II, 153 suggests that eleven men were lost on 13 September). And the Royalists seem to have been preparing for larger scale raids since two 6-pounder cannon were sent to Pershore on 14 September (ROP, B177).

Chapter Ten

1 'Lloyd's Memoires', 627–8; Washbourn, clxxiv; Newman, 'Royalist Officers', 92.

2 POffA, 240–1; Foster, 262–3; Codrington, 230; Corbet, 57; Luke, II, 150–4; MA, 15 Sep; Clarendon, IV, 231–2. POffA, 241 identifies Colonel Alexander Brackley as leader of the commanded foot, perhaps Lt. Col. Alexander Bayley of Barclay's Regiment.

3 POffA, 241 (40 cartloads); Foster, op cit (27 cartloads); Corbet, op cit (30 cartloads); Luke, II, 153–4.

4 Clarendon, IV, 231–2; Digby, 2; Byron, Clar MSS, 1738; Money, 15; WRO, 413/444; Warburton, II, 287–8.

5 Clarendon, IV, 232; ROP, B175 (for Lisle's musketeers to have accompanied the cavalry, double mounted, would be inconsistent with later events at Aldbourne Chase and I have therefore concluded that they force-marched their way south); Foster, 263 (rain); Clarendon, ibid; Digby, op cit; Luke, II, 154; Pythouse Papers, 16; 'Diary of Henry Townsend', II, 134 (Sandys); Warburton, II, 289–90; Money, 26.

6 Luke, op cit; POffA, ibid; Foster, 263; TT E69/2.

7 Earlier that year, Marlborough had been one of only two Wiltshire towns not controlled by Parliament (Adair, 'Roundhead General', 53). Luke's spies reported a Royalist cavalry regiment there on 22 July and that the king was expected to stay there on 8 August, *en route* from Bristol to Oxford; there is no recorded report from the spy sent to the town on 1 September (Luke, II, 123, 130, 154). Hopton was quartering overnight in Marlborough with last minute reinforcements when he learned of the outcome of Newbury (Hopton, 61).

8 Digby, op cit, is the exception, writing that the action took place two miles north-west of Aldbourne; Money, 17, recorded local tradition that the site was close to Dudborne Lodge, where a cannon ball and other relics had been found; WRO, 413/444; Foster, 263–4; 1773 Andrews and Dury map of Wiltshire, sheet 15; Ordnance Survey Drawings of Swindon, BL OSD 166, 9, accessible on www.collectbritain.co.uk.

9 Estimates: MA, 19 Sep; POffA, op cit; Foster, 264; Digby, op cit; WRO 413/4. Royalist sources for Aldbourne Chase are Digby, 2–3; Byron, op cit; Prince Rupert's Diary at WRO 413/444; Clarendon, IV, 232–4; *Mercurius Aulicus*, op cit; Warburton, II, 289–92. Parliamentarian sources are POffA, 241–2; Foster, 263–4; Codrington, 230–1; TT E68/5, E69/2, E69/12, E69/17. Descriptions of the landscape are drawn from these accounts, the *Victoria History of Wiltshire, Vol XII, 71–8, and the maps at viii above.*

10 This interpretation of Royalist squabbling reflects Digby, 2; Clarendon, IV, 232; MA, op cit; Byron, op cit; WRO 413/444.

11 For the initial clash between Urry and Middleton, see in particular POffA, 241 (including a list of the Parliamentarian regiments involved – Middleton, Gray, Sheffield, Harvey and Meldrum); and Digby, op cit. I have suggested that Sheffield's Regiment was overrun because muster records in Turton, 'Chief Strength of the Army' suggest that it was about 200–300 strong before the march to Gloucester; and suffered relatively heavy losses during the campaign (one troop had 73 men on its books in August but only 42 in November); this was the only action in which it was likely to have sustained such casualties; and it lost a standard in the fighting.

12 I have suggested that Gerard's brigade took the lead in this stage of the action because of the role played by one of its units, the Queen's Regiment, WRO 413/444 and because Warwick, 262, recorded that at Aldbourne Chase 'the Lord Gerard appeared eminent'.

13 The level of personal detail of this action is one of the most persuasive justifications for attributing the 'official Royalist' account to Digby. For the Queen's Regiment to have been committed alone in this way, it must have been numerically strong as well as brimming with self-confidence (the figure of 500 comes from Stoyle, 'Soldiers and Strangers', 95). On the Parliamentarian side, Norton's Regiment was 220 strong later in the autumn of 1643 (Goodwin, 'Civil War in Hampshire', 140).

14 EHR 13, 734; Money, 26.

15 For Essex's night march and the Royalist response, see POffA, 242; Foster, 264–5; MA, op cit; Digby, 3.

Chapter Eleven

1 'Journal of Prince Rupert's Marches', EHR, 13, 734; Luke, II, 154; Warburton, II, 291; Hopton, 61; Belasyse, 383; Clarendon, IV, 234; Gwyn, 52–3; Luke, II, 155.

2 MA, 19 Sep; Digby, 4; Money, 33–4; Washbourn, clxxvi.

3 MA, ibid; Foster, 264–5.

4 Foster, 263; MA, ibid; Codrington, 230–1; Money, ibid. For evidence that the road ran south of the river, see Chapter Nine, footnote vii.

5 Luke, II, 150–4; TT, E69/2; Andriette, 'Devon and Exeter in the Civil War', 95; CJ, vol 3, 20 September 1643.

6 Codrington, 231; POffA, 242–3; Foster, 265; Prince Rupert's Diary, WRO413/444; MA, ibid. Codrington's reference to the narrowness of the lane ('in which but six men could march on breast') suggests that the ground on either side was either too enclosed and/or too damp for troops to deploy in large scale formations. Landscape evidence (eg Baker's 1775 map of Enborne manor) seems to support this.

7 Foster, ibid; Codrington, ibid; Digby, 4–5; Clarendon, IV, 234–5; Rupert's Diary, WRO413/444; Washbourn, ibid.

Chapter Twelve

1 Money, chapters 3–5; Gardiner, I, 209–19; Burne, 202–5.

2 Anon, BL Add. MS 18980; Luke, II, 142; Lloyd, 658. Feilding died on board Rupert's flagship in 1649–50. Professor Wanklyn suggests the author was Thomas, Lord Wentworth but I cannot agree with his interpretation of the evidence. Wentworth was son of the Earl of Cleveland, Major General of Dragoons and soon to command the Prince of Wales' Horse. He was an unlikely candidate for routine picket duty and I can find no reason for senior officers to refuse him a remount, for the king to ignore him or for him to feel the need to vindicate his actions. He is not, as far as I can see, mentioned in Prince Rupert's Diary as commanding the cavalry in the first assault on Round Hill while Byron explicitly has him in joint command of Lisle's musketeers. As for similarities in handwriting, I would be interested in a graphologist's opinion (Wanklyn, 'Decisive Battles of the English Civil War', 64, 214; Newman, 'Royalist Officers', 404; WRO, 413/444; Byron, Clar MSS 1738).

3 Enclosure maps and awards are on BRO New Landscapes @ www.berkshireenclosure.org.uk/. Enborne tithe map is at BRO, D/D1 51/1. There is a good selection of pre-18th century maps of Berkshire on Genmaps @ freepages.genealogy.rootsweb.com/~genmaps.

4 Ordnance Survey Drawing of Hungerford, BL OSD 78,7, accessible on www.collectbritain.co.uk; Rocque, 'Topographical Survey of the County of Berkshire in 18 sheets', 1761, sheets IV & V; Willis, 'Plan of Country Ten Miles Around Newbury', BRO PM 123; Baker, 'A Map of the Manor of Enborne ... 1775', BRO D/EC E/11; Northcroft, 'A Plan Survey and Admeasurement of St Bartholomew's Hospital ... 1757', BRO D/E2 80/10; Ballard, 'A Plan of The Estate Belonging to Mr Henry Grace ... 1777', BRO D/EZ 80/11; J R Wordie, 'Enclosure in Berkshire 1485–1885', 60–61, 111–113.

5 These maps can all be found on HantsMap @ www.geog.port.ac.uk/webmap/hantscat/htm/mapmenu.htm.

6 Digby, 5; Codrington, 231.

7 M Gelling, 'Place Names of Berkshire', Vol 1, 9 & Vol 2, 294–6. The River Enborne was the Aleburne in 1335 and the Auborn in 1695 and 1761. Surprisingly its origin ('alder stream') seems to differ from that of Enborne village ('duck stream').

8 VCHB, IV, 179–81.

9 VCHB, IV, 142.

10 Digby, op cit; TT E69/2.

11 Wanklyn, 'Decisive Battles', 59–60, uses the field pattern set out by Rocque to argue that the enclosures facing the Kennet were quite large fields. In fact, as shown above (iv refers), Rocque's interpretation was illustrative only and Baker's more detailed survey paints a very different picture. The only unenclosed ground was West Field, behind the Royalist front line.

12 As examples of Money's continuing influence, Barratt, 'Newbury', repeats the Bigg's cottage story uncritically and places it in the centre of the Parliamentarian position (84), and has the army drawn up on 20 September on a two mile front (86–7); Roberts, 'First Newbury', has Stapleton's cavalry advancing onto the Wash Common plateau past Bigg's Hill cottage and extends the Parliamentarian line from the Kennet almost to the River Enborne (69–76); Wanklyn & Jones, 'Military History', extend the Parliamentarian line even further south, beyond Enborne Street Road (120–2); Wanklyn, 'Decisive Battles', 69, expands on this to have the Blue and Red Regiments advancing onto the plateau by this route.

13 Foard, 'Naseby', 193, gives a credible methodology: 4,000 horse moving four abreast = 2 miles; 9,000 foot moving eight abreast = 2 miles; 100 carriages = 1.25 miles.

14 Money, 33–42. His theory derives from an earlier analysis in 'History and Antiquities of Newbury and its Environs', published anonymously by Edward Gray in 1839. My counter-argument draws on the maps at iii–v above, plus Foster, 264; POffA, 242–3; Codrington, 231; TT E69/2, 69/17, 68/5; Digby, 4–5; Clarendon, IV, 235; Byron, op cit; Anon, BL Add MS 18980; BRO, Parish Records, various; Gelling, Vol 2, 294–6. Wanklyn, 'Decisive Battles of the English Civil Wars', 59, suggests an alternative possibility, that Biggs Hill was used in the 17th century to describe the entire Wash Common plateau. I can find no evidence for this.

15 Wanklyn, 'Decisive Battles', 69, argues that the initial assault was carried out along all three lanes onto the plateau, with the Blue and Red Trained Band Regiments advancing along Enborne Street Lane in parallel with Essex's Regiment on Cope Hall Lane and Barclay and Holburn on Wheatlands Lane. Setting aside the tactical challenge of coordinating such a complex operation, and the dangers of dispersing a relatively small force over such a wide area, POffA, 243, makes clear that the initial assault was carried out by Essex's 'own regiment, Colonel Barclay's, and Colonel Holburn's brigades' only, and that the two trained band regiments arrived on the common after the vanguard had already seen considerable action. Foster, 266, confirms that fighting had started before the trained bands arrived, and that they were used first to reinforce Lord Robartes' brigade (Wanklyn suggests that this reference is to Essex's Regiment but Foster consistently calls him the Lord General, never Lord Robert). He is also clear that when the trained bands arrived on the common, Royalist foot, horse and artillery were already in place opposite them.

16 This analysis is based primarily on POffA, 243–7, which gives a detailed account of the order of battle and is generally corroborated by other Parliamentarian sources and by Digby, 4–5, plus material in Peachey and Turton, 'Old Robin's Foot' and Turton, 'Chief Strength of the Army' (frontages are approximate and use the methodology in Foard, 'Naseby', 237–40); CSPV, 1643, 26–7; Foster, 265.

17 There is no Royalist equivalent to the POffA. My analysis draws on a multitude of sources including Digby, Prince Rupert's Diary, Byron, Belasyse, Gwyn, MA, Clarendon, Lloyd and more recent research. For attrition, see Clarendon, IV, 232, 234; Byron, op cit; Young, 'Atkins and Gwyn', 52 and JSAHR, 1964.

18 Belasyse: see his 'Memoirs', 383. Sir Gilbert Gerard: see 'Hurt Soldiers', JSAHR, 1964. Sir Nicholas Byron: see Byron, op cit. Darcy: ROP, B174, shows that he still had his brigade on 7 September; Digby, 6, and MA, 20 Sep, identified him as the senior officer wounded on Round Hill, and his northern regiments do not appear in 'Hurt Soldiers' among those in Sir Nicholas Byron's brigade, the other formation engaged on the hill. Vavasour: see BL Add. MSS. 18 980–2. In 'Hurt Soldiers' Vavasour's brigade is attributed to Lord Herbert, nominal commander of the Marcher army but not mentioned as having been present by other sources.

19 Reconstructing the order of battle is difficult because much of the Royalist foot was not organised on a regimental basis. This analysis differs from those of Young (JSAHR, 1964), Reid ('All the King's Armies'), Roberts('First Newbury') and Barratt (ECW N&Q 27 and 'First Battle of Newbury') primarily because I have presumed that 'Hurt Soldiers' is an incomplete list (it excludes units known to be present and Lisle's musketeers); Darcy commanded a fifth brigade; Charles Gerard's 'regiment' was a composite unit formed from the Oxford garrison; and Belasyse's twelve-regiment brigade included the four regiments from Bristol referred to by Hopton.

20 'Diary of Henry Townsend', II, 134; Byron, op cit; Clarendon, IV, 232.

21 Reconstructing the order of battle for the Royalist horse is even more difficult than for the foot. Unlike previous breakdowns (eg those in xix above), I have attempted to ascribe regiments to brigades. My analysis is necessarily speculative but based on past and subsequent deployments, and the sources in xvii above.

22 Guns: ROP, B183; Young and Adair, 'Hastings to Culloden', 148, 161. Powder: ROP includes orders for the despatch of c70 barrels from Oxford on 2 and 3 September (B171, 173) and deliveries from Bristol of 30 barrels on 27 August, 8 barrels on 6 September and the equivalent of 22 barrels on 10 September (A106, 110); Digby, 6–7, states that the army used 80 barrels on 20 September and could not maintain that level of consumption 'for half such another day'. Cannon balls: ROP show deliveries of 111 demi-cannon, 350 culverin, 202 12-pounder, 122 6-pounder and 300 5-pounder cannon balls plus 44 wooden case-shot and 21 iron bars (A105–8).

23 Clarendon, IV, 235; Codrington, 231; Young, 'Atkins and Gwyn', 52–3.

Chapter Thirteen

1 This section is based on POffA, 243–5; Foster, 265–6; Codrington, 231; TT E68/5, E68/8, E69/2, E69/9, E69/17; Vicars, 414–5; Byron, Clar MSS, 1738; Digby, 4–5; Feilding, BL Add MS 18980; Prince Rupert's Diary, WRO, 413/444; Clarendon, IV, 235; MA, 20, 21, 30 Sep, 6, 14 Oct. I have examined in detail whether the Royalists were taken by surprise or expelled from Round Hill because of the impact it had on their tactics and mindset, and on the course of the battle.

2 POffA, 243, makes clear that the lane entered the common at the top of the hill, which rules out the Bigg's cottage alternative, and Cope Hall Lane would have embroiled Essex's infantry in the cavalry battle, which both POffA and Digby are clear did not happen.

3 Based on Byron, op cit; Digby, op cit; WRO 413/444; Clarendon, op cit; Warburton, II, 292.

4 Warburton suggests that Rupert still favoured a defensive posture but his interpretation probably conflates the argument on the previous evening, when that made military sense, with the discussion on the morning of the battle, when it did not (Warburton, II, 292). Prince Rupert's Diary (WRO413/444) states that three infantry brigades were deployed on Newbury Common. Unless the Royalists possessed a sixth brigade, which is improbable, that means Darcy's brigade was there instead of Round Hill. All other evidence suggests that my interpretation is correct even if it is not, the only substantive difference is that would make to the narrative is to make the disparity of forces on Round Hill greater, Sir Nicholas Byron's failure to advance further even more explicable and the subsequent anger among senior Royalists at the failure of the Royalist infantry on the Common still more understandable.

5 Based on Money, 91, 95; POffA, ibid; Feilding, op cit; Digby, 6.

6 Based on POffA, 243–5; TT E68/3, 69/12; Lloyd's 'Memoirs', 366, 370, 465–6; Digby, 5–6; MA, 20 Aug; Clarendon, op cit; WRO 413/444; Warwick, 'Memoirs', 262. The difference between the Royalist accounts, which suggest a short, one-sided combat, and the Parliamentarian version, setting out the various strongly contested phases in much more detail, reflects the different agendas at play. Digby was emphasising the innate superiority of Rupert's cavaliers so for him the result was a foregone conclusion. POffA's authors wanted to show that Parliament's despised horse had in fact fought long and hard before being defeated by weight of numbers, in part to rebut allegations that they had provided inadequate support to the foot.

7 This argument applies whether or not the southern end of Wash Common was wooded. The stream and gulley would have made a cavalry charge impossible to mount successfully in any event.

8 There is no evidence that Stapleton's cavalrymen employed the complex caracole tactic of successive ranks firing and then peeling off to the rear to reload. Indeed, it is difficult to see how they could have done so if they did not open fire until the Royalists were at very close range. I am grateful to Stephen Ede-Borrett for this point.

9 Whitelock in Money, 71.

10 Muster details from Turton, 'Chief Strength of the Army'; Ware in TT E69/14; St Barbe in Money, 62; Ulrick in MA, 24 Sep and LJ 6, 22, 25 Sep.

11 Based on TT E69/2; Digby, 5; MA, 20, 21 Sep; POffA, 245–6; Foster, 267–8; JSAHR, 1939.

12 The hillock can be identified on modern OS maps. The king did not remain in the valley throughout the day since he is identified on Newbury Common later in the fighting, and his Lifeguard suffered casualties there; the complaints by Mercurius Aulicus seem to stem from this early stage of the battle.

13 Based on Byron, op cit; MA, 14 Oct; POffA, op cit; Foster, 266; JSAHR, 1939. I have identified Holburn's brigade as the target of Sir John Byron's initial attacks because their numerical strength tallies with Byron's description.

14 Wanklyn, 'Decisive Battles of the English Civil Wars', 67–80, proposes a very different order of events based, in my view, on a misreading of the main sources. In particular, he ignores the careful chronology of the Parliamentarian Official Account and Foster. But no writer on Newbury can be certain that they have got it entirely right.

15 Compare Clarendon, IV, 240–57 with Aubrey, 'Brief Lives', 64.

Chapter Fourteen

1 This section is based on Byron, Clar MSS, 1738; POffA, 245–6; MA, 14 Oct. In my view, this stage of the battle was Essex's point of greatest danger. POffA gave due credit to Barclay and Holburn because there was a political imperative to demonstrate that the outlander officers were pulling their weight. The contrary would be true later in the war when the focus shifted to the role of the thoroughly English Trained Bands. This subsequently became the authorised version for both sides.

2 Wanklyn, 'Decisive Battles of the English Civil Wars', 72, goes furthest in this respect, arguing that Byron was attacking not Round Hill but 'a small hill 400 yards or so to the east of it' and that the lane reached at the end of the advance was Dark Lane.

3 POffA, 244–5; Lloyd, 'Memoirs', 475.

4 Based on POffA, 246–7; Digby, 5; Feilding, BL Add MS 18980.

5 Based on POffA, 243, 246–7; Foster, 266–9; TT E68/3, E69/2; E69/12, E69/17; Codrington, 231–2; Digby, 5–6; Byron, op cit; Belasyse, 383; Young, 'Atkins & Gwyn', 53; JSAHR, 1939; Lloyd, 'Memoirs',

475; Clarendon, IV, 235–6. The various accounts of the afternoon's fighting are more difficult to reconcile than for the earlier part of the day. I am, however, satisfied that this chronology is most consistent with the major, most reliable sources.

6 Roberts, 'London & Liberty', 29, 36.

7 Had case shot been used, the Trained Band regiments would quickly have been destroyed, but it appears to have had a range of no more than c150m (conversation with Glenn Foard, Aug 2006).

8 Based on MA, 5 Oct; Gardiner, 217; Digby, 6–7; Byron, op cit; ROP, B183.

9 Based on Foster, ibid; Rupert's Diary, WRO, 413/444; Clarendon, IV, op cit; Digby, 5; Codrington, ibid; TT E68/5; E69/8.

10 Stuart Reid has suggested that forming a square in this way was impractical under combat conditions and that it is more likely that the pikes closed up and charged their pikes forward, with the musketeers lined along the flanks, protecting themselves with their musket butts (ECW N&Q 45, 21–23). That is not my reading of Foster's account, which is not to say that the squares would have been parade-ground perfect rather than huddled schiltrons with musketeers firing at will.

11 Based on POffA, 246–7; Digby, 6; TT E68/5, E69/12, E69/17; WRO, 413/444; Vicars, 414–5; Foster, 268–9.

12 Based on Clarendon, IV, 236–9; Bulstrode, 'Memoirs', 96; Digby, 6–7; WRO, 413/444; Byron, op cit; Luke, II, 154–5.

Chapter Fifteen

1 Foster, 268; TT E69/12; Money, 93; Aubrey, 'Brief Lives', 64–65; Digby, 5–6; JSAHR, 1939; Newman, 'Royalist Officers', 292 (Pinchbeck); Reid, 'Officers and Regiments' 4, 176–7 (Tyldesley's horse and foot together lost four captains); Hopton, 60 (Thomas Randall, one of the captains of the Bristol commanded musketeers); Clarendon, IV, 235–9; Prince Rupert's Diary, WRO, 413/444; Byron, Clar MSS, 1738.

2 Foster, op cit; TT E69/2, E69/12, E69/17; Luke, II, 155; CSPV, 1643, 27; MA, 24, 28 Sep, 7 Oct (including the implication that Essex claimed 5,000 Royalist dead); Belasyse, 383.

3 The Red Regiment lost Major Tucker, Captain Hunt and Captain Lieutenant Mosse; the Blue Regiment's Captain Lieutenant Stoning was shot in the heel and died at Reading; Captain Lieutenant Juxon from the Green Regiment died in London. Two other captains with fatal wounds, Bolton and Willet (the latter received at Aldbourne Chase), may have been Auxiliaries.

4 POffA, 242–7; Foster, 266–9; TT E69/2; Peachey & Turton, 'Old Robin's Foot', 58 and Turton, 'Chief Strength of the Army', 15–69 (muster rolls); Money, 'Popular History of Newbury', 49 (Springate); MA, 28 Sep, 7 Oct; Snow, 'Essex', 392 (Whitelocke). The Trained Band figures assume Mainwaring's regiment was 600 strong. The reference to post-battle attrition among Trained Band units relates to the action on Greenham Common and the likelihood that some of Foster's comrades will not have waited for Essex's leisurely march back to London to return to their families.

5 Clarendon, IV, 239; POffA, 247; Foster, 268; TT E69/2, E69/12, E69/17.

6 POffA, 247–8; Foster, 268–9; TT E68/5, E69/2; Money, 62; MA, 21 Sep.

7 Digby, 6–7; Warburton, II, 297–8; WRO, 413/444; Clarendon, IV, 237; MA, 21 Sep; POffA, 248.

8 Money, 66–7, 80–2; TT E68/5; MA, 21 Sep; Foster, 269; POffA, 248; Wordie, 'Enclosure in Berkshire', various.

9 Rocque, 'Topographical Survey of the County of Berkshire in 18 sheets', 1761; BL OSD 79,1 accessible on www.collectbritain.co.uk. Subsequent nineteenth century OS maps at all scales show the common in the same way.

10 MA, 21 Sep; POffA, 248; TT E68/5, E69/2, E69/17; Foster, 269–70; Luke, Intro, vi–vii; Codrington, 233; WRO, 413/444. The only clues as to Rupert's cavalry are the references in MA to Wilmot and Northampton commanding the pursuit at the outset; and in Prince Rupert's Diary, which refers to 'the Earl of Worcester's troop', 'my Lord Bernard's troop' and a squadron under Major Legge. The former was probably in Vavasour's regiment, and therefore part of Northampton's (ex Carnarvon's) brigade. The latter could be the King's Lifeguard under Lord Bernard Stuart. Legge was Rupert's own major but played a wider role.

11 Foster, 270; POffA, 248; CJ 3, 23 Sep (the letter was written by Essex's secretary, Mr Baldwyn).

12 MA, 21 Sep; Luke, II, 154–7; TT E69/12; Money, 63; Digby, 1; Hopton, 61.

Chapter Sixteen

1 TT E67/3; Washbourn, clxx, lxx–lxxii, 275–9, lxxv–lxxvi; CSPV, 1643, 21, 23, 25; CJ 3, 12, 15, 18, 19 Sep; MA, 19 Sep.

2 TT E68/3; CJ 3, 21–3 Sep; MA, 24 Sep.

3 Luke, II, 156; POffA, 248; CSPV, 1643, 25, 29; Foster, 270–1; CJ 3, 26, 28 Sep; LJ 6, 22, 25, 26, 28 Sep; Snow, 'Essex', 393; MA, 24, 28 Sep.

4 Foster, 253; POffA, 235; TT E68 & 69, various. Wanklyn, 'Decisive Battles of the English Civil Wars', 65, argues that the Official Account was published primarily to counter criticism in the London news

books. My reading is that this criticism was muted compared to the vitriol poured on Essex in the summer and that the aim was rather to put an authorised version on record in response to Royalist claims of victory at Newbury in Mercurius Aulicus.

5   CSPV, 1643, 27; TT E69/12, E69/8; Adair, 'Roundhead General', 120–2.

6   Green, 'Letters', 227–8; Digby, 1; MA, 20 Sep–25 Oct, various; Luke, II, 154–7; Hutton, 'Royalist War Effort', 65, 115; ROP, B184; Warburton, II, 314.

7   Clarendon, IV, 258, 314–5; Hopton, 61; Luke, II, 156–7; CSPV, 1643, 29; Warburton, II, 322; EHR 13, 735.

8   Clarendon, IV, 258–62, 301–2. Bulstrode was also critical of Rupert's failure to impede Essex's advance: 'though the Prince had then a brave army, and was most commonly in a race campagne, and that we still marched before Essex, to eat up the provisions, and to attend his motions, yet we took no advantage of him' (Bulstrode, 'Memoirs', 94–5).

9   Money, 62; Newman, 'Royalist Officers', 292; Fassnidge, 'English Civil War Documents', 1, 23. Taken overall, the campaign was not especially costly in lives. Probably no more than 5,000 soldiers and civilians involved in the fighting were killed, wounded or stricken by disease (compared, for example, to the 190,000 deaths attributed to the Civil Wars in England and Wales in Carlton, 'Going to the Wars', 211).

10 CJ 3, 15 Sep, 7 Oct; Clarendon, IV, 257; Washbourn, 59–61; Corbett, 56–63. My downplaying of Gloucester's strategic significance will be controversial but I have no doubt that the evidence supports it.

11 The performance of Essex's cavalry in successive engagements suggests that a reappraisal may be needed. The traditional view of their poor quality may rely unduly on the partial accounts of the Royalists, Essex himself (who was painting a bleak picture to secure extra funding) and Cromwell (who wanted to talk down rival armies).

12 See Scott Wheeler, 'The Making of a World Power', chapter 4.

13 Percy is an unattractive personality but here too a re-evaluation is called for, including about the suitability of landowners as generals of artillery – their main role was as an army's chief of logistics and experience of running estates, businesses etc may have been as valuable as any in an un-martial society.

14 It has been the norm to dismiss the performance of Luke's spies (Philip concluded that their activities "do not appear to have had any effect on operations during this period . . . [and] failed to get information of immediate tactical value" Luke, Intro, ix). I disagree. The evidence is that the network of around fifty agents, a dozen of whom were operating with the army during the campaign, produced much good material and that it was often influential in decision making.

15 As I have made clear throughout, Massey was another difficult personality but the recent revisionism in the DNB and Warmington, 'Civil War . . . in Gloucestershire', goes too far.

16 Gardiner, 217: "The charge against the Royalist gentry is that they had ceased to lead. The contrast between the infantry which followed Essex and the infantry which followed Charles is their bitterest condemnation". He was making a broader and now outdated political point, but from a purely military perspective his conclusion stands.

17 I have been surprised at how often Rupert was unsuccessful in getting his own way during this period. It puts his attitude during the rest of the war in a rather different light.

18 Wedgwood, 'King's War', 383.

19 I am especially grateful to Peter Ryan for his comments on this section and the introduction.

20 Stoyle, 'Soldiers and Strangers' is an excellent analysis of this aspect of the civil wars; Atkin & Laughlin, 155; Worden, 'Roundhead Reputations', 300. Although I can find little evidence for the prior careers of the Scottish colonels, except for a brief summary of Middleton's early years in the DNB, their subsequent histories in English service until the formation of the New Model Army can be traced fairly easily and their roles in later Scottish operations are fully documented in Furgol, 'A Regimental History of the Covenanting Armies'.

21 For a fascinating counter-factual speculation, see Adamson, 'King Charles I wins the English Civil War' in Roberts, 'What Might Have Been'.

Bibliography

Seventeenth-century sources

Anonymous, 'Royalist Account of the Battle of Newbury' (I have attributed it to Colonel Richard Feilding), BL Add. MSS. 18980, printed in Money, *The First and Second Battles of Newbury and the Siege of Donnington Castle* and the English Heritage battlefield report.

Anonymous, 'A Journal of the Siege of Gloucester', printed in *Gloucestershire Notes and Queries*, Volume III and Warburton, *Memoirs of Prince Rupert and the Cavaliers*, Volume II.

Anonymous, *A True Relation of the Late Expedition of His Excellency, Robert Earle of Essex, for the Relief of Gloucester, with the Description of the Fight at Newbury*, the Parliamentarian official account published London, 1643, reprinted in Washbourn, *Bibliotheca Gloucestrensis*' and by Partizan Press, Leigh on Sea.

Anonymous, 'A true Relation of the manner of the Seigh before the Citty of Gloster by his maties forses with Prince Rupert & Prince Mauris', printed in *Gloucestershire Notes and Queries*, Volume III (Washbourn believed that Dorney was the author).

Anonymous, 'A True Relation of the Severall Passages Which Have Happened to Our Army, Since it Advanced Towards Gloster', London, 1643, reprinted in Washbourn, *Bibliotheca Gloucestrensis*.

Anonymous, 'Hurt souldiers of Newberry', printed in P Young, 'King Charles I's Army of 1643–5', *Journal of the Society for Army Historical Research*, (1939).

Anonymous, 'Journal of Prince Rupert's Marches', printed in *English Historical Review*, Volume 13 (1898).

Anonymous, 'On a Manuscript List of Officers of the London Trained Bands in 1643', printed by A Dillon in *Archaeologia*, Volume II, (1890).

Anonymous, 'Prince Rupert's Diary', Wiltshire Record Office, 413/444 (manuscript plus notes and transcript).

Atkyns, R, 'The Vindication of Richard Atkyns' – in *Richard Atkyns, John Gwyn*, edited by P Young (London, 1967).

Aubrey, J, Brief Lives' (Woodbridge, 1993).

Belasyse, John Lord, 'A Briefe Relation of the Life and Memoires of John Lord Belasyse', Historical Manuscripts Commission, Manuscripts of the Marquess of Ormonde, NS2, (1903).

Bulstrode, Sir Richard, *Memoirs and Reflections* (London, 1721).

Byron, Sir John (later Lord), account of Aldbourne Chase and Newbury, Clar MSS 1738, printed (in part and with inaccuracies) in Money, *The First and Second Battles of Newbury and the Siege of Donnington Castle*, and the English Heritage Battlefield Report.

Clarendon, Edward Earl of, *The History of the Rebellion* (Oxford, 1826).

Codrington, R, 'The Life and Death of the Illustrious Robert, Earl of Essex' (London, 1646), reprinted in *Harleian Miscellany*, Volume I, (London, 1808).

Corbett, J, 'An Historical Relation of the Military Government of Gloucester', (London, 1645), reprinted in Washbourn, *Bibliotheca Gloucestrensis*.

De Gomme, B, 'The Journall of the Seige of Bristoll', printed in *The Storm of Bristol, De Gomme's Account*, edited by S Ede-Borrett (Leeds, 1988).

Digby, George Lord, 'A True and Impartiall Relation of the Battaile Betwixt, His Maiesties Army, and that of the Rebells neare Newbery in Berkshire', (Oxford, 1643), TT, E. 69.10.

Dorney, J, 'A Briefe and Exact Relation of the Most Materiall and Remarkeable Passages that Happened in the Late Well-formed (and as Valiently Defended) Seige Laid Before the City of Gloster', (London, 1643), reprinted in Washbourn, *Bibliotheca Gloucestrensis*.

Foster, H, 'A True and Exact Relation of the Marchings of the Two Regiments of the Trained Bands of the City of London', (London, 1643), reprinted in Washbourn, *Bibliotheca Gloucestrensis*.

Gwyn, J, 'The Military Memoirs of John Gwyn', in *Richard Atkyns, John Gwyn*, edited by N Tucker (London, 1967).

Hopton, Sir Ralph, *Bellum Civile, Sir Ralph Hopton's Memoirs of the Campaign in the West, 1642–44*, edited by A. Wicks (Leigh on Sea, 1988) also in Clarendon MSS, Volume 23, No 1738 (1).

Lloyd, D, *Memoires of the Lives, Actions, Sufferings & Deaths of those Noble, Reverend and Excellent Personages that Suffered for the Protestant Religion in Our Late Intestine Wars 1637–1660*, (London, 1668).

Rushworth, J, *Historical Collections*, Part III, Volume II (London, 1691).

State Trials, Volume IV, 'Trial of Colonel Fiennes for Surrendering the City of Bristol' (London, 1816).

Symonds, R, *Richard Symond's Diary of the Marches of the Royal Army*, edited by C E Long, (Cambridge, 1997).

Townsend, H, *Diary of Henry Townshend of Elmley Lovett 1640–63*, Part II, edited by J W Willis-Bund, Worcestershire Historical Society (1916).

Vicars, J, 'England's Parliamentary Chronicle' (London, 1643–6).

Warwick, Sir Philip, *Memoires of the reign of King Charles I* (London, 1702).

Later collections of seventeenth-century material

Berkshire Record Office, Parish Records for Aldermaston and Enborne.

Calendar of State Papers Venetian Series, 1642–3 and 1643–7.

Gloucester Record Office, Royalist papers in D115 10/10/4.

'Journal of the House of Commons, Volume 3' (online at www.british-history.ac.uk).

'Journal of the House of Lords, Volume 6' (online at www.british-history.ac.uk).

'Journal of Sir Samuel Luke', Volume II, edited by I G Philip, Oxfordshire Record Society (1950).

The Letters of Queen Henrietta Maria, edited by M Green (London, 1857)

Mercurius Aulicus, in *The English Revolution III*, Newsbooks 1, Oxford Royalist, Volumes 1 & 2 (1971).

The Pythouse Papers, edited by W A Day (London, 1879)

Royalist Ordnance Papers 1642–46, Volumes I & II, edited by I Roy, Oxfordshire Record Society, Volumes 43 & 49 (1964 & 1975)

Ruthven Correspondence, edited by W D Macray (London, 1868)

'Thomason Tracts', British Library, Parliamentarian newsbooks in E64, 65, 67, 68, 69, 70.

Memoirs of Prince Rupert and the Cavaliers, E Warburton (London, 1849).

Bibliotheca Gloucestrensis: A Collection of Scarce and Curious Tracts Relating to the County and City of Gloucester; Illustrative of, and Published During the Civil War, edited by J Washbourn (Gloucester, 1825).

Later sources – books

Adair, J, *Roundhead General: A Military Biography of Sir William Waller* (London, 1969).

Adair, J, *Cheriton* (Kineton, 1973).

Adair, J, *A Life of John Hampden* (London, 2003).

Adamson, J H, & Folland, H F, *Sir Harry Vane* (Boston, 1973).

Ashley, M, *Rupert of the Rhine* (London, 1976).

Atkin, M, *The Civil War in Worcestershire* (Stroud, 1995).

Atkin, M, & Laughlin, W, *Gloucester and the Civil War: A City Under Siege* (Stroud, 1992).

Barratt, J, *Cavaliers: The Royalist Army at War* (Stroud, 2000).

Barratt, J, *The First Battle of Newbury* (Stroud, 2005).

Burne, A H, *The Battlefields of England* (London, 1950).

Carlton, C, *Charles I: The Personal Monarch* (London, 1983).

Carlton, C, *Going to the Wars: The Experience of the British Civil Wars* (London, 1992).

Dictionary of National Biography (Oxford, 2004).

Disbury, D, *Beef, Bacon and Bag Pudding: Old Berkshire in the Civil War* (Reepham, undated).

Duffy, C, *Siege Warfare: The Fortress in the Early Modern Age* (London, 1979)

Eales, J, *Puritans and Roundheads: The Harleys of Brampton Bryan* (Cambridge, 1990).

Edgar, F T R, *Sir Ralph Hopton* (Oxford, 1968).

Emberton, W, *Skippon's Brave Boys* (Buckingham, 1984).

Emberton, W, *The English Civil War Day By Day* (London, 1995).

Firth, C H, *Cromwell's Army* (London, 1992).

Foard, G, *Naseby* (Guildford, 1995).

Furgol, E M, *A Regimental History of the Covenanting Armies* (Edinburgh, 1990).

Gardiner, S R, & Hill, C, *History of the Great Civil War* (London, 1987).

Gaunt, P, *The Cromwellian Gazetteer* (Stroud, 1987).

Gelling, M, *Place Names of Berkshire* (Cambridge, 1974)

Godwin, G N, *The Civil War in Hampshire* (Southampton, 1904).

Gray, E, *History and Antiquities of Newbury and its Environs* (published anonymously) (London, 1839).

Haythornthwaite, P, *The English Civil War: An Illustrated Military History* (London, 1983).

Hexter, J H, *The Reign of King Pym* (Harvard, 1941).
Hutton, R, *The Royalist War Effort* (London, 1982).
Hyett, F A, *Gloucester in National History* (London, 1906).
Kenyon, J, *The Civil Wars of England* (London, 1988).
Kenyon, J & Ohlmeyer, J, (eds.), *The Civil Wars* (Oxford, 1998).
Kitson, F, *Prince Rupert: Portrait of a Soldier* (London, 1994).
Lynch, J, *For King and Parliament: Bristol and the Civil War* (Stroud, 1999).
MacLachlan, T, *The Civil War in Hampshire* (Salisbury, 2000).
Massie Collins, R J, *Major General Sir Edward Massie: A Cavalier Among the Roundheads?* (Broadway, 2002).
MacNair-Wilson, M, *Battle for a Kingdom* (Reading, 1993).
Money, W, *The First and Second Battles of Newbury and the Siege of Donnington Castle* (London, 1881).
Money, W, *The History of Newbury* (Oxford, 1887).
Money, W, *A Popular History of Newbury* (1905).
Newman, P R, *Atlas of the English Civil War* (London and New York, 1998).
Newman, P R, *Royalist Officers in England and Wales* (London, 1981).
Ollard, R, *Clarendon and his Friends* (London, 1987).
Porter, S, *Destruction in the English Civil Wars* (Stroud, 1994).
Reid, S, *All the King's Armies: A Military History of the English Civil War* (Staplehurst, 1998)
Ridsdill Smith, G, & Toynbee, M, *Leaders of the Civil Wars* (1977).
Roberts, K, *First Newbury: The Turning Point* (Oxford, 2003).
Roberts, K, *Cromwell's War Machine: The New Model Army* (Barnsley, 2005).
Rogers, H C B, *Battles and Generals of the Civil Wars* (London, 1968).
Scott Wheeler, J, *The Making of a World Power: War and the Military Revolution in Seventeenth Century England (Stroud, 1999)*.
Seymour, W, *Battles in Britain* (London, 1975).
Sherwood, R E, *Civil Strife in the Midlands* (London, 1974)
Smith, R, *The Utility of Force: The Art of War in the Modern World* (London, 2006).
Smurthwaite, D, *The Ordnance Survey Complete Guide to the Battlefields of Britain* (London, 1987).
Snow, V F, *Essex the Rebel* (Lincoln, 1970).
Stoyle, M, *Soldiers and Strangers: An Ethnic History of the English Civil War* (New Haven and London, 2005).
Tennant, P, *Edgehill and Beyond* (Stroud, 1992).
Thomas, P W, *Sir John Berkenhead 1617–1679* (Oxford, 1969).
Toynbee, M & Young, P, *Cropredy Bridge* (Kineton, 1970).
Toynbee, M & Young, P, *Strangers in Oxford* (London, 1973).
Van Creveld, M, *Supplying War: Logistics from Wallenstein to Patton* (Cambridge, 2004).
Victoria County History of Berkshire, Volumes II, III, IV (London).
Victoria County History of Gloucestershire, Volumes IV, VI (London).
'Victoria County History of Wiltshire, Volume XII, (London).
Wanklyn, M, *Decisive Battles of the English Civil War* (Barnsley, 2006).
Wanklyn, M, & Jones, F, *A Military History of the English Civil War* (Harlow, 2005).
Warmington, A R, *Civil War, Interregnum and Restoration in Gloucestershire* (Woodbridge, 1997).
Webb, J & T W, *Memorials of the Civil War as it Affected Herefordshire and the Adjacent Counties* (London, 1879).
Wedgwood, C V, *The King's War* (London, 1958).
Whiting, J R S, *Gloucester Besieged* (Gloucester, 1984).
Worden, B, *Roundhead Reputations: The English Civil Wars and the Passions of Posterity* (London, 2001).
Wordie, R, (ed.), *Enclosure in Berkshire 1485–1885*, Berkshire Record Society (Reading, 2000).
Wroughton, J, *An Unhappy Civil War: The experiences of Ordinary People in Gloucestershire, Somerset and Wiltshire* (Bath, 2000).
Young, P, *Edgehill* (Kineton, 1967).
Young, P, & Adair, J, *From Hastings to Culloden* (Kineton, 1979).
Young, P & Emberton, W, *Sieges of the Great Civil War* (London, 1978).
Young, P & Holmes, R, *The English Civil War* (London, 1974).

Later sources – articles, essays, pamphlets, web sites, etc

Adamson, J, 'King Charles I Wins the English Civil War', in *What Might Have Been*, edited by Andrew Roberts (London, 2004).
Atkin, M, 'The Civil War Defences of Gloucester', in *Fortress*, No 10, (August 1991).
Clark, P, 'The Ramoth-Gilead of the Good: Urban Change and Political Radicalism at Gloucester 1540–1640', in *The Tudor and Stuart Town*, edited by J Barry, (London, 1990).
Dawson, A, 'English Civil War Artillery, New Evidence Unearthed' in *Miniature Wargames* (October 2005).
Dils, J A, 'Epidemics, mortality and the Civil War in Berkshire', in *The English Civil Wars – Local Aspects*, edited by R C Richardson (1997).

English Civil War Notes and Queries and *English Civil War Times,* – various issues and authors (Leigh-on-Sea).

'English Heritage Battlefield Report: Newbury I, 1643' (online at the English Heritage web site, www.english-heritage.org.uk).

Fassnidge, J, 'English Civil War Documents', four volumes, (York, 1984).

Frampton, D, & Garnham, P, 'The Forlorn Hope Guide to the First Battle of Newbury' (Leigh-on-Sea, undated).

Hazell, M, 'Fidelity & Fortitude: Lord Capell, his regiments and the English Civil War' (Leigh-on-Sea, 1987).

Morris, R, 'The Siege of Gloucester' (Bristol, 1993).

Pafford, J H P, 'Accounts of the Parliamentary Garrisons of Great Chalfield and Malmesbury 1645–46' (Devizes, 1940).

Peachey, S, 'The Mechanics of Infantry Combat' (Bristol, 1992)

Peachey S & Turton, A, 'Old Robin's Foot: The equipping and campaigns of Essex's infantry 1642–1645' (Leigh-on-Sea, 1987).

Reid, S, 'The Finest Knight in England: Sir Thomas Tyldesley, his regiments and the war in the north' (Leigh-on-Sea, 1987).

Reid, S, 'Gunpowder Triumphant' (Leigh-on-Sea, 1987).

Reid, S, 'Officers and Regiments of the Royalist Army' (Leigh-on-Sea 1988).

Roberts, K, 'London & Liberty: Ensigns of the London Trained Bands' (Leigh-on-Sea, 1987).

Roy, I, 'George Digby, Royalist intrigue and the collapse of the cause', in *Soldiers, writers and statesmen of the English Revolution,* edited by I Gentles, J Morrill & B Worden (Cambridge, 1998).

Turton, A, 'The Chief Strength of the Army: Essex's Horse (1642–45)' (Leigh-on-Sea, undated)

Wanklyn, M, 'Royalist Strategy in the South of England 1642–1644', in *Southern History 3* (1981).

Young, P, 'King Charles I's Army of 1643–5' in *Journal of the Society for Army Historical Research* (1939).

Young, P, 'Royalist Army at the Battle of Roundway Down' in *JSAHR* (1953).

Young, P, 'Order of Battle of the Parliamentarian and Royalist Armies at the First Battle of Newbury', in *JSAHR* (1964).

Index